THE SPATIAL
ORGANIZATION OF SOCIETY

Second Edition

4·11-74

THE SPATIAL
ORGANIZATION OF SOCIETY

Second Edition

Richard L. Morrill
University of Washington

DUXBURY PRESS
North Scituate, Massachusetts
A Division of Wadsworth Publishing Company, Inc.
Belmont, California

Duxbury Press
North Scituate, Massachusetts
A Division of Wadsworth Publishing Company, Inc.

© 1974 by Wadsworth Publishing Company, Inc., Belmont, California 94002. All rights reserved. No part of this book may be reproduced, stored in a retrieval system, or transcribed, in any form or by any means, electronic, mechanical, photocopying, recording, or otherwise, without the prior written permission of the publisher, Duxbury Press, a division of Wadsworth Publishing Company, Inc., Belmont, California.

ISBN-0-87872-057-X
L. C. Cat. Card No.-73-89884
Printed in the United States of America

1 2 3 4 5 6 7 8 9 10 — 78 77 76 75 74

CONTENTS

PART TWO
STRUCTURE OF LAND USE:
EXTENSIVE SPACE   41

CHAPTER 3
COMMERCIAL AGRICULTURE   45

PART THREE
STRUCTURE OF THE SYSTEM OF
PLACES   67

CHAPTER 4
TOWNS AS CENTRAL PLACES   69

CHAPTER 5
INDUSTRIALIZATION: TOWNS AS
PROCESSING CENTERS   93

PART FOUR
SPATIAL INTERACTION   125

CHAPTER 6
TRANSPORTATION AND
TRADE   127

Preface

The great contrasts that exist in the human and physical world are intriguing and at times disturbing. The traveler to distant places is often struck by the differences he observes between the familiar and the new. Descriptions of neighboring cities and towns as well as tales about exotic lands focus on the unusual and the unexpected.

The Spatial Organization of Society proceeds, nonetheless, from the premise that in one respect — its use of territory — human society is surprisingly the same from place to place. The similarity appears not in physical resemblance but rather in the predictable, organized pattern of locations and interrelations. This structure results from the operation of a few simple principles of human behavior and not from a unique man-to-space relationship in a particular location. Essentially, this structure derives from the necessity of using space efficiently. Specific features of the environment can be viewed as modifying the basic structure rather than as fundamentally controlling our use of the earth. Perhaps, after all, local physical and human variation will prove more significant than the ordering principles I stress. Even so, I feel that it is valuable to seek out the commonality in seemingly disparate landscapes.

For their helpful comments and suggestions, I would like to thank Brian J. L. Berry, University of Chicago; Warren E. Hultquist, Sacramento State College; Edward J. Taaffe, Ohio State University; John D. Nystuen, University of Michigan; Forrest R. Pitts, University of Hawaii; William L. Thomas, Jr., California State College, Hayward; and Phillip Wagner, Simon Fraser University. Of course, I alone am responsible for any possible errors or omissions.

PREFACE TO THE SECOND EDITION

The Spatial Organization of Society has succeeded in introducing the notion that men arrange themselves and their activities in fairly regular and predictable ways. Students and reviewers have suggested many useful ways in which the presentation could be improved. More important, they point out how the emphasis of geography has changed, since the time the book was conceived, from developing general theory to a greater concern with the limitations of these theories, particularly in dealing with human and environmental problems. This revision does not dilute the emphasis on theory, but rather expands the discussion of problems of the real world, especially with respect to the contemporary American landscape and to the concept of regional development.

Introduction

The face of the earth proclaims the presence of man. Once the realm of nature alone, it has for over 2 million years comprised both natural and human elements. Geography seeks to understand how these elements interrelate to produce the observed landscape. Traditionally, geographers have studied the ways in which specific elements of a particular region, such as natural resources, towns, and trade routes, interact to form an individual landscape. Now we also observe striking similarities among landscapes, recurring patterns that suggest underlying principles about the way people organize space to serve their needs and desires.

In *The Spatial Organization of Society* we shall examine and define the general principles that constitute a theory of spatial organization. These will be presented in the light of current theoretical research in the field of geography.

Our analysis rests upon certain assumptions that we feel are sound. Basically, we assume that spatial organization is the outcome of man's attempt to use his territory efficiently. This is not the only organizing principle, but it is the one that will be stressed here. We also assume that the wide variety of landscape patterns, and the theories constructed to account for them, can be unified by three common principles guiding man's use of space. Briefly, these are that man tends:

— *To maximize the net utility, or productivity, of areas and places at minimum effort.*
— *To maximize* **spatial interaction*** *at minimum effort (or cost).*
— *To bring related economic activities as close together as competing aims permit.*

The first principle implies that man tries to use land efficiently to get the maximum return (or productivity) for the least possible effort. The second suggests that man tries to maximize trade and communication among people and places at the lowest cost or for the least effort. Taken together, these two principles ought to ensure patterns of

---

* Terms printed in boldface are defined in the Glossary at the back of the book.

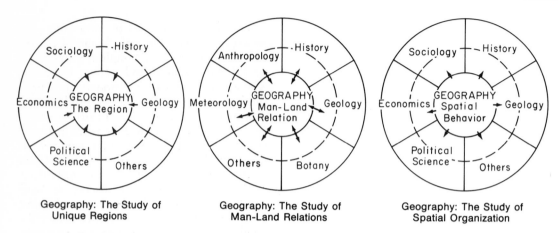

Geography: The Study of
Unique Regions

Geography: The Study of
Man-Land Relations

Geography: The Study of
Spatial Organization

Figure .01   Three approaches to the study of geography.

land use and interaction that give the greatest economic return for the least effort. The third principle follows from the other two: man usually locates related activities as close together as possible, depending on the nature and strength of the relationship. The application of these principles tends to produce predictable patterns and order in the **landscape.**

The natural **environment** is another force that shapes the particular landscape and influences the arrangement and success of human activities. But contrary to more usual practice, we give the environment, or tangible quality of space, only a secondary role. We do not mean to diminish the importance of environmental variation; but in order to demonstrate the underlying pattern of the landscape, we begin with the ideal patterns that would result from the more abstract qualities of space alone. Then, to return to the real world, we show how environmental factors modify or distort the theory.

Once the assumptions noted above have been accepted, we can distinguish the objective of geography in our view from the objectives defined in other approaches.

OBJECTIVES OF GEOGRAPHY

Geography may claim at least three distinct objectives:

— *To understand the unique characteristics of a place or region.*

— *To discover the relation between man and his environment.*

— *To explain systematically patterns of* **location** *and spatial interaction.*

(See figure .01 for a discussion of these alternative goals.) This book is committed to the last objective, not because the others are less valid, but because the idea of geography as **spatial relations** and **spatial organization** has been but little developed in an introductory context, and also because this viewpoint has been fruitful in formulating current geographic theory.

Geography as the study of spatial organization attempts to explain how physical space is structured, how man has organized his society in space, and how man's conception and use of space undergo change. In short, this book views geography as the study of location and spatial realtions.

A location is simply an area where human activities take place: it may be a cornfield, a hospital, or a bridge. The area may be as small as an office or as large as a city or national park. A set of similar or related locations is called a **region.**

Connections between locations, such as roads and railways, facilitate interaction between individuals and groups. These connections may be considered linear locations. It is more useful, however, to disregard the literal shape of connections and to focus attention instead on (1) the process of interaction and the costs associated with that interaction; and (2) the decisions that lead to the specific locations of places seeking to interact.

Space derives its structure from patterns of location and interaction. The area occupied by man and nature varies in quality, use, and potential, and it separates man from the activities and people he wishes to relate to. Our goal is to describe, classify, and compare the use and character of territory across the earth's surface; to define and distinguish general patterns of land use, towns, transport networks, and levels of economic development; and to formulate and test theories of the observed patterns of location, interaction among locations, and locational change. Our basic thesis is that space is not just a void to be filled, but that its very existence and dimensions induce both predictable individual behavior and collective order in location and interaction.

PLAN OF THE VOLUME

We begin our discussion by examining how people choose locations for their towns, farms, factories, and other activities (chapter 1). What geographic factors influence people's decisions to locate in particular places? How do natural environments and such spatial characteristics as distance and **relative location** interact to make one place more attractive or useful than another? What is the influence of technology, economics, and politics on the development of a location? We find that much of man's decision making with respect to land use is motivated by the desire both to maximize the utility of places (that is, to increase their value to people) at least cost and to maximize interaction (flow of goods or information between people or places) at least cost. We also point out some restraints that prevent the achievement of these goals.

The efficient use of space produces regular patterns of spatial organization that characterize developed industrial and commercial societies. In less developed societies, however, local physical environment and cultural traditions exert the major influence on the way land is used (chapter 2). But even the most technologically "primitive" people try to make the best use of their territory, resulting in observable, ordered patterns.

The goals noted above, maximizing the utility of places and maximizing interaction at least cost, motivate many groups of people in advanced societies. One such group is that of commercial farmers. In the context of commercial agriculture, we study the spatial relationships that develop between farms and their market areas, and discover how environment and government modify patterns of agricultural land use (chapter 3).

Next, we describe how space is organized into a **hierarchy** of trade areas, varying in importance and in the kinds of services they offer, around central places (towns or cities offering services to surrounding areas). Again, these patterns result from the goals of maximizing place utility and minimizing the costs of interaction and are modified by environmental and other factors (chapter 4).

The final patterns of location we discuss are those formed by the industrial sector in pursuit of the same goals (chapter 5). The predictable spatial patterns of industries and industrial towns vary according to the relative importance of transportation, **resources, markets,** or **processing costs.**

After outlining the major spatial patterns of location, we focus our attention on spatial interaction. Interaction implies the development of **transport networks** and flows of trade, as people seek to make the best use of their locations and to exchange goods at least cost (chapter 6). Not only do we consider the flow of goods, but we also look into the movement of people and ideas, a vital source of fundamental change in human society (chapter 7).

The last part of the volume attempts to show how spatial organization comprises all the ideal patterns examined in the previous chapters. The most highly developed patterns of goal-seeking activities converge in the city, which is itself a complex topic for study (chapter 8). After investigating urban structure, we make a general statement about the spatial organization of the agricultural and urban landscape and about the factors that distort "ideal" landscape patterns (chapter 9).

Ideal landscapes, of course, do not exist. We bring our discussion to an end with a brief survey of possible reasons for and consequences of man's failure to achieve a more efficient and equitable structure of society (chapter 10).

Part One

Geography:
Spatial Behavior,
Process,
and Structure

Location: Factors and Principles

Chapter 1

PATTERNS OF WORLD POPULATION AND DEVELOPMENT

To begin our study of spatial organization, we shall examine briefly two patterns of human society — the distribution of people and the distribution of wealth. These patterns form a complex spatial organization, the result of profound spatial change in settlement and economic development. Population is distributed very unevenly on both a large scale (over the entire world) and a small scale (within an area or town). The bulk of the world's population is contained in just a few areas that occupy only a fraction of the earth's land surface; much of the rest is distributed in several smaller nodes of population **concentration**, leaving a remainder of vast, scarcely inhabited areas (figure 1.01). The distribution of per capita income is even more irregular, from a few areas of relatively high economic development to many areas of relatively low development (figure 1.02). Geography is concerned with exploring world patterns of population and development, and the rest of this book may be viewed as an attempt to do so.

SPATIAL EXPERIENCE

Not only do societies differ in population and economic development, but they also vary in the extent of their **spatial experience,** that is, in their knowledge of the space around them (spatial awareness) and in their relationships with other areas (spatial **interdependence).** In technologically primitive societies, the individual's awareness of space and of areas and peoples far from him is limited to his direct experience. A small organizational unit, such as a village or tribal area, can be self-sufficient for most purposes; thus spatial interdependence and awareness are confined mostly to the village and its lands and to neighboring villages. The villager knows this local area intimately and can differentiate it in detail.

As societies develop technologies and grow more aware of distant places, they often become more specialized and more dependent upon other areas. In the most technologically developed societies, such as the United States, essentially all regions de-

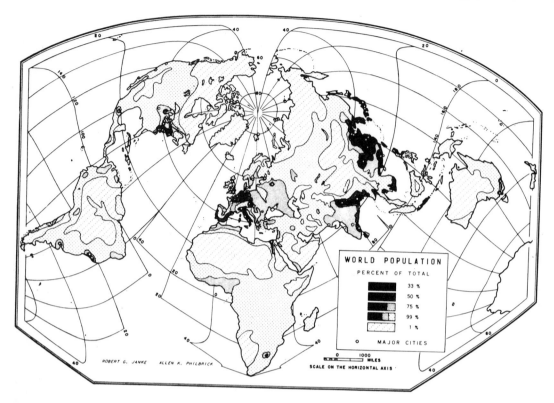

Figure 1.01 Distribution of world population. Associated densities per square kilometer are approximately as follows: greater than 120 for areas containing 33 percent of the world's population; 60-120 for areas containing the next 17 percent; 20-60 for areas containing the next 25 percent; 1-20 for areas containing the next 24 percent; and less than 1 for areas containing the last 1 percent of the world's population. (Reprinted by permission of John Wiley & Sons, Inc., from Allen K. Philbrick, *This Human World*, 1963.)

pend upon one another. As the economic development of a nation progresses, given kinds of production are concentrated in given regions (regional **specialization**), and thus regional **self-sufficiency** is abandoned. If the nations of the world were arranged along a spectrum of spatial interdependence, the most specialized and mobile societies would be the most interdependent.

In nations such as these, an individual person is keenly aware of and affected by events in distant places. Indeed, his very survival depends upon the goods and services produced by others. At the same time, however, he may be ignorant of events in his own neighborhood: although individual experience remains largely local, "local" means a radius of 50 miles rather than the 5 miles of the villager in a **subsistence** economy (figure 1.03).

Communications instantly link the individual in an advanced society with the rest of his country and the world. His mobility is enhanced by a greater freedom of choice, higher income, and better transportation than in less developed nations. Thus he is more likely to change his residence, and his trips are more likely to be frequent and to cover greater distance in less time. His field of acquaintance widens, and the distant and different no longer seem so strange or threatening.

FACTORS INFLUENCING LOCATIONS AND SPATIAL INTERACTION

Geography has traditionally pointed out that certain areas are more useful or attractive than others. They might be favorable

GROSS NATIONAL PRODUCT, 1970 estimates

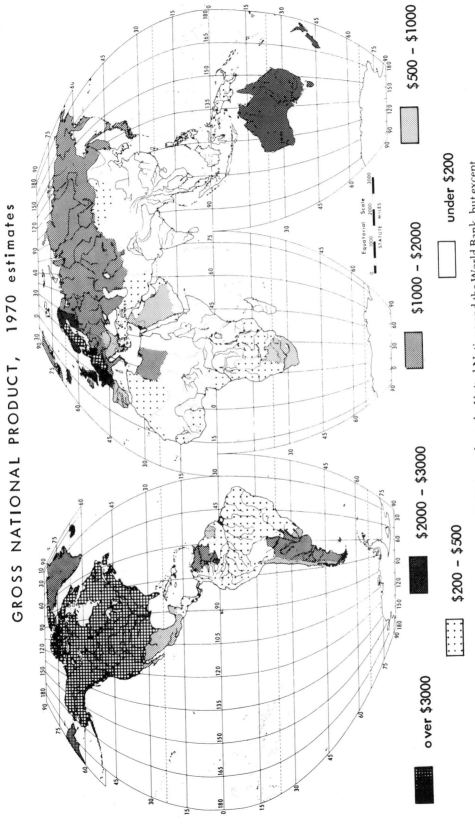

over $3000

$2000 – $3000

$200 – $500

$1000 – $2000

$500 – $1000

under $200

Figure 1.02 Estimated per capita income of countries, 1970. Data are from the United Nations and the World Bank, but except for the more affluent countries, estimates are not considered highly accurate. No account is taken of differences in the cost of living, which tends to be higher in wealthier countries. Levels of wealth, industrialization, and interdependence differ extremely from area to area; only a few have reached a relatively high level of economic development.

Figure 1.03 Individual travel patterns. Daily pattern of a sample of individual trip origins (+) and destinations (-) within Durham, North Carolina, in 1963. Longer-distance commuting or other trips into and out of the city are not included. (Reprinted by permission of the University of Illinois Press, from Stuart Chapin, Jr., *Urban Land Use Planning*, 2nd ed., 1965.)

for specific economic activities, or they might be focal points for trade and communication. These benefits are due in part to geographic factors, which can be classified as (1) the abstract characteristics of space (for example, distance and **accessibility**), and (2) the variable quality of the earth's surface. Whether the advantages of a location are realized, however, depends upon other factors that are not strictly geographic. These include economic, political, and cultural determinants, and will be considered here as indirect geographic factors influencing location and interaction. Perhaps the most important determinant of all is the sheer force of historical inertia, or what might be called the precedent of past patterns of development.

The Precedent of Past Patterns of Development

Undoubtedly the greatest influence on the future location of people and activities is their present location. Most human locational decisions depend so much on previous experience that existing patterns are strongly reinforced (figure 1.04). Economically, the large investment in the physical structures and human resources used in existing locations militates against radically changing location. Psychologically, the individual's investments in the area, in his home, and in his associations tend to make him immobile; he would rather modify existing locations than create entirely new settlements. Thus, new investment is concentrated in existing locations. For instance, a large proportion of investment in manufacturing is devoted to modifying and modernizing existing plants rather than to constructing new ones. Explaining the present on the basis of past patterns, however, begs the question of why these patterns came about, so let us now turn to more fundamental influences.

Spatial Characteristics and Location

Space is required of all economic activities, from fisheries to finance. The area needed for houses, factories, fields, and forests involves most of the earth's land surface — an immense territory. Distance, or spatial separation, inevitably separates people who may wish to interact for their mutual benefit and the products that they could profitably exchange. Space, as territory to be efficiently used and organized, and distance, as a spatial barrier to be overcome, are fundamental geographic factors influencing location and interaction.

Because man's activities require specific location in space, distance plays a role in determining the ideal locational pattern for these activities. Further, because activities require different amounts of territory, a particular structure is given to what was originally homogeneous space: space is differentiated into a structure consisting of areas, points, and interconnecting lines. Locations can thus be characterized by their relation to the whole, for example, according to their accessibility. This relation tends to determine each location's future potential as much as do its inherent characteristics. The following analysis will describe how location and development are influenced by the abstract characteristics of space — distance, accessibility, **agglomera-**

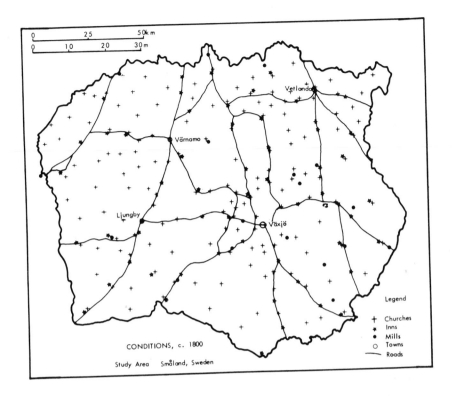

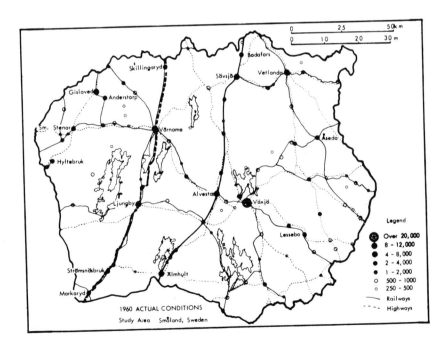

Figure 1.04 Past development as reinforcement for future development. Shown are major settlements and roads in a small area of Sweden in 1800 and 1960. The 1960 settlement was greatly influenced by the earlier one.

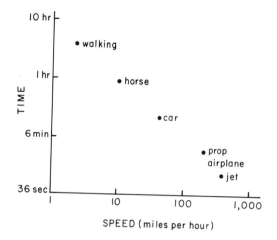

Figure 1.05 The cost in time of traveling 10 miles. Distance is often measured in terms of its time cost.

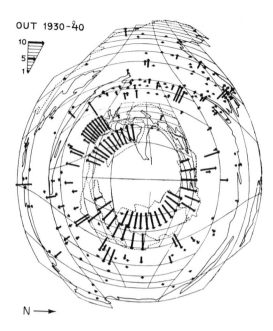

Figure 1.06 Hägerstrand's logarithmic projection closely expresses the way people perceive the space around them, greatly exaggerating the importance of nearby areas. This example shows the number (indicated by size of arrow) and destinations of migrants leaving a small area in central Sweden (at center of projection) in 1930-40. Note that most settled in nearby regions. (Reprinted by permission of the Department of Geography, University of Lund, Sweden, from T. Hägerstrand, "Migration in Sweden," *Lund Studies in Geography*, No. 13, Series B.)

tion, size, shape, and the relative location of parts in the whole.

Distance. Distance is the spatial dimension of separation, whether measured physically or by the time, effort, and cost required to overcome it. Historically, distance limited the area of the earth that man could utilize. Inability to cover distance encouraged man to make more **intensive** and specialized use of the territory familiar to him.

Distance has always been viewed primarily as a barrier to communication, movement, and trade, and has often been measured by cost (figure 1.05). The cost of crossing the same physical distance may vary greatly: in one direction it may be high enough to discourage travel completely, in another it may be low enough to invite interaction. Persons at greater distance from a major center of control must pay extra costs and thus are at a disadvantage. Costs of shipping to markets limit the scale of production at a single place, so the same combinations of activities must be repeated again and again over space. Therefore, distance has been a check on concentration of economic power or production at a single point.

Frequently, the time required to cover distance is the most meaningful measure of spatial separation. Much of economic history concerns gradually overcoming dis-

tance by improving transport (figure 1.05), thus cheapening spatial interaction. But this change is relative; distance is still costly. It has become less of a barrier, however, because we have invested so heavily in reducing its effects.

Individuals or groups may not perceive distance accurately. In figure 1.06, for instance, a peculiarly distorted view of the world is revealed. People tend to exaggerate the importance of closer areas, which they know well, and to diminish the more distant, less familiar areas. Figure 1.07 shows that people perceive certain streets to be very stressful, and so the distance across them seems much greater than it actually is.

Accessibility. Since man is social and many of his activities entail coming together to exchange goods and to exercise control, an area that is accessible — or central — to customers and citizens has many advantages. An area may be central because of its position within a natural basin, but more generally it is central with respect to the distribution of people or activities to which it is related.

The concept of **centrality** implies its opposites, isolation and location on the periphery. Location at the edge of settlement has traditionally hindered development, weakened loyalty and unity, and discouraged interaction. Provincial areas may be sparsely settled and deprived culturally and materially, providing a stark contrast to the cultural capital.

Agglomeration. Agglomeration refers to the grouping of people or activities for mutual benefit; in other words, it minimizes the distance separating them. Because the benefits of agglomerating activities are at once economic, geographic, and psychological, they constitute extremely important locational factors. From the clusters of dwellings in the tribal village to the concentration of population in the modern metropolis, agglomeration of people in one area enhances social satisfaction and interaction, and facilitates the exchange of **information**.

Economically, production efficiency is increased by associations of related industries, such as the clustering of small subcontractors around large automotive and aircraft complexes. Distribution efficiency is gained by grouping the buyers and sellers of goods and services in such places as the fair, the market town, and the shopping center. The proximity of various shops stimulates impulse-buying, thus increasing business turnover and regional consumption in the area. Not only does agglomeration reduce the total distance that people travel, satisfying a geographic goal, but it enables them to satisfy many purposes with little effort (figure 1.08).

The concept of agglomeration is perhaps best demonstrated by the structure of a city; but the existence of many cities shows that the extent of agglomeration is limited by the large territorial requirements of man's activities, especially agriculture.

Size. The size (and complexity) of organizational units ranges from tribe to nation. Since larger areas often contain a variety of peoples and interests, they may lack

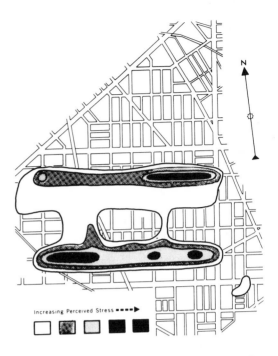

Increasing Perceived Stress ━━▶

Figure 1.07 Perceived environmental stress surface for residents living in part of the inner city of Philadelphia. (Courtesy of D. Ley, "The Black Inner City as a Frontier Outpost: Images and Behavior of a North Philadelphia Neighborhood." Ph.D. dissertation, Pennsylvania State University, 1972.)

unity, be subject to internal dissension, and thus find it difficult to develop rapidly and to act as a unit. On the other hand, a larger area may also have many different types and qualities of resources, which may be complementary to each other, allowing further specialization and greater **efficiency**. The presence of larger internal markets and labor pools promotes larger scale production, reduces the cost per unit of production, and so gives larger areas greater economic potential for the same relative effort (figure 1.09). As will be more clearly explained later, larger size also makes possible more efficient specialization and more theoretically ideal patterns of location.

Shape. The shape of organizational units significantly affects the costs of maintaining control, transporting goods efficiently, and communicating with other people. These activities are clearly cheaper and easier within a compact territory. In such a territory, a given effort results in greater unity, and a compact shape makes it

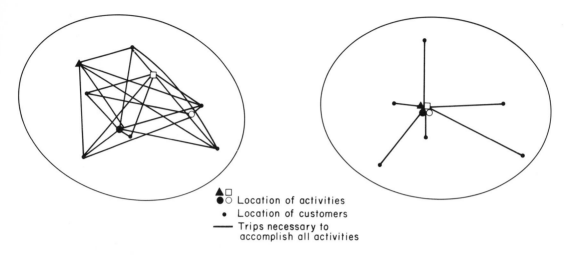

▲□
●○   Location of activities
 •   Location of customers
———   Trips necessary to
       accomplish all activities

Figure 1.08   Agglomeration: distance savings. Travel is reduced by nucleating activities. In the two figures, the customers are in fixed locations. If the activities are dispersed, more travel is required to visit all of them. For even greater convenience customers tend to move into or near an agglomeration.

easier for one center to dominate cultural life. In contrast, an irregular shape may foster regionalism, diversity, and multiplicity of control.

Relative Location. Location on natural routeways, such as that of Singapore and Gibraltar on straits, may give a site many communication advantages. Positions at gaps within natural barriers, such as at mountain passes, or at ends of large lakes (like Chicago, on the shore of Lake Michigan) also promote development.

Location on a transport network has a tremendous impact on the economic potential and viability of a place, no matter what its own resources may be. For example, some junctions on the new U.S. Interstate Highway System may well develop into new towns.

Location near existing centers of development also favors economic growth. The potential of any site depends as much on its position with respect to stable, more populous areas as on its own natural qualities.

The spatial characteristics described above are only some of the factors that influence location and interaction. Another factor is the environment; however, nearly all theory of spatial organization assumes that the structure of space is based solely on the principles of minimizing distance and maximizing the utility of points and areas within the structure, without taking the environment, or variable content of space, into account. Although environmental variation is interesting and has a significant effect on location and interaction, most observable spatial patterns result from the efficient use of **uniform territory.** In fact, the theoretical structures for agricultural location, location of urban centers, and the internal patterns of the city are all derived from the principle of minimizing travel on a uniform plane.

Environmental Factors

So visible is the natural landscape that its elements alone might seem responsible for man's economic development. Indeed, landforms, water features, climate, soils, vegetation, and natural resources have been vital to man's existence throughout most of history. Yet we must guard against overstating the importance of nature; after all, technology has enabled man to prosper in what had been inhospitable environments, while comfortable climates have proved no guarantee of development.

The natural environment affects development insofar as it either facilitates or hinders economic activity in a given place. Man often evaluates the environment in terms of the cost that it might impose on his activities. In this sense, the role of the environment in contributing to the advantages or disadvantages of a location can be measured. The cost of development in difficult environments may be great; take, for example, the polder development in the Netherlands, where people reclaimed land from the sea. In other cases, development may be possible only at the expense of severe damage to the natural landscape, as in massive open-pit mining.

Much the same as we analyzed the influence of spatial characteristics, we shall now look into the effects of environmental factors on location and interaction.

Landforms. The slope and ruggedness of the terrain often determine whether a particular location can be used for economic activities, such as forest exploitation or, especially, agriculture. Farming is easier and far cheaper on nearly level land, whereas sloping hills add not only the risk of erosion but also higher labor costs. Moreover, mechanized agriculture depends on level land, and after its introduction farming has been abandoned in many rugged areas. Thus, most of the world's farmland is contained in plains and valleys. To be sure, population pressures may force farmers to use hilly land, but only at increased cost.

Landform conditions also affect transportation: as slope and curvature increase, the costs of constructing and operating roads and railways mount too. Routes are usually concentrated in passes of least grade, so it is often necessary to construct costly tunnels, canals, or causeways to reduce transport cost and time. Transport in rough terrain is so difficult that mountains may constitute effective barriers between lowlands regions and even foster cultural and economic isolation.

Urban and industrial settlement in rugged land is prohibitively expensive unless highly desirable resources (mineral, timber, recreational) can be exploited.

Water Features. When land transport was poor, lakes and large rivers served to unite people and activities and were main sites for settlement. Even today lakes and rivers provide fairly cheap transportation, and most major cities are located on their shores.

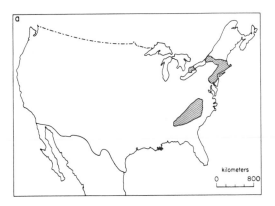

Figure 1.09 Effect of size and political fragmentation on production. The many borders (separate national economies) in Europe led to many local zones of successful textile production, whereas free movement in the United States promoted greater concentration. (Courtesy of F.E.I. Hamilton, "Models of Industrial Location," in R. J. Chorley and P. Haggett, eds., *Models in Geography*, London: Methuen, 1967.)

Land transport frequently follows the relatively level river valleys. River junctions and especially river mouths, the focal points of waterways, are advantageous locations for exchange and processing. Also favored for settlement are points where waterways can be crossed at little cost, such as at a shallow ford; a narrow, bridgeable canyon; or the first bridgeable point after an estuary. Such crossings are chosen partly because transport can shift from water to land at these points, but mainly because land routes tend to focus toward them. Transport being so vital to urban economy, location by a river is especially advantageous for larger towns and cities. But sometimes the location alone cannot ensure success: many river junctions are devoid of towns, and some successful cities were founded away from rivers to take advantage of other qualities.

Climate. Economic development is often attributed to favorable climate. Looking back in history, the survival of agricultural man depended upon climate hospitable to human life; our existence still ultimately depends upon it. Agriculture is limited to locations where the climate is suitable, but the limitation is indirect, operating through economic constraints as much as through those of plant physiology.

Temperature extremes set limits on the spatial range of a particular crop, whereas normal temperature patterns affect the *cost* of obtaining a given yield. Subject to the level of technology, the growing season (length of time between frosts) generally controls the variety of crops that can successfully be grown in a particular area. Another important factor is precipitation. Yields typically increase with moisture, while areas of extreme drought (perhaps one-fourth of the earth's land surface) are barren unless man interferes with nature in some extraordinary way.

If temperature and precipitation were mapped (as in figure 3.01, p. 44), one could see that good climatic conditions increase yields and lower costs, while poor conditions reduce yields and raise costs. In large areas of the world, costs are prohibitive for growing most crops; other areas permit only a limited range of activities. Some areas, however, are favorable for even more agriculture and other economic activities than the available space can hold, which means that some of these activities have to be carried on elsewhere under less than the best conditions. The actual locations of settlements, however, do not necessarily reflect the pattern of favorable climates. Although few people live in the extremes of desert and permafrost, some of the better areas are scarcely used, and some of the mediocre areas can be made to support dense concentrations of people by applying superior technology. For example, land is used much more intensively in Japan and Western Europe than in areas of comparable climate in New Zealand or North America. Man has been somewhat freed from the

locational limits of climate by irrigation, drainage, erosion control, and the development of new food crop species. Often these victories have released immense latent productivity at relatively low cost. In other cases, however, nature has been remade at high cost under difficult conditions. Many "naturally unfavorable" areas still exist that need only a small human investment — in irrigation or drainage or disease control — to become profitable. But man's desire to remain in other inherently inferior and unresponsive environments may lead to wasteful and costly efforts to transform nature.

Climate influences the location of industry in more limited ways. Warmer locations, for instance, may be preferred in order to reduce heating costs and workdays lost because of illness. On the other hand, hot and humid conditions can lower the productivity of some people and increase spoilage problems. The technologies of heating and air conditioning are about equally costly. They can free man from the limitations of climate, but only by increasing his costs.

Finally, climate affects location through the availability of water supplies. In arid areas, water shortages limit agricultural and urban development. Even in humid areas, local water supplies often cannot keep up with the demands of large concentrations of people, and sufficient water must be obtained at high cost.

Soils. Soils vary in their productivity for various crops, in their stability for supporting structures, and in their direct usefulness for construction. Areas that are poorly drained as a result of uneven glacial deposition or location on river or tidal floodplains have always been strong barriers to settlement and are settled only because of population pressures — at high cost.

Vegetation. Primitive agricultural technology limited early man to the use of natural vegetation, such as grassland for grazing, easily cultivated soil or river basins for planting, and forests for hunting game, cutting timber, and gathering fuelwood. But natural vegetation was also a barrier to intensive agricultural settlement: the tough sod made grasslands hard to till, and forests were difficult to clear.

When improved technology provided more efficient plows for working the sod and better techniques for cutting forests, large areas were freed for agricultural location. Particularly in the case of cleared forests, ample moisture and easily worked soils invited agricultural settlement. Forests themselves were not a significant resource until the sixteenth century, when the charcoal-based iron industry and large-scale ship construction developed.

Natural Resources. Natural resources are the elements of nature that man uses to help satisfy his needs and desires. A few are "free" but undependable, such as climate. To use most resources human effort and capital must be expended; but because resources increase man's productivity, this cost is usually considered worthwhile. For instance, although it is costly to irrigate land, the cost may be far exceeded by the benefit of increased productivity.

Many resources valued today were considered valueless three centuries ago. For example, the chief sources of power today are coal, petroleum, gas, and uranium, whereas formerly they were wood, water, animals, and men.

Much of man's recent progress is due to industrialization, which requires natural resources, particularly the fuels. Since these resources have been utilized mainly in modern times, their location was **random** with respect to the existing patterns of agricultural settlement and land productivity. In some cases, notably in northwestern Europe, high-quality coal and suitable metal ores were found near areas of dense population, so these fields were the first to be used. Gradually the coal fields, and, to a lesser extent, the other resource areas attracted industry and settlement, and population shifted locally to these places from agriculturally richer areas.

From a spatial point of view, the most significant facts about resources are that they are unevenly distributed, are often concentrated in small areas, and are depletable.

Because resources are unevenly distributed, there is striking variation in the resource endowment of different areas of the world. Since economies are contained within national boundaries, a country with a variety of internal resources has a great asset. A nation that lacks needed resources must purchase them from other nations and risks military or political embargoes on essential supplies.

A nation's resource endowment largely determines the kind of industrialization that is possible and its cost. Until fairly recently, industrialization was closely tied to the presence of raw materials, especially coal. During this century, fuels have been used far more efficiently than before. Moreover, industry has developed processes in which fuels and raw materials have become less important, thereby giving nations increased freedom from the limits of their own resources.

Because resources are concentrated in specific locations, clusters of small hamlets or villages designed to exploit them are typical. Since any given resource may be depleted, however, these settlements are often impermanent — in the United States there are thousands of such "ghost towns."

How much a given resource is used depends on its quality and its distance from markets. The quality of the resource determines the cost of processing. Naturally, the resources that cost the least, either because they are closest to markets or highest in quality, are used first. A slight change in either factor can force a given resource out of competition (figure 1.10). However, the better nearby resources will gradually be depleted, and resource suppliers will probably need to use fairly remote sources before industry and population are located near them. Resource exploitation is thus a major source of growth, if an uncertain one, of regions remote from the center of the economy.

In summary, the effect of environmental factors may be calculated in terms of the cost of carrying on a particular activity, such as agriculture, commerce, or industry. The environment places limits or controls on the possibilities of economic development, governs the costs of exploiting or altering natural conditions, and facilitates or hinders interaction in certain areas. Environmental factors alone, however, do not account for the difference between developed and less developed countries, for there are many areas with high-quality environments that are underdeveloped and

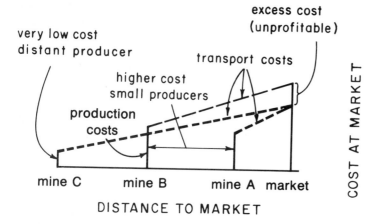

Figure 1.10   Resource use related to transport and production costs. Distant mine *C* can compete equally at the market with close mine *A* because of low production costs. Intermediate mine *B* incurs costs that are too high, and thus cannot compete profitably.

This kind of graph will appear often in this book. Typically, the *x*-axis (horizontal) will measure increasing distance, volume, or time, and the *y*-axis (vertical) increasing cost or value (from the bottom up). These graphs are designed to indicate how values on the *y*-axis (or cost) change (increase, decrease, fluctuate) with increasing distance or volume. In this example we are comparing the cost at which mines *A*, *B*, and *C*, at increasing distances, are able to deliver ores to the single market at the right. The vertical lines above *A*, *B*, and *C* represent production costs per unit, and the sloping lines represent transport costs. The lesser slope from *C* indicates a lower rate per unit distance than from *B* or *A*, but the total transport costs from *C* are higher than from *A* because of the greater distance. Note that the cost at the market is the sum of site production costs and transport costs to the market.

many areas with meager ones that are successful.

Technology allows industries in settled areas to produce needed goods without having to move to unsettled but naturally superior areas. Technology thus provides the main alternative to environmentally determined development.

The environmental forces that are important to man change through time. Early agricultural man needed suitable land and climate to survive. Modern man, through technology, has been able to make use of agriculturally poor but minerally rich areas. Our improved technology permits the natural beauty of landforms to influence location, not because it is necessary for survival, but because it enriches human life.

Comparative Advantage

As we have seen, spatial and environmental factors make some locations more advantageous than others for certain activities, subject to the technological level of a given people. In favorable locations, the net productivity, or excess of returns over costs, of a specific activity is greater than in other places. In other words, certain locations have a **comparative advantage** over others. For instance, the spatial qualities of good accessibility or centrality give a market town comparative advantage over more **peripheral** areas. Environmental factors can also provide comparative advantage: a natural harbor has comparative advantage over a potential manmade one, which would cost a tremendous amount of money to construct.

Assuming that we can measure costs and returns, an analysis of economic activities in a sample of areas would reveal two main characteristics:

— **Complementarity** *of location or areas: The requirements of different activities vary so markedly that areas with the greatest advantages for some activities are poor for others, which might find an ideal location in yet other areas. These different areas can benefit each other through trade.*

— An uneven endowment of "advantages": Some areas have greater comparative advantage in many activities, while other areas are less productive in most or even all activities. This may result in strong competition for the preferred areas and extremely intense use of land within them. There may be no room for less profitable activities that might be carried on there better than anywhere else. Unfavorable areas, if they are to develop at all, must be satisfied with activities that will survive, even though such activities might be more profitable elsewhere. For example, cattle grazing would be more productive on the lush prairies near urban markets than on the western high plains, but it survives on the plains and is squeezed out from the prairies because activities that are more productive, such as raising corn, preempt the better land.

Advantage may result from human decisions to group activities into mutually beneficial systems, even though individual activities alone may not appear so profitable. Comparative advantage is relative, not absolute. For instance, although one activity may have an absolutely higher yield in area *A* than in area *B*, the *relative* price levels and land costs must be considered in determining which area really has the greater comparative advantage. Another important point is that the comparative advantage of an area is never static: changes constantly occur in the relative influence of land, climate, resources, transport position, and concentration of development; and the demands of society change too. History is filled with examples of once-profitable locations rendered obsolete by change and poor areas invigorated by new technologies.

OTHER LOCATIONAL FACTORS

Comparative advantage and past development do not alone explain the complexity of locational patterns and change. Psychological, cultural, political, and above all, technological and economic factors help determine how space is used and whether it even has value to people at all. These factors can be spatially differentiated and therefore may be considered indirectly geographic.

Cultural Factors

Cultural attitudes, beliefs, and practices often determine the economic and social potential of peoples and are changed only slowly. Attitudes toward work; toward eating certain foods and using certain products; toward birth control; toward the role of the individual, family, and society; toward willingness to migrate and to change occupations — all are affected by cultural tradition.

Technological and Economic Factors

The location of an industrial activity is partly a function of the technological and developmental level of the economy. The nature and organization of activities are influenced by the supply, quality, and price of labor, the availability and price of capital, and the available technology. The possibility of **substitution** between labor and capital depends on their relative availability, cost, and quality. If the labor supply is abundant or cheap, less capital is needed. But if a location contains few skilled workers, more capital must be spent for mechanized equipment, or higher wage levels must be offered to attract specialized labor.

The quality of transportation within an economy also helps govern locational decisions. Since transport connections must be available if a location is even to be considered for some specialized activities, many locations of great potential productivity lie undeveloped, awaiting improved access to the larger economy.

Economies of Scale

Production efficiency (that is, cost per unit), depends in part on the volume of the good produced in a particular plant. Larger volume generally results in lower unit costs because overhead costs are spread over more units, cost of larger quantities of raw

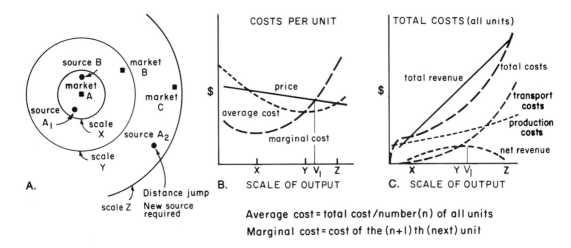

Average cost = total cost/number(n) of all units
Marginal cost = cost of the (n+1) th (next) unit

Figure 1.11 Economies of scale and spatial implications of scale. A. Plant is at market *A*. At scale *X*, sources A_1 and *B* and market *A* are required. At scale *Y*, market *B* is added, but no new sources are required. At scale *Z*, however, a new source of material, A_2, is required in order to penetrate market *C*. B. For a while, as volume (sales) increases, the marginal cost (cost of producing the next unit) falls more rapidly than price; thus the average cost of all units falls, and net revenues (profits) increase. In this example, marginal costs again rise because of increasing transport costs to the farther market, *B*. If volume rises to *Z*, marginal costs rise above the price because of excess transport costs to market *C*, and net revenue falls. Unit production costs are lowest at scale *Z*. Note that the net revenue curve is obtained by subtracting the total cost curve from the total revenue curve. C. In the right-hand diagram, total costs are divided into transport-cost and production-cost components in order to illustrate that as production increases, production costs tend to rise less quickly than revenues, but transport costs tend to rise more quickly, as more distant sources or markets are needed. The optimum scale of output is at *V*, where marginal cost equals price and net revenues are maximum.

materials are lower, and bulk shipment costs are lower. When economies result from greater **scale,** the plant may be able to afford more efficient processes or more specialized labor, and less fluctuation in output may be expected.

Such advantages, however, do not accrue indefinitely. Internal-cost increases, or **diseconomies**, can result from increasing **congestion**, in-plant organizational problems, or input-supply limitations. Most important from a geographic viewpoint, as scale increases, the lower unit-production cost must also be balanced against probable increases in distribution and **assembly costs**, for supplies must be brought from more distant sources, and products must be sold in more distant markets. (Figure 1.11 illustrates these crucial relations.) Transport cost and time have historically been the primary obstacles to increased scale. One of the chief benefits of improved transport is the opportunity to realize economies of greater scale.

The economies achieved by large-scale production strongly encourage regional specialization, but the possibilities are limited by the cost of overcoming spatial separation. However, society has moved toward realizing such economies: farms and factories have increased in size, ships and trucks have increased in capacity, schools have enlarged their physical plant, metropolitan areas have expanded, and common markets (such as the European Economic Community) have been created.

Political and Economic Systems

In contrast to industrialized societies, tribal groups, usually small in size and somewhat communal in character, demonstrate relatively simple levels of technology, economy, and spatial organization. Location of activities follows repetitive patterns; decision making is little affected by outside influences and therefore tends to be local, small scale, and traditional.

In some countries, feudal economic and political systems still exist in which a large number of peasants support a small ruling group. Under such systems, there is little incentive for growth or change. So long as control is maintained and the expectations of the peasants remain low, there is little reason to increase production. Locational change is minimal, consisting of further subdivision of land as population grows. Feudal systems usually break down under either a need for the state to defend itself, which requires greater total wealth, or a demand for more goods, greater power, and broader freedom accompanying the growth of the middle classes.

In individualist capitalist economies, highly differentiated locational patterns evolve. Indeed, most of our theories of the way people use space **(spatial behavior)** include such individual goals as the short-term maximization of profit. Locational decisions are made by individuals or small groups under conditions of risk and uncertainty. Since a small entrepreneur cannot survive years of losses in order to realize long-term profits, the optimal location for new business tends to be near already successful enterprises and locations. The incentive of profit, however, may still be sufficient to induce acceptance of fairly great risks.

In a rather pure capitalist system, then, investment reinforces and only gradually extends existing patterns of settlement. Economic growth in capitalist societies has traditionally originated in a fairly small region, from which development has only gradually spread. Even after much government intervention, the pattern of development is extremely uneven (for example, see figure 10.09, showing the distribution of poverty in the United States). Since investment and locational decisions are individual, however, an abundant variety of goods and services are offered, and the response to local needs is fairly rapid.

In a market economy, the price of land, labor, and capital in all their forms fluctuates according to supply and demand. Competitive prices provide a mechanism for achieving efficient use of space. In contrast, a monopoly often reduces efficiency: if a single decision maker controls the production of a good, he can preserve imperfect location through fixed prices. On the other

hand, competition can lead to excessive numbers of enterprises and thus to inefficiency and chaos. Take, for example, the inefficiency of electric power distribution when it was in the hands of competing systems or, similarly, the high cost of milk delivery today. Carefully planned and regulated monopolies, where costs could be honestly calculated and excess profits prevented, could result in better locational patterns.

In a socialist economy, investment and prices are centrally planned and controlled, and locational patterns different from those in capitalist economies can be expected. The goal of efficient use of space and resources may be identical, but since decisions are made by a few, who have greater knowledge of all areas and who view the system as a whole, greater efficiency should result. Also, since the state is better able and perhaps more willing than individual investors to sustain losses for longer periods, it should be possible to achieve more rational and regular development and use of resources. In the long run, regional differences in a socialist economy will probably reflect more closely the actual potential of a region rather than its economic history, and regional income differences should be less than in capitalist societies.

When decision making is by a few, however, the potential for both good and ill effect is increased. In spite of superior information and power, no system is immune from error, and a poor decision under central planning can have far-reaching and ruinous effects. Evidence is also strong that central planning agencies are in fact, if not in theory, much less responsive to the demands of local citizens. Finally, monopoly power in the hands of the state makes it more difficult to use price as a test of efficiency.

Political Factors

Nationalism. The world consists of national economies, each with its own banking and monetary system, tax system, and other attributes of economic and political independence. Although many nations are too

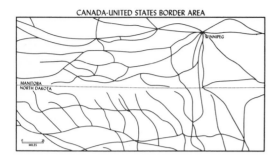

Figure 1.12   Broken railroad network in the Canadian - U.S. border area. Political boundaries often diminish interaction. (Reprinted by permission of Yale University Press, from August Lösch, *Economics of Location*, 1954.)

small to constitute easily viable economic units, feelings of nationalism often give rise to the desire to be self-sufficient. The attempt to create a fairly self-sufficient economy generally requires the imposition of protective measures, such as tariffs and subsidies for internal industries. These measures often work against the utilization of comparative advantage and the achievement of economic efficiency over the entire world.

Administrative Structure. An administrative structure inherited from an earlier era may prove inadequate to later needs; examples are the conflicts between central city and suburb and the ineffective administration of many counties laid out by arbitrary geometry prior to settlement.

Boundaries. National boundaries normally signify a sharp break in political and economic authority. Sometimes they follow natural physical features, but often they artificially separate areas that would otherwise be united physically and economically. For example, the United States-Canada border separates nearly identical areas, imposes a $1,000-per-family income differential, and radically alters transport and settlement patterns (figure 1.12). Thus, borders are likely to weaken the economic strength of contiguous areas. Yet national boundaries also foster the development of specialized locations, like military posts and customs-service areas; in addition, border towns, such as those between the United States and

Mexico, may spring up to take advantage of differences in prices, wages, or products between two countries.

Governmental Systems. Centralized authority produces greater economic uniformity than does a federalized system of government. Nations with a strong central government may impose nationwide wage, banking, and taxation rates. They tend to have a uniform economic and cultural life and usually place national interests above local ones. Countries developing from several smaller states or containing radically diverse elements tend to form federal systems in which economic power is divided. Regional interests thus supercede national ones in many economic decisions. This diffusion of power preserves regional differences in culture and development; for example, by controlling banking and local taxes, U.S. states influence the nature of their industry, the quality of their schools, and the viability of their agriculture.

Changing Roles of Locational Factors

The nature and impact of factors influencing location and interaction constantly change. For instance, the oceans were once impenetrable barriers to interaction, but the invention of the sailing ship enabled man to trade across water even more easily than over land. With the **innovation** of trains and trucks, land transport became more feasible, and economic development again focused internally. Today, air transport broadens the potential of interrelations, and the world seems to shrink as traveling cost and time decrease. Although distance may still hinder interaction, improvements in transport have enabled man to travel farther with less effort and have made possible relations that could never have existed before.

Locational Factors and Predicted Patterns

Our explanation of spatial organization will proceed from the deductive — what would occur under the simplest conditions — to the inductive — how local variation distorts this "pure" structure. If we were to begin by discussing all the local variation, we would risk missing the underlying spatial structure. Most theory of location and spatial organization, therefore, stresses the way spatial characteristics (especially distance) interact to produce regular and repetitive patterns. In this book environmental variation, rather than playing the dominant role in explaining location, acts as a distorting influence on the ideal patterns that would occur on a uniform surface.

GOALS AND RESTRAINTS

Goals of Spatial Behavior

If there is an underlying order in human geography, it is because man and society try to organize space efficiently, to locate activities and use land in the "best" way. As noted earlier, man's goals can be expressed as three principles: To maximize the net utility of places at minimum effort; to maximize spatial interaction at minimum cost or effort; and to bring related activities as close together as possible.

In maximizing the net utility of places at minimum effort, man attempts to get the maximum return from the sum of all parcels of land within an economy for the least possible effort. This does not mean that *each* parcel is to be used to its *absolute* maximum, but that after weighing the comparative advantages of all parcels, each should be used for the best purpose that can be sustained by technology, resources, and the demand for goods and services. For instance, land most remote from the economic and cultural center may not be used at all even if it is inherently productive, while the use and value of land close to the center may be intensified by demand.

In maximizing spatial interaction at least cost, man tries to maximize the profitability of his activities by taking advantage of the possibility of regional specialization. This aim is subject to controls of technology, cost and time of transportation, and possible risk of overspecialization. A balance exists

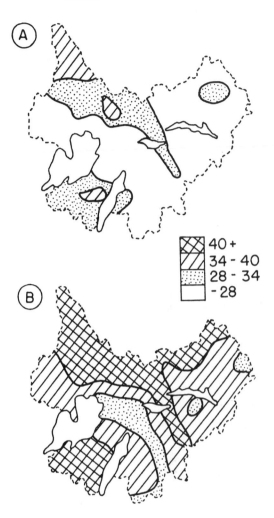

Figure 1.13 Actual and potential **labor productivity**. In this example from middle Sweden, indices of actual labor productivity shown on map A (in 10 Swedish kroner per hour) fall far below the maximum potential productivity shown on map B. The deficiency was due partly to inadequate information, but more to the unwillingness of farmers to take the risk or make the effort required for greater productivity. (Reprinted by permission of the Association of American Geographers from Julian Wolpert, "The Decision Process in Spatial Context," *Annals of the Association of American Geographers*, Vol. 54, 1964.)

between the possibility of reducing transport costs by developing more regional self-sufficiency and the possibility of reducing production costs by using more transport to encourage greater regional specialization.

Following the first two principles should result in a pattern of land use, a degree of specialization, and a volume of trade that maximize productivity at least cost. The third principle, that related activities should be as close together as possible, is a corollary of the other two.

Restraints on Spatial Behavior

The principles defined above ought to lead to ideal and efficient patterns of location and interaction, but they are not so easily followed. Individuals, groups, corporations, and governments may lack the knowledge, ability, or motivation to make the optimal decision. Men and societies are often willing to achieve a good or simply profitable level of satisfaction rather than the maximum level (figure 1.13). For example, the best resource use may be a long-term rate of use, but because of risk and uncertainty a less favorable short-term rate may be chosen. The achievement of optimal decision making may be prevented or destroyed by natural disasters like floods, fires, and earthquakes, or by irrational and self-destructive human behavior, such as distrust, hatred, and war.

More commonly, most locational decisions have a short-term horizon and their efficacy is subject to erosion as conditions change. As technology continues to advance and dramatic social changes develop (like the reduction of social discrimination in the United States), a decision that was optimal yesterday becomes imperfect today. Yet the investment in a location, whether in terms of plant or people or fields, is very important to the people concerned. So long as the investment continues to pay for itself, people or firms may feel it is better to operate at less than peak profit than to abandon the investment altogether. Although most locations are probably less than optimal, only the really inefficient will fail. It is also possible that an activity situated in a poor location can profitably adjust to the environment.

Some locations are inefficient to begin with. Such locations may or may not fail, depending on the degree of inefficiency. Typically, the decision maker has acted on insufficient or poor information and has made an error in the location, scope, and size of the investment. However, a nonoptimal location, which is at the same time profitable or satisfactory, may be deliberately chosen. Many investors are willing to incur higher costs and to accept lower profits. They may be unsure of long-term possibilites and thus are content to achieve satisfactory rather than optimal levels of efficiency; or they may have overriding social or personal reasons for choosing a less profitable location.

This chapter has described how man attempts to use space efficiently. We have examined the role of spatial factors influencing location and interaction, and also the role of environmental, cultural, political, and economic factors. All these help structure the spatial organization of society, especially technologically advanced and spatially interdependent society. In the next chapter we digress a bit to look at location and interaction in **spatially restricted** societies. Because the content of chapter 2 is not absolutely essential to the discussion of the book, the reader may wish to proceed directly to chapter 3. However, we feel that the background provided by chapter 2 will greatly enrich the reader's understanding of the material that follows, and thus we urge him to read on.

REFERENCES

General References

Abler, Ronald, John S. Adams, and Peter Gould, *Spatial Organization: The Geographer's View of the World*, Englewood Cliffs, N.J.: Prentice-Hall, 1971.

Alexander, J.W., *Economic Geography*, Englewood Cliffs, N.J.: Prentice-Hall, 1963.

Berry, B.J.L., and D. Marble, eds., *Spatial Analysis: A Reader in Statistical Geography*, Englewood Cliffs, N.J.: Prentice-Hall, 1968.

Bunge, W., "Theoretical Geography," *Lund Studies in Geography*, Series C, 1, 1962.

Chorley, R., and P. Haggett, eds. *Models in Geography*, London: Methuen, 1967.

De Blij, Harm J., *Geography: Regions and Concepts*, New York: John Wiley and Sons, 1971.

Friedmann, J., and W. Alonso, eds., *Regional Development and Planning: A Reader*, Cambridge, Mass.: The M.I.T. Press, 1964.

Haggett, P., *Locational Analysis in Human Geography*, New York: St. Martin's 1966.

Hawley, A.H., *Human Ecology*, New York: Ronald Press, 1950.

Hoover, E.M., *Location of Economic Activity*, 2nd ed., New York: McGraw-Hill, 1972.

Isard, Walter, *Location and Space-Economy*, New York: Technology Press, 1956.

Jones, E., *Human Geography*, London: Chatto and Windus, 1964.

Lösch, A., *The Economics of Location*, translated by W. Stolper, New Haven, Conn.: Yale University, 1954.

Pred, A., Behavior and Location, *Lund Studies in Geography*, Series B, 27, 1967; and 28, 1969.

Stea, D., "Space, Territory, and Human Movement," *Landscape* 15 (September, 1965): 13-17.

Thomas, W.L., Jr., ed., *Man's Role in Changing the Face of the Earth*, Chicago: University of Chicago Press, 1956.

Nature of Geography, Economic Geography

Barrows, H.H., "Geography as Human Ecology," *Annals of the Association of American Geographers* 13 (1923): 1-14.

Boesch, Hans, *A Geography of World Economy*, Princeton: van Nostrand, 1964.

Bunge, W., "Spatial Relations: The Subject of Theoretical Geography," in *Voprosy Geografii*, edited by Y.G. Saushkin, Moscow: University of Moscow, 1964.

Burton, I., "The Quantitative Revolution and Theoretical Geography," *Canadian Geographer* 7 (1963): 151-162.

Dicken, S.N., and F.R. Pitts, *Introduction to Human Geography*, New York: Blaisdell, 1963.

Fryer, D.W., *World Economic Development*, New York: McGraw-Hill, 1965.

Hartshorne, R., *The Nature of Geography: A Critical Survey of Current Thought in the Light of the Past*, Washington, D.C.: Association of American Geographers, 1959.

Hartshorne, R., *Perspective on the Nature of Geography*, Association of American Geographers, monograph series 1, Chicago: Rand McNally, 1959.

Harvey, David, *Explanation in Geography*, New York: St. Martin's Press, 1970.

Hoffman, L.A., *Economic Geography*, New York: Ronald Press, 1965.

Isard, W. et. al., *Methods of Regional Analysis: An Introduction to Regional Science*, New York: Technology Press, M.I.T., 1960.

James, P.E. and C.F. Jones, eds., *American Geography: Inventory and Prospect*, Syracuse, N.Y.: Syracuse University Press, 1954.

Lukermann, F., "The Role of Theory in Geographic Enquiry," *Professional Geographer* 13 (1961): 1-6.

McCarty, H.H. and J.B. Lindberg, *A Preface to Economic Geography*, Englewood Cliffs, N.J.: Prentice-Hall, 1966.

Morgan, W.B. and R.P. Moss, "Geography and Ecology: Concept of the Community and Its Relationship to Environment," *Annals of the Association of American Geographers* 55 (1965): 339-350.

Philbrick, A.K., *This Human World*, New York: Wiley, 1963.

Progress in Geography. General editors: C. Board, R. Chorley, P. Haggett and D. Stoddart, Vol. 1, 1969; Vol. 2, 1970; Vol. 3, 1971, New York: St. Martin's Press.

Schaeffer, F.K., "Exceptionalism in Geography: A Methodological Examination," *Annals of the Association of American Geographers* 43 (1953): 226-249.

Smith, R.H.T., E. Taaffe, and L.J. King, eds., *Readings in Economic Geography*, Chicago: Rand McNally, 1967.

Taaffe, Edward J., ed., *Geography*, Englewood Cliffs, N.J.: Prentice-Hall, 1970.

Thoman, R.S., *The Geography of Economic Activity*, New York: McGraw-Hill, 1962.

Tornqvist, G., "Flows of Information and the Location of Economic Activities," *Lund Studies in Geography*, Series B, 30, 1968.

Wagner, P., *The Human Use of the Earth*, New York: Free Press, 1960.

Warntz, W., "Global Science and the Tyranny of Space." *Papers and Proceedings of the Regional Science Association* 19 (1967): 7-22.

Watson, J.W., "Geography — A Discipline in Distance," *Scottish Geographical Magazine* 71 (1955): 1-13.

Woytinsky, W.S. and E.S. Woytinski, *World Population and Production*, New York: Twentieth Century Fund, 1953.

Environmental Factors

Amiran, D.H.K., "Arid Zone Development: A Reappraisal under Modern Technological Conditions," *Economic Geography* 41 (1965): 189-210.

Borchert, John R., "The Dust Bowl in the 1970's" *Annals of the Association of American Geographers* 61 (1971): 1-22.

Bridger, M.K., and B. Greer-Wootten, "Landscape Components and Residential Urban Growth in Western Montreal Island," *Revue de Geographie de Montreal*, 19 (1965): 75-90.

Burton, I., R. Kates, and R. Snead, *Human Ecology of Coastal Flood Hazard in Megalopolis*, University of Chicago Department of Geography, Research Paper 115, 1969.

Clarkson, James D., "Ecology and Spatial Analysis," *Annals of the Association of American Geographers*, 60 (1970): 700-716.

Detwyler, Thomas R., *Man's Impact on Environment*, New York: McGraw-Hill, 1971.

Gould, P.R., "Man against His Environment: A Game, Theoretic Framework," *Annals of the Association of American Geographers* 53 (1963): 290-297.

Hidore, J.J., "The Relations between Cash-grain Farming and Landforms," *Economic Geography* 39 (1963): 84-89.

Kates, R.W., "Industrial Flood Losses," University of Chicago Department of Geography, Research Paper 98, 1965.

Pepelasis, A.A. and K. Thompson, "Agriculture in a Restrictive Environment," *Economic Geography* 36 (1960): 145-157.

Quinn, F., "Water Transfers: Must the West be Won Again?" *Geographical Review* 58 (1968): 108-132.

Semple, E.C., *Influences of Geographic Environment*, New York: Henry Holt and Company, 1911.

Taylor, G., "Environment, Village, and City: A Genetic Approach to Urban Geography," *Annals of the Association of American Geographers* 32 (1942): 1-67.

Ullman, E.L., "Amenities as a Factor in Regional Growth," *Geographical Review* 44 (1954): 119-132.

Other Factors,
Abstract Geography

Bachi, R., "Standard Distance Measures and Related Methods for Spatial Analysis," *Papers and Proceedings of the Regional Science Association* 10 (1963): 83-132.

Boyce, R.B. and W.A.V. Clark, "The Concept of Shape in Geography," *Geographical Review* 54 (1964): 561-572.

Brown, Lawrence A. and Frank E. Horton, "Functional Distance: An Operational Approach," *Geographical Analysis* 2 (1970): 76-82.

Buttimer, A., "Social Space in Interdisciplinary Perspective," *Geographical Review* 59 (1969): 417-426.

Clark, P.J., and F.C. Evans, "Distance to Nearest Neighbor as a Measure of Spatial Relationships in Populations," *Ecology* 35 (1954): 445-453.

Dacey, M.F., "Analysis of Central Place and Point Patterns by a Nearest Neighbor Method," *Lund Studies in Geography*, Series B, 24, 1962.

Dikshit, Ramesh D., "Geography and Federalism," *Annals of the Association of American Geographers* 61 (1971): 97-115.

Duncan, O.D., R.P. Cuzzort, and B. Duncan, *Statistical Geography: Problems of Analyzing Areal Data*, New York: Free Press, 1961.

Getis, Arthur and Barry N. Boots, "Spatial Behavior: Rats and Man," *Professional Geographer* 23 (1971): 11-14.

Golledge, R., and L. Brown, "Search, Learning, and the Market Decision Process," *Geografiska Annaler* 49B (1967): 117-124.

Gould, P., "Problems of Space Preference Measures and Relationships," *Geographical Analysis* 1 (1969): 31-44.

Hamilton, F.E. Ian, "Aspects of Spatial Behavior in Planned Economies," *Papers of the Regional Science Association* 25 (1970): 83-108.

Holzner, Lutz, "The Role of History and Tradition in the Urban Geography of West Germany," *Annals of the Association of American Geographers*, 60 (1970): 315-339.

Hudson, J., "A Model of Spatial Relations," *Geographical Analysis* 1, (1969): 260-271.

Hudson, J.C., "Pattern Recognition in Empirical Map Analysis," *Journal of Regional Science* 9 (1969): 189-200.

Jones, David R.W., "The Caribbean Coast of Central America: A Case of Multiple Fragmentation," *Professional Geographer* 22 (1970): 260-266.

Jones, S.B., "Boundary Concepts in the Setting of Place and Time," *Annals of the Association of American Geographers* 49 (1959): 241-255.

Karabenick, Edward, "Djerba: A Case Study of the Geography of Isolation," *Journal of Geography* 70 (1971): 52-57.

Kasperson, Roger E., and Julian V. Minghi, *The Structure of Political Geography*, Chicago: Aldine-Atherton, 1971.

King, L.J., "Analysis of Spatial Form and Its Relation to Geographic Theory," *Annals of the Association of American Geographers* 59 (1969): 573-595.

Kolars, John and Henry J. Malin, "Population and Accessibility: An Analysis of Turkish Railroads," *Geographical Review* 60 (1970): 229-246.

Mackay, J.R., "The Interactance Hypothesis and Boundaries in Canada," *Canadian Geographer* 11 (1958): 1-8.

Mayer, H.M., "Politics and Land Use: The Indiana Shoreline of Lake Michigan," *Annals of the Association of American Geographers* 54 (1964): 508-523.

McConnell, Harold and David W. Yaseen, eds., *Models of Spatial Variation*, Volume 1 *Perspectives in Geography*, De Kalb: Northern Illinois University Press, 1971.

Nystuen, J.D., "Identification of Some Fundamental Spatial Concepts," *Papers of the Michigan Academy of Science, Arts, and Letters* 48 (1963): 373-384.

Olsson, G., "Trends in Spatial Model Building," *Geographical Analysis*, 1 (1969): 219-229.

Olsson, G., and S. Gale, "Spatial Theory and Human Behavior," *Papers and Proceedings of the Regional Science Association* 21 (1969): 229-241.

Rushton, G., "Analysis of Spatial Behavior by Revealed Space Preference," *Annals of the Association of American Geographers* 59 (1969): 391-402.

Warntz, W. and D. Neft, "Contributions to a Statistical Methodology for Areal Distributions," *Journal of Regional Science* 2 (1960): 47-66.

Webber, M., "Culture, Territoriality, and the **Elastic Mile**", *Papers and Proceedings of the Regional Science Association* 13 (1964): 59-70.

Wolpert, J., "The Decision Process in Spatial Context," *Annals of the Association of American Geographers* 54 (1964): 537-558.

Zipf, G.K., *Human Behavior and the Principle of Least Effort*, Cambridge, Mass.: Harvard University Press, 1949.

Resources

Borchert, J.R., "The Surface Water Supply of American Municipalities," *Annals of the Association of American Geographers* 44 (1954): 15-32.

Church, M., "The Spatial Organization of Electric Power Territories in Massachusetts," University of Chicago Department of Geography, Research Paper 69, 1960.

Ehrlich, Paul R. and Anne H., *Population, Resources, Environment: Issues in Human Ecology*, San Francisco: Freeman, 1970.

Firey, W., *Man, Mind, and Land: A Theory of Resource Use*, New York: Free Press, 1960.

Ginsburg, N., "Natural Resources and Economic Development," *Annals of the Association of American Geographers* 47 (1957): 196-212.

Guyol, N.B., *Energy in the Perspective of Geography*, Englewood Cliffs, N.J.: Prentice-Hall, 1971.

Henderson, J.M., *The Efficiency of the Coal Industry: An Application of Linear Programming*, Cambridge, Mass: Harvard University Press, 1958.

Krutilla, J.V., "Water Resources Development: The Regional Incidence of Costs and Gains," *Papers and Proceedings of the Regional Science Association* 4 (1958): 273-312.

Linton, D.L., "The Geography of Energy," *Geography* 50 (1965): 197-228.

McNee, R.B., "Centrifugal-Centripetal Forces in International Petroleum Company Regions," *Annals of the Association of American Geographers* 51 (1961): 124-138.

Manners, G., *The Geography of Energy*, London: Hutchinson University Library, 1964.

Melamid, A., "Geography of the World Petroleum Price Structure," *Economic Geography* 38 (1962): 283-298.

Roepke, H.G., "Changing Patterns of Coal Production in the Eastern Interior Field," *Economic Geography* 31 (1955): 234-247.

Van Burkalow, A., "The Geography of New York City's Water Supply," *Geographical Review* 49 (1959): 369-386.

White, G.F., "Industrial Water Use: A Review," *Geographical Review* 50 (1960): 412-430.

Conservation

Burton, I. and R. Kates, eds., *Readings in Resource Management and Conservation*, Chicago: University of Chicago Press, 1965.

Ciriacy-Wantrup, S.V., *Resource Conservation: Economics and Policies*, Berkeley: University of California Press, 1965.

Krutilla, J.V. and O. Eckstein, *Multiple Purpose River Development*, Baltimore: Johns Hopkins, 1958.

Zobler, L., "An Economic-Historical View of Natural Resource Use and Conservation," *Economic Geography* 38 (1962): 189-194.

Location and Interaction in Spatially Restricted Societies

Chapter 2

Most theories of spatial organization (and the goals of "best use of space" that suggest theory) seem to relate primarily to urbanized, industrial and commercial societies. In a subsistence farming society with limited technology, nature appears to determine how land is used. Yet it is apparent that man has always sought to use territory efficiently and productively, within the constraints of environment and technology, in order to survive. The landscape patterns in less developed societies may seem quite different from those in highly technical ones, but the goals are nearly the same. Moreover, in areas where technology is limited the patterns of land use are relatively simple, and therefore provide a useful point of departure for our study of the spatial organization of man's social and economic life.

Although the emphasis of this book is on societies that are technically advanced, mobile, and interdependent, it is a fact that about half the world's population lives in spatially restricted, largely self-sufficient, and near-subsistence societies. In such societies, only the smallest surplus is produced for exchange, and thus spatial experience is limited. Life is confined to local areas; agriculture is the main livelihood. Social and economic relations over distances are restricted, and the local area, the village, or perhaps a tribal group of villages constitutes the **social space**, the area in which most activities take place. Today's advanced nations evolved from such societies, so it is enlightening to compare the characteristics of the two kinds of societies (figure 2.01).

CHARACTERISTICS OF SPATIALLY RESTRICTED SOCIETIES

Life in spatially restricted societies reflects both the population's close ties to the land and the poor state of its transport system. The landscape seems miniaturized, with small fields, narrow roads, and a very local pattern of movement. Agriculture and handcrafts are also organized on a small scale. The community usually achieves a fair degree of self-sufficiency in food and in goods that can be manufactured by hand, but the production and trade of specialty

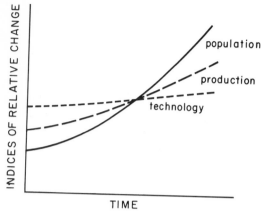

A. Spatially Restricted (Traditional) Society

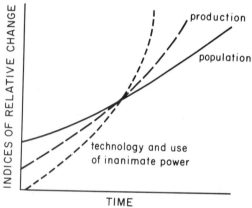

B. Spatially Interdependent (Commercial) Society

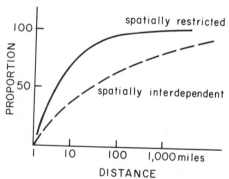

C. Proportion of Economic and Social Activities Conducted Within a Given Distance

goods are limited in scope, volume, and variety. Since transport is poor, distance is a strong barrier to trade and travel.

The pattern of life is repetitive in both time and space: the seasons often enforce a rigid regimen of work, and a family's ties to its land are strong. Migration tends to be circular (ending back in the home village), motivated largely by a desire to find brides outside the village, to seek temporary work, or to visit relatives and friends.

Regional dialects, customs, and character tend to develop in such societies; note, for example, the many language areas in a small part of New Guinea, each representing a small geographic region (figure 2.02).

Markets and Exchange

Societies vary in level of commercialization — the degree to which they exchange goods and services (see figure 2.01). The farm in Western society is a business: the farmer's activities and success are governed by the national market, by prices on land and labor, and by the exchange of goods. The peasant in a subsistence society, however, operates a small household economy, whether he cultivates rice intensively or farms in the traditional European way. He also functions as part of a larger kinship group, and his activities are governed by the needs of the group and by a strong social and economic order. Exchange often occurs because of compulsory rent or tax; any surplus from this exchange is very small. Increased productivity results more from the peasant's desire to improve the well-being of his household than from external demand. In these nonmarket economies, economic exchange is linked to personal needs, so the change from primitive cultivator to modern farmer involves a radical shift from a personal con-

Figure 2.01 In spatially restricted (traditional) societies, population tends to grow faster than production (A), while in spatially interdependent (commercial) societies, the rapid increase in technology and especially in the use of inanimate power allows production to grow faster than population (B). One measure of spatial interdependence is the distances over which economic and social activities are carried out — rather limited in traditional societies and extensive in technically advanced societies (C).

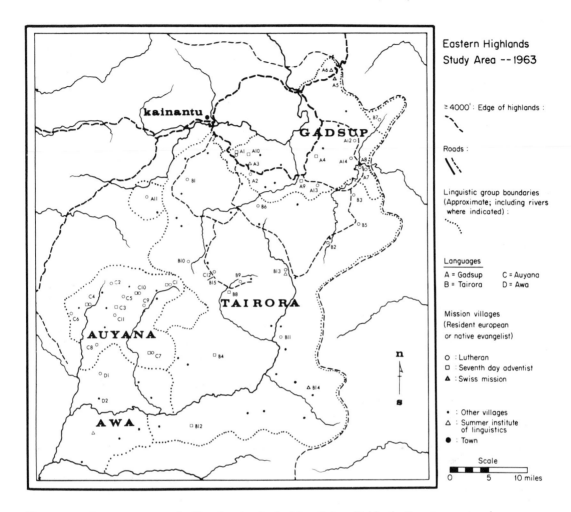

Figure 2.02 Language areas and village location in the New Guinea highlands. Poor transport and physical isolation partly account for the presence of the different languages in such a small area. (Reprinted courtesy of K. Pataki.)

cept of economics to an impersonal one.

Most near-subsistence societies do support, often by means of the small surpluses of many peasants, a small aristocracy, whose members are educated, relatively wealthy, and have broader outside contact and experience. The system is efficient and convenient for such an aristocracy and is perhaps even a necessary stage in development in the sense that the aristocracy could concentrate capital and introduce modern technologies; but resistance to change is very great, since the aristocracy can maintain its position only by owning extensive lands and by exploiting the labor of hundreds or thousands.

SPATIALLY EXTENSIVE ACTIVITIES

Hunting and Gathering

Some groups that are restricted to a small territory may nevertheless engage in **extensive** activities, in which the productivity per unit area is low. Few people today live under very primitive socioeconomic systems; simple hunting and gathering societies are fast-disappearing remnants in the areas most remote from centers of "civilization." Probably only a few million persons ever lived in such societies at any one time, since only a small number of people, at best, can

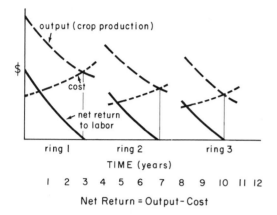

Net Return = Output – Cost

Figure 2.03 Shifting cultivation: costs and benefits. Productivity of an area falls over time and with distance of the gardens from settlement. Here ring 1, closest to the settlement, is first cultivated. After four years productivity falls, and cultivation shifts to the more distant ring 2, where initial productivity may not be as great, owing to the greater distance from the settlement. Note that the net return to labor is derived by subtracting cost from output.

depend upon nature to provide animals, skins, fish, and shelter. Indeed, some recent evidence suggests that as man entered new and rich territories, his numbers grew rapidly, almost as quickly decimated or destroyed other animal populations, and in turn moved on or were reduced by famine.

As the better lands have been taken over by crop agriculture, the hunters have been forced into the poorest and most remote areas of the earth, where the productivity of the land is even lower. A square mile (2.59 km²) or more per person is required today for such societies to exist, even though poor transport makes it hard to cross such distances. Thus, small hunting groups of 50 persons need an area with a radius of up to 6 miles (10 kilometers) and a food margin (ratio of potential food to needed food) of as much as 40 to 1. Hunting and gathering activity survives among some Eskimos in areas too cold for farming, and also in remote hilly forests or deserts in temperate or tropical areas, where neither the technology of agriculture nor animal domestication has yet been successfully introduced.

The social organization of hunting and gathering groups is normally tribal. Permanent settlement is limited by the need for access to large land areas and by the group's need to move frequently despite poor mobility. The group is isolated physically and culturally, although it is seminomadic and larger gatherings occasionally occur. Certainly in these societies where survival is always difficult, the pursuit of goals of efficient use of territory is essential and is indeed apparent in the carefully worked-out locations for semipermanent camps, in hunting circuits, and in group numbers.

Technologically Primitive Agriculture

Forms of agriculture in which tools are limited to digging stick, hoe, and shovel still survive in fairly wide areas, although relatively few people are involved. Either because they have been forced there or because they have long existed in such remote locations, technologically primitive agricultural societies are generally located in poorer areas unwanted for technically superior activities.

Shifting Cultivation. **Shifting cultivation**, known also as *swidden* or "slash and burn" cultivation, is not a very productive kind of agriculture, and its practitioners are almost totally removed from the commercial world. Where there is a small population and plentiful land but little technology, shifting cultivation may be a fairly efficient method. It involves making a short migration and creating new gardens and villages as the fertility of an area becomes exhausted. From 5 to 25 persons per square mile can be supported; villages usually have only 30 to 300 inhabitants, since productivity is so low.

Figures 2.03 and 2.04 illustrate a typical pattern of shifting cultivation. A new village is founded in virgin forest. Patches of adjacent land are cut and burned for nutrients, and fields and gardens are cultivated with a variety of crops. Since no fertilizer is used and few animals are kept, nutrients are exhausted very rapidly, and satisfactory crops may be grown for only three or four years. Yields typically drop about 30 percent the second year, 50 percent the third (figure 2.03). These fields are then returned to fallow, and rings of gardens farther from the village are cultivated, until the distance between fields and villages becomes excessive. The village then migrates to a new area, probably a few miles away, and the depleted land is left to recover its fertility over a long period of fallow, which may be up to 40 years. By continually shifting to more fertile land, more people can be supported at a fairly consistent level. Totally new villages may be founded if the old ones become too large or are disrupted by severe internal conflict.

Shifting cultivation is subject to increasing restrictions. Population growth must be relieved either by migration of part of the population from the area, perhaps to settle in more intensively farmed regions, or by adoption of a stationary and technologically improved agriculture. Moreover, further population increase and the lack of unoccupied land may force a group to find a permanent location for its villages and fields, especially after some contact is made with advanced cultures.

Shifting cultivation well illustrates how the concept of "efficiency" differs in the perception and lives of groups with different technologies and experiences. For spatially restricted groups with very limited technology, the pattern of shifting field and village locations may be an optimal spatial structure. Yet to people in the wider, more technological and commercial society, the practice appears wasteful, inefficient, and environmentally damaging.

Nomadism (Migratory Husbandry). Nomadic herding is also an extremely old type of occupance, first developed in Southwest Asia and Northeast Africa. It is usually practiced in natural grassland areas in arid and semiarid regions, where crop agriculture cannot be supported, at least with available technologies.

Productivity from herding is very low relative to yields from crop agriculture, partly because the climate is arid, partly because animals are an inefficient source of food. Such regions can support only one or two persons per square mile.

Nomadic herdsmen operate in tribal or extended-family units. They tend many different animals, which provide both transport and a wide variety of products:

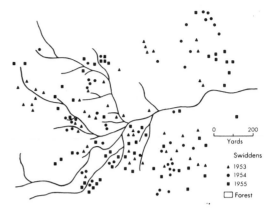

Figure 2.04   Shifting of gardens. Location and year of clearing of swiddens (gardens) among the Hanunoo, Mindoro, the Philippines. Hamlet locations are not given. In this area the cycle of reuse is about 12 years. (Reprinted by permission of the McGraw-Hill Book Company, Inc., from Donald W. Fryer, *World Economic Development*, 1965.)

milk, cheese, and butter; meat, skin, and hides; and bones for tools. Such a diversity of articles available within the group is very desirable for a society that must be largely self-sufficient.

Given limited technology and resources of variable quality, nomadism is a remarkably efficient system of location. Herds move from one pasture and water hole to another. When one area is fully grazed, the range is left to recover. Because nomadism allows fairly quick adjustment to variation in weather and in grass quality, it can support a larger average herd and a greater population than can a settled livestock industry with the same technology, where average herd size is restricted by the quality of the range in the poorest years.

Nomadic migration often exhibits a regular circular pattern (figure 2.05), but this may be distorted by the randomizing effects of weather and by peculiarities of topography. Groups tend not to cross paths, since they usually operate in "traditional" territories. The migration may be both horizontal and vertical. In vertical migration (**transhumance**) animals move to mountain pastures for the summer and to lowland pastures for the winter, using land efficiently.

Most arid zones have a few oases, or

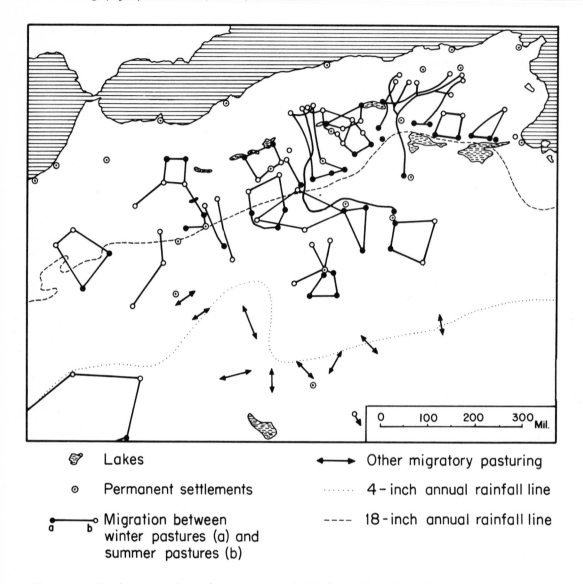

☞ Lakes

⊙ Permanent settlements

●━━━○ Migration between
  a   b   winter pastures (a) and
          summer pastures (b)

◄━━━► Other migratory pasturing

········ 4 - inch annual rainfall line

- - - - 18 - inch annual rainfall line

Figure 2.05 Simple patterns of nomadic movements in far Northwest Africa. Many groups move in restricted areas, and a few move rather great distances. Many move from lower arid zones in winter to more humid mountain areas in summer. (Reprinted courtesy of D. Van Nostrand Company, Inc., from Hans Boesch, *A Geography of World Economy*, 1964.)

larger water spots, supporting both towns and areas of intensive agriculture, and having many times the population of the larger regions of nomadic herding. Oases occasionally supplement the needs of the herdsman, supplying him with vegetables, fruits, grain, tools, water, and a market for his limited surpluses of animal products.

There are many restraints on nomadism. A strong national administration and boundary defense tend to eliminate cross-border movements, thereby limiting the free movement necessary to maintain a herd successfully. Nomadism is weakened also when a society makes an effort to commercialize agriculture and concentrate herds to produce meat for new urban markets. In this case, settled commercial-livestock ranching gradually takes over.

In conclusion, nomadic ways of life are neither irrational nor inefficient, but for their environment and technology represent an efficient and productive use of territory.

SPATIALLY INTENSIVE ACTIVITIES: INTENSIVE SUBSISTENCE AGRICULTURE

Today about one-third to one-half of the world's population (in the past the proportion was much higher) is supported by intensive, rather self-sufficient farming. Intensive subsistence agriculture is distinguished here from the technologically primitive (extensive) agriculture previously discussed by the greater human alteration of nature, the greater dependence on human labor, and the higher productivity per unit area. Most of East and South Asia and parts of Africa and Latin America are supported by intensive subsistence agriculture, and until the Industrial Revolution, Europe, too, was so supported. Indeed, the rise of the early civilizations depended on successful intensive farming to support greater and greater concentrations of people. Thus, population growth both necessitated and made possible intensive agriculture.

The village is the dominant social and economic unit in most traditional peasant societies. As a political unit it may include several small settlements, together with their surrounding fields. Villages tend to be distributed in a fairly efficient and uniform pattern. Their frequency originally was determined by the distance easily reached and returned from in a day. But new villages have been created as old ones succumb to population pressure, and larger consolidated and fortified villages have been established in some areas for defense.

Life on a subsistence farm was and still is repetitive. Change comes only gradually when new methods and crops, such as the recent "miracle rice," are introduced, making it possible to intensify further and support a larger population. More common are gradual improvements in existing technology. Since change is so slow, however, subsistence agriculture — where the needs of the family or village are just barely met — remains characteristic of such economies until a change in the political-economic organization permits industrialization and commercialization.

Subsistence Agriculture in European History

The typical pattern of European subsistence agriculture was a mixture of communally held woodland and pasture and several hundred long, narrow strips surrounding a small village. An average family might cultivate up to 50 strips of diverse quality at various distances from the village, totaling about 5 to 15 acres. These strips were sometimes held as private property, but could still be reallocated by the village; the inner strips were generally used more intensively and frequently. A traditional fallow rotation system was employed: a strip was planted for two years, then allowed to lie fallow. Often the village lands were part of a large estate. Rents due to landlords and taxes and interest usually claimed half the crop, so that no surplus was available for the peasant to sell.

The population expansion of the seventeenth to nineteenth centuries led to excessive land division, extreme poverty, and **underemployment**, and the demand for food by the growing cities could not be met by the existing farm organization. Governments and large landowners forced enclosure and consolidation of strips and communal lands into separate farms. These remained too small, however, and peasants were soon differentiated into rich and poor: the more successful often acquired the holdings of the less successful and, thus, having a surplus, made the transition to a commercial economy. Those forced off their land either became farm laborers, migrated abroad, or moved into the growing cities.

East and South Asia: Dominance of Rice

East and South Asia are today the main areas where intensive, self-sufficient farming predominates. There is great variety of landscape and climate in this vast area, but the warm, moist, "tropical" rainy conditions of the long summer monsoon are most characteristic. Rice is best suited for maximum yields under just these conditions, and it has long been the staple and preferred grain of the region. Further inland, where there is less moisture or where the growing season is too short, rice is replaced by hardier grains.

The distribution of population in South and East Asia closely follows the concentration of rice in the lowlands and floodplains.

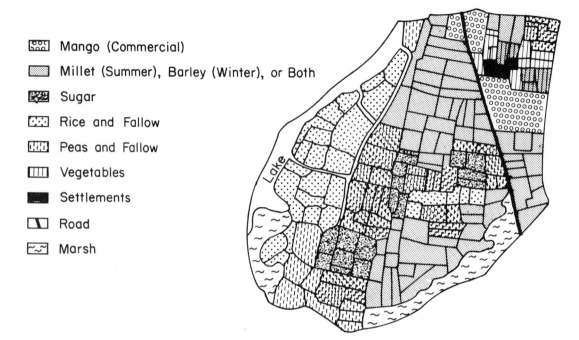

Mango (Commercial)

Millet (Summer), Barley (Winter), or Both

Sugar

Rice and Fallow

Peas and Fallow

Vegetables

Settlements

Road

Marsh

Figure 2.06   A village and its lands: Bauria, India (about two miles in length). Note the concentration of more intensive vegetables and mangos near the villages; rice is grown along the lake and canals for easiest irrigation.

Severely sloping land is not used very intensively, despite the high density of population in Asia. Floodplain locations are the most preferred, since fields can be larger and the labor needed to construct fields and supply water is reduced.

Organization of the Farm and Means of Intensification. Intensity of rice production — greater productivity per acre and the ability to support a larger population — is partly achieved by paddy irrigation. The paddy represents a significant and costly human modification of nature. Carefully constructed, absolutely level rice fields are flooded at crucial times to obtain the maximum yield. Double-cropping (two crops per year) of rice is possible in near-tropical and more continuously moist areas. Rice and a small grain crop alternate in wet-dry areas, rice in the warm summer, wheat, millet, or other grains in the cooler winter. Efficiency of land use is further increased by using separate fields to produce seedlings while the main fields continue to be used for other crops.

Patterns of fields reflect minor topographic variations, ease of irrigation, and the tendency of larger units to fragment into smaller ones as the population increases (figure 2.06). The reduced size of the fields makes mechanization technically difficult, and the small size of farms and the meager surplus makes mechanization economically impractical. Where fields are very small, even an animal cannot compete with hand labor. Where fields and farms are fairly large, however, an animal such as a water buffalo becomes profitable; the **marginal productivity**, or extra output, more than pays for the animal. In Japan, where transport is good, rice prices are high, and more than half the rice crop is typically sold, farmers have found it economic to use hand tractors even in rather small fields.

Heavy fertilization is a basic aid to high yields of rice and continuous land productivity. In China and especially Japan, human waste is a principal fertilizer; mud from the bottom of fish ponds and canals is also important in China. Yields are further increased by careful weeding.

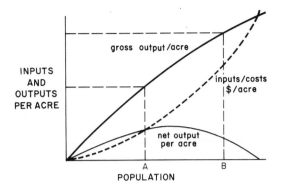

A. Low population pressure; moderate farm size

B. High population pressure; small farms

Figure 2.07 Population and productivity: intensive subsistence agriculture. As population increases in a finite area, additional output is achieved by greater inputs. At lower population levels (as at *A*) a significant net output, that is, output over and above the minimum needs of the farmer, can be achieved at moderate cost. At a higher population level (as at *B*) very great inputs are needed to raise output only moderately, and the net output, or surplus, falls.

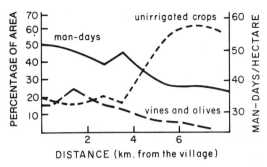

Figure 2.08 Distance to fields and farmer attention (Canicatti, Sicily). The left scale shows the percentage of area devoted to vines and unirrigated crops. The right scale shows man-days per hectare (labor per unit area). Crops requiring more effort (including fertilizer) are located near the village, and labor per unit area therefore decreases with distance from the village. (From data in M. Chisholm, *Rural Settlement and Land Use; An Essay on Location*, Hutchinson University Library, 1962.)

All these means of intensifying rice yield depend on the use of a great deal of labor, chiefly for spring transplanting and for the fall harvest (when only a single crop is grown each year). At other seasons, farm labor is often underemployed without enough work to keep fully occupied, and is therefore available for construction or other temporary jobs. Labor productivity and farm income would rise if a farmer were able to obtain more land. Land productivity is high at present, but productivity per man-hour is extremely low. (See figure 2.07, which illustrates the idea that production per man-hour at first increases as population increases, probably because of better technology, but then decreases as population levels require excessive subdivision of land.)

All these efforts to increase productivity result from the need to sustain the family with only a small — and possibly diminishing — farm, rather than from the desire to increase cash sales. If a farmer has sufficient land, however, he will probably be eager to take advantage of commercial demand.

Problems of Subsistence Agriculture

The Problem of Land.   In all areas of intensive, subsistence agriculture, the small size of farms severely limits the productivity of labor. Division of land upon inheritance and transfers owing to debts and marriage result in complex ownership patterns and small farms. Such reduction in farm size tends to increase the amount of tenancy (dependence on rented land) as farmers seek to add to their holdings. Since rents may be from one-third to two-thirds of the crop, however, the marginal return to the operator on such land is exceedingly poor.

Land division can also mean that an individual's fields are extremely fragmented (separated in space). Small fields can result from adapting paddy fields to local topography and, when village communal lands are of varying quality, from the practice of allotting fields of each kind to every family; for example, every family may be allotted some irrigable paddy and some upland fields. The unfortunate consequence is increased labor for reduced yields on a given quantity of land, since the farmer can give less attention — especially in fertilizing — to more distant fields (figure 2.08).

The Problem of Transport.   Transport is local, slow, and irregular in most regions of subsistence agriculture. Footpaths and canals are used for local travel, and rivers and major canals provide a means of long-distance transport, supplemented in Japan and India by railway systems. In general, however, local access to transport is so poor that movements beyond 20 miles are very costly, and most movements are much shorter than that.

The Growth of Markets and the Commercialization of Agriculture

Peasant subsistence societies have weak local or regional, rather than national, markets. Much exchange of goods, in fact, is a function of legal and social obligations. Exchange for economic reasons is not absent, however. Although individual farm surpluses are small, there is a collective demand for exchange of grains, meat, vegetables, handicrafts, and outside food products and manufactures. Traveling merchants and seasonal fairs help satisfy these demands, as do occasional village markets. Market towns also exist, perhaps one for every 200,000 people; because of the high density of the rural population, such market towns may be within 5 to 10 miles of most farmers.

Subsistence agriculture is changing, however, even in remote areas. In most regions the proportion of rice and other products sold commercially is increasing as new transport is built and the urban population grows. Special commercial crops for exporting have been developed, such as cotton in China and India and jute in Pakistan. In Japan, development of a commercialized agriculture has accompanied the evolution of an urban-industrial society; on the average, more than half the rice crop is now sold, and more farmers are specializing in meat, poultry, and even dairy products. Commercialization has also permitted the farmer to increase fertilization, utilize hand tractors and other modern tools, and raise productivity to the highest known levels. Agriculture in Japan, however, still yields such a low return per family that an economic dualism exists — there is on the one hand a fully modern urban-industrial sector and, on the other, a half subsistence, half market-oriented agricultural society.

Intensive subsistence agricultural landscapes, evolving under a feudal social, economic, and political order, did and do now exhibit regular patterns of settlement and land use, representing the greatest productivity possible under technical and cultural constraints.

Fragmentation of holdings into areas of varying quality and into zones of varying distance is inefficient in comparison to the separate farmsteads in the United States, but given limited technology and transportation, the idea of self-sufficiency, and the great social importance of the village, it may be an optimal solution for a subsistence society.

SPATIALLY INTERDEPENDENT ENCLAVES: WESTERN ESTATES

Following the European voyages of discovery, demand in Europe for tropical products like sugar, spices, and fruit grew rapidly. The supplies purchased from local rulers soon proved inadequate, and European companies established estates and plantations dedicated to efficient, fairly modern production of specific crops. Although these estates helped commercialize the local economy, they were at the same time part of the agricultural economy of the European mother country.

Estates, typically located in tropical environments suited for growing the desired exotic products, were subject to three restraints: location in an area in which the mother country had sufficient influence and power to protect the estate; availability of a sufficient labor supply, whether indigenous or imported; and location, if possible, in coastal areas, for easy access to ocean transport. Gradually, railways and roads were built, and greater advantage could be taken of better lands farther from the ocean (figure 2.09).

Estate Products

Major plantation products are sugar, rubber, coffee, tea, cocoa, copra, bananas, fibers (hemp, abaca, sisal, cotton, henequen), oil palm, and spices. Production of each tends to be concentrated in certain

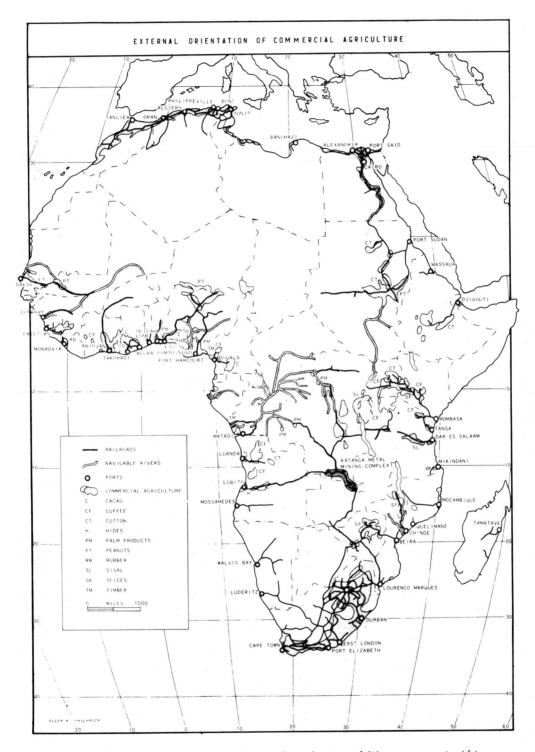

Figure 2.09 External **orientation** of commercial agriculture: location of Western estates in Africa around 1955. Most commercial agriculture (in large part carried on by Western estates) depended upon foreign markets and located along coasts or railways, which provided external access rather than internal connections. (Reprinted by permission of John Wiley & Sons, Inc., from Allen K. Philbrick, *This Human World*, 1963.)

regions or districts devoted to that specialty, even though production could be located in a much greater area if environmental constraints or advantages were the only factors that had to be considered.

Marketing, consumption, and prices are largely controlled by interests in Europe and the United States. Since these crops can be raised in much greater quantity than is justified by demand, the bargaining position of suppliers is weak. In order to stabilize production and prices, the supplying and receiving countries have jointly created marketing and quota agreements setting production and trade patterns.

Estate agriculture requires considerable labor. Where local labor supplies proved insufficient, workers have been brought great distances, either on contract (from Japan or the Philippines to Hawaii, for instance) or as slaves (Negroes to the American colonies and to the Caribbean estates). These groups radically altered the composition of the population in the areas to which they were transported. The concentration of adequate labor, local or imported, is an important reason why estates have a particular and limited distribution. Where local population pressure is great, estates must compete for land and labor with the agriculture needed to provide local food supplies.

Mining

Western-controlled mining activities also form commercial enclaves competing for local labor. Exploitation of products begins with the discovery of a particularly rich resource, usually of such high quality that the expense of building costly transport lines, usually railroads, is warranted. Even with this expense, profits may still be higher than those received for exploiting resources in the home country. Cheap local labor for mining and refining sometimes determines the use of specific mines, but the discovery of scarce resources is the major factor in mining location.

Significance of Estates and Mining Enclaves

Estates and mines have brought greater commercialization to colonized countries by paying wages — no matter how low — to workers. They have also induced greater development by building the railways and roads necessary to export goods. Secondary development, however, has generally been minimal, since investors have preferred to locate in their home country the **processing activities** that produce the most wealth. Since the railways were built to penetrate the country and to aid in exporting goods rather than to facilitate internal circulation, they tend to create a bias toward economic relations with — if not dependence upon — the mother country.

In these colonies a **colonial** trading pattern was developed in which most of the cash income of the colony derived from export activities. Since power, banking, investment, and trade were largely controlled by the colonial administration, this income was typically spent on costly consumption goods from the home country, rather than on economic development. In fact, official policy usually discouraged general industrialization, since colonies were more useful as captive markets. The contrasts between the small landed aristocracy and the large body of subsistence peasants thus became aggravated.

Nevertheless, sanitation facilities and other health measures were introduced by colonial nations, along with more formal educational systems. As a result, population in colonized nations increased spectacularly — without corresponding radical changes in the economy. Thus, more and more people have had to be supported by an agricultural system that uses only limited technology, and standards of living may have actually declined in the last few centuries in such areas as India, China, and the Caribbean. Estates have helped redistribute the local population, concentrating people in coastal estate areas and associated towns. When estates have moved (because of disease, for example) severe short-run social and economic disruption has occurred.

Urbanization and Migration

Widespread urbanization has accompanied or even preceded the commercialization of agriculture in most lesser developed, spatially restricted societies. The growing cities usually include both some modern industry and an extensive small-scale commercial, service, and handicraft economy; but in general the population exceeds available employment opportunities. Much of the labor force from rural areas is better described as circulating between rural homes and urban jobs than as migrant. People tend to maintain a very strong tribal, kinship and "home town" loyalty and social network, often as a means of adjustment to the radical change from a subsistence village society to an urban one.

PRINCIPLES OF LOCATION AND GOALS OF SPATIAL BEHAVIOR IN SPATIALLY RESTRICTED SOCIETIES

We may summarize this discussion of less commercial societies with reference to the locational principles and goals discussed earlier.

— **Repetitive patterns in time and space:** *Spatial patterns of behavior are more likely to be repetitive in noncommercial than in commercial societies. Still, the more successful forms of land use gradually spread out from their points of origin — the diffusion of wet-rice culture is one example.*

— **Environmental control:** *Environment sets strong limits and channels the development of an agricultural economy. Thus, wet-rice cultures tend to be present where there is level land and plentiful water. The combination of relief, soil, and climate makes many areas useful only for nomadism or for shifting cultivation.*

— **Role of distance:** *Given the limited technology and dependence on agriculture, distance is a strong barrier. Mobility and travel are limited, so both surpluses and deficits are difficult to alleviate. The local area must be self-sufficient, and regions tend to become greatly differentiated in language and custom.*

— **Role of tradition:** *Religious and cultural traditions influence spatial behavior in several ways — by favoring repetition of past methods of organization, by favoring or rejecting certain foods, goods, and methods,*

and by placing relatively little emphasis on innovation and change.

— **Level of technology:** *The less mechanized technology of spatially restricted societies is reflected in their dependence on human and animal labor; in their poorer transport system; and in their smaller scale of operations, from the size of fields and buildings to the distances typically traveled.*

— **Scale:** *Inadequate transport and high population growth in these societies have prevented the realization of benefits that would accrue from larger firms and enterprises. In fact, scale has been reduced. Per capita productivity is very low and may even have fallen in the last two centuries.*

— **Socioeconomic system:** *Semifeudal forms of organization in some areas have tended to stifle change. The high degree of tenancy and land fragmentation associated with semifeudal society reduces productivity.*

— **Goals and restraints:** *(a) Maximizing the productivity of each area. This goal has been avidly pursued, with some degree of success, since output per acre is fairly high. The effect of intensifying production has been to support more people performing the same activities rather than to free part of the population for different activities or to raise the level of living. Whereas in a commercial society productivity is achieved by specializing and differentiating land use and labor, in a subsistence society greater productivity depends upon intensifying local production. (b) Maximizing interaction with minimum travel. As a result of pursuing this goal, the size and spacing of settlements are efficient, although land fragmentation and tenancy are a problem. But interaction (interchange of people and goods) is often limited to the area of the village and its fields. Even if trade is highly valued, poor transport and low farm productivity hinder the exchange of goods.*

In conclusion, a self-sufficient agricultural society with low technology produces a repetitive and miniaturized landscape pattern — a spatial structure consisting of independent but look-alike cells. The patterns of village organization are similar over much of the world. Still, there is little interrelation between areas because language and culture are often different. In contrast, in commercial societies the same transport system that sustains the economy fosters greater cultural unity, even though the economy is extremely diversified through specialized land use.

Subsistence societies, then, do pursue the same goals of organizing space in the best way, but given the limited technology, the specific patterns may appear quite different (especially in scale) from those in commercial societies, to which we now turn.

REFERENCES

Nomadism, Shifting Cultivation

Brookfield, H.C., "Local Study and Comparative Method, Central New Guinea," *Annals of the Association of American Geographers* 52 (1962): 242-254.

Clarke, J.I., "Summer Nomadism in Tunisia," *Economic Geography* 31 (1955): 155-167.

Harris, David R., "The Ecology of Swidden Cultivation in the Upper Orinoco Rain Forest, Venezuela," *Geographical Review* 61 (1971): 475-495.

Igbozurike, Matthias U., "Ecological Balance in Tropical Agriculture," *Geographical Review* 61 (1971): 519-529.

Johnson, D., *Nature of Nomadism*, University of Chicago Department of Geography, Research Paper 118, 1969.

Melamid, A., "Political Boundaries and Nomadic Grazing," *Geographical Review* 55 (1965): 287-289.

Rasmussen, T.F., "Population and Land Utilization in the Assam Village," *Journal of Tropical Geography* 14 (1960): 51-74.

Sonnenfeld, J., "Changes in an Eskimo Hunting Technology," *Annals of the Association of American Geographers* 50 (1960): 172-186.

Watters, R.F., "Some Forms of Shifting Cultivation in the Southwest Pacific," *Journal of Tropical Geography* 14 (1960): 35-50.

Intensive Subsistence Agriculture

Ahmad, N., "The Pattern of Rural Settlement in East Pakistan," *Geographical Review* 46 (1956): 388-398.

Blaikie, P.M., "Spatial Organization of Agriculture on Some North Indian Villages, Part 1," *Transactions of the Institute of British Geographers* 52 (1971): 1-40.

Clark, C. and M. Haswell, *Economics of Subsistence Agriculture*, New York: St. Martin's, 1954.

Dobby, E.H.G., "The North Kedah Plain — A Study in the Environment of Pioneering for Rice Cultivation," *Economic Geography* 27 (1951): 287-320.

Hale, R.A., "The Origin, Nature, and Distribution of Agricultural Terracing," *Pacific Viewpoint* 2 (1961): 1-40.

Ho, R., "Mixed Farming and Multiple Cropping in Malaya," *Journal of Tropical Geography* 16 (1962): 1-17.

Hore, P.N., "Rainfall, Rice Yields, and Irrigation Needs in West Bengal," *Geography* 49 (1964): 114-121.

Kakiuchi, G.H., "Recent Development and Trends in the Cultivation of Wet-Rice in Japan," *Land Economics* 41 (1965): 69-73.

Matui, I., "Statistical Study of the Distribution of Scattered Villages in Two Regions of the Tonami Plain," *Japanese Journal of Geology and Geography* 9 (1932): 251-256.

Shafi, M., "Measurement of Agricultural Efficiency in Uttar Pradesh," *Economic Geography* 36 (1960): 296-305.

Sopher, D.E., "The Swidden Wet-Rice Transition Zone in the Chittagong Hills," *Annals of the Association of American Geographers* 54 (1964): 107-126.

Stevens, Richard E., "Land Tenure and Agricultural Productivity in a Basotho Village," *Proceedings of the Association of American Geographers* 2 (1970): 132-135.

Vermeer, Donals E., "Population Pressure and Crop Rotational Changes among the Tiv of Nigeria," *Annals of the Association of American Geographers* 60 (1970): 299-314.

Estates

Brookfield, H.C., "Probelms of Monoculture and Diversification in a Sugar Island, Mauritius," *Economic Geography* 35 (1959): 25-40.

Hill, P., *Migrant Cocoa-Farmers of Southern Ghana*, Cambridge, Eng.: Cambridge University Press, 1963.

Hodder, B.W., "Tin Mining on the Jos Plateau of Nigeria," *Economic Geography* 35 (1959): 109-122.

Ward, R.G., "Cash Cropping and the Fijian Village," *Geographical Journal* 130 (1964): 484-506.

Development and Change

Chang, Jen-hu, "Sugar Cane in Hawaii and Taiwan: Contrasts in Ecology, Technology and Economy," *Economic Geography* 46 (1970): 39-52.

Coi, J.B., "Rural Development in Tropical Areas," *Journal of Tropical Geography* 12 (1958): (entire issue).

Floyd, Barry, "Agricultural Innovation in Jamaica: The Yallahs Valley Land Authority," *Economic Geography* 46 (1970): 63-77.

Fryer, D.W., "Development of Cottage and Small Scale Industry in Malaya and Southeast Asia," *Journal of Tropical Geography* 17 (1963): 92-98.

Good, Charles M., "Rural Markets and Trade in East Africa," University of Chicago, Department of Geography, Research Paper 128, 1970.

Johnson, E.A.J., *The Organization of Space in Developing Countries*, Cambridge, Mass.: Harvard University Press, 1970.

Knapp, Donald, "Marketing and Social Patterns in Rural Taiwan," *Annals of the Association of American Geographers* 61 (1971): 131-155.

Kolars, J.F., "Tradition, Season, and Change in a Turkish Village," University of Chicago Department of Geography, Reserach Paper 82, 1963.

Lentnek, B., "Economic Transition to Commercial Agriculture: El Llano, Mexico," *Annals of the Association of American Geographers* 59 (1969): 65-84.

Ojo, G.J. Afolabi, "Some Observations on Journey to Agricultural Work in Yorubaland, Southwestern Nigeria," *Economic Geography* 46 (1970): 459-471.

Riddell, J.B., *The Spatial Dynamics of Modernization in Sierra Leone: Structure, Diffusion and Response*, Evanston: Northwestern University Press, 1970.

Smith, R.H.T. and A.M. Hay, "Theory of the Spatial Structure of Internal Trade in Underdeveloped Countries," *Geographical Analysis* 1 (1969): 121-136.

Stouse, Pierre A.D. Jr., "Instability of Tropical Agriculture, the Atlantic Lowlands of Costa Rica," *Economic Geography* 46 (1970): 78-97.

White, H.P., "Internal Exchange of Staple Foods in the Gold Coast," *Economic Geography* 32 (1956): 115-125.

Part Two

Structure of Land Use: Extensive Space

In part 2 we develop the theory that man's attempt to use territory most efficiently should result in a continuous **gradient** of intensity of use, density of population, and value of land, from a maximum at the society's center to virtually nothing at its most remote reaches. While the theory applies equally well to urban uses of land (chapter 8), only its application to agriculture is developed at this point.

Commercial Agriculture

Chapter 3

THE ROLE OF AGRICULTURE IN SPATIALLY INTERDEPENDENT SOCIETIES

Of all man's economic activities, agriculture is the most fundamental and has altered the natural landscape the most dramatically. For this space-consuming activity whole portions of continents have been deforested, cultivated, and reordered by man. So dominant is the imprint of agriculture on the landscape, so intimate the relationship between man and environment, that the agricultural landscape has long been a focal point of geographic study. Although in the most advanced countries its role has been eclipsed by the urban activities that support much of the population, it is essential as a supplier both of food and of raw materials for industry. Agricultural production constitutes less than one-fifth of the national income in these advanced countries, but it provides the raw materials needed by about one-fifth of industry. In turn many industries and indeed thousands of villages, towns, and cities exist mainly to serve the agricultural sector.

Indirectly, as much as half of most advanced economies depend upon agriculture. In advanced commercial societies, farming is a business rather than a way of life — as opposed to farming in subsistence societies — and is subject to economic controls even more than to the special relations of a man to the land he uses.

Agriculture has not responded as well as urban activities to improved, more efficient technology. There are several reasons for this lag: many farmers are unable or unwilling to adopt mass-production techniques; their lack of organization puts them in a weak competitive position; and low and unstable prices discourage them from making improvements. Income levels are consequently not as high for agricultural occupations as for urban ones, except perhaps in occasional years of very short supply. Nevertheless, agricultural productivity has increased remarkably over time; in a few countries, less than 10 percent of the population provides all the agricultural needs of the country.

Commercial agriculture has a fascinating geographic distribution resulting from the

OPTIMA AND LIMITS SCHEMA

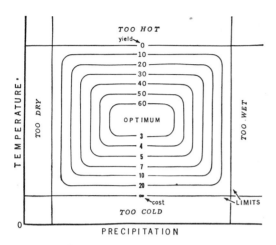

Figure 3.01 Optima and limits schema. This diagram illustrates hypothetically that for any given crop there is an optimal combination of temperature and moisture. Nonoptimal combinations reduce yields and raise costs until, at the limit, yields drop to zero and costs are prohibitive. (From Harold H. McCarty and James B. Lindberg, *A Preface to Economic Geography,* © 1966. Reprinted by permission of Prentice-Hall, Inc., Englewood Cliffs, N. J.)

interplay of environmental, market, transport, and human factors. In the self-sufficient societies examined in chapter 2, environmental and cultural preferences often dictated farm organization and land use. When transport improved and regional and national markets became concentrated in small areas, however, specialization became possible — and location with respect to major markets became very important.

The relative location of land with respect to the largest market provides the basis for a fundamental theory of spatial organization — the land-use intensity gradient. The theory is abstract — how space would be organized, that is, what the pattern of land use would look like, if there were no natural variation in land or climate. In reality, environmental differences are great and obviously affect agriculture. However, if the role of spatial factors — distance and relative location and the sheer demand for land — had not been examined separately, their importance in understanding real landscapes might never have been recognized.

FACTORS INFLUENCING THE LOCATION OF AGRICULTURAL PRODUCTION

Major controls over use of land for agriculture are:

— *Location relative to major markets and the resulting transport costs for different crops.*

— *Environment, especially landforms, soil, temperature, moisture, and growing season, all of which influence the production cost of various crops.*

— *Consumer demand for various products.*

— *Inherent characteristics of the crop — productivity and labor required, for instance.*

— *Productivity of the crop in response to inputs such as fertilizer or machinery.*

— *Regional differences regarding labor quality and costs, form of ownership, population pressure on the land, and presence of alternate employment opportunities.*

— *Government policies.*

Environmental Influences. For most crops, the range of conditions in which survival is possible is wide, but the range where maximum productivity can be achieved — where the value of the crop harvested exceeds the cost of production — is much narrower. For any given crop there is a preferred location; preferred locations vary sufficiently to allow a diversity of crops (complementarity of production).

Unusual pressure, however, is placed on lands of the best quality. Production outside optimal conditions means extra effort and costs for the farmer, although these will not necessarily prohibit agriculture. One model of agricultural land use could be constructed on the basis of the suitability of the environment for different crops. Figure 3.01, for instance, illustrates the notion of optimal conditions and limits for crops. If we could construct such diagrams for several crops, we would find some areas in which one crop is

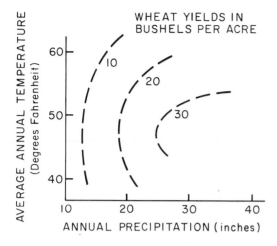

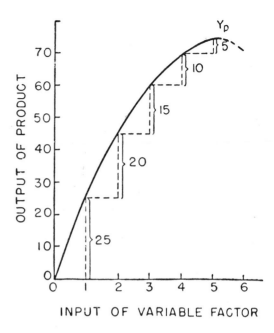

Figure 3.02 Effect of temperature and moisture on wheat yields. This figure illustrates the response of yields to temperature and moisture. Other factors, of course, may make it profitable to grow wheat under less than highest yield conditions. Note that yield does not have a simple linear relation to precipitation and/or temperature. Yield increases with moisture, but not much after 25 inches, and it first increases then decreases with higher average temperatures.

best, and others in which several can compete.

Strong relationships can be found between the yield of crops, handling costs, and environmental factors. For instance, yields are reduced and handling costs increased in areas where sloping land is accompanied by thinner soils and greater erosion risk. Soil quality also affects yields and production costs because of variations in acidity or alkalinity, organic content, moisture and air absorption and retention, lightness for working, drainage, and so forth. Other factors clearly influencing crop growth and quality are temperature, both the long-range average and the daily temperature range, and moisture supply, especially at critical periods (see figure 3.02).

Consumer Demand for Crops. Prices are a function of both the costs of production and consumer demands and preferences. When consumer demand creates a structure of crop prices partly independent of the costs of production, the consumer modifies agricultural location. A high price on a low-yield product, for instance, permits production in a remote area.

Figure 3.03 Inputs and yields. Normally, yields increase rapidly with the first inputs, then increase more slowly, and may finally decrease with additional, excessive inputs. (From Earl O. Heady, *Economics of Agricultural Production and Resource Use*, © 1952. Reprinted by permission of Prentice-Hall, Inc., Englewood Cliffs, N. J.)

Crop Characteristics. Crops vary in their inherent productivity (volume of output for a given effort), perishability and transportability, labor requirements, and adaptability to machinery. Under the same conditions some crops, such as vegetables, produce a much greater usable volume and thus, given sufficient demand, have a much higher value than, say, grains. On the other hand, grain is less perishable, can be stored longer and handled more easily and roughly, and is therefore cheaper to transport than fresh vegetables, fluid milk, and fresh eggs. However, the higher valued and less transportable crops are usually able to compete for better land.

Yield in Response to Inputs. There is a crucial relationship between yield and the application of extra inputs — investments to increase production. Figure 3.03 depicts a typical pattern of rapidly increasing yields with initial inputs, giving way to a slower increase in yields, and finally diminishing returns with excessive inputs. The differen-

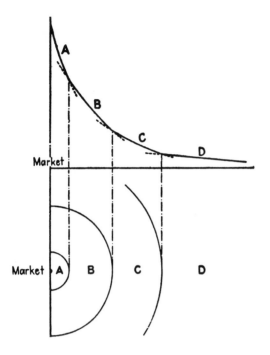

Figure 3.04 The ideal pattern of agriculture. The *x*-axis indicates distance from market, the *y*-axis net return per acre. Those crops that are relatively most costly to transport bid the highest price (rent) for land and obtain the land closest to the market, in zone *A*. Within this zone, increasing transport costs lessen net return per acre, and the dashed line tangent to the curve between *A* and *B* indicates that at this distance, a new crop (or set of crops) becomes more profitable, creating a second crop zone, *B*. These have relatively lower transport costs than the *A* zone crops, but higher costs than those in zone *C* (see text and caption to figure 3.07). (Reprinted by permission of McGraw-Hill Book Company, Inc., from Edgar M. Hoover, *Location of Economic Activity*, 1948.)

tial response of crops to inputs such as extra water, fertilizer, weeding, and spraying affects how intensively they can be raised and how well they can compete for quality land and accessible locations. So long as extra inputs raise revenues more rapidly than they raise costs, such intensification pays. Price is important also, since producers of low-value crops cannot afford to add many inputs without diminishing their returns.

Mechanization and Farm Size. Mechanization can dramatically raise agricultural productivity by permitting a farmer to handle much greater acreages. In addition to powerful and efficient tractors, all kinds of specialized equipment for weeding, spraying, drilling, harvesting, and picking are available for most farm specialties. Many farmers, however, cannot take full advantage of this machinery because their farms are too small.

Increasing farm size certainly enables the farmer to achieve greater economies by making more productive use of labor and equipment. Unfortunately, many farmers do not have the capital or land necessary to bring production to its optimal level. In addition, economies of scale do not always increase smoothly with size; at the point where a hired man must be employed, for example, the economies will temporarily decrease. The farmer must also consider the risk of price variation if he grows only one product. Long-run profitability may be greater with two products, even though fewer economies of scale will be realized.

THE THEORY OF AGRICULTURAL LOCATION

The owner of a piece of land in a commercial society presumably wishes to achieve the maximum possible productivity. The problem for the farmer is to choose the products, inputs, and markets that will best satisfy this goal. Thünen, who formulated classical agricultural location theory, recognized earliest the gradient aspect of spatial organization: The ability of crops to compete for access, or location nearer major markets, is determined by the level of demand for a given crop, its inherent productivity, its response to inputs, and its transport cost. Variation in ability to compete for access results in a spatial ordering of crops.

Where little or no agricultural produce is marketed, as in subsistence farming, the most productive use of land would be determined only by the character of the land itself. In a commercial society, however, most produce is sold, and because of transport costs, location relative to large, concentrated urban markets influences what is most productive at any particular location. For a simplified illustration, consider two farms with equally good land located 10 and 100 miles from a large market. Suppose that the price of milk is 50¢ a gallon in the city (wholesale), the price of cheese 50¢ per pound; that the farmer at 10 miles pays 10¢ per gallon to ship the milk, and 8¢ per pound to ship cheese; the farmer at 100 miles pays 25¢ a gallon to ship milk, 15¢ a pound to ship cheese (cheese is somewhat easier to ship longer distances than milk). For both the cost of producing a gallon of milk is 20¢, and a pound of cheese 25¢; but they can produce the same total value of milk or chesse for the same effort. The farmer at 10 miles will certainly choose to ship milk, since his net price is 20¢, that is, 50¢ less production cost of 20¢ and transport cost of 10¢; whereas for cheese it is 17¢ (50¢ - 25¢ - 8¢). The farmer at 100 miles will choose cheese, for which his net price is 10¢ (50¢ - 25¢ - 15¢), whereas for milk it is only 5¢ (50¢ - 20¢ - 25¢). From a production-cost point of view, both would prefer milk, but it is more profitable for the more distant farmer to ship the "less productive" cheese, simply because the transport cost for milk rises so rapidly with distance from the market.

More generally, as one goes out from the market center, production becomes less intense, fewer inputs are added, and returns per acre fall.

Agricultural products that are unusually productive per acre, that cannot be transported easily, or that respond unusually well to inputs compete for the limited space available around a market center. Growers of crops such as these, for which the transport rate is highest in relation to net price, will bid a very high price (rent) for this land, since easily accessible land is necessary to make production feasible. Thus, because there is limited land near the market and rents are high, the farmer must employ very intensive methods.

Farmers who grow crops with relatively lower transport costs can use more land at a greater distance from the market. The precise distance at which a particular crop is competitive is a function of prices, yields, and transport costs. As distance increases, transport costs become greater and greater and net revenue lower and lower until a point is reached — the **economic margin —** where revenues equal costs. For example, in the above illustration, the absolute margin for milk would be at 150 miles if transport

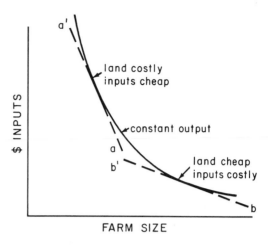

Figure 3.05   Substitution between land and other inputs. To achieve a given level of output, one may use more land at less intensity (fewer inputs per acre) or less land at greater intensity (more inputs per acre). If the land is relatively costly, and inputs, such as labor, relatively cheap (dashed line *aa'*), the less land-greater intensity course is best; if land is cheap and inputs costly (line *bb'*), however, the more land-less intensity course is best. The dashed lines indicate the ratio of land cost to input cost per unit of output.

rates were 30¢ a gallon (50¢ - 20¢ production cost - 30¢ transport cost.).

Figure 3.04 depicts the net return per acre for different crops with respect to distance from the market. Note that crops in zone *A* have a very high return initially, but that the high transport costs reduce the net return rapidly. Rather quickly, the profitable crops change. Although the crops in zone *B* were less profitable near the market, in *B* they become more profitable, since their transport costs reduce net returns less rapidly. Because they do not need easy market access, the less perishable and more transportable crops (*C* and *D*) are pushed farther from the market, where they remain profitable. The agricultural system thus extends outward until no activity exists for which transport and production costs do not exceed revenues. At its simplest, the ideal pattern of agriculture is one of concentric rings surrounding a market, with decreasing returns per acre in each ring (as in figure 3.04).

This agricultural gradient has many theoretical effects on the pattern of farm production. Size of farm and amount of inputs will vary with the return per unit area and distance from the market. The farmer who is close to a market relies on high response to inputs to raise productivity high enough to compensate for the low transportaility of his product and the high cost of his land. The distant producer, on the other hand, often finds it easier to maximize his income by cultivating more land. Land and inputs can be substituted for each other to some degree; variations in inputs can equalize income among farms of different size at a given distance (figure 3.05). Where land is cheap, a farmer uses more acres with a lower level of inputs; where land is expensive, more inputs make up for the smaller acreage that he can afford.

The more intensive and perishable goods can sometimes be produced at a distance from a market if an intermediate processing step improving transportability is feasible. A dairyman at a greater distance, for instance, processes less transferable fluid milk into cheese or butter. Canning, freezing, drying, and refining in effect place distant producers of fruit, vegetables, and sugar beets a .thousand miles closer to a market. Thus, greater advantage can.be taken of distant but high-quality land.

Short-run stability in the location of crops is maintained by the interplay of productivity and transport costs. If a farmer located near a market attempts to raise a less profitable crop, for instance, the opportunity cost (the higher price he could have received for an alternate crop) will tend to force him to shift to the more profitable crop or sell the land to someone who will raise that crop. If, on the other hand, a more distant farmer attempts to raise a more productive, but less transportable crop, the higher transport costs will reduce his net revenue. A long-term stable **equilibrium** between transportability and productivity and for the location of different crops is actually never reached, since ownership, technology, and demand change continuously.

The gradient is more visible because there are different crops of varying productivity and transportability, but, in theory, there should be a gradient of net returns, inputs, and farm size even if there were only one product! Very simply, a more distant producer using the same production method as one closer to market will have a lower net return per acre because of his higher transport costs. To obtain the same income the distant producer requires more land, but handling more land in the same way as the closer producer would increase his costs and thus decrease his revenues. If the more distant producer, however, can reduce his inputs and lower his production costs more rapidly than his yields fall, so that his labor is spread over more land, he can compete with the closer farmer. For example, very low production costs can allow a wheat farmer who owns 1,000 acres of crop in a semiarid area to earn more than a farmer with 200 acres in a humid area close to markets, despite the first farmer's higher transport costs and lower yields.

Rent. The value of agricultural land (in the absence of governmental, psychological, and other influences) should closely reflect the average net return per acre. Net return (value of produce less production and transport costs) includes both return to the farmer's labor and *rent*, which a farmer pays for the use of land if he does not own it (normally rent is about one-quarter of net return). This rent, or payment for the use of a unit of land for a period of time, is very high close to the market because of the limited amount of such land. Sometimes farmers must bid a high price for the use of this closer land in order to raise products that would otherwise incur prohibitively high transport costs. This in turn forces them to seek high yields and to utilize a high level of inputs, thus raising returns to acceptable levels. Conversely, land in remote locations attracts little demand or competition, so for the same total rent per farm, a farmer can afford more land, on which he will only be able to grow those products that can be raised and shipped very cheaply.

Additional Markets

Additional markets and markets for varying ranges of products create landscapes like the theoretical one shown in figure 3.06. Such additional markets are the result of the repetitive, dispersed location of some urban centers (to be subsequently discussed). **Rent gradients** and a zonation of crops will also surround these lesser centers, but the smaller demand will result in a steeper gradient and smaller market area. The intersection of the gradients (that is, the locations at which rents are equal out from the major market and any lesser market) will ideally result in circular market areas around lesser centers; however, environmental and transport variations may lead to variably shaped market areas.

The amount of land that is planted with a given crop is, in part, a function of the size of the market. Theoretically, products sold at smaller markets have lower net returns (partly due to higher handling costs with lower volume). Hence, smaller markets may receive produce only from a small region that is completely surrounded by a larger region supplying a very large market. Smaller markets may also be incomplete. For example, in figure 3.06, the small markets 2 and 4 demand only milk, markets 3 and 5 demand milk and beans, and only market 1 demands all three — milk, beans, and wheat. Thus, markets 2 through 5 are incomplete.

The extent of the region serving a market increases, of course, as the demand in the market rises and as transport costs become cheaper. Historically, then, although the environment has (in general) remained unchanged, land has shifted from less intensive to more intensive crops as consumer demands have increased; the entire gradient has moved upward and outward (figure 3.07). The American wheat belt, for example, shifted from New York, to Ohio, to Illinois and Wisconsin, to Iowa and Minnesota, to Kansas and the Dakotas. In addition, in less than 100 years the Los Angeles basin evolved from a region of livestock-hide production to one of the world's most intensive fruit-vegetable-dairy regions.

With the possible exception of the very local dairy (a case of near monopoly), isolated farms growing any kind of crop are rarely successful. Competitive strength seems to require the agglomeration of like producers, directly or indirectly sharing techniques and marketing. The advantages

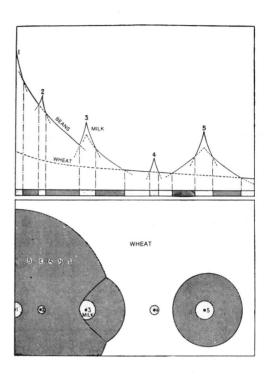

Figure 3.06 Effects of additional markets. In this hypothetical example, smaller markets 2 through 5 disrupt the pattern of land use around the main market, 1. The smallest, 2 and 4, have a demand for milk only. Markets 3 and 5 contain demand for beans as well. The dashed cones under 3 and 5 indicate the return if the farmer grew beans instead of producing the more profitable milk close to the market. The demand in these smaller markets is great enough to cause nearby farmers to supply them rather than the main market. Still, the markets are incomplete; they are surrounded by farmers shipping directly to market 1. The lesser demand at smaller markets also means less competition for access to them and thus lower land prices, reduced intensity, and lower return per acre in the land immediately surrounding them. (Dollar return per acre is indicated on the y-axis.) (Reprinted by permission of McGraw-Hill Book Company, Inc., from Edgar M. Hoover, *Location of Economic Activity*, 1948.)

gained by grouping producers of the same crop in clusters have also favored the concentration of specialties in local areas. For example, such minor crops as peppermint and hops are highly concentrated in small regions in the United States, and even significant crops, such as rye and potatoes, are grown in relatively small areas. Some moderate to small urban centers may thus be major markets for one or two less common products.

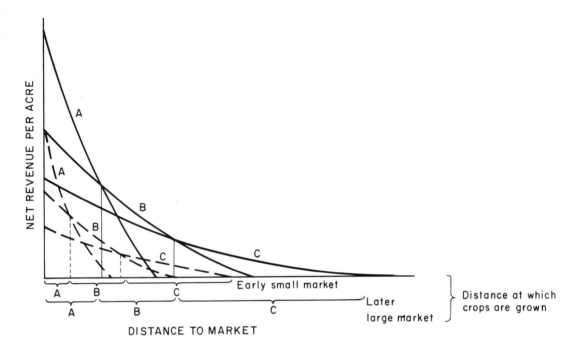

Figure 3.07   Shift of gradients over time. This figure illustrates the competition for land among three crops (*A, B,* and *C*) when a market is small (dashed lines) and later when it becomes large (solid lines). The three lines for each period indicate the decline in net return for the three crops as distance from the market increases. Crop *A* is less transportable than *B* or *C*; hence its growers bid a higher rent for land close to the market and must be more productive. Where lines *A* and *B* intersect, for example, crop *B* becomes more profitable than crop *A*. Even though the net return from *B* is not as high as for *A* near the market, the net return of *B* declines more slowly because of less significant transport costs.

When the market is small, producers do not need to bid as high a price for the closest land, or to use as much land, or to use it as intensively as they do later when the market is large; higher market demand requires both that more land be used for crops and that land be used more productively. Thus, land has shifted from less to more intensive crops, and the gradient has moved upward and outward.

The Role of the Environment

The gradient theory we have just developed assumes that activities take place on a uniform plain, with the same environment, equal entrepreneurial ability, and identical level of technology at all points. The quality of real landscapes, of course, varies notably even in small areas. Such variation is reflected in the costs of production and thus distorts the ideal gradient (figure 3.08). For instance, an enclave of above-average land permits a farmer either to obtain greater profits on a crop typically grown in that zone or to cultivate a more intensive crop if the greater yield or price of the new crop can offset the increased transport costs. Thus, irrigated land in distant but exceptional environments yields up to five times as much cotton as average land

and can compete successfully against much closer cotton-producing land. Similarly, in an enclave of poorer than average land relative costs are higher; the farmer on rugged land, for example, may replace wheat with livestock grazing. If cost variations due to environment are combined with the gradients around a market, an ideal crop pattern might appear, as in figure 3.09.

Improvements in transportation have radically reduced marketing costs, and improvements in inputs and crop and animal technology have boosted productivity. Therefore, distance from markets may become less decisive in agricultural location, and environmental quality more so. Indeed, as distant producers in far superior environments are able to compete against closer producers, more and more low-quality land near markets is being aban-

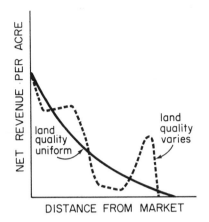

A. Effect of variation in land quality on revenue per acre

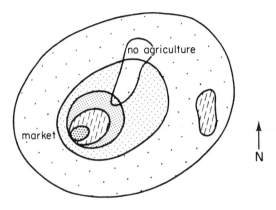

B. Distortion of ideal concentric pattern of crops due to land quality variation

Figure 3.08   A. Variation in land quality (slope, soil, climate) can cause an inversion of farm intensity and net return.   B. In this figure, land quality falls much more rapidly to the southwest, and the three most intensive zones disappear. To the northeast, an island of poor quality reduces crop intensity, but farther to the east, a zone of very intensive production is possible because of superior land.

doned. At the same time, modern technology is transforming seemingly poor environments into highly productive areas, as when irrigation is introduced into arid or semiarid regions with inherently rich soils. Great intensity of production, however, achieved by applying extra inputs and growing valuable crops, is usually required to compete in distant markets and to pay for the cost of water (figure 3.10). Irrigation projects are costly, large-scale investments. The success of many such projects can be partly attributed to the secondary benefits derived from irrigating an area — crop concentration, cooperative marketing, and disease control. Moreover, some irrigation projects are subsdized, usually from power revenues, either for the initial construction or for water costs (see figure 3.10).

The Decision Process

The individual farmer has many difficult decisions to make when he attempts to achieve the highest possible profits from his location. By evaluating the quality of his land and its position near markets and by applying his knowledge of crops, the farmer should ideally be able to determine an expected level of return from specific crops and products, and then should select the most profitable ones.

Most behavior lags far behind this ideal. Inefficiency results from lack of knowledge, uncertainty, and — often — the farmer's willingness to achieve satisfactory rather than optimal levels of production. Furthermore, uncertainty is always present in agriculture: weather is somewhat unpredictable, as are the behavior of prices and other farmers. A cautious response to uncertainty may minimize year-to-year fluctuations, but it also tends to reduce the farmer's long-run profits, since he will reject risky but potentially profitable choices. (See also figure 1.13.)

Summary

Agricultural space consists of patterns of crop locations and intensities resulting from efforts to reduce transport costs and to maximize returns. These patterns are modified by environmental variations, such as temperature, moisture, and soil quality.

How closely does the "real world" follow such patterns? The largest concentrated markets are in northwestern Europe and the northeastern United States, which are also the areas of highest productivity, highest in-

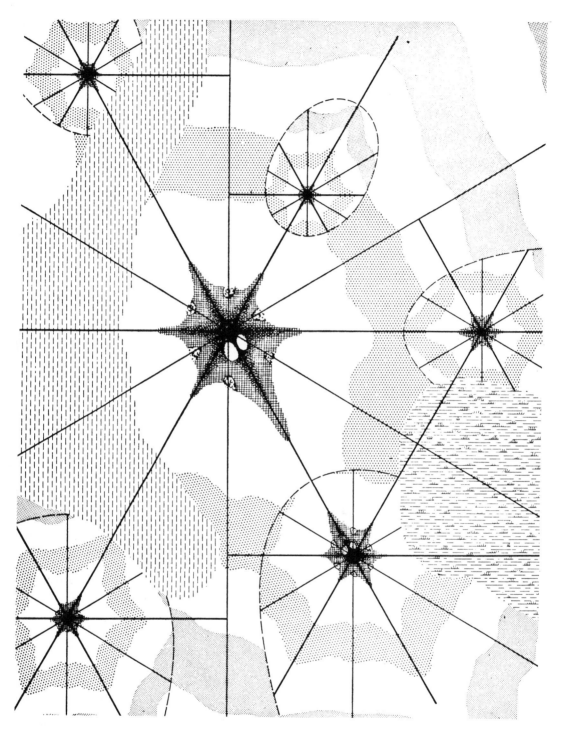

Figure 3.09   A composite agricultural landscape. An idealized picture of the land use in a region, with large zones of decreasing density and radial transport out from the major city and smaller patterns of land use and transport out from smaller cities. (Reprinted from *Location and Space Economy* by Walter Isard by permission of the M.I.T. Press, Cambridge, Mass. Copyright © 1956 by the Massachusetts Institute of Technology.)

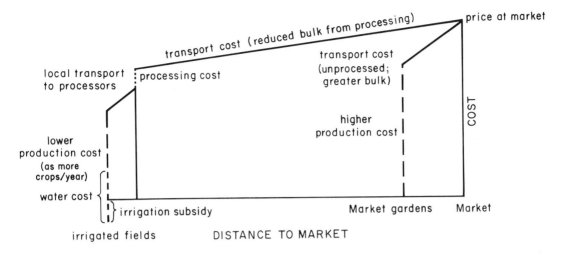

Figure 3.10 Competitiveness of distant irrigated crops. Areas distant from markets can compete in production of fruits and vegetables with nearby market gardens. For example, in this figure the irrigated fields enjoy lower production costs and have their water costs subsidized somewhat. In addition, the produce is processed locally, thereby reducing the volume to be transported. Note that, in this example, the producer whose fields are irrigated could not have competed against the market gardener without government subsidy.

tensity, and greatest rent — even though the natural fertility of these areas is not the best. Yields decline from the market centers. Fluid milk, horticulture, and feed-lot operations* dominate the regions near the markets. A generalized zone of intermediate productivity, emphasizing animal-crop combinations, occurs next. Beef and pork are the major products of this zone, but butter and cheese will replace them in more suitable environments. A predominantly cash-crop zone occurs next, such as wheat in the American plains. Land rents are lower, farm size is larger. A fourth zone emphasizes livestock ranching, thus completing a national pattern of Thünen rings. On a smaller scale, separate supply areas, especially for milk, can be distinguished for major regional urban markets.

To understand the locational pattern of agriculture, one must recognize the role of relative accessibility to markets (as measured by transport costs).Recognition of the importance of accessibility has given rise to a basic theory of spatial organization, namely, that the competition of activities for access to markets leads to an ordering of ac-

tivities and to a gradient of land values, rent and, usually, intensity. As we shall see in chapter 8, the same competitive process occurs within cities, and helps explain why certain land uses occur in given areas. But rather than the perfect geometry of concentric rings, the important principle is that the relative location of a farm to a market strongly conditions, through transport costs, what the farmer may profitably do, whatever the environment, governmental influences, or his own personal preferences.

TRENDS AND PROBLEMS IN AGRICULTURE

Part-time and Residential Farmers

Part-time farmers are common in America and Europe (20 percent of U.S. farms are operated by them). They often farm remote areas, such as the hilly isolated valleys of Appalachia. These small farmers can do little more than maintain their food supplies. Part-time nonfarm jobs supplement family income.

Another class of farmer, the **residential** farmer (15 percent of U.S. farms), works in the city but lives on a small nearby farm.

---

*Near-market fattening of beef cattle or hogs mainly with purchased feed brought in from outside.

Contributing little to output, and inefficient, he may withhold land from intensive and efficient agricultural use. Although over a third of all American farms are either residential or part-time, the value of their total output is only two percent of total American farm production.

Farm Ownership and Tenure

Because modern society is mobile and much of the rural population has migrated to the cities, ownership of farm land has become complex. Much is held as an investment by banks, business, and individuals located in cities. The average farm holding of individuals 50 years ago would be too small to compete in the modern economy. To secure a reasonable income a farmer must rent additional land, often again as much as he owns. Those without any land who wish to farm must rent all their land, paying as much as one-third of their crop for rent. Since holding farm land as an investment is popular, however, land values are too high, making it difficult to buy sufficient land to maintain a good income. "Tenure" as such is not inefficient; but given the prevailing low level of farm prices, the shift of farm income through rents to city owners aggravates the problems of inadequate farm income.

A recent trend in the United States and Europe is for urban investors to buy many farms and transform them into highly technical and specialized corporate farms. The operation of these farms conflicts with notions of traditional family farming, since workers are paid wages, but it may be a means of making farming competitive with industry.

The Effect of Government Policies

Probably no country exists in which political influence on commercial agriculture is not felt. Through construction of reservoirs, drainage schemes, flood control measures, and massive support of research, governments try to make agriculture more productive. Through agricultural experiment stations, extension or other agents, farmers are introduced to better technologies, seeds, and methods of weed, disease and erosion control. Less directly, but as important, the state affects commercial agriculture by regulating transport rates on railroads and trucks. Since accessibility to markets is a function of transport rates, any such arbitrary rate structure interferes with "ideal" location.

A more pervasive influence, though, stems from governmental attempts to stabilize production and prices and to guarantee a reasonable income to farmers. Agriculture remains more popular than is warranted by typical farm incomes. Because of family tradition, lack of other skills, and a desire to own land, too many farmers remain on the land. Too many farmers means that there is too little income per family, land value and prices are inflated, farms are too small, production costs are excessive, and overproduction is a possible risk. Government policies only add to the problem by guaranteeing the right to be a farmer and by increasing arable land with irrigation projects.

The free competition which underlies a theoretical landscape (as depicted in figures 3.06 and 3.07) is interfered with by very large subsidies of irrigation projects, by differential production and export subsidies, and by discriminatory transport rates among crops, regions, and carriers. Both transport-rate structures and irrigation subsidies, for example, tend to discriminate in favor of more distant producers in the United States.

Partly because farmers are spatially dispersed, they have failed to form strong organizations that might reduce competition among themselves, restrict entry, and improve their bargaining position with the larger industrial buyers. Overproduction, low prices, and low income may result. The government attempts to protect farm income by erecting barriers against foreign imports, by using guaranteed quotas, such as the quota for domestic sugar production, and by stabilizing and supporting prices. Higher support prices tend to encourage greater production and more intensive inputs, but to avoid a surplus, acreage must be restricted. Acreage restriction reduces proportionately the cultivated land of all farmers — the less efficient **marginal farmers** as well as the most efficient producers —

resulting in inefficient land use and higher than necessary prices. Rising demand and prices for grain and meat, however, may well make support prices and acreage restrictions unnecessary.

The government to some degree thus induces overproduction and supports inefficient location; but measures that would restrict entry to agriculture would reduce rural employment and would be politically difficult. The best solution seems to be to strengthen alternative opportunities to agriculture in or near the agricultural areas, if possible.

Over the last 50 years, a massive move out of farming has occurred. However, the move has not been fast enough, even though in the United States, for example, the average farm size increased from 170 to 303 acres and the number of farms declined from 6.7 million to 3.8 million between 1939 and 1959.

Agricultural Location under Socialist Central Planning. A centrally planned economy strongly affects agricultural organization and location. Ideally, high efficiency should result from the widespread information and the capital and technology available to the state. The goal that all land be used to the best possible advantage would seem to be more easily met under socialism than under a capitalistic system, and one would expect the gradient pattern to be even more regular. But centralization has its shortcomings: misjudgments may be applied to all the agriculture of the state and have extremely widespread effects — at least compared to an individual farmer's errors.

After the Russian revolution, the Soviet Union broke up the large estates of the aristocracy and distributed the land to the peasants. During the late 1920s and 1930s, about 200,000 collectives were created from this land. Collective lands as a whole were allocated for different uses, and individuals received a share of the earnings in proportion to the work they had done. Mechanization was hastened, given the very limited supplies of machinery available, by allocating machines to specialized Machine Tractor Stations and later to collectives, rather than to individual farm families. A trend toward large state farms technically matches the trend in the United States

toward large corporate farms.

Soviet agriculture, like American, has subsidies. The most significant represent compromises with the past, that is, with the traditional peasant organization of general farming. Small private plots for collective farmers are tolerated, on which is produced a high proportion of Russia's meats, poultry, and vegetables. The greater attention paid by the peasants to making these inefficiently sized plots productive represents a large indirect subsidy in time and equipment from the collective sector of the Soviet economy to the private sector.

The Soviet policy of regional self-sufficiency is reflected in a lower degree of specialization and in less clear-cut zones of different types of farms than in the United States. About a third of the Soviet population works in agriculture - far too many people - and the return per man-hour is very poor. Factors reducing productivity are:

- *Inadequate investment in agriculture — insufficient fertilizer, inadequate buildings, poor farm-to-town roads, lack of storage, inadequate disease control, and backward animal breeding.*

- *Lack of specialization (as in poultry, vegetables), although this is changing rapidly.*

- *An inadequate labor force, resulting from the manpower losses of World War II.*

- *A less favorable environment overall, compared to the United States and France, for instance.*

- *Inadequate incentives and discretion allowed to individual collectives.*

Agriculture and Urban Use

Urban activities, including residences, are of such productive intensity and pay so well that agriculture cannot compete. Therefore, land is constantly changing from farm to urban use in the fringes of towns and cities. Around U.S. cities there is a peculiar pattern of land use: some land is used for intensive farming near or even inside city limits; much land is used for "farm" residences for urban workers as far as 40 miles out; and much land is bought for speculative purposes, which raises taxes above what farmers can pay.

EXAMPLES OF AGRICULTURAL SYSTEMS

The more prevalent types of agriculture in North America and Europe are briefly discussed in this section, beginning with the least intensive and competitive activity of livestock ranching, generally relegated to the outer reaches of the density gradient, through cash-grain farming, which normally occupies the next most intensive zone, through the dominant grain-animal combinations (beef, hogs, broilers, butter, cheese), which can compete for land relatively near markets, to intensive fluid-milk dairying, eggs, and market gardening, which need and thus bid for the land nearest major markets.

Extensive Agricultures

Livestock Ranching. Livestock ranching is the only possible response to the physical conditions in most of the areas where it is carried out - areas of naturally short grassland with inadequate moisture for crop production and a topography too rugged for mechanized agriculture. Not all these areas are so used, however. The market price of livestock and the costs of caring for livestock and transporting it to markets govern the maximum distance from the market at which livestock can be profitably raised. Some territory suitable for cattle or sheep may be beyond these limits and thus lie unused. Since this activity is relegated to land naturally poor in vegetation and since livestock do not convert grass to meat efficiently, productivity per acre is extremely low. Hence an adequate farm return requires very large ranches, averaging almost 2,000 acres in the United States and in the drier areas as much as 20,000 acres or more (over 30 square miles).

In contrast, there are areas (for example in Argentina and Uruguay) quite suitable for crops, but devoted to livestock grazing because of the relatively great demand for the latter.

In the early days of American livestock ranching, transport was so poor that only highly concentrated and light weight products, such as hides and dried meats, could be shipped out. With the development of the railroad and refrigeration around 1880, long-distance livestock shipments became possible and a complementary system began to emerge. Raising the mature animals for meat greatly reduced the number of animals that could be accommodated on the range. The livestock rancher thus found it advantageous to specialize in breeding and in yearling production, shipping the cattle at a young age to the feed-grain centers near major markets for fattening. In the United States today, about one-third of all cattle are fattened through this dual ownership, and the range is thus used to fuller capacity.

Commercial-Grain Farming. Since grain production is the staple of subsistence economies, it dominates a general farming agriculture in much of the world. But in advanced commercial economies, feed-grain-animal combinations have priority, and production of cash grains for human food without raising animals becomes a specialty.

Commercial-grain farming produces a variety of crops, including rye and barley, but our discussion will emphasize wheat, the primary commercial-grain crop in the world.

Wheat is extraordinarily tolerant of a wide variety of natural conditions, can be easily stored for long periods of time, is readily transportable, and is relatively unresponsive to extra inputs. Therefore, wheat is often grown in locations far from markets. Less tolerant crops, such as corn, oats, soybeans, and hay, tend to preempt the land closer to markets for the priority purpose of providing animal-feed grains. About one-half the world's wheat comes from specialized farms in subhumid areas. These distant lands may be profitably used so long as the better lands closer to market are required for more intensive purposes and the demand for wheat keeps prices high enough to provide the farmer with a normal margin. The extensive wheat farm is generally profitable because the efficient but lower yield methods used have such low production costs that the low-yield wheat can compete successfully against higher yield wheat located closer to the market. This success in spite of marginal location and environmental conditions is due to efficient farm organization; successful wheat farmers handle vast amounts of land and develop special soil- and moisture-conservation methods.

Grain-producing areas in the United States and Soviet Union have been progressively pushed outward into more marginal country. Mechanization in the 1890s made this kind of location practical for farming. Most grain fields are composed of wide tracts of flat land, and large specialized farm machinery can easily be used to provide very high man-hour productivity. Even though the return per acre is small, the net income to farmers can be unusually high for agriculture.

Labor requirements for raising wheat are concentrated in the summer months. As a result, some wheat farmers — called **suitcase farmers** — have winter jobs in town and neglect their land during those months. (This practice is resented by farmers who must earn their entire income from farming.)

Intensive Agricultures

General Farming. American and European agriculture evolved from traditional general farming, in which many different crops and animals were raised in order to ensure the family's self-sufficiency. Any surplus grain, meat, eggs, or vegetables were taken to a market for sale. The productivity of medieval European agriculture significantly increased with the development of this general-farming system, in which the production of fodder for animals was part of the crop rotation.

General farms are not uncommon even today. In the United States and Canada perhaps one-third of the farmers live on farms of this type, but they produce only 5 percent of total farm output; in Europe the proportions are higher. The persistence of general farming reflects the isolation, conservatism, preference for traditional ways, and fear of specialization — even when specialization might mean far higher income — characteristic of many farmers. General farming prevails in much of Appalachia and the Ozarks and in smaller areas elsewhere where physical and cultural isolation combined with very small farms and fields, has hindered modernization.

Commercial Dairying. During the past century, general farming has evolved into dairy farming in many areas. Dairying is an efficient response both to environmental conditions and to the influence of markets on location, given a demand for milk and related products.

In much of northwestern Europe and the northeastern United States there is a dense urban population (often over 500 persons per square mile) in an environment characterized by year-round humidity and cool summers — an environment favorable to the hay, pasture, and small grains customarily used for feeding cows. Where the land is rugged or ill-drained, it can be used for permanent pasture. Given the urban demand for milk in these areas, dairying has a comparative advantage over, for example, commercial grazing or beef and hog raising. In addition, the greater weight and cost of transporting milk requires its producer to bid for land closer to market.

The spatial variation within dairying is striking. Around cities, especially larger ones, there are rather well-defined **milksheds** (or milk-supply areas), their extent governed by the total demand of the city, by the price, cost, and technology of fluid-milk shipment, and by any legal restrictions placed upon production. In a few areas where dairying competes strongly for very limited land (for instance, near Los Angeles), the density of cows is so great that most feed must be brought in from other areas.

Beyond the zones from which it is most profitable to ship fluid milk, the dominant products are cheese and butter (figure 3.11). Although both are commonly produced in an area, cooperative production arrangements and local traditions often lead to specialized cheese and butter districts.

Dairy farms in the United States have on the average been less prosperous than wheat and beef-hog farms. This difference is probably due to the smaller mean size of dairy farms and their small stock, which make it difficult to realize scale economies

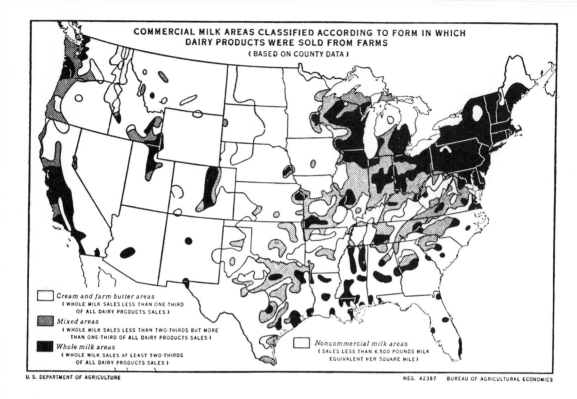

Figure 3.11   Areas farther from large markets sell more cream and butter than whole milk, since these concentrated products are relatively cheaper to transport. (From Earl O. Heady, *Economics of Agricultural Production and Resource Use,* © 1952. Reprinted by permission of Prentice-Hall, Inc., Englewood Cliffs, N.J.)

on the necessary equipment for refrigerating, milking, and the like. Furthermore, labor requirements are heavy, man-hour productivity is fairly low, and rolling topography, inadequate cropland, and fields that are too small also inhibit productivity.

Intensive Livestock - Grain Farming. The most common — and indeed the "classic" — kind of farm in Europe and America is the livestock-grain farm, whose primary product is meat, especially pork and beef. It developed as the commercial, more specialized heir of the subsistence family farm after commercial dairying and grain-production specialties were established. It remains the most self-contained and self-sufficient farm system. The farmer produces the bulk of his own seed and most of the stock in which he specializes, and in many areas he raises enough poultry and dairy products for his personal needs as

well. Competitively livestock-grain farming occupies the middle zone between the extremely market-oriented milkshed and the more export-oriented cash-grain farming.

The corn belt of the United States has the unequaled combination of vast stretches of level or slightly rolling land, moderate and even moisture, warm temperatures, and rich soils; and the livestock-grain farm here is based on corn as the dominant feed crop. (Although this farming system is also present in southeastern Europe, most of Europe has cooler summer temperatures and utilizes a hay and small-grain combination, supplemented by intensive root crops (turnips, beets, and potatoes).

Corn has many advantages. It provides the highest protein and bulk per acre of any feed grain, and this yield can be obtained with only reasonable effort, provided the climate is right. Hybridization has at least doubled corn yields since the 1930s. Corn therefore occupies close to one-half the cropland in many areas, dominating the entire landscape.

Raising corn alone, however, gradually depletes the fertility of the soil. This can be prevented by using crop rotation systems, which provide feed variety and extra cash income in addition to conserving the soil. Common rotations over a four-year period are corn-corn-wheat-hay, corn-hay-pasture-wheat, and corn-corn-soybeans-hay. Wheat and soybeans have a moderate yield, can be sold for high prices, and require little labor; they thus provide extra cash income. Soybeans have become very popular: they improve the soil and are especially valuable as a cash crop. Indeed, soybeans are both the chief source of edible oil in the United States today, especially for margarine, and a major export crop as well. Hay, alfalfa, clover, and wheat-grass are sources of alternate feeds, and when partly plowed under they improve the nitrogen and organic content of the soil, its structure, and its capacity for retaining moisture.

The typical farm raises beef cattle, and/or hogs, a combination that is often preferred because it brings in a stable income and maximizes the use of feed. Up to one-third of the cattle produced in the United States are purchased from western ranchers as yearlings and fattened on corn-belt farms. A feeder-in-transit privilege, providing a through rate even though the cattle are stopped and fattened on the way, encourages the practice. Farms average about 250 to 350 acres, and mechanization has permitted a rapid increase in farm size and income.

Feed grains such as corn sell for a lower price than food grains such as wheat. Yet the transport rate is similar for both grains, so corn is primarily consumed on the farm or shipped only short distances. Corn does become a cash crop in areas of very level land where a high degree of mechanization is practical, such as in North Central Iowa and near some major feeding areas, such as Chicago and Omaha (figure 3.12). East Central Illinois is also a cash-corn region because of preferential transit rates.

In Europe, farms are generally more self-sufficient and varied, and they tend to in-

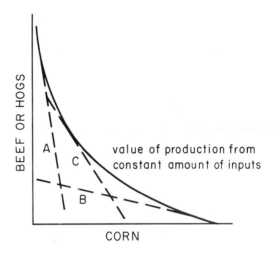

Figure 3.12 Feeder, cash-corn, or balanced livestock farming. The relative importance of animals and crops varies within the corn-beef-hog farm type. Where the value of beef or pork is high compared to the value of corn (dashed line *A*) — very close to markets and on costly land for instance — feeders should be emphasized. Where the relative value of corn is greater (line *B*) — on large, level, highly mechanized farms, and where special transport rates exist — there should be an emphasis on corn. More commonly, on moderate-sized rolling farms, a balanced mix of corn and animals is preferred (*C*).

clude poultry-raising as a sideline rather than making it a separate specialty. Population pressure and a tradition of subsistence agriculture have resulted in an excessive farm population and in farms too small or fragmented for efficient production (European farms average 100 acres, U.S. farms, 300 acres). More intensive production and subsidized prices are necessary for a farmer to make a reasonable living.

Other Agricultural Specialties — Horticulture. Other farm specialties tend to reflect unusual local and regional characteristics and advantages, and occasionally entrepreneurial aptitude. Location of a farm near large urban markets justifies intensive production of horticultural specialties: flowers, fruits, vegetables, and berries. In the United States, for instance, the rather urbanized belt from Hartford to Washington, D.C., is an area of very specialized vegetable, flower, fruit, and seed production. Inputs are great — fertiliza-

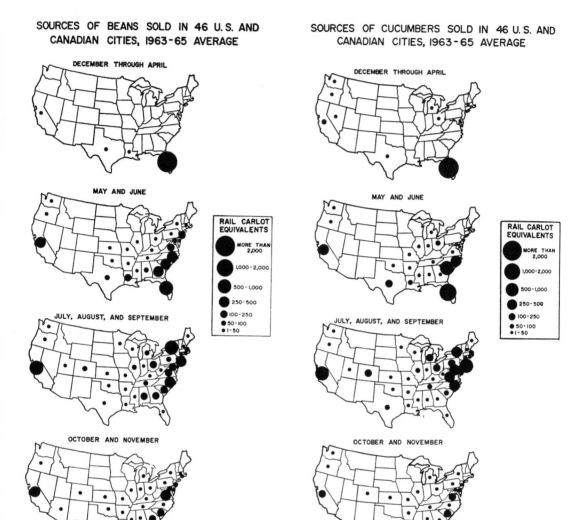

SOURCES OF BEANS SOLD IN 46 U. S. AND CANADIAN CITIES, 1963-65 AVERAGE

SOURCES OF CUCUMBERS SOLD IN 46 U. S. AND CANADIAN CITIES, 1963-65 AVERAGE

Figure 3.13 Sources of fresh vegetables. These maps of bean and cucumber sources illustrate the importance of seasonal differences and the advantages of large-scale, efficient production in subtropical areas, especially Florida and California, which have long growing seasons. Volume discounts in transportation help these distant areas compete successfully with horticulture near the northeastern markets. (Reprinted by permission of Sidney Jumper, "The Fresh Vegetable Industry in the U.S.A.," *Tijdschrift v. Economische en Sociale Geografie*, Vol. 60, 1969.)

tion is over three times the national average.

Environmental factors, however, have caused the location of horticulture to shift from traditional areas to places more remote from urban markets. Because of their year-long growing seasons, California and Florida and, in Europe, parts of the Mediterranean basin have a winter monopoly on fruits and vegetables. This advantage has permitted these areas to specialize, in-

crease their output, and reduce their costs. These areas have also had lower labor costs — Mexican bracero labor (temporarily imported on contract), for example, helped make California and Texas competitive. Thus, even though remote from final markets, these areas have come to dominate production of fruits and vegetables. Although perishable and bulky fruits and vegetables are expensive to transport, these areas can successfully compete against local suburban producers because their production costs are so low (figure 3.13). The growth of the canned- and frozen-foods industry has also aided this shift.

Areas with a winter growing season usually have distinct specialties — crops that won't grow in other parts of the country. Subtropical crop specialties such as citrus fruits and some kinds of grapes and olives are sources of cash income to farmers.

Cotton.   Cotton is inherently only a fairly productive crop, but it has the advantage of being highly transportable. If it had not originally developed under the plantation slave system, a labor-intensive system (one where labor costs are a high proportion of total cost), it could readily have been grown on larger, more mechanized, and distant farms, comparable to wheat farms. Cotton is now in fact being raised on such farms in the western United States.

Since the land available for cotton far exceeds that required by demand for the crop, the risk of overproduction always exists. Government price supports have encouraged excessive planting and at the same time have increased the competition from cheaper foreign cotton for traditional American markets. In order to reduce production in the United States, acreage restrictions on cotton presently limit the farmer to as little as one-fourth of his available cotton acreage, and the result is that cotton planting is often inefficiently dispersed among countless small fields comprising the best land of each farmer, whether he is an efficient or inefficient producer.

Poultry.   In the United States poultry has become a specialized agricultural product, displacing the raising of poultry as a sideline on the general, dairy, and livestock farm. Chicken, once a Sunday luxury, has thus become one of the relatively cheaper foods except during periods of grain shortage and high grain prices. This trend has also begun to emerge in Europe. Near large U.S. markets, eggs are the dominant commodity produced — on a rather industrial basis, using grain imported from outer zones. Egg production is the most obvious example in agriculture of a response to economies possible with greater scale.

In other areas (largely the southern United States), chicken raising has developed on some formerly poor, marginal general farms on a contract basis. Feed companies supply the chickens and much of the feed, and guarantee to buy the full-grown birds. There is more security for both farmer and distributor under this system, but prices remain low because of excessive competition, and the farmer typically remains poor.

Summary: The Spatial Arrangement of Agriculture.   In general the most intensive zone is occupied by highly productive, single-purpose specialties, like horticulture, fluid milk, and feed lots, which often require feed imported from other zones. The least intensive zone similarly is occupied by efficient, but less intensive single-purpose specialties like livestock grazing or cash grain. The dominant intermediate intensity and distance zone is occupied by more balanced combinations of grains and animals, with the primary purpose of supplying meat and dairy products. Depending on climate, topography, and other factors affecting competition, the zone is differentiated into dairying (especially butter and cheese), hog or beef raising, and poultry raising.

Rural Life and Settlement

Although in most commercially advanced countries rural population has declined and been surpassed by urban population, about a third of the people remain rural dwellers. In Europe, rural settlement was and is largely village-oriented; people prefer living in villages for reasons of protection, conservation of land, and ease of social contact.

The spacing and size of villages reflects the density of population, cultural preferences, and available transportation, modified by natural conditions. The spacing between villages used to be influenced by the mere need for sufficient people to support a parish priest and by the desirability of being close to one's lands — if fields were more than a few miles away, they risked being neglected.

In England, in parts of Scandinavia, and especially in the United States, the individual homestead has become the norm.

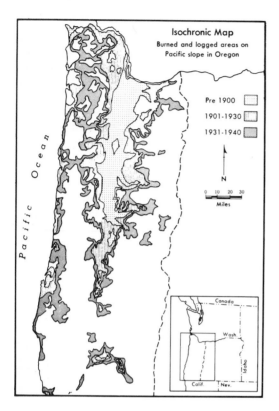

Isochronic Map
Burned and logged areas on
Pacific slope in Oregon

Pre 1900
1901-1930
1931-1940

N

0   10   20   30
Miles

Figure 3.14 Use of forests over time. Resources are first taken from more accessible areas. As resources in these areas are used up, logging shifts to less accessible areas. Since this map was made, the area of active logging has shifted more into southwestern Oregon, continuing the process of diffusion (see chapter 7). (Reprinted by permission of the Association of Pacific Coast Geographers, Vol. 19, 1957).

In the United States, greater emphasis on individual freedom, the sheer abundance of space, and the larger size of farms made living on individual farms more attractive than grouping in villages. Naturally, the pattern of farmsteads reflects the adaptation of the farm to the distribution of arable land. In the American interior, however, where the land was previously uncultivated and most of it was arable, areas were settled according to the regulations of the Homestead Act: each adult family member was given a quarter section in a square township. As a result, farmstead spacing is amazingly uniform.

Farm hamlets and villages in the United States grew up more as service centers than as residential centers for farmers, although now that schools have been consolidated in some areas there has been a tendency for farmers to move to town to obtain better services.

Commercial Forestry

Forestry represents the least intensive use of farmland in humid areas. Individual land holdings are large, and net return per acre is low to moderate. In rugged areas, however, where soils are poor for crops or where forests are of especially high quality, use of land closer to markets for forests can compete with other uses. Forestry is also becoming increasingly agricultural — trees are planted, thinned, and sprayed for disease.

About 40 percent of the world's managed land consists of forests. About one-third of the original forest, which covered one-quarter of the land surface of the earth, has been cleared, largely because the land is more valuable for farming, which can support many times more people on the same amount of land than forestry. The land remaining as forest is normally more remote or more rugged than that used for agriculture.

Although wood is valuable for construction, chemicals, paper, and other purposes, the basic raw material derived from the forest, the log, is of such weight and bulk that long-distance shipment is discouraged. Because they are remote and not accessible to good transportation, large areas of good forest are left untouched, at least so long as forests closer to market remain sufficient for man's needs. High transport costs have encouraged the development of alternate materials, especially for construction.

Production costs for lumber vary tremendously. Within the United States, for example, because logs have a large mean size, costs per board foot are low enough in the Pacific Northwest to justify transporting lumber to eastern markets. In both Europe and the United States, the quality forests near settlements were exploited first until today the major forest activity is on the periphery (figure 3.14). The older exploited forests may be used again as trees begin to regrow, but the newer peripheral forests will probably continue to be dominant because conservation and sustained-yield methods (where new growth equals or exceeds timber removed in the long run) were adopted before the peripheral forests were destroyed. Also, in the peripheral areas there are few or no competing activities, and land ownerships are large and efficient.

In the earliest days, logs were transported to the sea by river. Logging railroads soon provided access into the great interior to the virgin forests of America, Russia, and Scandinavia; today the less costly, more adaptable logging truck has taken over. Logs are brought very short distances to forest roads by cable or tractor and are then moved a short distance to a sawmill, where excess weight is removed (figure 3.15). In some forest areas, such as in Scandinavia and Russia, logs are still floated down rivers, and in others, floated along the coasts, as in Canada, Sweden, the United States, and Siberia.

Different logging patterns are used for different kinds of trees. For many species (such as pines and hardwoods) selective cutting of mature trees, although fairly costly, is the most efficient method of maintaining a sustained yield. In douglas fir-hemlock regions, stands are so regular that clear cutting (removal of all trees) is most efficient although unesthetic. A checkerboard pattern (where alternate sections are cut) is favored for quick reseeding and minimum erosion and watershed damage, but larger cut areas are less costly and preferred by lumbermen.

To be commercially successful forestry must be able to compete with possible alternate uses of land, labor, and capital. The return is generally sufficient to be competitive if the forest is fairly close to centers of demand and if the lumber is of high quality and quantity per unit area. Thus, some forests very near major markets are not used because higher production costs in these areas outweigh the higher transport costs from more distant but better quality sources.

Forestry alone cannot support a dense population. Exploitation of forests, however, may generate sufficient capital to permit the establishment of a secondary industrial economy. Thus, early New England had few resources except for trees and fish, but these yielded the capital to create textile and other industries.

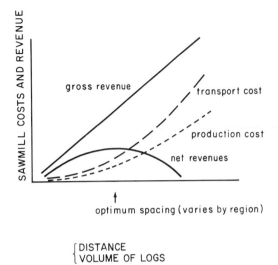

Figure 3.15 Optimum spacing of sawmills. As the volume of logs through a sawmill increases, production costs increase more slowly than gross revenues. Because the logs must be brought in from greater distances, however, transport costs increase more rapidly than gross revenues, outweigh the savings in production costs, and reduce net revenues. The optimum spacing of sawmills is that which allows each sawmill the maximum net returns. Sawmills will tend to be closer together in areas of very dense and rich forests.

In the diagram, the net revenue curve is found by subtracting the transport and production cost curves from the gross revenue curve. Improved transportation and sawmill processing technologies have increased the optimal spacing, and therefore the size and permanence of sawmills have increased too. The x-axis measures increasing distance and, in this case, also implies a more rapid increase in volume.

Extensive Use of Space: Conclusion

In the ideal economic world, all activities would be at a single point. In the real world, activities, especially food and wood production, demand vast amounts of space and require separation of production from centers of consumption. Differential competition for access to these centers results in a gradient ordering of activities and a consequent decay in density and land value, rather obviously distorted by environmental variation. The outcome satisfies the underlying goals of maximizing the utility of the set of all locations and permitting the maximum interaction at the least total cost. The same process occurs within cities, but discussion of urban gradients is deferred to chapter 8.

REFERENCES

Agriculture:
General and Regional

Chisholm, M., *Rural Settlement and Land Use: An Essay in Location*, London: Hutchinson University Library, 1962.

Gregor, H.F., "Regional Hierarchies in California Agricultural Production," *Annals of the Association of Geographers* 53 (1963): 27-37.

Grigg, D., "Agricultural Regions of the World," *Economic Geography* 4͜C (1969): 95-132.

Haystead, L. and G. Fite, *The Agricultural Regions of the United States*, Norman, Okla.: University of Oklahoma Press, 1955.

Higbee, E.C., *American Agriculture: Geography, Resources, Conservation*, New York: Wiley, 1958.

Highsmith, R.M., "Irrigated Lands of the World," *Geographical Review* 55 (1965): 362-389.

Jensen, R., "Regionalism and Price Zonation in Soviet Agricultural Planning," *Annals of the Association of American Geographers* 59 (1969): 324-347.

Kendall, M.G., "The Geographical Distribution of Crop Productivity in England," *Journal of the Royal Statistical Society* 102 (1939): 21-62.

Sauer, C.O., "Agricultural Origins and Dispersals," American Geographical Society, Bowman Memorial Lectures 2, 1952.

Spencer, J.E. and R.J. Horvath, "How Does an Agricultural Region Originate?" *Annals of the Association of American Geographers* 53, (1963): 74-92.

Weaver, J.C., "Crop Combination Regions in the Middle West," *Geographical Review* 44 (1954): 536-565.

Whittlesey, D., "Major Agricultural Regions of the Earth," *Annals of the Association of American Geographers* 26 (1936): 199-240.

Locational Factors
in Agriculture

Baker, O.E., "Increasing Importance of Physical Conditions in Determining the Utilization of Land for Agriculture and Forest Production in the United States," *Annals of the Association of American Geographers* 11 (1921): 17-46.

Chisholm, M., "Economies of Scale in Road Good Transport: Off-Farm Milk Collection in England and Wales," *Oxford Economic Papers* 11 (1959): 282-290.

Fielding, G.J., "The Role of Government in New Zealand Wheat Growing," *Annals of the Association of American Geographers* 55 (1965): 87-97.

Grigg, D., "The Geography of Farm Size: A Preliminary Survey," *Economic Geography* 42 (1966): 205-235.

Hudson, J., "Irrigation Water in the Utah Valley," University of Chicago, Department of Geography, Research Paper 79, 1962.

Reitsma, Hendrik J., "Crop and Livestock Production in the Vicinity of the United States-Canada Border, *Professional Geographer* 23 (1971): 216-223.

Schuh, G.E. and J.R. Leeds, "A Regional Analysis of the Demand for Hired Agricultural Labor," *Papers and Proceedings of the Regional Science Association* 11 (1962): 295-308.

Agricultural Location
Theory: Models

Birch, J.W., "Rural Land Use and Location Theory: A Review," *Economic Geography* 39 (1963): 273-276.

Dunn, E.S., *The Location of Agricultural Production*, Gainesville, Fla.: University of Florida, 1954.

Garrison, W.L. and D.F. Marble, "The Spatial Structure of Agricultural Activities," *Annals of the Association of American Geographers* 47 (1957): 137-144.

Grotewold, A., "Von Thunen in Retrospect," *Economic Geography* 35 (1959): 346-355.

Harvey, D.W., "Theoretical Concepts and the Analysis of Agricultural Land Use Patterns in Geography," *Annals of the Association of American Geographers* 56 (1966): 361-374.

Heady, E.O., *Economics of Agricultural Production and Resource Use*, Englewood Cliffs, N.J.: Prentice-Hall, 1952.

Henderson, J.M., "The Utilization of Agricultural Land: A Regional Approach," *Papers and Proceedings of the Regional Science Association* 3 (1957): 99-117.

Horvath, R., "Von Thünen's Isolated State and the Area around Addis Ababa, Ethiopia," *Annals of the Association of American Geographers* 59 (1969): 308-323.

Peet, J.R., "Spatial Expansion of Commercial Agriculture in the Nineteenth Century," *Economic Geography* 45 (1969): 283-301.

Extensive Agricultures: Ranching, Cash Grain

Beyer, J., "Integration of Grazing and Crop Agriculture," University of Chicago Department of Geography, Research Paper 52, 1957.

Calef, W., *Private Grazing and Public Lands: Studies of the Local Managements of the Taylor Grazing Act*, Chicago: University of Chicago Press, 1960.

Hewes, L., "Causes of Wheat Failure in the Dry Farming Region, Central Great Plains, 1939-1957," *Economic Geography* 41 (1965): 313-330.

Hoag, L.P., "Locational Determinants for Cash-Grain Farming in the Corn Belt, *Professional Geographer* 14 (1962): 1-7.

James, P.E., "The Process of Pastoral and Agricultural Settlement on the Argentine Humid Pampas," *Geographical Review* 49 (1950): 121-137.

Kollmorgen, W.M. and G.F. Jenks, "Sidewalk Farming in Toole County, Montana, and Traill County, North Dakota," *Annals of the Association of American Geographers* 48 (1958): 209-231.

Mather, E., "The Production and Marketing of Wyoming Beef Cattle," *Economic Geography* 26 (1950): 81-93.

Grain-Animal Agricultures

Coppock, J.T., "Crop, Livestock, and Enterprise Combinations in England and Wales," *Economic Geography* 40 (1964): 65-81.

Durand, L., Jr., "The Major Milksheds of the Northeastern Quarter of the United States," *Economic Geography* 40 (1964): 9-33.

Edmondson, M.S., "Hybrid Corn and the Economics of Innovation," *Science* 132 (1960): 275-280.

Fielding, G.J., "The Los Angeles Milkshed: A Study of the Political Factor in Agriculture," *Geographical Review* 44 (1964): 1-12.

Gregor, Howard F., "The Large Industrialized American Crop Farm: A Mid-Latitude Plantation Variant," *Geographical Review* 60 (1970): 151-175.

Henderson, D.A., " 'Corn Belt' Cattle Feeding in Eastern Colorado's Irrigated Valleys," *Economic Geography* 30 (1954): 364-372.

Lentnek, Barry, George P. Patten, and Richard Jones, "A Spatial Production Function Analysis of Corn Yield," *Proceedings of the Association of American Geographers* 2 (1970): 85-87.

Schrader, L.F. and G.A. King, "Regional Location of Beef Cattle Feeding," *Journal of Farm Economics* 44 (1962): 64-81.

Weaver, J.C., L.P. Hoag, and B.L. Fenton, "Livestock Units and Combination Regions in the Middle West," *Economic Geography* 32 (1956): 237-259.

Agricultural Specialties: Horticulture, Cotton

Gregor, H.F., "Farm Structure in Regional Comparison: California and New Jersey Vegetable Farms," *Economic Geography* 45 (1969): 209-225.

Jumper, S.R., "The Fresh Vegetable Industry in the U.S.A.: An Example of Dynamic Interregional Dependence," *Tijdschrift voor Economische en Sociale Geografie* 60 (1969): 308-318.

Large, D.C., "Cotton in the San Joaquin Valley: A Study in Government in Agriculture," *Geographical Review* 47 (1957): 365-380.

Loeffler, M.J., "Beet Sugar Production in the Colorado Piedmont," *Annals of the Association of American Geographers* 53 (1963): 364-390.

Rural Settlement

Brown, R.W., "Upsala Community: A Case Study in Rural Dynamics," *Annals of the Association of American Geographers* 57 (1967): 277-300.

Golledge, R., G. Rushton, and W.A.V. Clark, "Some Spatial Characteristics of Iowa's Dispersed Farm Population and Their Implications for the Grouping of Central Place Functions," *Economic Geography* 42 (1966): 261-272.

Hudson, J.C., "A Location Theory for Rural Settlement," *Annals of the Association of American Geographers* 59 (1969): 365-381.

Johnson, H.B., "Rational and Ecological Aspects of the Quarter Section: An Example from Minnesota," *Geographical Review* 47 (1957): 330-348.

Zelinsky, W., "Changes in the Geographic Patterns of the Rural Population in the United States, 1790-1960," *Geographical Review* 52 (1962): 492-524.

Part Three

Structure of the System of Places

If activities and people did not require space, everything and everybody would be clustered in a single place — a one-point world. The demand for space forces the dispersion of people and activities. In part 2 the gradient of intensity of activities out from central places (markets) was demonstrated. In part 3 we explain how the ordered arrangements of central places themselves are developed: first we discuss the patterns that result from the competition of places for the marketing of agricultural products and for the supplying of goods to people who live in the rural hinterland (chapter 4), and second, we examine the patterns that develop from the competition of places for the processing of resources and for the distribution of manufactures (chapter 5).

Towns as Central Places

Chapter 4

The most obvious physical contrast in man's organization of space is between rural and urban patterns of land use. In the more advanced countries, the vast majority of the population lives in dense concentrations covering small portions of territory. Such concentrations began to develop long ago when towns arose to serve the needs of the population. In particular, towns enabled people (1) to exercise control from a central place, (2) to have a center for the exchange of goods, and (3) to process resource materials efficiently. The first two items constitute, in a broad sense, service or "central place" functions — those provided from a center for a surrounding territory or hinterland. We will discuss these two central place functions in this chapter.

Locations compete to serve as centers for the marketing of rural produce and the selling or provision of goods and services that rural people cannot supply for themselves. This competition produces regular patterns of central place size and location — patterns that provide the best access for the most people at the least effort, thus satisfying the dual goals of maximizing the utility of places and maximizing interaction at least cost.

THE EXISTENCE OF SERVICE CENTERS

Service centers exist to fulfill basic human desires and needs. Even in the most primitive societies, people desire goods and services that they themselves do not or cannot produce. Indeed, all people at one time or another want greater material security and luxury, typified by the possession of products made by others. To obtain such products, a place is needed where goods can be exchanged. Moreover, human societies require direction, military protection, and religious or ethical control — functions performed most efficiently in central locations.

The Agglomeration Principle

Agglomeration, as illustrated earlier in figure 1.08, pp. 10, refers to the grouping of people and activities for mutual benefit.

Man is a social animal, banding with his fellows for mutual security, work, and pleasure. In addition, he tries to accomplish tasks with the least possible effort. Early man attempted to achieve these goals by agglomerating into villages — the most efficient social and spatial forms for his semicommunal life. A village located at the center of the group's lands minimized the distance men had to walk to their fields and to meet one another — provided that the group had many joint activites, held some lands in common, and continually changed the plots tilled by any one family. The extent of agglomeration and the size of villages were limited by the very poor means of transport and by the low productivity of hunting and early forms of agriculture.

Towns grew up later as an extension of the same principle of minimizing distance. The local village had specialized in some activities, or service functions, but could neither provide nor support a large number of them; some functions might require, for adequate support, the combined purchasing power of several villages, for instance. Each village might provide one needed activity, but since persons in all the villages would want to use each of the services, they would eventually have to travel to every village. It is obvious that if all the functions could be located in one village, the total distance all villagers would need to travel could be greatly reduced. In fact, one village that would minimize traveling distance for all villagers could be found — and, ideally, given free competition and efficient behavior, such a central village would attract and hold all the service functions and thus become a town. Agglomeration of services in larger centers adds the benefit of impulse buying — a person coming to town for one purpose is likely, by the proximity of additional services, to use some of these as well. Finally, relationships between the services themselves, as between banks and retailers are enhanced by centralization. The city, as a large agglomeration, can bring together a greater number and variety of buyers, sellers, and producers; but the benefits of agglomeration are achieved at a cost — as the city exercises influence over an ever-larger area, time and cost incurred by transport increase as well.

The purpose and benefit of agglomeration is to minimize the time and distance people must travel to carry out desired activities. Why, then, is there not one "world city"? Simply because agriculture, as man's basic activity for survival, requires the dispersion of man over much of the globe and because other needed resources are equally scattered. Furthermore, while the metropolis reaps tremendous benefits from agglomeration, even the small village is a rational and efficient agglomeration, minimizing distance for those activities for which people are least willing to travel far.

CENTRAL PLACE THEORY: THE SPATIAL STRUCTURE OF CENTRAL PLACES

Specialized non farm activities will group, for spatial efficiency, in a central place. But how many activities can be so grouped? How much territory can one center efficiently control? If more centers are needed, how will they be arranged? Why do various centers exist as either hamlets, villages, towns, cities, or metropolises? Walter Christaller provided a simple yet elegant theory of an entire system, or landscape, of central places, predicting ideal numbers, spacing, and arrangement of a hierarchy of places ranging in size from the local hamlet to the central metropolis (see page 79). Along with the gradient order of agricultural activities discussed in the previous chapter, the central place concept is a basic element of the theory of spatial organization.

Spatial Equilibrium of a Central place

By "spatial equilibrium" we mean the balance that exists between the location of a place and its customers. The fundamental question of central place theory is the optimum spacing or separation of sellers and hence the places where they are located. Imagine that you are operating a local store or tavern. Intuitively, you realize that an ideal location would be where the largest number of paying customers will have to

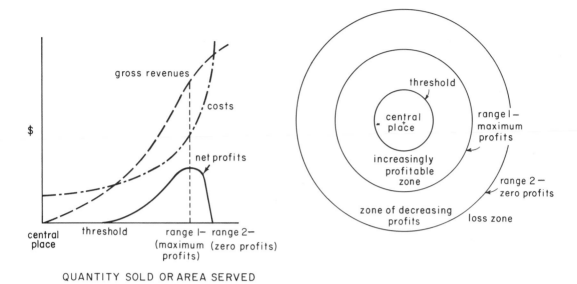

Figure 4.01 Threshold and range of a central place activity. An activity will typically have greater costs than revenues until a threshold volume and market area are reached, say the customers within one-half mile. Profits will then increase so long as revenues from more distant customers exceed the cost of serving them (if the store pays for delivery), until at range 1, the point of maximum profits is reached, say at two miles. After this, profits decline until the maximum range of sales, range 2, is reached; here costs equal revenues, say at three miles. Presumably, no rational seller would offer goods to customers beyond the maximum-profit range. If the customer pays for his own transport, the maximum range is simply the distance from which no further customer will come.

travel the least. Losses are typically incurred until the volume of sales reaches the critical level, or **threshold** (say 50 customers a day, that is, those within one-half mile), where sales exceed costs. Profits then increase as long as the revenues from new customers reached by extending the market area exceed the costs of serving them (assuming the store pays for the delivery costs). This defines the optimum market size (range 1 in figure 4.01). Beyond that point, the cost of serving additional customers will increase more rapidly than the profits derived from their purchases. A distance will be reached at which the cost of service will equal the income derived from providing the service (range 2 in figure 4.01). For example, if the average customer buys $10 worth of groceries, and the profit margin is $1, this range will be where delivery costs $1. If the customer pays for his own transport to the store, he will have less income available for goods and services. Thus the optimum market size is defined by how quickly the demand for goods falls off and by how far

the customer is willing to travel, since there is a limit to the time and transport cost an individual is willing to spend when seeking goods or services. For example, if a potential customer allows 50¢ for beer and spends 25¢ for transport to get to the store, he will only be able to buy half as much as a customer who lives next door. In this case, the maximum range will be that distance from which no customers will travel to the store.

The time limit that people are willing to allow is especially important to certain kinds of central place activities. Services such as those provided by police, taxis, public transport, doctors, hospitals, and schools can hardly be postponed; families cannot stock groceries or gas for long periods; so people demand that such activities be reasonably close. Declines in demand due to time limitations or the cost of transport thus define the maximum **range** at which a good may be profitably offered; but this range or distance will vary greatly from the close range for the most constantly sought goods

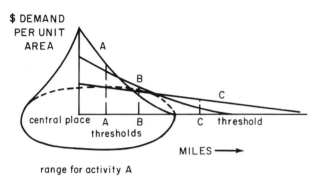

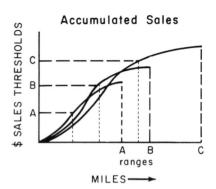

Unit Area Sales, Threshold and Range

Accumulated Sales

range for activity A

Figure 4.02 Demand, sales, threshold, and range. Demand for goods falls with distance from the seller, and thresholds vary for different activities, *A*, *B*, and *C* (left-hand figure). For example, curve *A* could represent the dollar sales of groceries, *B* of gasoline, and *C* of furniture for those customers in a unit area at an increasing distance from the sellers. Dollar demand for groceries is highest near the stores, and threshold sales are achieved at a short distance; but transport cost, as a proportion of the value of groceries, is high, and demand soon falls to zero as customers feel they are spending too much of the grocery budget on transportation or too much time. This defines the range (area within which customers will buy) for groceries (activity *A*). Dollar demand for furniture (*C*) is much lower, since it is a less frequently needed good, and the minimum threshold market area is larger than the maximum distance people will go for groceries. They are willing to travel much farther, because transport costs are small relative to the value of the furniture. The implication of this variability in threshold and range is that grocery stores (or groups of them) tend to be closer together than furniture stores. In the right-hand diagram, the demand per unit area is multiplied by the increasing area at greater distances to yield total sales, and then these are accumulated. Note how sales at first increase very rapidly with distance, and then more slowly, as the demand per customer becomes very small despite the many potential customers.

or services to the farther range for those rarely, if ever, demanded.

In figure 4.01, the increasing transport costs that result from enlarging the market (when the store pays for delivery) gradually outweigh the additional revenues. The threshold, the market area of optimum profits, and the maximum range of the activity are partly a function of population density and income level. Lower density or lower income, or both, means fewer sales per unit area and an increase in the ratio of transport cost to net revenue. In a sparsely settled or very poor area, the minimum threshold sales, say $100 per day, might require that customers come from a distance greater than they are willing or able to travel (the customers' maximum range), thus the service could not be offered at all.

Central place activities are essentially distributional; that is, they are located at a point, and the customers are spatially diffuse. The problem of locating a central place is thus one of minimizing the distance traveled by customers while maximizing the profitability of the activity. The larger the

sales, the larger the potential profits, but more sales require more customers and therefore a larger territory. However, customers who come from a greater distance incur greater transport costs; even if they spend the same total amount as nearby customers, they will receive fewer goods and services. As a result, demand for a service falls with distance from the service. Figure 4.02 summarizes the concepts of threshold, maximum range, and optimum level for a central place activity in cases where the customer pays the costs of transportation.

The Spacing of Central Places

Now consider the competition between two suppliers of the same activity (figure 4.03). What will be the efficient separation or spacing between them? Presumably, each seller would locate at a point where each could obtain maximum profits (that is, serve customers and monopolize business) within a range where customers will still come (or

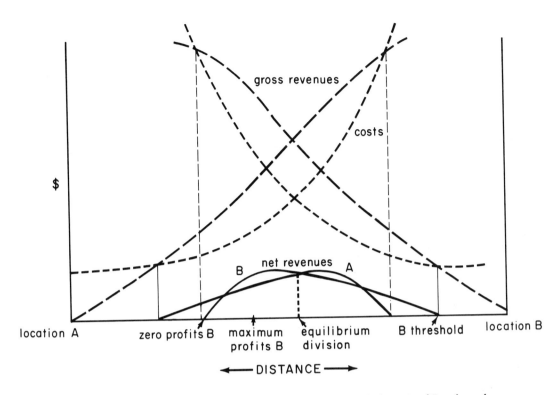

gross revenues

costs

$

net revenues

B   A

location A   zero profits B   maximum   equilibrium   B threshold   location B
                            profits B   division

◀— DISTANCE —▶

Figure 4.03 Equilibrium spacing between two sellers (central places). Central places *A* and *B* are located far enough apart so that each achieves satisfactory profits (at the equilibrium division). They do not locate farther apart (to achieve maximum profits), for then a competitor might enter midway between them and reduce all to minimum profits or to losses. See figure 4.01 and text for further explanation.

where delivery cost is less than the extra revenue). But because of the risk that a competitor might enter the market midway between the two suppliers, reducing all three to marginal thresholds and minimum profits, or even losses, a closer spacing often results, forcing sellers to accept satisfactory but not maximum profits — to the customers' benefit. In fact, competition will tend to bring about a spacing close enough to yield only minimally acceptable profits.

Central place theory could be called a theory of **spatial monopoly.** Each center has a competitive advantage in a given piece of territory because of the factor of distance — transport costs are significantly less for customers close to the centers. This spatial monopoly, however, is strictly limited by competition. If one center raises prices, its cost advantage within its spatial monopoly or "captive market" is in part eliminated, and neighboring centers can capture portions of its market and either destroy the

first center or force it to return to its original price level. On the other hand, one center may resort to price discrimination by offering a fairly low uniform price everywhere in order to capture more distant markets and to destroy competing centers. With a uniform price, nearby customers are "discriminated against" in the sense that they are charged more than the price warranted by the cost of serving them, although still less than a competitor charges (figure 4.04). The extra profits are used to subsidize sales to distant customers. The greater total sales may lead to lower cost operation and permit further price reduction. Since all central places can use the same weapon, however, equilibrium will tend to be restored.

The market areas within which stores make a profit (threshold to maximum range) are similar for many activities. For example, groceries, taverns, and gas stations each need but a small market area to survive. Indeed, many central place establishments,

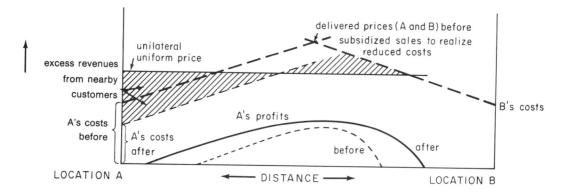

Figure 4.04 The sellers at places *A* and *B* originally divide the market between them at the point where delivered prices are equal. When *A* unilaterally adopts a uniform price, distant customers are subsidized by the extra profits *A* receives from nearby customers. The greater sales enable *A* to reduce costs, and when it reintroduces delivered prices, it has increased profits and extended its market at the expense of *B*. *B*, of course, could use the same tactics and perhaps restore the original equilibrium.

such as variety and department stores, contain within them goods and services with varying — but overlapping — threshold requirements. The precise combination of activities that can theoretically occur together is determined by; (1) the similarity of their thresholds and ranges, (2) the population density and average income of the region, and (3) the nature of transport costs in the area. Ideally, if an activity with a given threshold is successful at a given point, all activities with a lesser threshold should also be successful there. If groceries have a threshold higher than taverns and gas stations, neighborhood centers with groceries should also be able to support the other two activities; but it is possible to find even more local gas stations and taverns at locations which cannot support a grocery.

Having considered in some detail the relation of a seller at a central place to its hinterland and nearest competitor, the problem now is to discover how a set of such sellers or places is organized in space.

*Theoretical Hexagonal
Central Place Structure*

The simplest central place theory assumes: (1) a uniform plane of constant population density and purchasing power, (2) transport costs varying linearly with distance, and (3) no attenuation of demand with distance. Given these assumptions, im-

agine a whole set of small central places or sellers each with its own spatial monopoly, It is geometrically obvious that only a triangular arrangement of competing centers and markets will, for any one center, make all its competing centers (six of them) equally distant, so that the ideal separation suggested in figure 4.03 can be maintained with all. Such an arrangement is theoretically the most efficient (figure 4.05A): the "unserved" area is minimized, and all persons are as close to a center as possible. But there are unserved areas remaining outside the circles. If instead, the centers move a bit closer together, so that market areas will overlap, and if the overlap area is divided between the closest centers, a hexagonal pattern of market areas emerges (figure 4.05B). The appearance of the hexagon as the optimal form within a large structure of areas is demonstrated over and over again in nature. An isolated circle is more efficient than a single hexagon, but a set of circles or any other structure is not as efficient as a set of hexagons. Total distance from customers to centers is minimized, and the disparity between the farthest customers at the corners and those midway between centers is the least possible.

An orthogonal (rectilinear) arrangement has four equally close neighbors, but also four other more distant neighbors (see figure 4.10, p. 80). The unserved area is relatively larger. Overlapping of such a packing of circles results in square market

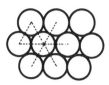

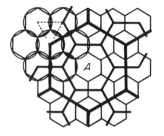

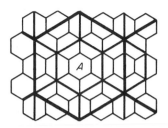

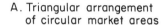

A. Triangular arrangement of circular market areas

B. Collapse of circular trade areas into hexagons; development of hierarchy according to the "marketing principle"

C. Development of hierarchy according to the "transportation principle"

Figure 4.05 Development of central place patterns. See text for explanation.

areas, the next best structure after hexagons, but one that involves higher total travel and greater disparities in distance traveled.

What activities will the smallest central places contain? Because of the benefits of agglomeration, the smallest places will include the less demanded activities with the highest threshold (customer sales and therefore size of market area required) that does not exceed the maximum range (market area) within which the most demanded activities with the lowest threshold will still remain profitable. For example, if the minimum threshold market area for a grocery requires the customers within one and one-half miles, while the maximum distance from which customers will come to a tavern or gas station is two miles, then the smallest places should contain all three activities, and be spaced between three and four miles apart. If less than three miles, grocers could not survive in each hamlet, and if spaced at more than four miles, some customers and business would be lost.

Hierarchical Structure of Central Places: The Marketing, Transport, and Administrative Principles. Suppose that one place (such as *A* in figure 4.05B) succeeds in adding higher threshold activities, such as a drive-in, drugstore, and cleaners, that require greater support than can be obtained from the smallest market areas. Suppose these were hamlets three miles apart, with a grocery, tavern, and gas station. The new activities will then require

support from the markets of the six surrounding hamlets in order to reach threshold levels, which might be the area within two miles of *A*. None of these surrounding hamlets can possibly add these new village-level activities, too, since part of their customer market is needed to support the first village at *A*. The closest villages that can compete — that can also offer the higher threshold activities — will be the six labeled *x* in figure 4.05B, located beyond and exactly as far from the neighboring hamlets as is *A*. Now if boundaries are drawn midway between these seven more important "higher level" places, a larger set of hexagonal **trade areas** will be revealed. Each of the larger places, or villages, has a spacing of 5.5 miles and serves one-third of the trade areas of its six surrounding hamlets as well as its own area, so that the total area and population served is three times that of the smaller places. Similarly, if one of these larger, second-level places (which could be called villages) adds additional town-level activities requiring even larger trade areas, a third level of trade area will be created in the same way — this time with a spacing of nine miles, and an area and population nine times that of the hamlets.

The **marketing principle** diagram at the top of figure 4.06 illustrates this pattern. Here the large black dots are the towns, the thin lines depict the boundaries of their trade areas, and the small city in the center is seen to require one-third of the trade areas of the surrounding towns for its larger trade

The System of Central Places
After The
Marketing Principle

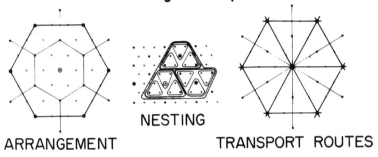

NESTING

ARRANGEMENT   TRANSPORT ROUTES

Administrative Principle

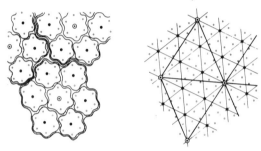

ARRANGEMENT AND NESTING   TRANSPORT ROUTES

Transportation Principle

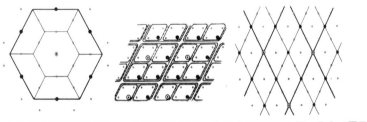

ARRANGEMENT   NESTING TRANSPORT ROUTES

○ Hamlets
● Villages
● Towns
◉ Small city

Figure 4.06   Ideal central place patterns according to Christaller. One ideal pattern for the hierarchy of central places follows the marketing principle: in the figure in the upper left, the relative location of hamlets, villages, towns, and a small city are shown, and the market areas for the towns and the city are indicated. If smaller places were nested wholly within larger ones, the middle pattern might occur. The upper right diagram shows the more important (thicker lines) and less important transport routes. Patterns for the relative locations of hamlets, villages, towns, cities, and major transport routes may alternately follow the administrative principle or the transport principle. Note that the former principle avoids dividing the market areas of smaller places, and that the latter has the most efficient transport pattern (see text for details). (Reprinted by permission of the Regional Science Association from B.J.L. Berry and A. Pred, "Central Place Studies: A Bibliography of Theory and Applications," Series No. 1, 1965, Regional Science Research Institute.)

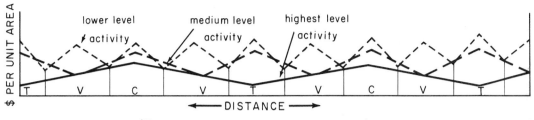

(Traverse across a central-place landscape)

Figure 4.07 Pattern of **demand in space**. In this cross section through an ideal central place landscape, one passes through this sequence of central places: *T* (town), *V* (village), *C* (city), *V*, *T*, *V*, *C*, *V*, *T*. The lower or village-level activities are of high volume, but decline quickly with distance from a central place. Customers will travel farther for medium- or town-level activities, which are available in towns and cities, and farthest for city-level activities. The city-level activities have the lower volume of sales per unit area, but because of their greater market area, they have higher total sales. Note that the towns and cities also offer village-level activities to a village-level market area, and that cities offer town-level activities to a town-sized market area.

area (thicker lines). This arrangement, in which each more important place and trade area is three times as large as the one smaller, describes the hierarchy according to what Christaller called the marketing principle, because every customer is as close as possible to a center at every level of the hierarchy.

Observe, however, that a transport system to serve such an arrangement is not efficient (see figure 4.06, top) — the important transport links between larger places do not pass through intermediate ones. If, instead of the arrangement in figure 4.05B, every other village in a line (in figure 4.05C, those labeled *x*) were to add the second-level town functions, the trade area of the smaller places would be equally shared by two larger places. As a result, the trade area of each larger place would be four times as large as the trade areas of smaller places. In this theoretical arrangement, transport is more efficient, since routes connecting the largest places pass through the next largest (see figure 4.06, bottom right), although customers must travel farther to reach a center at a given level of the hierarchy than in the "marketing" arrangement. This hierarchy is therefore said to be arranged according to the **transport principle.** It has also been observed that, historically, places of a next lower order tend to develop midway along a road between two places of a higher order, suggesting that this hierarchical structure is the most likely to occur in the real world.

Figure 4.06 depicts patterns of places and roads as seen from the air. An alternative view is to look at what happens to the level of sales across such a landscape. In figure 4.07 we see a cross section of sales per unit area along a main transport route for a landscape according to the transport principle. For the lower level activities (villages), sales per unit area fall rapidly from each center. From the less closely spaced towns, sales fall less rapidly, and for the highest level activities, sales fall least rapidly and extend over the widest area. The rate of decline in demand is steepest for frequently needed village-level activities like groceries because transport and time costs are high, and it is less steep for less frequently used city-level activities like clothing stores and banks because transport and time costs are not so important.

In the hierarchical arrangement according to both the marketing principle and the transport principle, smaller places or market areas between larger centers are divided — equally among three centers in the case of the marketing principle, and between two centers in the case of the transport principle — rather than being contained completely within the market areas of the larger places. See figure 4.10 and the diagram of figure 4.06. This split may seem confusing from a planning point of view, but much evidence demonstrates the "torn loyalty" of smaller places in such a median position. For example, residents of Hartford, Connecticut, shop in both New York and Boston. Indeed,

Figure 4.08 Development of new central places. This example from the southern Swedish province of Skane shows the proliferation of central places over time. The market-area boundaries shown are for local bus service around towns (irregular black blobs). Note that many new centers are at the edge of the earlier market areas. (Reprinted by permission of the Department of Geography, University of Lund, Sweden, from S. Godlund, "The Function and Growth of Bus Traffic within the Sphere of Urban Influence," *Lund Studies in Geography*, Series B, 18, 1956.)

new towns have frequently developed midway between existing towns. Economically, when purchasing power increases to the point where only one-third or one-fourth as much territory is needed to achieve threshold sales, competing centers may arise to take advantage of the interstitial purchasing power (figure 4.08). Many studies, however, present evidence that although new centers may arise midway between existing centers, there is a tendency for **nesting**, that is, the capture of the intermediate center by one of the larger centers (see figure 4.09). This suggests that the economies which wholesalers, retailers, and customers achieve by having fewer main destinations outweigh the disadvantages of increased distances (figure 4.09).

For purposes of administration, such as for school districts and governments, the division of smaller areas between larger ones is not convenient. Obviously, if smaller ones are not to be divided, the only logical arrangement is for the larger place (town) to serve the entire market area of the six surrounding areas. Under this ideal arrangement, called the **administrative principle,** each larger market area is seven times as large as the next smaller one (see figure 4.06, center). Nesting is automatic, but the transport system is relatively inefficient and customers travel farther than in the marketing- and transport-principle arrangements (figure 4.10).

In an economy where regional self-sufficiency is a planned goal, an administrative structure would tend to develop where lower order centers were nested under higher ones. In national economies or in small, isolated regions, which one larger center could easily dominate, one would expect to find only a single ring of provincial satellite cities around the primary center, following the administrative principle, as found in England, France, Sweden, Denmark, and other countries. At lower levels of the hierarchy, however, the transport or marketing principle, or both, might dominate, as is true in the countries mentioned above. Each principle suggests one ideal arrangement of service centers. In most landscapes, evidence for all three principles may be found. During a period when economic exchange is limited but govern-

Figure 4.09 The nesting process. The town and its trade area, midway between the two cities, are served entirely by one city rather than being divided. A cross section is shown below it; height of bars may be interpreted as number of central place functions. (Reprinted by permission of the Regional Science Association, from B.J.L. Berry, H.G. Barnum, and R. Tennant, "Retail Location and Consumer Behavior," *Papers and Proceedings of the Regional Science Association*, Vol. IX, 1962.)

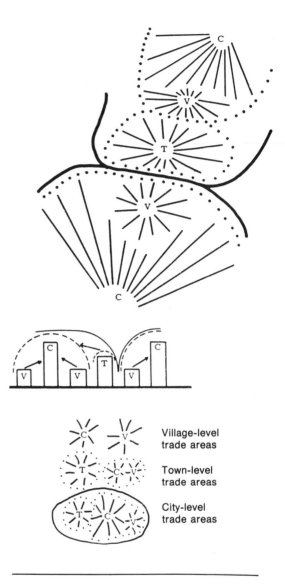

ment is strong, goals of administrative efficiency would be expected to affect arrangements most. As economic efficiency becomes more important, an arrangement may arise that violates political boundaries (for example, cities like Kansas City, which straddles state boundaries), and improved transport, in turn, may tend to readjust places in greater conformance to the transport principle. All three principles act together in a real landscape, creating many composite patterns — which are not so ideal. (See, for an example of one urban pattern, figure 8.03.)

The hierarchical arrangement of service centers and market areas according to the three theoretical principles has a significant bearing on the actual size, number, and spacing of places. Christaller suggested theoretically, and observed empirically in studies of Southern Germany, seven levels of central places and market areas — from hamlets to metropolises. The ideal sizes, numbers, and spacing of these places, according to the transport principle as applied *only* to central place activities, may be approximated as follows:

Level	Type of Place	Size Range* (population)	Number of Places A**	Number of Places B**	Spacing Range***(km²)
1	Hamlet	250 - 1,000	3072	12,288	3 - 10
2	Village	1,000 - 4,000	768	3,072	6 - 20
3	Town	4,000 - 16,000	192	768	12 - 40
4	Small city	16,00 - 64,000	48	192	24 - 80
5	City (District capital)	64,000 - 256,000	12	48	50 - 160
6	Small metropolis	256,000 - 1,024,000	3	12	100 - 320
7	Large metropolis	1,024,000 - 4,096,000	1	3	200 - 640
8	World city	4,096,000 - 16,000,000		1	640 - 1280

*Size Range: The ideal sizes for a national economy would depend on its total population and degree of urbanization.
**A, a nation of perhaps 50,000,000 people; B, a nation of perhaps 200,000,000.
***Spacing Range: Spacing depends largely on density (varies between and within economies).

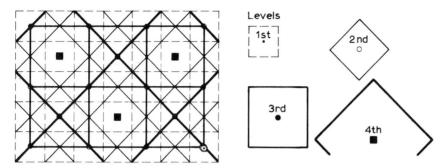

Each higher level center serves an area twice that of a lower level center.

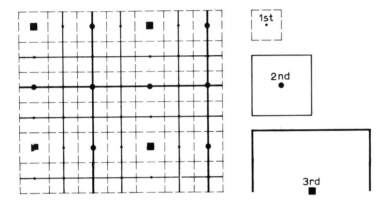

Each higher level center serves an area four times that of a lower order level center.

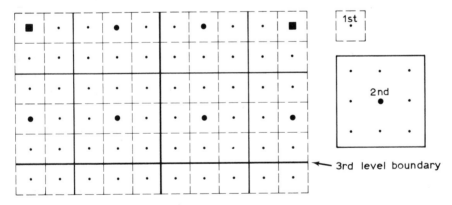

Each higher level center serves an area nine times that of a lower level center. An "administrative principle" nesting of entire areas.

Figure 4.10 Rectilinear central place patterns. These represent three fairly simple patterns of a hierarchy of central places developed on a rectilinear land and transport grid. In the first, in which each higher level center serves an area twice that of a lower level center, the packing is very tight, implying a poor transport system. Trade areas at one level are set at a 45° angle to levels just above or below. In the second case, every other place in line is of a higher order, as in the hexagonal "transport principle" case. This is also the closest approximation to real conditions. Similarly, an "administrative," fully nested structure can be formed.

Central Place Theory and Reality

Central place theory has been widely criticized because neither research nor maps show the "pure" patterns of development that should result from the marketing, transport, or administrative principles. Not only is the geometry of the real landscape imperfect, but the sizes of places are not what they should be, density varies, rivers and mountains distort the landscape, and mining and manufacturing towns seem to intrude any place. What then is left of our theory?

First of all, one must recognize that searches for pure geometric patterns are naive. Central place theory as formulated is, of course, incomplete. Many functions give rise to and help support towns. The real contribution of central place theory lies in its description of spatial behavior, which suggests reasons for the different functions, sizes, numbers, and spacings of places. The crucial test of the truth and validity of central place theory is not the observation of strict geometric forms, but answers to these questions:

— *Do groups of entrepreneurs seek to serve the available purchasing power of an area and to carve out somewhat monopolistic service areas for themselves? Certainly they do. This is the fundamental planning or decision problem that faces any prospective shopping center, for example.*

— *Do places with similar activities in similar physical and cultural environments tend to be regularly spaced? Experimental research does provide evidence that the distance between places offering a certain scope of activities does not vary much within a region of physical and cultural homogeneity.*

— *Do individuals tend to minimize the distance traveled to satisfy their desires? Many researchers have observed the tendencies of individuals to minimize travel, although for a variety of reasons they will often travel beyond the closest opportunity.*

— *Does one individual have available and use a hierarchy of service centers — does he go to different places for different types of goods and services? The answer to this question is complex, and is discussed at length below.*

Debate has raged over whether a hierarchy of central places actually exists, in view of observed *continuum* of central place sizes. Each of us is aware, from our own shopping behavior, of the existence of a hierarchy. We go to the local store or gas station often, less frequently to a larger town or shopping center, and infrequently to the downtown shopping area of a large city, (unless we live there). Yet, if all the places in a nation like the United States are ranked according to population, it will be seen that a fairly continuous gradation of population occurs, rather than, say, places of 40,000, 160,000, and 640,000. Where in the hierarchy do real places of 80,000 fit — with the level - 4 "small cities" or with the level - 5 "cities"?

The fact that places of different sizes exist is explicit evidence of a hierarchy, but we cannot expect a clear hierarchical division of places, for three major reasons: (1) Almost half the support for cities comes from other than central place activities, that proportion varying widely from city to city. That is, our place of 80,000 may have one-half its labor force in manufacturing for export out of the region, so that the population dependent on central place services actually approximates 40,000. (2) The density and relative purchasing power of the surrounding population varies. For example, centers of about 50,000 in the sparsely populated intermontane West of the United States, because they are so widely spaced, offer the kinds of activities (though perhaps less profitably) found only in places of about 100,000 in the densely populated Northeast. (3) Entrepreneurs and individuals often make mistakes. The net effect of these and other factors is to cause much variation around any theoretically expected size, resulting in a continuum rather than a strict hierarchy of central place sizes.

To determine whether a hierarchy exists, one must examine a territory that is meaningful, that is, a territory within a range of distances actually used by individuals. If we examine any areas within which most trips to **central place functions** can be made, we discover that there is a fairly clear-cut hierarchical division of place sizes, despite varying industrialization and other factors. Examine your own area — part of a state or even part of a city — and discover whether a hierarchy of places (or business centers) exists, which you visit for goods and services.

The theory of central place hierarchy, then, is a statement of how the pursuit of the goal of maximizing interaction (exchange of goods) at the least effort (distance traveled and cost of services) tends to produce a hierarchical regularity in the size and spacing of places. This optimum organization of space cannot be observed in pure form, but that it exists is constantly demonstrated by the behavior of firms and people and by the relative success and importance of places.

Central place theory is useful for the private planning of warehouses, stores, or shopping center locations, and for the public planning of health facilities, schools, and other services. Recognition of the practical and theoretical value of locating services at more than one hierarchical level and spacing has been particularly important — for example, knowledgeable city planners allow for neighborhood health centers as well as large, specialized ones.

Modifications of Central Place Theory

Research on central place theory in recent years has brought to light significant evidence of the variation in the thresholds, ranges, and groupings of central place functions; of the mutually repellent pattern of places at a similar level; and of zones of spatial monopoly and the existence of a hierarchy of places. The fact that pure central place landscapes cannot be observed in the real world, however, has led to frequent criticism; consequently, central place theory has been modified, following these changes:

— *The assumption that an area is a uniform plane was relaxed to permit physical and cultural variation, such as varying population density or a particular settlement pattern, for example, a rectilinear land survey.*
— *The assumption of simultaneous development over limitless space was relaxed to allow for the gradual development of central place patterns from areas of early settlement.*
— *The assumption that people will always make an optimal response and have perfect information was relaxed.*
— *It was recognized that places of greater size dominate larger areas than do smaller places, even if the smaller ones offer the same goods.*
— *It was recognized that central place theory conflicts with agricultural rent theory, requiring mutual modification.*
— *It was recognized that other economic activities, especially manufacturers, contribute to the growth of towns.*

Variations in the physical quality of space and in population density required the modification of classical theory to recognize that the size of hexagonal market areas varies, hence their shape is distorted, both within a local area and over very large regions (for example, as in extreme southeast Florida).

Locally, conditions of poor topography and irregular transport, as in Appalachia, have led to many small settlements with a very limited variety of goods and services. A small set of these settlements, known collectively as a **"dispersed city"** occurs in many mining or logging areas. Some consequences are increased travel, decreased consumption, and reduced demand for higher level activities.

It has been observed, too, that even if land quality is constant, transport quality is superior between large places. As a result, corridors of greater development are included, as along major railways, producing sectors of greater and lesser population and settlement density (the city-rich sectors of figure 4.11), for example, the Mohawk corridor in New York State. Transport routes distort the patterns postulated by central place theory in still other ways: in much of the United States, for instance, development of a central place system occured in the context of a rectilinear land-survey system. Transport routes thus tend to be north-south and east-west, settlement patterns tend to be square and trade areas tend to be square or diamond-shaped rather than round or hexagonal (for example, in Iowa or Southern Minnesota).

Viewing central place development as a gradual process in time as well as in space introduces two main complications:

— *Changes occur in the nature and price of goods and services, in population and in purchasing power, and in the quality and cost of transportation; that is, the parameters determining threshold, range, and profitability change; and*

— *It is quite possible that the entire central place system develops gradually as settlement itself spreads across a territory.*

Experimental studies have shown both that the hierarchical pattern of places gradually develops as purchasing power increases and, more recently, that the smallest settlements decline as transport improves. Theoretically, changes in parameters such as an improved transport system will make the existing settlement pattern nonoptimal. For instance, with improved transport, older places of any size that are too close together will lose some importance as central places, and some will be more successful than others in adapting to the altered transportation or population conditions. Where settlement spreads gradually, as in the United States, places beginning in a later period should, because of improved transport, theoretically be farther apart and also more dependent on the transport system. Thus, the passage of time has an important effect on the arrangement of settlements.

People usually do not possess enough information or care enough about costs and profits to behave in a truly optimal fashion. Building a theory as if people did or could behave in such a way is valuable, however, because it depicts the state toward which people are moving, even though imperfectly. When **nonoptimal behavior** and uncertainty are included in central place theory, the following effects occur:

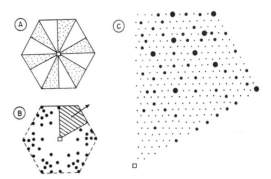

Figure 4.11 City-rich and city-poor sectors around a metropolis. Sectors of denser population and larger places (stippled areas in *A*, dots in *B*, detail in *C*) tend to develop. In *C*, note the concentration of the largest places along the lines connecting the vertices of the sector. (Reprinted by permission of the Yale University Press, from August Lösch, *Economics of Location,* 1954.)

— *There is variation around the optimal position for a place in the hexagonal structure.*

— *There is a variability in the mix of goods and services offered by places at a given level: some places will not take advantage of their opportunities, others will try to offer goods with a threshold that is too high.*

— *Customers will either not be able to distinguish between small differences in distance or other personal considerations will at times be more important than efficiency. The result is that theoretically clear-cut market areas will become overlapping fields (see figure 4.12).*

Central place theory uses a strict geometric approach to the delineation of market areas. Thus, with respect to a given level (say, towns), the trade areas are all considered to be identically sized hexagons — despite the fact that some of the trade areas will contain centers (small cities, perhaps) offering higher level goods and services. Studies of actual shopping behavior indicate that larger places having greater quantities of given goods (due to their larger internal

RURAL

1st CHOICE SHOPPING

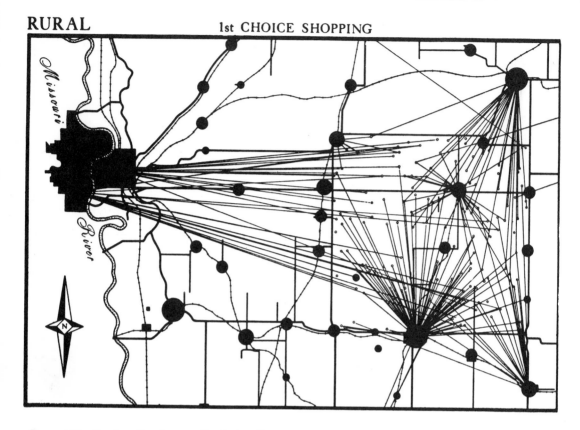

Figure 4.12 Overlap of trade areas. "Desire lines" connecting rural customers (small circles) with urban places (larger black dots and Omaha, to the left) where furniture is usually bought indicate that centers do not monopolize all nearby customers, but rather that their trade areas overlap. (Reprinted by permission of the Regional Science Association, from B.J.L. Berry, H.G. Barnum, and R. Tennant, "Retail Location and Consumer Behavior," *Papers and Proceedings of the Regional Science Association*, Vol. IX, 1962.)

populations) will have a competitive advantage over neighboring smaller places offering the same goods. Even setting aside the fact that larger places are better known, the benefits of greater scale for sellers in the larger place should enable them to extend their trade area. The result is a reduction in the range of goods that smaller surrounding places offer. Larger places thus alter the basic central place structure by tending to make intermediate-order places drop to a lower order.

One major problem with the uniform-plane assumption is the existence of the rural population-density and land-rent gradients from major markets as developed in chapter 3: because a larger trade area is needed when population density decreases, it is not possible to maintain the ideal hexagonal shape. This density change is often accompanied by a change in the population of places at a given level and by a change in the mix of goods and services offered at that level. For example, Salt Lake City, in a low-density area, has a much smaller population than cities in high-density areas with a comparable variety of activities.

An attempt to preserve hexagonal market-area shape while adjusting to the declining density away from metropolitan areas produces "distorted" central place patterns, although they may be in fact very regular and produced by the same principles of competition for territorial monopoly. Figure 9.01 on page 212 illustrates a possible surface on which a central place system is developed as geometrically faithfully as possible over a constantly changing density gradient.

Finally, one should be aware that central

place theory explicitly excludes other town-building activities that produce goods for "export" rather than for serving the town itself. These activities — most typically, processing — directly affect central place theory, however; if there is an initial growth of manufacturing towns, for instance, these towns will develop a demand for services. Since the industrial population is not diffuse, but concentrated in clusters of settlements, the central place pattern will have a rather different spatial appearance than the theoretical arrangement that occurs with uniform population density.

Historical Development of Urban Patterns

In early subsistence societies, permanent markets could not be supported because there was not enough demand for and supply of goods. The small surpluses of individual families could best be exchanged locally by barter. Still, there was always demand for some outside products, and the problem was how to meet such small amounts of demand scattered over such a wide territory. One solution was the itinerant peddler, who did most of the moving himself. Another was the annual or occasional fair, where even people from an area with the poorest transport could get together once a year to exchange goods.

As specialization, productivity, and the demand for trade and outside goods gradually increased, fairs took place more frequently and became closer in space. Less spectacularly, groups of farmers, together with small merchants and service people, developed the periodic market. These markets circulated among a set of nearby villages, spending perhaps a day or two in each. Gradually, the fairs of larger places became permanent, and the villages that were favored because of better average accessibility to a wider area became permanent market towns. All these were rational and efficient means of maximizing interaction, given the constraint of limited productivity and mobility.

With industrialization and the growth of cities, agriculture became commercial. Improved roads and railroads increased rural accessibility, and higher personal income reduced thresholds, permitted the rise of new service centers closer to the population, and stimulated the growth of existing places as well.

Commonly Recognized Levels of Settlement

As settlements grow in size and in functional complexity (providing a greater variety of services), they require a larger population for support and a wider spacing between themselves and other centers. (Figure 4.13 illustrates the relation between population, area, and functional level.) Thus, a village becomes a town, a higher level in the spatial hierarchy. The terminology we use to describe settlements, in fact, reflects the existence of a central place hierarchy. The following paragraphs define the levels of settlement that we distinguish.

A *hamlet* may contain up to 500 persons, but more typically its population is around 100 to 200. Hamlets usually serve about 2,000 persons and offer such everyday **convenience goods** and services as taverns, gas stations, and small grocery stores. As a rule, people do not wish to travel more than five minutes or so (about three miles) to reach these activities. As transport improves (by paving rural roads, for instance), more distance can be covered for the same effort, and many of the lowest order places have disappeared as more people can travel easily to larger places.

The *village*, containing from 500 to 2,500 persons (mean population about 2,000) and serving an area that may include up to 10,000 persons, offers a greater number of functions, including some which an individual may use only occasionally but for which the demand is constant: bakeries, several churches, schools, a restaurant or drive-in, a post office, a general clothing store, a hardware store, auto repair shop, farm implements, feeds, and perhaps a doctor, dentist, or bank.

The *town* has a population that may range from 2,5000 to 20,000 (mean size, 10,000) and serves 25,000 to 100,000 persons. The American town, often the county seat, is the traditional urban place. It dominates regional life and is the familiar social

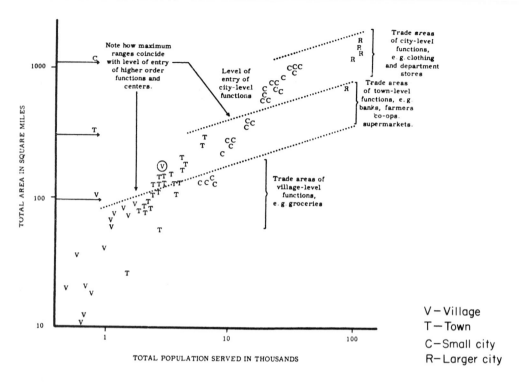

Figure 4.13   Relationship between population, area, and the functional level of central places. Note that the maximum population (range) served by villages is about the same as the minimum population (threshold) supporting a town. Because of variation in population density, however, there is much overlap in the area served by villages and towns, towns and small cities, and so forth. (Reprinted by permission of the Regional Science Association from B.J.L. Berry, H.G. Barnum, and R. Tennant, "Retail Location and Consumer Behavior," *Papers and Proceedings of the Regional Science Association*, Vol. IX, 1962.)

and economic center of American life. It is also the usual place of entertainment; it has the nearest hospital, newspaper, big high school, lawyers, and courts; it has doctors, dentists, veterinarians, large churches, many restaurants; it is a place where cars, farm equipment and supplies, appliances, furniture, and jewelry are usually bought; and it is where insurance and real estate agents, cleaners, and hotels can be found.

The town is probably no more than a half-hour to an hour, or 12 to 15 miles, away from most of the people it serves. In both Europe and the United States the large metropolis has replaced the town as the chief power in our lives; but the town heritage is still with us, and, even in the city, much individual activity is focused in town-sized shopping centers.

The *small city* contains from 20,000 to 200,000 people and serves a million people. It is the district capital, whose geographic

significance lies in its role as center for distribution and communication. It is at the bottom of the wholesale distribution ladder, the smallest market that can efficiently support a middle exchange between manufacturer and retailer. Here may be a college, a department store, medical specialists, much retail and service specialization (for example, stores, specializing in music, sporting goods, photography); in a sense small cities are the outposts of "metropolitan life." These cities are served by good roads, railroads, and fairly good air connections, and they are so located that in a day a family can travel to and from the center, have time to shop, and do business.

The *large city*, a regional, state, or provincial capital, includes from 200,000 to 500,000 persons and serves a population of from one to three million. These cities are more self-contained than are smaller ones, possess a range of local manufactures, and have perhaps a university, major department stores, specialized hospitals, and more sophisticated shopping and entertainment. Wholesale trade and finance may exceed local retail trade and banking in volume. These large cities are the highest level cities that most people need to reach — almost all necessary goods and services can be found here.

The *metropolis*, with near or over a million residents, dominates a large area containing from 5 to 30 million people. The metropolis is the controlling center of the modern economy, the place where most decisions are made and where much of a country's manufacturing is carried on. The metropolis dominates distribution, culture, education, innovation, and communication, and it generates expansion of the economy and the culture. People living up to 500 miles away may rarely or never visit the metropolis, but they feel its influence through the agricultural market, the banking structure, mail-order houses, wholesale-retail relationships, and so forth.

CENTRAL PLACE ACTIVITIES

Retail Trade

Of the many central place activities, retail trade is the most important and the most obvious. An individual spends much time and money buying goods from the various shops and using the repair services located in central places.

To keep in business, the retail outlet chooses a location where it can be seen and will attract customers. This is accomplished in three ways:

— *A retail decision maker places a premium on central accessibility — on being at the center of a transport subsystem. For instance, lower order activities like groceries and drug stores are often located at the center crossroads of a hamlet or village or at arterial crossings in a city; higher level activities are in larger places or at intersections of more important roads.*

— *Retail activities locate together in mutually beneficial groups. The activities that especially seek to form*

such clusters include clothing, jewelry, stationery, confection, and shoe stores.

— *Each group will try to locate as far from like competing groups as possible, in order to assure each retailer a fairly secure home market.*

While the majority of retail trade is grouped together and does best in locations where routes come together, large sectors of business are increasingly oriented toward traffic arteries and depend on traffic moving along a major road. Motels, auto and trailer sales and service, rent-all dealers, drive-in restaurants, and most gas stations have a largely linear marker — the vehicles traveling along a road. Since these facilities are automobile-oriented, they need much parking space for customers and cannot easily afford the rents of nucleated commercial centers.

Trade Areas. The store and the business district or shopping center to which it belongs have a trade area, defined by the shopping trips of its customers. Pure central place theory defines these areas absolutely and geometrically. We realize, of course, that individuals do not have perfect information and do not always behave optimally — they do not always go the shortest distance for a good or service. More realistically, then, we discover a field, or pattern of shoppers, about the store or center. The extent of the field is governed by the distance to competing centers of similar or larger size, and its intensity is controlled by the concentration of consumers in the area. Trade areas or shopping fields that are derived from asking customers the "place usually frequented for shopping" are found to overlap (see figure 4.12).

This lack of precisely delineated trade areas reflects not only the inability of customers to distinguish small differences in distance, but also the conflict between the goal of minimizing distance and that of maximizing quality or quantity of goods or services received and the subtle differences between supposedly identical mixes of goods and services.

Multipurpose Trips. Multipurpose trips help explain both the apparently inef-

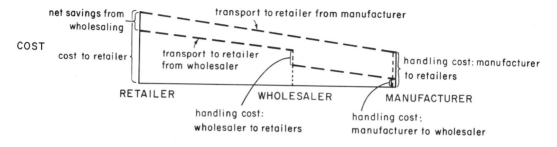

Figure 4.14   The spatial efficiency of wholesaling. If the manufacturer sells directly to retailers, his handling and distribution costs are very high because of the many retailers and the small size of his shipments. However, handling and distribution costs are small when manufacturers sell to only a few wholesalers, and retailers save by dealing with a few wholesalers rather than many manufacturers.

ficient overlap of trade areas and the efficient behavior of consumers, who, by combining several purposes in one trip, save time and distance. People make short, one- or two-purpose trips more frequently, but multipurpose, longer trips may accomplish much more.

Many trips involve travel to more than one retail location, either because the shopper was frustrated at the first center or, more usually, because he perceived that each center offered some items the other lacked. A multipurpose trip to two locations will still save time and distance over two single-purpose trips to one closer center.

Multipurpose trips provide one of the theoretical bases for the agglomeration of functions at few, larger centers. Agglomeration makes it easier for a business to maximize the availability of its service to the most people. Not only do shopping centers make possible the satisfaction of planned multipurpose trips, but the presence of other stores can often induce greater consumption than is originally planned by the individual.

Wholesale Trade

Wholesale trade is both spatially and economically efficient, and it is a necessary intermediary between the manufacturer or farmer and the retailer (figure 4.14). The producer, who specializes in a few items for very wide distribution, can neither spend the time on nor afford to handle countless small orders from retailers. The retailer, who stocks an immense variety of items, does not

have the time to order small amounts from countless producers. Furthermore, dividing large shipments into smaller lots would be a bookkeeping nightmare to both producers and retailers and would result in extremely high distribution costs.

The spatial and economic hierarchy of central place theory is well illustrated by wholesaling. With wholesaling, costly long-haul shipments of small lots are avoided; long-haul, large-volume movements from producers to wholesalers make possible economies of scale with respect to transport. At the same time, the retailer enjoys much quicker delivery from regional centers.

Wholesale trade is concentrated in the largest central places, although not only the size, but also the relative location of a place is important, (figure 4.15). In the United States, for example, wholesaling thrives in those metropolises on a border between the northeastern manufacturing region (the core) and the more agricultural periphery, as well as in regional centers of the periphery.

Transportation

Transportation facilities within towns are central place activities, since they make possible distribution and exchange. Warehousing (temporary storage), especially associated with the wholesale trade and marketing of local produce, constitutes a ''time cushion'' between producer and consumer — if a month's goods are stocked, producers do not have to adjust to day-by-day changes in consumption, and consumers do not have to wait long for goods.

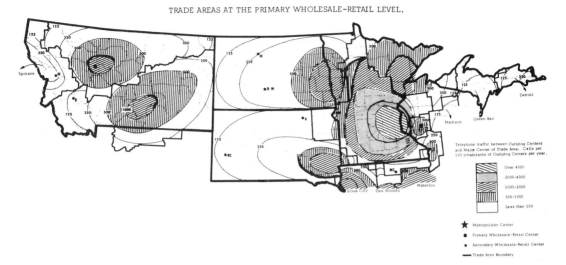

Figure 4.15   Major wholesale-retail trade areas in the upper Midwest. Note that many trade areas cross state lines. Telephone traffic is a fairly good indicator of wholesale-retail trade-area boundaries. (Reprinted by permission of John Borchert and Russell Adams, "Trade Centers and Trade Areas in the Upper Midwest," Urban Report 3, Upper Midwest Economic Study, Minneapolis, 1963.)

A special problem of warehousing and exchange is **queuing,** that is, finding the best coordination of activities to simultaneously minimize waiting, costs and time of storage, and taxes on inventories. The merchant or wholesaler wishes to meet all requests, but he has a limited storage capacity and finds it impossible to have enough stock to meet every contingency. Queuing theory permits minimum levels of stock to be estimated that will meet all but the most peculiar and, therefore, expendable demands. The spatial implications of queuing are great. The cost of having to turn away customers is both the ill will caused by having to send and wait for goods and the likelihood that the customer will shift to a new dealer at a new location.

Other Central Place Activities

Financial Services.   Financial and related services — banking, real estate, and insurance — are especially vital control services. They are often associated with other medium-threshold goods in multipurpose trips and hence are found in all towns and district shopping centers. However, there are higher level components of such services, such as commercial-industrial bank-

ing and investment services, that seek large-city downtown locations for the convenience of the most important customers and to ease interoffice transactions.

Real-Estate and Insurance Offices. Real-estate and local insurance offices have low thresholds and find it relatively easy to enter a market. Since they depend on advertising and selling in the home, their locational preferences are not very strong, and many of them are tenants of low-rent stores on lesser arterials.

Schools.   Schools are central place activities that follow administrative principles of spacing, that is, higher level schools (such as high schools) draw their students from a few schools from the next lower level (junior high schools). Schools need to be located centrally for their pupils' convenience, but a policy conflict arises out of the desire for close accessibility and the economies in teaching staff, facilities, and materials that can be realized if schools are larger and more widely spaced. This conflict is seen in the constant battle between the proponents of the neighborhood schools and those who want to consolidate schools in order to permit access to better equipment, more specialization in teaching, and the like. Some towns have experimented with consolidating all schools on one central campus to realize maximum efficiency, but this involves costly bussing, time cost for students, and, especially for pupils in the elementary grades, real social costs.

Health Services. Health services, from physicians to clinics, community hospitals, and highly specialized teaching hospitals, well illustrate the central place principles of hierarchical structure and regularity of spacing that result from competition for secure trade areas. They also illustrate the conflict that may exist between the desire to benefit from the advantages of agglomeration in specialized centers and the desire to be as close to the population as possible in order to serve its needs more directly. Because of variations in income level, however, some communities are better able than others to support local health services.

Summary

Central places are important — and increasingly so — for the support of the economy. Since they arise to serve a dispersed, somewhat "captive" population, which is closer to one particular center than to competing ones, a regular pattern tends to form in which centers are as far from each other as possible. Since the demand for goods varies, this spatial structure becomes a hierarchical one as well, from a large number of smaller centers offering the most frequently demanded goods to a very small number of great metropolises requiring large portions of the national economy for support and offering the most esoteric goods and services. Distortion of the ideal spatial patterns is due to many factors, not the least of which is the location of resources and of processing activities, to which we now turn.

REFERENCES

General References

Berry, B.J.L., "Cities as Systems within Systems of Cities," *Papers and Proceedings of the Regional Science Association* 13 (1964): 147-164.

Berry, B.J.L., *A Geography of Market Centers and Retail Distribution*, Englewood Cliffs, N.J.: Prentice-Hall, 1967.

Berry, B.J.L., H.G. Barnum, and R.J. Tennant, "Retail Location and Consumer Behavior," *Papers and Proceedings of the Regional Science Association* 9 (1962): 65-106.

Berry, B.J.L. and A. Pred, *Central Place Studies: A Bibliography of Theory and Applications*, Philadelphia: Regional Science Research Institute, Bibliographic Series 1, 1965.

Boventer, E. von, "Christaller's Central Places and Peripheral Areas," *Journal of Regional Science* 9 (1969): 117-124.

Christaller, W., *Central Places in Southern Germany*, Translated by C.W. Baskin. Englewood Cliffs, N.J.: Prentice-Hall, 1966.

Clark, W.A.V., "Consumer Travel Patterns and the Concept of Range," *Annals of the Association of American Geographers* 58 (1968): 386-396.

Curry, L., "Central Places in the Random Spatial Economy," *Journal of Regional Science* 7 (1967): 217-238.

Dacey, M.F., "The Geometry of Central Place Theory," *Geografiska Annaler* 47B (1965): 111-124.

Harris, C.D. and E.L. Ullman, "The Nature of Cities," *Annals of the Academy of Political and Social Science* 242 (1945): 7-17.

Janelle, D.G., "Central Place Development in a Time-Space Framework," *Professional Geographer* 20 (1968): 5-10.

Morrill, R.L., "The Development and Spatial Distribution of Towns in Sweden: An Historical-Predictive Approach," *Annals of the Association of American Geographers* 53 (1963): 1-14.

Morrill, R. L., "Migration and the Spread and Growth of Urban settlement," *Lund Studies in Geography*, Series B, 26, 1965.

Parr, John B. and Kenneth G. Denike, "Theoretical Problems in Central Place Analysis," *Economic Geography* 46 (1970): 568-586.

Rushton, Gerard, "Postulates of Central Place Theory and Properties of Central Place Systems," *Geographical Analysis* 3 (1971): 140-156.

Thijsse, J., "Second Thoughts about a Rural Pattern for the Future in the Netherlands," *Papers and Proceedings of the Regional Science Association* 20 (1968): 69-76.

Ullman, E.L., "A Theory of Location for Cities," *American Journal of Sociology* 46 (1941): 853-864.

Woldenberg, M. L. and B. J. L. Berry, "Rivers and Central Places: Analogous Systems?" *Journal of Regional Science* 7 (1967): 129-139.

Empirical Studies: Central Places and Hinterlands

Applebaum, W. and S.B. Cohen, "The Dynamics of Store Trading Areas and Market Equilibrium," *Annals of the Association of American Geographers* 51 (1961): 73-101.

Bracey, H.E., "Towns as Rural Service Centers," *Transactions of the Institute of British Geographers* 19 (1953): 95-105.

Brush, J.E., "The Hierarchy of Central Places in Southwestern Wisconsin," *Geographical Review* 43 (1953): 380-402.

Dickinson, R.E., *City and Region*, New York: Humanities, 1964.

Green, H.L., "Hinterland Boundaries of New York City and Boston in Southern New England," *Economic Geography* 31 (1955): 283-300.

Hodgen, M.T., "Fairs of Elizabethan England," *Economic Geography* 18 (1942): 389-400.

Hoover, Edgar M., "Transport Costs and the Spacing of Central Places," *Papers of the Regional Science Association* 25 (1970): 245-274.

Illeris, S. and P.O. Pedersen, "Central Places and Functional Regions of Denmark," *Lund Studies in Geography*, Series B, 31, 1968.

Johnson, Lane J., "Spatial Uniformity of a Central Place Distribution in New England," *Economic Geography* 47 (1971): 156-170.

King, L., "A Multivariate Analysis of the Spacing of Urban Settlements in the United States," *Annals of the Association of American Geographers* 51 (1961): 222-233.

McCarty, H.H., "The Market Functions of Villages in Eastern Iowa," *Annals of the Association of American Geographers* 31 (1941): 63.

Olsson, G. and A. Persson, "The Spacing of Central Places in Sweden," *Papers and Proceedings of the Regional Science Association* 12 (1964): 87-94.

Preston, Richard E., "Structure of Central Place Systems," *Economic Geography* 47 (1971): 136-155.

Stafford, H.A., Jr., "The Functional Bases of Small Towns," *Economic Geography* 39 (1963): 165-175.

Thomas, E.N., R.A. Mitchell, and D. Blome, "The Spatial Behavior of a Dispersed Non-Farm Population," *Papers and Proceedings of the Regional Science Association* 9 (1962): 107-133.

Webber, M.J., "Empirical Verifiability of a Classical Central-Place Theory," *Geographical Analysis* 3 (1971): 15-28.

Retail Trade

Bacon, R.W., "An Approach to the Theory of Consumer Shopping Behavior," *Urban Studies* 8 (1971): 55-64.

Berry, B.J.L., "Ribbon Developments in the Urban Business Pattern," *Annals of the Association of American Geographers* 49 (1959): 145 - 155.

Campbell, W.J. and Michael Chisholm, Local Variation in Retail Grocery Prices," *Urban Studies* 7 (1970): 76-81.

Clark, W.A.V. and Gerard Rushton, "Models of Intra-Urban Consumer Behavior and Their Implications for Central Place Theory," *Economic Geography* 46 (1970): 486-497.

Golledge, R.G., "Some Equilibrium Models of Consumer Behavior," *Economic Geography* 46 (1970): 417-424.

Harries, Keith B., "An Inter-Ethnic Analysis of Retail and Service Functions in Los Angeles County, California," *Proceedings of the Association of American Geographers* 2 (1970): 62-67.

Huff, D.L., "Ecological Characteristics of Consumer Behavior," *Papers and Proceedings of the Regional Science Association* 7 (1961): 19-28.

Johnston, R.L. and P. J. Rimmer, "Consumer Behavior in an Urban Hierarchy," *Journal of Regional Science* 7 (1967): 161-166.

Murdie, R., "Cultural Differences in Consumer Travel," *Economic Geography* 41 (1965): 211-233.

Reilly, W.J., *The Law of Retail Gravitation*, New York: Knickerbocker, 1931.

Rose, Harold M., "The Structure of Retail Trade in a Racially Changing Trade Area," *Geographical Analysis* 2 (1970): 135-148.

Simmons, J., *The Changing Pattern of Retail Location*, University of Chicago Department of Geography, Research Paper 92, 1964.

Vance, James E., Jr., *The Merchant's World — The Geography of Wholesaling*, Englewood Cliffs, N.J.: Prentice-Hall, 1970.

Yuill, R.S., "Spatial Behavior of Retail Customers," *Geografiska Annaler* 49B (1967): 105-116.

Other Services

Earickson, Robert J., "The Spatial Behavior of Hospital Patients: A Behavioral Approach to Spatial Interaction in Metropolitan Chicago," University of Chicago, Department of Geography, Research Paper 124, 1970.

Godlund, A., "Population, Regional Hospitals, Transport Facilities, and Regions: Planning the Location of Regional Hospitals in Sweden," *Lund Studies in Geography*, Series B, 21, 1961.

Kerr, D., "Some Aspects of the Geography of Finance in Canada," *Canadian Geographer* 9, 1965: 175-192.

Morrill, Richard L. and Robert J. Earickson and Philip Rees, "Factors Influencing Distances Traveled to Hospitals," *Economic Geography* 46 (1970): 161-171.

Morrill, R.L. and R. Earickson, "Variation in the Character and Use of Chicago Hospitals," *Health Services Research* 3 (1968): 224-238.

Morrill, R.L. and P. Kelley, "Optimal Allocation of Services," *Annals of Regional Science* 3 (1969): 55-66.

Teitz, M.B., "Toward a Theory of Urban Public Facilities Location," *Papers and Proceedings of the Regional Science Association* 21 (1968): 35-52.

Industrialization: Towns as Processing Centers

Chapter 5

In developing an ideal landscape based only on spatial principles, we have seen how a gradient of activities and density arises around large centers, and how competing centers of differing size and scope are spatially organized to provide demanded central services to a dispersed population.

Human societies also demand manufactured goods, transformed from a variety of raw materials. If these resources were ubiquitous, a given manufacturer would locate at the precise level of central place that would provide a profitable demand for his product. Resources, however, are sporadically located, and they vary in quality. Thus, manufacturing will appear as a factor distorting the ideal patterns previously described. Yet we will see that industry tends to locate according to the same goals of maximizing the utility of places (productivity of a plant) and maximizing interaction (sales of goods and assembly of materials) at least cost, and that consequently, several different patterns of industries can be observed, each of which is logical and predictable with respect to the location of the relevant resources and markets.

INDUSTRIALIZATION

Although increased commercialization, international trade, and internal exchange encouraged the development of market towns and ports, the town-building impact of industrialization — the growth of manufacturing — may have been even greater. Societies gradually began to demand more products than individuals could make at home and came to appreciate the efficiency and profitability of specializing in the conversion of raw materials into more finished products. Greater profits required greater productivity, so industrialization was accompanied by rapid mechanization and a shift to inanimate sources of power, vastly increasing production. The demand for resources, which were both converted into other goods and used as fuels, also grew rapidly.

The spatial impact of industrialization was enormous. Metal ores, wood, and fuels, rather than good farming land, became the resources most sought after, and the location of the two kinds of resources rarely coincided. Thus, towns frequently developed in areas of low agricultural productivity in order to exploit valuable local resources. Since industrial towns did not depend on a spatial monopoly over scattered rural customers, they often grouped in clusters rather than dispersed over a wide territory in the manner of market towns. This new basis for towns effected a large-scale redistribution of population from areas of rich farming to areas with rich resources. Not all industry, however, exploited these new resources: processors of agricultural products and makers of goods demanding high craftsmanship tended to locate in the older market towns.

Industrial activities typically utilized first the new resources closest to areas of existing development, but when these were depleted, often through wasteful and inefficient procedures, more distant sources had to be used.

In the early stages of industrialization, **primary industries** — making the simplest conversions of raw materials — tended to be dominant. In more affluent economies, secondary industries — manufacturing of more complex products (appliances, computers) from primary products (steel, paint) — have become dominant. The primary base of production is no less necessary in advanced economies, but a high standard of living depends on the willingness of the consumer to pay for increasingly elaborated products — clothes, for instance, not just cloth.

General Significance of Industrialization

Although some manufacturing can be done in the home, industrialization enables a firm to specialize in a limited range of products with specifically trained labor and management, thereby vastly increasing per capita productivity. Moreover, mechanized energy can be substituted for animal and human energy, a step which increases per capita production far more than does specialization alone. Although in the very short run the substitution of machines for men may cause **technological unemployment,** the long-term effect is to increase production and wealth. It is this ability to

produce goods with only a fraction of the labor force that permits a higher standard of living for all to develop: mechanized industrial production is 50 to 100 times more productive than is handicraft production. For instance, it might seem cheaper for an American family to buy flour and make its own bread, but it is far more efficient for society and saves time for the family if the bread is bought ready-made. The apparent savings of handicraft production are illusory, because the economy — and the standard of living — can grow only by increasing specialization and thus raising the productivity per worker. Once an efficient and productive industrial base is built, however, society tends to rediscover handicraft production. Also, in developing countries with very large underutilized labor forces, labor is relatively cheaper than capital, and therefore optimally used more extensively.

Spatial Significance of Industrialization

Industrialization brought about these major geographic changes:

— *Previously unvalued mineral resources, particularly coal, petroleum, and natural gas, became as important as land, climate, and animal resources.*

— *The population became generally concentrated in cities.*

— *Areas with clusters of urban settlements were created.*

— *Sharper distinctions became evident between prosperous and poor areas.*

— *Goods were moved increasingly long distances between regions.*

Mineral resources, more than agricultural ones, are the basis for our present industrial and service structures. Mineral resources have attracted industries, and cities have been built around them, whatever the surrounding agricultural potential. Since mineral resources are concentrated in small areas, and large-scale production is most economic, population has become concentrated in a few favored industrial areas. Industrial settlements have formed spatial patterns that are different from market towns, such as clusters of mining settlements and larger clusters of textile, steel, and other industrial towns.

Another major spatial effect of industrialization has been the weakening of regional and local self-sufficiency by the great demand for long-distance movement of raw materials, fuels, and foods. Because resources are located in diverse, specific places and industrial enterprises are large scale, industrialization requires great spatial interdependence. Industrialization has also made available both better mining equipment to permit use of lower quality ores, previously considered valueless, and more efficient farm machinery to permit previously marginal lands to be cultivated.

FACTORS DETERMINING INDUSTRIAL LOCATION

Processing (manufacturing) activities are the main alternative to central place activities for the support of towns and cities. Processing typically provides about one-fourth to three-fifths of the employment and value of products in a town. The total value of processing activities — manufacturing and construction — is about one-third to one-half an advanced nation's gross national product.

Processing activities involve a high level of spatial complexity. While central place activities mainly involve distributing goods to local consumers, and efficient location thus depends upon having the best access to customers, processing has different constraints on location. Distribution is to consumer markets that may be distant and large, rather than local, small, and dispersed. Materials must be collected from specific points within a wide area. Many processing costs vary from place to place and with size (scale) of operations. The manufacturer's desire to maximize his profit (the difference between revenues and total costs) means that he must be located so as to minimize total costs of obtaining materials, of processing them, and of marketing his output to customers. He must also be located favorably with respect to competing producers of the same goods. While regional variations in labor costs, taxes, and the like,

only slightly affect central place locations, they strongly influence processing locations, often changing the optimum site for a plant away from a more central location.

Industrial location, even in theory, is more complicated than central place location because variation in the quality of space — the location of specific resources, for example — is an explicit part of the theory. Decisions are more complex — and more interesting — because it is possible to vary the relative amounts of labor or capital and the specific kinds of products or materials. Before attempting to summarize the theory of industrial location, we shall review the elements included in the theory.

Location of Resources and Markets. Resources and markets do not exist in all places, but rather at sporadic, specific sites. They are spatially separated, and a successful manufacturer must overcome these distances.

Transport Costs and the Transport System. Assembling, or collecting raw materials, and distributing the finished goods to markets are subject to specific transport charges and costs in time. Even where the unit cost of transport is not great, the presence of a quality transport system is essential.

Spatial Variation in Processing Costs. Another factor that complicates finding the ideal processing location is the considerable spatial variation in the price and quality of land and labor, in corporate and inventory taxes, construction costs, and maintenance, heating, and cooling costs. The cost of labor, however, is a function of the expenditure per unit of product, not of the wage rate, and many companies are thus willing to pay high wages for highly productive workers. Variations in labor costs are also a function of the degree of economic development in a given area and of the relative labor supply.

Demand. For a new industry to be created and for existing ones to survive, consumers must be willing to pay a price that will more than cover manufacturing

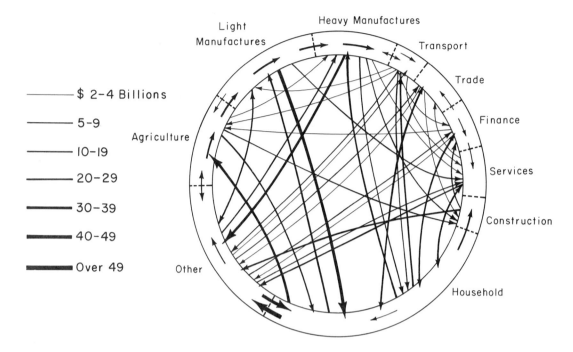

Figure 5.01   Input-output: interindustry flows of goods and services (after Isard). Shown is the value of goods and services flowing between and within major economic sectors in the United States, about 1955. (The chart is partly hypothetical.) Flows to households represent retail consumption; flows from households represent labor costs and family savings. Such a diagram reveals the significant linkages between sectors of the economy.

costs. Demand changes fairly rapidly, and industries must learn to adapt their technical processes and spatial behavior in order to survive.

Technology.   A feasible process to produce a good must exist if costs are to remain below prices. Internal production efficiency results from standardization of products and processes, mechanization, labor — management cooperation, and reduced turnover of labor. Extreme specialization in production reduces costs and simplifies both assembly and distribution (in other words, it simplifies the problem of finding the right location for the firm); but it also increases the short-run risks caused by price fluctuation, by change in consumer demand, and by increased competition for supplies and markets. Thus, although a firm may standardize its products, it also usually finds it beneficial to diversify and manufacture a small set of products; **diversification** may complicate manufacturing, but it reduces the economic

and locational risks of the firm. The main contribution of technology, however, lies in its development of more efficient and automatic forms of mechanized processes, which at the same time permit some flexibility of inputs and outputs.

Capital.   Processing industries usually require large outlays of capital, but are somewhat less risky than service activities. New plants typically require at least $100,-000, and may run to $10 million or more, whereas a new shop can be opened for only a few thousand dollars. Hence, lending agencies for processing activities are large and rather cautious. Since capital is generated in the largest amounts in already successful industrial locations, the most available capital is within large financial-industrial centers. Such capital may theoretically be mobile, but lenders are inclined to be more willing to invest in known areas in accepted lines of activities. Also, in an economy that is predominantly private, the lender and the prospective manufacturer

Table 5.01. *INPUT-OUTPUT OR INTERINDUSTRY*
FLOWS TABLE FOR WASHINGTON STATE, 1967
Sales to major purchasing sectors (in millions of dollars)

Selling sectors	Agriculture	Food products	Forest products	Metals, machinery	Aerospace	Services	All Washington industries	Washington consumers	Government	Exports	TOTAL SALES
Agriculture	87	303	151	6	....	20	585	104	10	356	1055
Food products	34	72	....	....	....	28	135	610	56	642	1442
Forest products	2	26	343	3	2	159	555	105	28	1143	1836
Metals, machinery	2	65	17	55	42	200	414	5	102	747	1298
Aerospace	....	....	....	....	59	5	63	....	495	1979	2536
Services	77	85	164	87	62	1074	1671	4045	972	816	8895
Washington Sales	238	577	708	161	173	1878	3952	5155	2143	6011	18695
Imports	130	400	298	578	1274	1503	4787	1524	175	....	8080
Value added	687	466	830	559	1089	5514	9955	1220	1658	....	12733

Source: William Beyers, Philip Bourque, Warren Seyfried, and Eldon Weeks, *Input-Output Tables for the Washington Economy, 1967*, Graduate School of Business Administration, University of Washington, December 1970.

Note: Table is incomplete. Columns will not add up to totals because some sectors have been omitted ("other industries," "investment," and so forth).

Interpretation: Consider agriculture, for example. As a selling sector it sells mostly to food products industries and to forest products industries (timber sales from farms); it sells directly to Washington consumers; and it exports to other regions and countries. As a purchasing sector, it buys from itself (interfarm transactions), and it buys some services and imports (machinery, fertilizer, etc.). The difference between these purchases and sales is the value added from farming (returns to the farmer's labors, etc.).

Note the heavy interindustry transactions of food and forest products, hence the great indirect benefits and costs of growth or decline, as well as their importance in the balance of payments (exports less imports). Also note, in contrast, the very limited ties of aerospace to other sectors, its high imports, value added, and exports.

must seek fairly short-run profitability, reducing the likelihood of either developing radically new processes and products or of placing manufacturing plants in totally new locations.

Agglomeration Economies. The economic relationships that have the strongest spatial element are the economies of agglomeration and the economies of scale. The benefits of agglomeration have already been discussed with reference to central place activities (see figure 1.08). For industries, agglomeration (clustering of industries in a given location) is spatially and economically efficient when the industries share identical resources or markets or have strong interindustry **linkages** (many sales to

each other). As with central place activities, however, even unrelated activities may enjoy indirect benefits when located together. These benefits may be due to the availability of better transport, more capital, or a larger labor pool, or to the use of a common technology. Also, light industries (such as candy) employing mostly women are attracted to places where heavy industries (such as steel) employing mostly men are predominant.

If transport costs are low and brand loyalty is high, competing producers of the same good frequently are located in a cluster. Here, they may take advantage of a common skilled labor force, spin off ideas and personnel from competitors, and, above all, make comparison purchasing easy for customers.

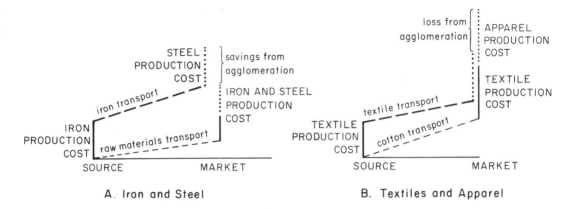

Figure 5.02 Agglomeration of industries: economies and diseconomies.   A. In the case of iron and steel, agglomeration (or integrated production) is usually cheaper than separated production because of savings on both processing (less fuel, shared overhead) and transport. B. Agglomerating textile and apparel production, however, does not result in such savings, because their labor and marketing requirements are different.

Industrial Interrelations and Industrial Complexes. A valuable short-term description of the linkages between industries is given by an account of **input-output** flows — the dollar amount that each industry purchases from every other industry (see figure 5.01 and table 5.01). It is also possible to construct a similar table for the interindustry flow of goods. These tables are particularly useful in estimating the short-term effects of change in demand or supplies in some sectors on the entire pattern of interindustry flows. Analysis of such tables also reveals that industrial complexes exist, in the sense that industries within a complex have more relations with each other than industries outside the group; but the existence of such a complex does not necessarily imply spatial agglomeration of these industries. However, if a set of related plants, for example, oil fields, refineries, synthetic fibers, and perhaps clothing or tire manufacturers, is isolated, the structure of the location of all the plants taken together will be more optimal than the location of any one type of plant considered separately.

One typical **industrial complex** consists of integrated iron and steel, by-product chemicals, fabricated metals, and machinery; another includes sawmills, pulp mills, and so forth. When these industries are located close to each other, transport costs are reduced and less handling is re-

quired for raw materials (figure 5.02A). Detroit, for example, is a rapidly growing steel producer because of the huge consumption of steel by the auto industry.

Textile and clothing manufacturers also form an industrial complex. Textile plants, however, are typically separate from apparel plants because their labor and marketing requirements are very different (figure 5.02B). Similarly, alumina processing (smelting of bauxite ore to aluminum dioxide), which does not use much electricity, tends to be separate from aluminum refining if savings from cheap electric power for refining more than offset the increasing transport costs for raw materials and the finished aluminum.

In general, the spatial concentration of related activities increases the total distance required for assembling basic materials and for shipping the final products, but it is justified so long as savings in the shipments between activities and in other relations between industries more than offset the increases from basic suppliers and to final markets (figure 5.02).

Economies of Scale. Economies of scale refer to the expected reduction in average unit cost when more units of the same product are manufactured. As scale increases, the costs of development, new machinery, plant, and overhead are spread over more units; labor productivity is rais-

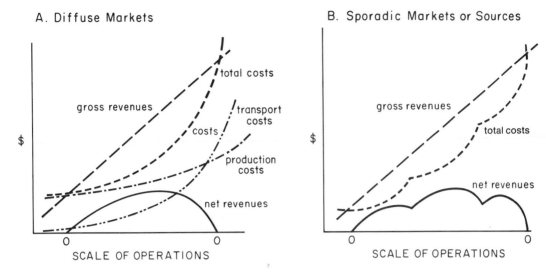

A. Diffuse Markets

B. Sporadic Markets or Sources

Figure 5.03 Economies of scale and market and source location. A. Where customer markets are small and diffuse, profits gradually increase and later decrease. B. Where customers or material sources are few, large, and sporadically located, several levels of output may be relatively profitable.

ed; more internal specialization is possible; the large quantities of inputs needed can be obtained at a reduced price and shipped at a lower rate; the large shipments of the goods produced receive lower bulk transport rates; machinery and specialized personnel are more fully utilized; and inventories of raw materials and products can be relatively lower.

As scale increases (see figure 1.11) the cost of the next unit produced (marginal cost) at first falls rapidly, and average costs fall. Eventually, the marginal cost begins to rise and comes to equal the average cost of all units, after which average costs per unit rise. Depending on the behavior of prices, another point occurs (when marginal costs equal marginal revenue, or the price of the next unit sold) at which total profit is maximized and then declines.

Costs rise internally (within the plant) and profits fall as plant reconstruction, labor shortages, internal transport inefficiency, congestion, and managerial confusion raise production costs; and costs rise externally (outside the firm) as the necessity for seeking more distant resources and markets raises transfer costs excessively.

If internal processing inefficiencies do not occur, however, average costs will decline with increasing scale while a firm remains within a spatially restricted market. Since most markets are in fact located at points and spatially separated (in cities), increased scale will sooner or later force a firm to use more distant markets or suppliers. The accompanying rise in transfer costs may more than offset any economies due to scale. Figure 5.03 illustrates two situations: In *A*, internal diseconomies and increasing transport costs due to serving more distant, diffuse customers eventually reduce profits. In *B*, the need to utilize large material sources and to serve large but sporadic markets gives more than one fairly profitable level of output, but also results in an eventual decline in profits.

Industries for which transport costs are high tend to seek protected market areas, and thus tend to become either monopolies or **oligopolies** (where only a few producers control supply and demand). Scale is limited by the size of regional markets and by the diseconomies of transportation over great distances. There are other industries for which transport costs play only a small role in determining optimal scale (see figure 5.04). The aircraft and machinery industries are typical examples. For these industries no significant spatial monopoly is possible: firms must share virtually the entire market. Scale is usually limited by the firm's competitive share of the market rather than by diseconomies. As a result, prices are likely to

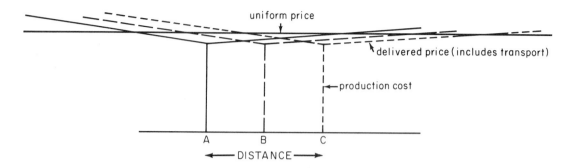

Figure 5.04   Shared markets. Where costs of delivery are low and delivered prices virtually the same, even widely separated firms like *A*, *B*, and *C* can compete over a wide area. The firms will prefer to quote a uniform price and will not attempt to capture a local market.

be fairly uniform, and plants will be located in places that minimize spatially varying processing costs. These industries are likely also to benefit from the processing-cost benefits of agglomeration discussed earlier in the chapter.

Substitution in Manufacturing.   Every kind of manufacturing involves a complex variety of inputs, and there can be many different processes for a number of specific products. Indeed, many possibilities for substitution are available to the firm when finding an optimal location or attempting to maximize profits.

Substitution among inputs is common — for example, coal, oil, gas, or nuclear material can all be used to produce electric power, and both plastics and wood can be used for containers. Figure 5.05, for example, illustrates a substitution between pig iron and scrap; the one used largely depends on its relative price and available supply. When substitution is made between two inputs, one located in a remote region and the other near major markets, the significance of location is most important. Thus steel, paper, and other industries exhibit a dual spatial orientation, locating either at resources or at markets.

Substitution between processes is closely tied to substitution between inputs — for example, the kind of wood used tends to dictate which pulping process can be used to make paper — but even while using the same inputs and making the same outputs, some variety may be possible; for example, steel is made in various kinds of furnaces:

electric, Bessemer, open hearth, basic oxygen, and so forth.

Substitution among outputs involves either finding the optimum combination of products or varying the details in a single product. Product substitution is especially important in adapting behavior in the existing location to meet changes in consumer demand. It is a limited method, however, because industrial machinery can do only specific tasks.

Capital and labor may also be substituted for one another to some extent; an investment in machinery, for instance, reduces labor requirements and labor costs, and where labor is scarce or expensive, such capital investment is indicated. Where labor is cheap, however, there is less pressure for automation. If machinery cannot be substituted for labor, an industry is limited to locations where labor is sufficiently cheap or uniquely skilled.

Substitutions between revenues and costs are common because of spatial variations in prices and in the importance of transport costs. Areas where higher prices can be obtained for goods may also be areas where higher transport costs are incurred. Thus profits are often equal in areas that have widely varying price levels. Substitutions between transport and other outlays are also of great interest geographically. By locating in remote areas, aluminum producers, for instance, may be willing to incur higher transport charges on materials and products in order to take advantage of the savings in electrical power that are usually available only far from major markets. Petroleum refineries can choose between transport charges for crude petroleum and those for the finished products. In general, when savings are made in processing costs, whether power, labor, or taxes, increased transport costs must be accepted.

One other fairly common substitution is between economies of scale and transport outlays. A large-scale producer can substitute his cost savings for higher transport costs and greater **market penetration** (greater distance at which he can profitably sell), but smaller, higher cost producers may also successfully compete by accepting a smaller market, especially if their plant is physically separate from any others.

THEORY OF INDUSTRIAL LOCATION

Industrial location theory, because of the greater number of variables, lacks the simple geometric elegance of central place theory — but, for the same reason, it is more challenging. The theory has developed from two directions: first, from concern with the optimal location of a single plant and, second, from the study of the equilibrium among a set of related firms.

Location of the Single Plant

As with any choice of location, the optimal site for a firm is one that is central, that minimizes the costs of spatial relations, and, if selling prices vary for the product, that maximizes profits (the difference between costs and revenues). A classical theory of firm location was formulated by A. Weber in 1909. Optimum location was seen primarily as the point where the transport costs of bringing the necessary raw materials and of supplying goods to the necessary markets were at a minimum. Because of transport costs, orientation to resources or markets was considered the normal case. However, if variations in other costs, particularly labor, were sufficiently great, a location determined solely by transport costs might not be the optimal one.

In its simplest form, the transport-cost approach compares the weight of a unit of

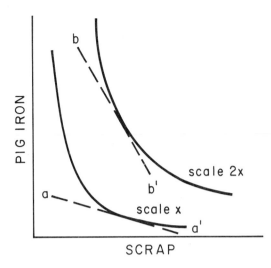

At scale x, cheaper scrap is substituted for pig iron

At scale 2x, limited scrap supply alters price ratio bb' in favor of pig iron

Figure 5.05 An example of input substitution: steel production. In this example, the solid lines indicate the combinations of pig iron and scrap that will produce a constant amount of steel. The slope of the dashed lines indicates the ratio of pig iron price to scrap price. Line *aa'*, for instance, shows that scrap is cheap if not too much is needed and the scale of steel production is limited, while *bb'* shows that if more is needed, pig iron is cheaper.

output with the weight of the raw materials necessary to produce that output. Transport costs are a simple linear function of weight and distance. Take the simple case in which there is just one product, one market, and one raw material: if the product is heavier and thus incurs higher costs, location will be at the market; if the raw material is heavier and incurs higher assembly costs, location will be at the material source. With multiple sources and markets, if the weight of one product or resource exceeds the sum of the weights of all the others, (usually a case where one is extremely heavy or has much bulk gain or loss in processing), location must be at the site of that dominant resource or market.

In figure 5.06, the weight and hence transport cost of raw material 1 exceeds that of the other raw material and of the product. If different transport rates are considered for different raw materials and finished

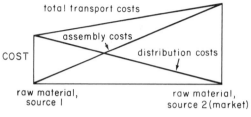

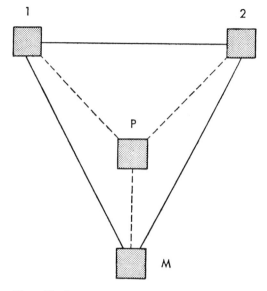

Figure 5.06 Simple raw material-transport orientation. The line labeled "assembly costs" shows the cost of obtaining raw material from source 1; the line "distribution costs" shows the combined cost of obtaining material 2 away from its source and of delivering the product to the market. Total transport costs (assembly plus distribution costs) are lowest at source 1 because the transport cost of raw material from source 1 exceeds the combined costs of transporting the raw material from source 2 and the finished product to the market.

M — Market

1 — Localized gross raw material

2 — Localized gross raw material

P — Production center

— — — Transportation route followed

Figure 5.07 The location triangle. In the simple case of a triangular arrangement of two material sources and one market (1, 2, and M), the ideal location for production (P), minimizing total costs, will be within the triangle bounded by the sources and markets and closest to the location that involves the highest transport cost (here M, since shipping the finished product is costliest). (Reprinted by permission of the Houghton Mifflin Company from R.J. Sampson and M.T. Farris, *Domestic Transportation*, 1966.)

products, it is necessary to compare the per-mile transport inputs — that is, weight times transport rate per mile — in order to compare costs.

Most often, no one cost alone determines location. Since, in this formulation, transport costs are strictly proportional to distance, the optimal site must be somewhere within the space bounded by the sources and markets. For two sources and one market or one source and two markets (or the "**location triangle**"), the optimal location shifts from a vertex of the triangle but remains closest to the point from which transport is most expensive (see figure 5.07). Thus total transport costs to and from the sources and market are minimized.

Since this simple model assumes that the transport surface is the same at all points — that is, that there is no existing transport network — finding the ideal location is equivalent to finding the bivariate median or "point of minimum aggregate travel" — the point where ton-miles for all the products and materials is the least.

The theory so far, then, is that the optimal location of a plant is at the point where transport costs to and from its necessary resources and markets are at the minimum.

Isodapanes. Fairly complex locational problems can be handled graphically by the **isodapane** method, as suggested by Weber and developed by others. The goal is the same — to seek the ideal location for produc-

tion, given a set of necessary sources and markets. In this method, one draws isolines (or isotims), where the cost of transportation for a raw material or a finished product is constant at every point on a line surrounding each source and market (see figure 5.08). At any point on the map we can then calculate total transportation costs for both materials and products. Lines showing constant total costs, called isodapanes, can then be drawn, and the optimum, where costs are lowest, can be found (figure 5.08).

The isodapane technique makes it possible to include variations in processing costs, whether occurring at single points or varying systematically over the surface (figure

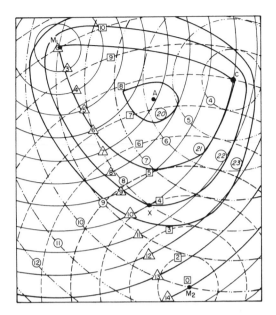

Figure 5.08 Lines of constant transport cost (isolines or isotims) are shown for assembly of material 1 away from its site (M_1); for material 2 away from its site (M_2); and for distribution of the product to the market (C). The italic numerals show the total of the three transport costs. Point A is the optimum location, where total cost is less than 20. (Reprinted from *Regional Development and Planning* by John Friedmann and William Alonso, eds., by permission of the M.I.T. Press, Cambridge, Mass. Copyright© 1964 by The Massachusetts Institute of Technology.)

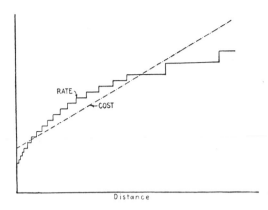

Figure 5.09 Realistic transport rates. A carrier's actual costs include a high terminal handling cost and perhaps a linearly increasing cost of hauling goods over greater distances. In setting rates, carriers average the two costs together, so that while rates increase over distance, they rise at a decreasing slope. Note, however, that short-distance and long-distance shipments are charged rates less than actual costs and are in effect subsidized by middle-distance shipments. (Reprinted by permission of the McGraw-Hill Book Company, Inc., from Edgar M. Hoover, *Location of Economic Activity*, 1948.)

5.08). Indeed, this is the use for which Weber originally intended it. Thus, lower labor cost may more than offset an increase in transport costs associated with shifting a firm from the optimal transport position. Although variations in processing costs are traditionally seen as deviations from transport optima, it is more realistic to seek from the beginning the point where total costs are minimum, since in fact transport costs are not always controlling ones.

Even with this elaboration, Weberian theory is still incomplete and in a sense unnecessarily complicated. It does not consider the serious questions of scale — whether there should be more than one plant, for instance — or the possibility that alternate or multiple sources of raw materials might be used, and especially, it considers neither the presence of a transport net which limits realistic plant locations to points on a network, nor realistic transport-rate patterns, which strongly militate against in-

termediate plant locations in favor of end points or **nodes**. Since transport rates are lower and connections better at nodes (towns or intersections) of a transport network, the problem of the best location is reduced to deciding among a finite set of points, rather than anywhere in an extended area. Realistic rate structures are illustrated in figure 5.09. The economies in rates for travel of longer distances and the steep initial rates favor end points for industrial locations. For example, in the triangle case (figure 5.07), even if the finished product were only a little costlier to ship than the raw materials, the market location would be optimal; that is, it is advantageous to eliminate one of the hauls completely.

For the case where there is one market and one resource, E. Hoover illustrates the role of realistic rates and transshipment costs (costs incurred from shifting carrier or transport mode). Terminal handling charges (loading, unloading, and the like), reflected in high transport rates near origins, clearly favor locations at markets or sources; one long haul at a lower rate per mile is cheaper than two shorter hauls at higher rates per mile. The classic cases of industrial orientation toward either the market, often because there are higher rates on finished products,

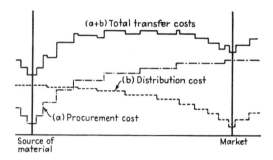

Figure 5.10   Realistic orientation to market or material end point. As in figure 5.06, assembly (procurement) costs are greater than distribution costs to the market, but, because of the structure of transport costs, a market location is better than any intermediate location beyond the immediate vicinity of the material. (Reprinted by permission of the McGraw-Hill Book Company, Inc., from Edgar M. Hoover, *Location of Economic Activity*, 1948.)

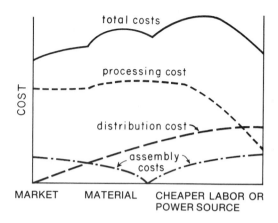

Figure 5.11   Processing or market orientation. In this example, a cheaper labor or power source, despite fairly high assembly and distribution costs, enjoys almost as low total costs as a location close to market (distribution-cost steps smoothed for simplicity).

or toward needed resources, often because great bulk or weight is lost if the raw materials are processed at the source, are illustrated in figure 5.10. Similar diagrams can be used to study the possible orientation of plant location toward cheaper labor (figure 5.11). Processing costs usually do not vary gradually in space, however; rather, they tend to change more sporadically.

Transshipment costs help explain the presence of industry in many port and river cities. A transshipment or **break-of-bulk** point may be an optimal site because often either the distribution costs of a firm include shipments to several markets, or because materials are assembled from several sources. Thus, we may view figures 5.10 and 5.11 as generalizations, where *material location* stands for a point central to all the necessary suppliers and *market location* for a point central to all markets. Either or both may be at transshipment points rather than at actual resource or market locations. The greater the number of suppliers and markets, the less dominant any one supplier or market becomes and the more likely it is that the optimal point will be a centrally located node, whether or not the node is itself a source or market of consequence. Between a single source and a single market, a transshipment point is less likely to be the best location, unless a processor's in-transit

privilege* is available or a shift from ocean to land transport is required.

The isodapane technique can be used to show locations on transport networks and realistic rate structures. As is evident from figure 5.12, it is primarily the nodal points (markets, sources, junctions) that need to be evaluated. The isodapane technique can also show fairly easily the cost of multiple sources of the same material so that each source can be evaluated at every point of the surface at which it is cheapest. Such problems can soon become graphically messy and arithmetically tedious, but a computer may evaluate costs for a finite system of places fairly readily.

The modified Weberian theory as developed may now be summarized: The optimal location for an industry is the point where transport and processing costs are at a minimum, satisfying the original goals of maximizing place utility and interaction at least cost and travel. This point is most likely to be an end point if there are very few markets and sources, and a central transportation node if there are many sources and markets.

---

*A through-transport rate from source to market is quoted, even though the materials are stopped and processed somewhere between.

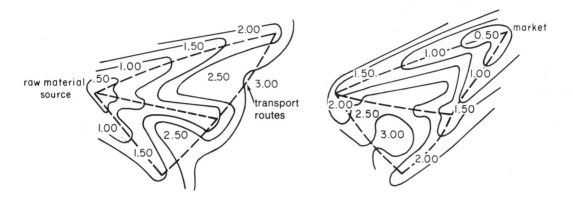

A. Cost of Raw Material Shipment

B. Cost of Product Distribution

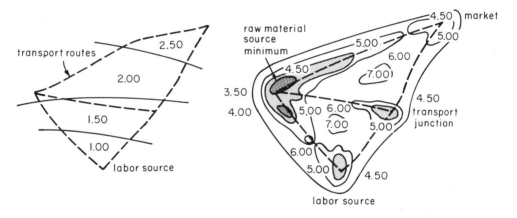

C. Variations in Labor Costs

D. Total Cost Surface

Figure 5.12 Cost surfaces and optimum location as modified by presence of transport routes. Isolines of cost are shown separately for raw material shipments, product distribution, and labor. Note that transport and total costs are relatively lower at nodes (market, material source, labor source, transport junction) and along transport routes. In *D*, the lowest total cost areas are shaded. Note that the lowest cost location is a point, the raw material source.

Spatial Behavior of the Firm: Economies of Scale

The Weberian approach determines the optimal location of industries as that which minimizes transport and processing costs. The effects of scale on these costs are ignored. Two examples of scale relations were given in figure 5.03, one the relations of a plant whose customer markets were small and diffuse (everywhere) and the other those of a plant whose customer markets were large and sporadic. In the first case, the scale of the plant may increase continuously

as the market expands to a greater distance and more customers become available. However, transport costs of serving more distant customers increase as a result and gradually outweigh the savings from lower unit processing costs, and the optimal scale and market size are thus found. If the customers pay an F.O.B. price (price at plant plus transport), then consumer demand falls with distance from the plant. In a setting where the number of potential customers falls off rapidly with distance, F.O.B. prices will yield maximum profits because the fewer distant customers can be ignored. If

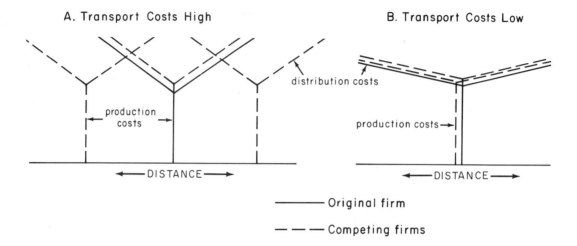

Figure 5.13   Entry and spacing of competitive plants. When distribution costs are high, new competitors will try to find a poorly served market and obtain a spatial monopoly (more than one firm may share it). Firms disperse because the scattered customers will not travel far or the firm cannot afford to deliver far. When distribution costs are very low, however, firms tend to cluster to take advantage of agglomeration economies or local low costs. Many firms may share even the national market from one best location.

the number of potential customers increases with distance, however, then it will usually pay the firm to quote a uniform delivered price to all its customers. Even though nearby customers will be penalized, in this way the firm can attract the largest number of customers and it can realize greater economies of scale. The plant in these examples acts like a central place: it expands to encompass as large a market as distribution costs will permit.

Cases of More than One Plant

Restricting the manufacture of a product to one firm or plant is unjustified; by admitting more than one plant into our landscape we may greatly reduce transport costs and thus raise profitability, despite possible scale benefits when there is only one large producer. As soon as we allow more than one plant, however, we are forced to estimate their number, their size, and their relative competitive position in space.

In the earlier example of the isodapane approach to problems of several markets and sources, a possible alternative would have been to establish more than one plant, whether branches of a firm or competitive plants. An infinite combination of numbers,

locations, and sizes of plants is of course theoretically possible. But a study of scale relations will yield a smaller range of profitable plant sizes. Thus, the approximately ideal number of producing units can be found for a given region. The problem can be reduced further by evaluating only a manageable set of locations of lowest cost and testing the appropriate scales and numbers of plants. For example, if the lowest cost locations were all markets and the optimal scale of production were fairly low, a plant could be established at each market proportional to the size of the market. Total costs could then be compared with those found with the one-plant solution. Still it is apparent that the problem of locating many plants in space is extremely difficult. Even with the largest computers, only very simple examples have been solved.

Consider the case of customers arranged along a line. If there is only one firm, the optimal location for distribution will be at the median customer. If there are two firms, H. Hotelling's equilibrium solution may apply: In his famous example of the location of two ice cream vendors along a stretch of beach, both will be located at the center; each may dominate the customers on its own side or the two may share the whole market. The truly optimal solution, if the two vendors are not competing (that is, if they work for the same firm), is at the two points one-quarter of the total distance from the two ends, where distance traveled by customers would be least. However, if the two vendors are competing, this solution will not last long — the firms are likely to move toward each other in an attempt to acquire a larger share of the market. The risk here, of course, is that the distant customer may be lost altogether, and more competition will develop on the edges. Also, one competitor may be content with a smaller, protected share of the market; in that case, the larger competitor should locate so as to minimize the distance traveled for the remaining customers.

For industries where the costs of transporting the final product are much greater than the costs of transporting raw materials, or where either customers or suppliers are spatially diffuse, plant location tends to follow the central place spatial-monopoly principle because customers will not travel far for products, and plants cannot afford to ship products very far (figure 5.13A). Within a firm, the number and size of the plants are determined by the balance between the economies achieved by having more customers and the costs of farther transport. Also, the spatial penetration (the market or supply area) of one plant is checked by the ability of the plant's competitors to collect materials, process them, and distribute products to closer markets at a lower delivered price. This pattern is most obvious on a local or regional scale — dairies, newspapers, and bakeries, for example.

On a national scale, the territorial size of the economy is so great that there are many markets and material sources for virtually every industry. For many industries, transport costs become significant only on a national scale. In industries such as machine tools or brewing, however, regional markets are large enough and transport costs great enough from any one location to bring some dispersal of plants and at least a limited degree of spatial monopoly.

Figure 5.14 illustrates a typical pattern of dispersed central place location. Each center of production may have plants from several firms, which together dominate the market

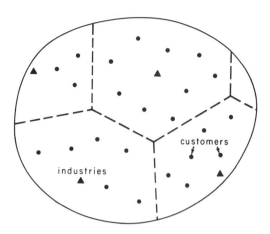

Figure 5.14   The spatially monopolistic firm: market areas. Where customers are small and diffuse, a central place pattern for industries tends to develop. Although each location has a monopoly over each area, there may be more than one plant in each location (see text).

area. This is an oligopolistic structure and often occurs when customers demand a variety of brands (television and cars, for instance).

As transport costs become relatively lower, location at resource concentrations (when raw-material transport is costlier) or at large markets (where distance provides a degree of spatial monopoly) becomes less advantageous and firms may seek the points of minimum costs over a wide territory. This frequently results in clusters of similar plants sharing large regional or national markets (figures 5.13B and 5.15). Moderate transport costs do not inhibit the increasing scale of production until great distances are reached.

Other constraints, however, such as internal processing diseconomies or, especially, division of the market by customer preference for various brands, may limit feasible scales of production much earlier. Hence, several firms may locate within a territory that one could dominate with respect to transport costs.

If the firms in a particular industry do not gain from agglomeration (see page 109), they will disperse so that each has a monopoly in a small area and shares a wider area where markets overlap (figure 5.15A). If agglomeration yields extra savings, then the clustering shown in figure 5.15B occurs, and spatial monopolies are abandoned.

A. Partially Shared Markets

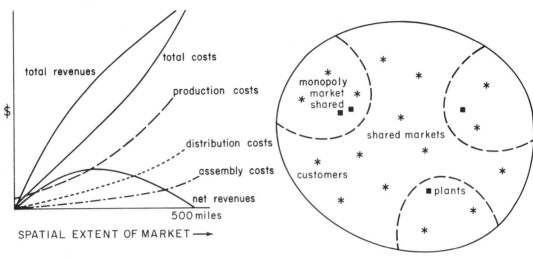

B. Totally Shared Markets: Clustered Production

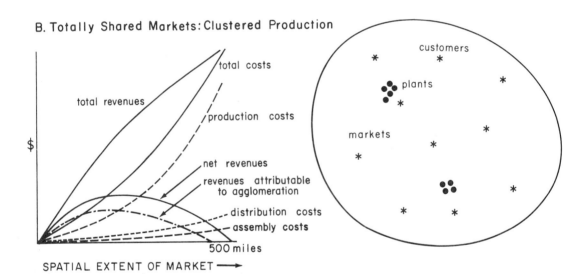

Figure 5.15   *A.* When transport costs are moderate and agglomeration benefits limited, plants may be either dispersed or clustered, but the area monopolized by a plant (or plants) is very limited. Most of the market customers must be shared.   *B.* When production costs are relatively important, transport costs relatively low, and agglomeration benefits great, plants tend to be highly clustered and share the entire market. The cluster will normally be associated with a major market.

Weber illustrated this by means of his critical isodapanes. Assume production occurs at a set of low-cost sites. If the savings incurred by carrying out all production at one location — that is, by agglomerating — exceed the additional transport costs, then all plants should be located at the point of minimum transport costs within the region. In figure 5.16, the circles represent the distance at which transport costs equal the savings gained by agglomeration. If these circles intersect, then the savings of agglomeration will exceed the additional transport costs.

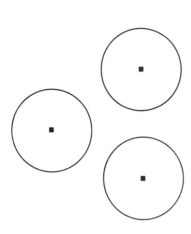

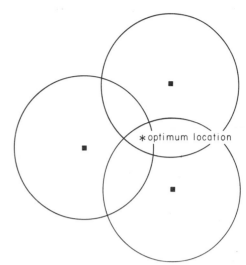

A. Relatively High Transport Cost
and/or Low Agglomeration Savings

B. Relatively Low Transport Cost and/or
High Agglomeration Savings

Figure 5.16 Agglomeration determined by critical isodapanes. The circles are isodapanes showing transport-cost equivalents of savings obtained from agglomeration. They are critical because if they intersect, the savings to each firm obtained by agglomerating will exceed the additional transport costs incurred from serving the more distant customers. In situation *B*, the firms should relocate to the optimum location, from which they can share the entire market more efficiently and profitably. In situation *A*, they should remain apart and serve local markets.

Frequently, the ideal point of location is not obvious. Many places within a region may have almost equal expected profitability, so that the ultimate locational decision within the set of places must be considered random from an economic-geographic point of view.

Summary: Location of Related Sets of Firms. The location of the firm represents an individual **spatial adjustment** to the existing pattern of the industry, but we may also analyze the spatial pattern of the industrial system as a whole. Plants in a single industry exist in a dynamic equilibrium with each other and with important sources and markets. If plants have identical inputs and outputs and significant transport costs, a spatial equilibrium may be determined in which plants and their areas of spatial monopoly are optimally located, scale is optimal, and total profits are maximized.

But solutions are far more complex if the plants do not have identical outputs and inputs or if markets overlap because of brand differentiation, low transport costs, and other factors. Operational models to analyze

these interrelations do not yet exist, but we can study changes in industrial locational patterns when the nature and location of demand, productivity, technology, or substitution possibilities change, in order to discover how variations in different factors affect location.

Spatial Adjustment of the Firm

Every firm has a significant investment in its existing plants, but changes in demand, in technology, and in transport routes and rates may render existing locations nonoptimal or even unprofitable if the plants fail to adapt. In fact, major behavioral changes at existing plants are far more common than establishment of new operations. If adaptation is limited or impossible, however, the factory may shut down. The older and lower the plant investment and the less restrictive the material and labor requirements, the greater will be the willingness of an industry to move. Thus, many New England textile plants with old structures and equipment have in recent decades found it easier to shift to southern locations than to adapt their old plants.

More often, however, substitutions among products, materials, sources, and markets, and between labor and capital, permit highly profitable if not optimal operations to continue. An investor who might wish to open a new plant in a better position than that of his competitors should carefully examine how far they might be able to adapt to the additional competition. As a result, a new plant is most likely to be located in areas where new demand has developed as a consequence of population shifts (for example, this is the main reason for the growth of industry in the Los Angeles area) or in areas of new supplies (such as a new petroleum field). New plants are nevertheless often located in areas of existing competition, especially if the product offered is somewhat new or different or if the demand for the product has increased beyond the capacity of competitors to meet it.

It is hard to adapt to changes in the location of demand. Price manipulation of nearby customers in favor of more distant ones (such as with uniform delivered prices) can work for a while, but either relocation or a change in the product mix may be necessary. Changes in the nature of demand may require costly retooling, a shift in the location of markets, or the manufacture of a higher quality product. Thus, textile makers who have successfully survived in New England have often shifted to new goods that require more highly skilled labor or more machinery.

Other kinds of changes also require major adjustment. Changes in the source and assembly cost of industrial raw materials are common, and are usually met by shifting to new sources, such as foreign materials of higher quality, or by using substitute raw materials, such as replacing pig iron with scrap (see figure 5.17). Increases in the relative cost of labor typically result in increased automation, if it is feasible. Changes in technology requiring a radical shift in the manufacturing process may force a plant to be abandoned, unless the location remains excellent for the new process. Reductions in transport rates, with an attendant rise in the optimal scale of the plant, have often weakened the position of many smaller producers; many survive, however, by shifting to custom production and by providing special services, such as quick delivery.

Interregional Input-Output. A valuable tool for estimating the regional impact of expected changes in production or demand among industries is the input-output or interindustry flows table introduced above (see p. 96). If a similar table were available showing the purchases each industry in a major region makes from the industries in every other region, it would be possible to estimate the consequence of changes in regional shares of demand or production. No such breakdown exists, but some single-region input-output tables include a slight regional breakdown of exports and imports by different industries, and some interregional analysis is thus possible.

Processing Location: Theory and Reality

Even if our theory encompassed all the factors that make a location optimal, we could never expect real locations to follow the patterns of the theoretically best ones. For one thing, as we have stressed before, locational decisions are often made by people who possess inadequate or misleading information and who thus make mistakes; not all decision making is rational; and entrepreneurs may be willing to accept suboptimal locations so long as operations are profitable. Moreover, rapid technological changes may render unsatisfactory once-optimal industrial locations. A plant is always faced with the problem of long-term locational weakness, hence if its owners are to realize their investment, the plant must be able to adapt to changing conditions.

Practical Plant Location. In practice, men choosing an industrial location take into account most of the concerns noted above and other factors as well, using a time-honored accounting, comparative-cost approach. Here, possible sites are narrowed to a finite number by the general considerations of competition for markets, transport position, and linkages to other industries. For each possible location, the expected total costs and revenues (considering the adjustment behavior of competitors to some degree), variations in output and input mix, and so on are compared in detail. While less mathematically sophisticated than some industrial theory, these practical methods based on accounting computations are behaviorally sophisticated in that reactions of competitors are estimated. Also, practical industrial location can and does take into account more personal and psychological constraints than are appropriate to a general location theory (such as the preference of owners for a location because of personal ties).

Centrally Planned Economies

Industrial location under centrally planned economies is subject to the same factors of costs, profitability, productivity, and opportunity costs. In practice, too, methods for choosing locations are probably nearly identical to those used by private individual firms. Yet, theoretically at least, a planned society might be expected to show some differences in the choice of an industrial location. For instance, if the state is the general owner of all industries, it might be willing to accept a longer period of loss before a new unit becomes established. A tendency for more rapid and extensive development in peripheral areas for egalitarian reasons — so that money is more evenly invested across the territory — should also result. Soviet experience supports these expectations at least partially. Also, an approach that maximizes benefits to society as a whole, rather than benefitting a single firm, could result in more efficient locational patterns, especially if investment capital is limited. Lack of competition within an industry on the one hand risks monopoly pricing, but on the other avoids unnecessary duplication. If it were not for a policy of regional self-sufficiency, common in many centrally planned economies, absence of competition would suggest that plants would tend to be fewer and larger.

The impact of large-scale industrial-planning errors may prove more damaging than the many small failures in a capitalist economy. For example, the "Great Leap Forward," China's 1959 industrialization

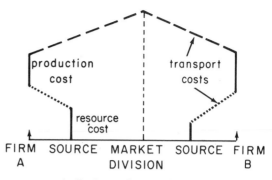

I. Before Depletion

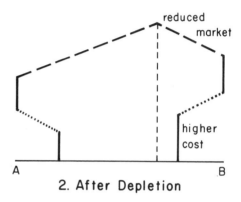

2. After Depletion

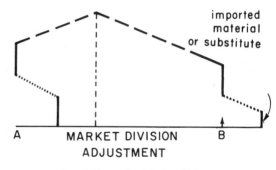

3. After Adjustment

Figure 5.17 Adaptation of individual firms to change: depletion of natural resources as an example. Before depletion, firms *A* and *B* use nearby resources at equivalent costs and they divide the market almost equally at the point where delivered costs are equal. When *B*'s source becomes depleted, however, its costs rise and its share of the market is reduced. To survive, firm *B* finds a cheaper imported resource or a substitute. This lowers its costs so much that it can expand its share of the market at the expense of *A*.

program, attempted to apply the technology and organization used for handicraft production to the manufacture of major industrial goods like steel. As a result, disastrous problems of lack of uniformity, waste of raw materials, transport congestion, and low productivity limited the plan's achievements. Since then China, with a large labor force, has found it preferable to encourage both a modern, standardized heavy industry and a more traditional handicraft sector.

Summary

Two very general theoretical statements about industrial location may be offered:

— *Manufacturing is so responsive to the benefits of increased scale of production that even the smallest industrial plant will tend to create small urban settlements around it.*

— *Manufacturing will be more concentrated in an economy than will population — that is, it will seek the largest, densest markets — because of scale benefits, because of the gradient in density of settlement, and because industry had spread historically from an early point of origin. Further, manufacturers will tend to be concentrated in larger, more populous places; except for cases where resources are available only in sparsely settled areas, most industries find that in isolated areas they cannot achieve sufficient scale economies without incurring excessive distribution costs. A much larger producer in denser urban areas may be able, because of very low unit-production cost, to serve the distant peripheral customer more cheaply than could a small plant in that area.*

In contrast to central place theory, which argues that a regular pattern of dispersed urban settlements is the most efficient and profitable way to provide almost all service, exchange, and collection activities, industrial location theory does not give us the satisfaction of a consistent spatial pattern. If the raw materials for industry were dispersed evenly and processing costs were invariate, industrial location theory could be reduced to central place theory. But precisely because space does vary in quality, because needed raw materials do exist only sporadically and are often costly to transport, and because labor and other processing costs do vary, industrial location patterns are inconsistent.

One could argue that industrial production would be carried out most efficiently within a central place structure, unless savings on processing costs or on transport costs for raw materials outweigh the savings in distribution costs obtained from locating at markets. Locating near resources in the situation where assembly costs are high is indeed analogous to the central place type of location at markets, except that in industrial location a spatial monopoly over a supply area — instead of over a market — is the most efficient solution, and the resulting spatial pattern is very different — more sporadic or randomly clustered than is a central place pattern — reflecting the more random location of resources. This resource-oriented structure is most efficient only when other costs, such as processing costs or transport costs on finished products, are less than the savings on transport obtained from location at the resource. These two kinds of industrial patterns represent the polar forms of plant location, in which transport costs for either resources or finished products are dominant, yielding a sporadic pattern of towns in the case of resources and a regular pattern in the case of markets.

It is easiest to view the other major industrial spatial location patterns by referring to these possible conditions:

— *Both assembly and distribution costs may be dominant, rather than one or the other.*
— *Transport costs may be balanced or outweighed by other costs, such as labor or power.*
— *Labor of sufficient quality, skill, and price may be sporadically located, like resources, and rather immobile.*
— *A profitable enterprise may have few, a moderate number of, or many suppliers and markets.*
— *The industry may need to be*

located near more powerful firms, for which a specific location is more important.

Perhaps four different spatial patterns result when industries seek an optimal location. Similar or identical patterns may occur for otherwise rather unlike industries. The first two polar types, as discussed above, are the regular lattice pattern of central place theory — call it type *A* (refer to figure 5.14) — and the cluster pattern of plants with small monopolistic resource supply areas — type *B* (figure 5.18).

If production requires, as in condition (3) above, a highly skilled and talented labor force, the industry will seek to locate in large places at the upper levels of the central place hierarchy, which attract such skilled labor. This condition develops a spatial pattern like type *A*, but it results from labor immobility rather than from high product-transport costs.

Cheap labor, power, and taxes are sporadically located, as are resources. If one of these factors is overwhelmingly important, a type *B* spatial pattern will result. Here, minimization of processing costs, rather than transport costs, is the key to optimal location.

If both assembly and production costs are high, the industry may attempt to attain a spatial monopoly for markets and supplies — as did the steel industry in Birmingham, Alabama, for example — or it may seek control over just markets or just supplies. In this case, a point of transshipment may be desirable. This third type of pattern (type *C*) is a kind of combination or compromise between types *A* and *B* (see figure 5.15A).

Finally, where processing and transport costs are somewhat balanced, where skill requirements are moderate, and, especially, where there are many suppliers and many markets — that is, where none of the polar conditions exists — then there is greater freedom in determining location, and, spatially, industries locate at random within any region rich in suppliers and markets (type *D*; see figure 5.15B).

EXAMPLES OF MANUFACTURING SYSTEMS

We intend to classify and analyze here the

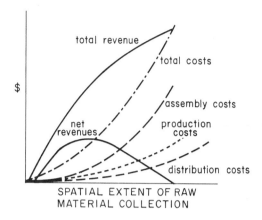

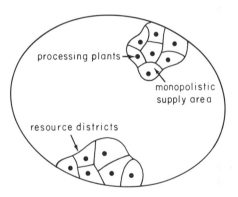

Figure 5.18 When assembly costs are very high, the zones from which plants can collect materials are limited, and each plant attempts to monopolize a local supply area. On a national scale, the plants appear to be clustered because of the concentration of the resource in certain regions.

various manufacturing systems with respect to the general principles of location and not to examine in much detail the precise nature of any one industry. Looking generally at manufacturing location, we can recognize these spatial orientations:

Transport Orientation

— *Location determined by a spatially restricted and/or relatively immobile material resource with high transport costs (resource orientation: pattern B).*

— *Location determined by high distribution costs, resulting in the market-oriented pattern of central places (market orientation: pattern A).*

— *Location determined by both high assembly and high distribution costs and related to a spatial complex of specific resources and markets (pattern C).*

Processing Cost and Agglomeration Orientation

— *Location determined by a spatially restricted and relatively immobile human resource with moderate to high labor costs (processing cost orientation: pattern B).*

— *Location determined by relatively restricted supplying or receiving industries (pattern A or B).*

— *Location determined by the agglomerative advantages of the largest markets (agglomeration orientation: pattern A).*

Complex Orientation

— *Location determined by spatially limited, but diffuse sources and markets, with moderate transport and labor costs (interindustry orientation: pattern D).*

— *Relative freedom of location (pattern D).*

Transport-Oriented Systems

Resource Orientation. Location near a spatially restricted material resource may be alternately thought of as transport orientation, since it is the high cost of transport that requires production at the source. This high transport cost is in turn a function of the low value per unit or high proportion of waste per unit of the raw material. Possible processing sites are dictated by the locations of such resources, but whether it is feasible to use such a resource depends on the spatial relationship among all these resource locations. For processing industries the variable quality of the environment has the greatest effect.

Mining. Mining operations are a special class of resource orientation, where the only process may be extraction of ores. The resource is typically a very impure ore, interspersed with valueless material. Extraction of the ore alone may be possible, but more often some simple processing is necessary to separate the more from the less valuable material.

Processing at the mine is done typically to reduce bulk to a point where it is possible to transfer the ore. Whether this point can be reached depends on processing costs (which are partly a function of the quality of the resource), transfer rate, distance to markets and to competing sources, and overall demand and price. Those mines succeed that can operate within these restraints. In figure 1.10 (page 14), for example, ores C and A can be sold at the market price; C is of high quality but is close to the market. Ore B, however, cannot compete because it is of such low quality that processing costs are excessive, even though its mine is moderately close. An increase in demand (price) or depletion of the sources of A and C might well change the situation, of course.

Smelting. The poorer the ore, the lower the metal content and the greater the likelihood that processing will be necessary at the mine. When the proportion of metal content approaches half the ore, such as with iron ore and some bauxite, little treatment is necessary; but many ores have proportions of metal as low as one percent, and the shipping of such raw ore is not feasible. Smelting — heat processing using coal, petroleum, or gas — is indicated whenever transfer costs for the ore exceed the combined cost of smelting, fuel transport, and metal transport. Smelting is a case of extreme orientation to resources and is the kind of manufacturing most likely to be found in remote, sparsely populated, perhaps rather inhospitable regions, which, despite all this, possess the coveted ore.

Food and Wood Processing. The largest group of resource-oriented manufacturers are those who process biotic raw materials, especially agricultural and forest products. Many of the best forest sources are located far from major population centers, and much agricultural production, because of its

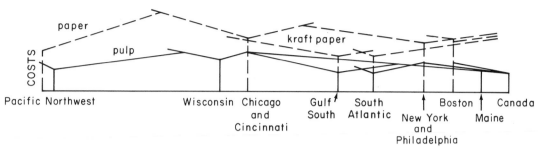

Major Pulp and Paper Locations and Zones

Figure 5.19 Spatial equilibrium of pulp and paper. This is a diagrammatic generalization of spatial competition. Only major features are depicted. Production costs (vertical lines) and transport costs (sloping lines) are shown for major locations of pulp, kraft (brown) paper, and other paper producers. Intersections of transport lines at peaks define the zones within which given producers are most competitive. Note that Chicago and New York, major paper producers, can receive pulp supplies from several sources at similar costs: Chicago from Wisconsin, Maine, and the Gulf South; New York from the South Atlantic, Maine, and Canada. Also, the Gulf South and South Atlantic produce both pulp and kraft paper.

space requirements, is also well away from more concentrated markets. Such raw materials are normally characterized by low **transferability:** they are bulky and perishable and are therefore costly to handle and ship. But after processing they often lose much bulk or weight and become much less perishable, thus increasing their transferability.

Canning and freezing plants, which frequently use riper, less transportable products, tend to be located as close as possible to their raw materials. Output per plant is rather low because each plant cannot assemble much material at the high cost of transport. Hence, processors of fruits, vegetables, sugar beets, and fish are likely to be found in remote and less-populated areas.

Another group of food processors — meat packers, creameries, flour and feed mills — locate largely in response to resources, but also must consider their ultimate markets. To reconcile these concerns, the agricultural resources themselves are located as close to markets as competition permits, and processing locations are midway between resources and markets. In the United states, for example, the most favored locations for these processors are the "gateway" cities, dividing the more rural from the more urban regions of the country — for example, the importance of meat packing in the set of cities in the United States from Fargo, North

Dakota, to Fort Worth, Texas, approximately along the western edge of the midwestern corn belt.

Wood processors, including sawmills, veneer-plywood makers, shingle mills, turpentine and rosin makers, and wood pulp manufacturers, are further cases where the bulk and weight lost in processing attract manufacturers to the specific resource locations (figure 5.19). Sawmills, for example, although not very responsive to scale benefits, are sensitive to transport costs; hence, they are small and widespread. However, depletion of local resources restricts the useful life of the sawmill, and an intermediate scale of processing with larger supply zones is becoming most profitable.

Aluminum. A special kind of orientation to a costly, relatively immobile resource occurs in the "power-intensive" industries which are optimally located in sites where the cost of electricity is lowest. Final aluminum, magnesium, and titanium refining requires vast amounts of electricity, which is the single largest or most variable element in costs. These refineries are commonly located in relatively remote areas with large hydroelectric resources, such as Quebec, Norway, the Pacific Northwest, and Ghana. The high value per unit weight of aluminum justifies the extremely long shipments of intermediate raw materials, alumina, and finished aluminum.

Market Orientation. Central place manufacturing can be considered extremely market-oriented because of the very high cost of final distribution. Transferability of the final product is poor, and processing often creates greater bulk or weight and increases perishability.

A typical example of a market-oriented industry is the beverage industry, particularly the bottling of soft drinks — water is obtainable everywhere, the syrup base has only a small bulk and is highly transportable, but the final product is very bulky. Other examples are the bottling of fluid milk; freshly baked soft goods, which have greater bulk and perishability than their ingredients; manufactured ice; and newspapers dealing with local affairs, for which demand is limited in time and space. Much of the construction industry, especially residential building, and production of many of the materials that go into construction, such as sand and gravel, brick, concrete, and concrete block, are similarly market-oriented.

Higher Levels of Market Orientation. For many industries, distribution costs are greater than assembly costs, but not so great as to limit delivery to a small area. However, in a large economy with vast distances between markets, such as the United States, the costs of distribution are sufficient to make possible somewhat protected regional markets. Many kinds of manufacturers have thus established branch plants in major regional centers. The successful broad industrialization of California illustrates indeed that most kinds of manufacturing can be successful if the regional market is large enough and far enough from the traditional centers of industry. Much of the automobile industry is highly concentrated, but there are assembly plants in the large cities of major regions. The same is true of much steel, cement, petroleum refining, food processing, furniture, and other industries, to be discussed below.

Orientation to a Spatial Complex of Resources and Markets. For some industries, both the raw materials and the finished products exercise some control over location, generally if the costs of transport tend to exceed possible differentials in processing costs. Use of several raw materials and many markets with significant transport costs may further complicate the location problem. In such cases, there is a complex of locational possibilities: an industry may locate in response to any one of the sources or markets or even choose locations between sources and markets. Rarely are the transport costs of any one raw material or finished product so great that it alone determines location. Location thus becomes essentially the point where total transfer costs are at the minimum.

Iron and Steel. The iron and steel industry is an especially **basic activity** because of its linkages to the fabricated metal, machinery, transport, military, hardware, and construction sectors of the economy. The industry is complex: it uses a mix of raw materials that allows for some substitution, and it has a variable processing technology, considerable product differentiation, and a wide variety of markets.

Material requirements for primary pig iron production in blast furnaces include coking coal, iron ore, and limestone. In the making of steel, scrap can be partially or largely substituted for pig iron, coking coal is not strictly needed, and a variety of power sources are usable. Modern techniques have greatly reduced fuel requirements. Thus, the location of steel production is freer than that of iron, although such freedom is limited by the advantages of integrated production with iron.

Historically the location of coal was the dominant factor for iron and steel manufacturing, since it was required in the largest volumes and not much scrap was available. The optimal location was near whichever coalfields were closest to steel markets. However, as requirements for coal have been reduced to one-third what they were in the 1830s, as demand has developed for more finished goods with higher transport costs, as scrap supplies have mounted, and as nearby iron-ore supplies have been depleted, a more complex locational orientation has evolved.

In the United States, when the chief ore supplies were in the Mesabi range in Minnesota, the locations that became profitable were lake ports fairly close to, but not on, coalfields — such as Cleveland, Erie, Chicago, Detroit, and the intermediate

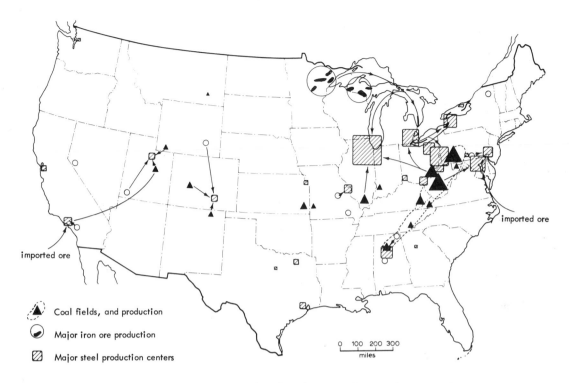

Figure 5.20 Relative location of iron ore, coal, and steel production in the United States, 1970. Major steel production exhibits a mixed orientation to raw materials and markets, with a marked concentration of both production and consumption of raw materials and steel in the Great Lakes-Pittsburgh region.

Youngstown — all major industrial markets (figure 5.20). More recently, the ever-increasing demand of concentrated metropolitan markets, their great supply of scrap, and the increasing dependence of the industry on imported ore have justified expansion of steel production into coastal markets like Philadelphia and Baltimore. Steel centers have arisen in new areas, too, when demand has grown sufficiently to permit production at a scale large enough to compete with older, distant centers.

Although integrated plants producing both pig iron and finished-steel products offer advantages such as fuel and transfer savings and single administration, separate production of finished steel is often profitable, particularly in regional markets such as Houston, Los Angeles, San Francisco, and Seattle, which lack readily available coal and are at a distance from large, integrated basic producers. These regional steel mills must purchase pig iron from other producers, but they can utilize much scrap. One of their main advantages is

much quicker delivery.

In summary, the pattern of iron and steel production reflects both historical inertia in its location near coal fields and the strong attraction of markets, which have dispersed the industry somewhat. Minimum costs can be found in many regional locations where distance from traditional industrial centers protects markets, and there are many ways in which processing techniques and products can be substituted for each other.

Petroleum Refining. Petroleum refineries and petroleum-based chemical products are located more simply than are iron and steel mills and they illustrate clearly the advantage of location at end points — the oil field, market, and certain intervening transit points. Processing of crude petroleum is efficient — there is little weight or volume loss — and the slightly higher cost of handling and shipping refined products, which are more varied and volatile, does not outweigh by too much the cost of handling and shipping the slightly greater bulk of crude petroleum. Hence, the advantages of locations near markets, while real, are not overwhelming, and with a few products of sufficiently large volume, field refineries can compete with those in markets. (The technical development of multiproduct pipelines and tankers was necessary, however, before an oil-field refinery location could become competitive.)

Electric Power. Generating electricity from steam involves high costs for both transporting fuel and transmitting electricity. Transmission costs have historically been higher than the costs for transporting fuel, thus large plants are usually located near major markets. But technological improvements in high-voltage long-distance transmission, as well as in fuel efficiency, are beginning to permit coal, gas, and petroleum power stations to be installed up to 300 miles from the final markets.

Processing Cost and Agglomeration Orientation

Orientation to Spatially Restricted and Relatively Immobile Human Resources. For industries in which the use of skilled labor constitutes a major part of the technology and adds most of the value to the products during their manufacture, spatial variations in the productivity, cost, skill, and scarcity of labor play a big role. Labor costs may also be important by default when transport of raw materials and products is relatively cheap. It is possible that this kind of orientation is not inherently necessary, but rather a matter of choice; some industries may choose locations with cheap labor rather than use a more automated technology that would enable them to pay higher wages.

Textile manufacturing, for example, has always been a labor-intensive industry, with a traditionally high ratio of women to men. The industry has long had some difficulty in competing for labor when other industries were close by, but found it possible to survive so long as workers could be hired who were willing to accept lower wages. Radical change in other industrial sectors thus forced radical change in the spatial pattern of textile manufacturing. In the United States, textiles were first made in New England, where capital, surplus labor, and many good water-power sites were

available. Machinery, shipbuilding, and other industries began to bid up the price for labor, and early welfare legislation was passed, restricting the hours women could work, for example. Unions developed, work stoppages were held, and many operations elected to shift their locations to clusters of small towns in the southern Piedmont, where the conditions of surplus labor were comparable to those in New England a century earlier. Other advantages of the South, especially in small towns, were lower taxes, less costly services, absence of unions, easier access to cotton supplies, and no competing industries. Certain segments of the textile industry resisted the shift — mostly those that required more highly skilled labor, were hesitant to move, or could continue to use immigrant and minority groups at lower wages. Such segments included some finishing, finer woolens, printing, carpetry, and some knitwear (see figure 5.21).

Furniture and luggage manufacturers are good examples of the conflict between markets, sources, and locations with lower labor or processing costs. The location of the early furniture industry was oriented toward the labor supply and the hardwoods of southern New England and the Michigan-Ohio region. As with the textile industry, competition for labor, superior southern hardwood sources, and similar factors led to a partial relocation of the industry, especially to North Carolina. The traditional northern centers, such as Grand Rapids, were forced to shift to higher quality furniture for which customers were willing to absorb the extra labor costs.

Certain mass-produced electronic goods made with a standardized technology, for example, some radios, electrical parts, and light bulbs, require considerable labor and have migrated gradually from the northeastern centers of innovation like New York to smaller cities with cheaper labor just outside the industrial core — in Iowa, Kentucky, Virginia, and Minnesota — and to depressed areas with surplus industrial labor, such as New England in the 1950s.

Secondary Location Determined by More Restricted Supplying or Receiving Industries. Industries with low transport costs and technical linkages to other industries that are strongly oriented toward

1 dot = Single plant hiring
        249 or fewer employees
1 square = Single plant hiring
           250 or more employees

Figure 5.21 Location of textile manufacturing. An example of dispersal to clusters of small towns. (Reprinted by permission of the McGraw-Hill Book Company, Inc., from Richard S. Thoman, *Geography of Economic Activity*, 1962.)

transport may locate near the related industries to obtain agglomeration benefits. Such a dependent location is common for two types of manufacturers: those using by-products and those that are small suppliers to larger industries. Many chemical concerns use by-products of iron and steel mills and petroleum refineries. Tin-can and other container companies are located where they can best supply the less flexible food-processing industry. Special-machinery manufacturing tends to be located in areas where the machinery is used; for instance, drilling equipment is made in Los Angeles and Houston. Aircraft components are produced in major airframe centers, and the very large auto-parts industry locates in a wide region around Detroit.

Location Determined by the Agglomerative Advantages of the Largest Markets. Many industries characterized by fairly high labor costs, high prices, and high value added during production are attracted to the largest metropolises and their satellite suburbs. Transport costs are not important in these cases, and markets may be somewhat diffuse even if located mainly in metropolitan areas. The higher labor costs are due to higher skill and education requirements, the significance of research, the importance of innovation and managerial skill, and, in some cases, the sheer volume of moderately paid labor. The kind of labor needed may prefer metropolitan regions, demanding a high level of urban **amenities** (cultural, educational, recreational). Thus, even if costs were much lower outside the city, the firm could not attract labor of sufficient quality.

Not only is the metropolis itself a sizable market containing a large, flexible labor pool, but it also has superior educational, recreational, and cultural facilities, and, for the firm, easier access to transport (including more frequent service), capital, advertising, communication, and other services.

A few industries with high labor requirements and moderate wages have not migrated but have remained in traditional locations, usually because a special skilled labor pool was immobile. In the United States, for example, cutlery, brassware, silverware, jewelry, fine stationery, and watches are all made in the areas of the earliest industry.

The apparel industry traditionally consists of small-scale enterprises with limited ranges of products and few employees (usually fewer than 50, in the United States). The location of this industry reflects extreme metropolitan concentration and inertia. In the United States over 40 percent of all clothes are made in New York City, notably within a small area of Manhattan; Moscow, Paris, and London are similarly dominant in their countries. The largest cities have the greatest pool of skilled workers who will accept only moderate wages — especially women and recent immigrants. In addition, the marketing and distribution advantages of a large metropolis are strong incentives for the apparel industry, which depends much on publicity — most easily disseminated from the largest city — and fashion — a product of the concentration of the wealthiest and most prominent segment of society in an economic capital.

The publishing and printing industries (except for local newspapers) similarly acquire special benefits by locating in a cultural capital and hence are also located in such places as New York City, London, Paris, and Moscow. The relative immobility of printers within the apprenticeship structure of their union also plays a role in the location of the printing industry, and transport privileges, such as low mailing rates for books, make centralization feasible. Thus, general book publishers and high-quality periodicals needing centralized or even cooperative distribution are concentrated in New York. Mass publishing of very high-volume material, such as Bibles, telephone books, mail-order catalogs, and mass-circulation magazines, are published in more central locations, such as Chicago. Current trends for much higher mailing rates for books and magazines will probably force the printing industry to decentralize.

Complex Orientation

Interindustry Orientation. The largest group of manufacturers in the more advanced countries makes machinery, transport and communications equipment, and other elaborated products. They use a variety of simpler manufactured inputs, especially formed steel, and ship to a fairly wide market composed of other industries (such as machine tools) or even to the entire national market (such as autos). Because these manufacturers are not tied to one particular source or market by transport costs, time requirements, or labor-cost advantages, they possess a limited freedom of choice: they can locate within a set of sources and markets that often have the same boundaries as the urban industrial core of the economy. In the long run, optimal location will be influenced by transport position, quality of labor pools, relationships to other industries and competitors, and benefits of agglomeration.

Motor Vehicles. The automobile is the single most valuable product and the largest user of steel, rubber, and glass in several advanced countries, especially the United States. As producers of a highly mobile and widely desired good, location at or near the center of the transport and industrial net would be optimal. In the United States, Chicago would probably be the best location if the industry did not already exist in Detroit; but Detroit and its environs were an optimal site when the industry developed 50 years ago and the greater market was near the Atlantic seaboard. Carriage manufacturers, boat-engine makers, a wood supply, and a skilled labor force were located in the Detroit area. Here, also, the market was divided between the wealthy East and the developing West. Finally, in Detroit were the early car-producing entrepreneurs who succeeded in defeating competitors in New York, Philadelphia, Chicago, and elsewhere. The decision of some Detroit builders to standardize and mass-produce vehicles was perhaps crucial to success. In any event, once the industry was well established, Detroit's advantages of agglomeration and experience overshadowed any transport or labor advantage of other cities. Detroit today remains very well located with respect to inputs, although not quite so well with regard to final markets. Population shifts and the increasing costs of final distribution have led to a partial dispersal of body-making and final-assembly operations to serve distinct regional markets.

Related industries are not far removed from Detroit. Parts suppliers in the United States are scattered throughout Michigan, Indiana, and Ohio. Glass production is concentrated in the nearby Toledo, Ohio, area, rubber tires in the Akron, Ohio, area. The rubber industry, which requires large coal inputs, is located near the eastern Ohio coal fields and is also reasonably close to Detroit.

Machinery. Machinery industries, both general and electrical, are very large and are basic to increasing the productivity of society. They consume much steel and other materials and add a high value during manufacture. A great variety of industries depend on their products, from primary producers such as smelters to the most consumer-oriented ones. Hence, it is difficult to speak of them as a group; their markets are diffuse and are spread throughout the industrial core. Although distribution costs on finished products are higher than on raw materials, the fact that there are many customers induces a plant to locate at their center. Electrical machinery is more dominant on the Atlantic seaboard; nonelectrical machinery, oriented to the automotive industries, in the central parts of the industrial belt; and agricultural and processing machinery at the western end. Almost all northeastern metropolises are strongly represented in machinery production, and the industry dominates many smaller and intermediate-sized cities as well.

Subdistrict specialties arose out of early inventions and spin-offs, and include the machine-tool industry centered around Cincinnati, the turbines and generators made near Milwaukee and Chicago, the textile machinery made in New England, paper machinery in Wisconsin and New York, mining equipment in Minneapolis, and printing machinery in New York.

Freedom of Location. True **locational freedom** is in fact nonexistent, although there are a few small specialty manufacturers in small, remote places who survive by the uniqueness of their brands and by employee loyalty. Large industries with powerful governmental influence, notably aircraft, ordnance, and missile and rocket development, may also be in peculiar locations, partly because of security requirements and partly because of the federal government's half-conscious desire to spread wealth to some of the less developed parts of the country or to aid politically powerful, but economically weak, peripheral areas.

The aircraft industry has always depended on rapid technological improvement, much at military instigation, for its growth. In its early days, locations were most common near spruce forests (whose lumber is noted for lightness and strength), such as in Michigan or the Pacific Northwest, and near large cities. Because of the good climate for experimentation and pleasure, the industry also grew rapidly in Los Angeles. Based on the preferences of early entrepreneurs and on World War I contracts, some dominant locations were set: Los Angeles, Seattle, Hartford, St. Louis. Although transport costs are trivial (hence the industry is called "footloose"), the need for large bodies of skilled labor enables established centers to remain dominant and metropolitan locations to be sites for future expansion. Only governmental pressure imposed in World War II created new centers at Wichita, Kansas; Marietta, Georgia; and Fort Worth, Texas.

Conclusion

The ideal location of manufacturing or processing activities results from the pursuit of goals of maximum utility of places and maximum interaction (sales, procurement) at least cost. Because the location of resources is sporadic, and because the importance of resources, transport costs, and processing costs differs from industry to industry, a variety of ideal locational types and patterns might be expected. If it were not for resources, manufacturing activities would tend to reinforce the central place structure, especially at higher levels. Thus it is clear that the sporadic location of needed resources distorts the patterns of transport, of settlement, and of central places themselves.

REFERENCES

Industrialization

Kerr, C. et. al., *Industrialization and Industrial Man*, Cambridge, Mass.: Harvard University Press, 1960.

Pred, A., "Industrialization, Initial Advantage and American Metropolitan Growth," *Geographical Review* 55 (1965): 158-189

Pred, A., "Manufacturing in the American Mercantile City, 1800-1840," *Annals of the Association of American Geographers* 56 (1966): 307-338.

Principles of Location: Manufacturing in General

Alampiyev, P.M., "New Aspects of the Location of Production in the Period of Full-Fledged Construction of Communism," *Soviet Geography: Review and Translation* 3 (1962): 49-59.

Alderfer, E.B. and H.E. Mich, *Economics of American Industry*, New York: McGraw-Hill, 1957.

Alexander, J., "Location of Manufacturing: Methods of Measurement," *Annals of the Association of American Geographers* 48 (1958): 20-26.

Bain, J.S., "Economies of Scale, Concentration, and the Condition of Entry in Twenty Manufacturing Industries," *American Economic Review* 44 (1954): 15-39.

Barloon, M.J., "The Interrelationship of the Changing Structure of American Transportation and Changes in Industrial Location," *Land Economics* 41 (1966): 169-182.

Dicken, Peter, "Some Aspects of the Decision Making Behavior of Business Organizations," *Economic Geography* 47 (1971): 426-437.

Dunn, E.S. "The Market Potential Concept and the Analysis of Location," *Papers and Proceedings of the Regional Science Association* 2 (1956): 183-194.

Fulton, M. and L.C. Hoch, "Transportation Factors Affecting Locational Decisions," *Economic Geography* 35 (1959): 51-59.

Goldberg, Michael K., "An Economic Model of Intrametropolitan Industrial Location," *Journal of Regional Science* 10 (1970): 75-80.

Harris, C.D., "The Market as a Factor in the Localization of Industry in the United States," *Annals of the Association of American Geographers* 44 (1954): 315-348.

Hayes, C.R. and N.W. Schul, "Why Do Manufacturers Locate in the Southern Piedmont?" *Land Economics* 44 (1968): 117-120.

Isard, W. and E.W. Schooler, "Industrial Complex Analysis, Agglomeration Economies, and Regional Development," *Journal of Regional Science* 1 (1959): 19-33.

Kadas, C., "The Impact of the Development of Transportation of the Optimal Size of Plants and on Optimal Regional Location," *Papers and Proceedings of the Regional Science Association* 12 (1963): 193-206.

Karaska, G. And D. Bramhall, eds., *Locational Analysis for Manufacturing*, Cambridge, Mass.: MIT Press, 1969.

Krumme, G., "Toward a Geographical Enterprise," *Economic Geography* 45 (1969): 30-40.

Krumme, G., "Note on Locational Adjustment Patterns in Industrial Geography," *Geografiska Annaler* 51B (1969): 15-19.

Lonsdale, Richard E. and Clyde Browning, "Rural-Urban Locational Preferences of Southern Manufacturers," *Annals of the Association of American Geographers* 61 (1971): 255-268.

McMillan, T.E., "Why Manufacturers Choose Plant Locations vs. Determinants of Plant Location," *Land Economics* 41 (1965): 239-246.

Maki, Wilbur R., "Spatial-Economic Decentralization and Mergers in a Metropolitan Region," *Papers of the Regional Science Association* 25 (1970): 119-132.

Manners, G., "Regional Protection: A Factor in Economic Geography," 38 (1962): 122-129.

Martin, V.E., "Size of Plant and Location of Industry in Greater London," *Tijdschrift voor Economische en Sociale Geografie* 60 (1969): 369-374.

Miller, E.W., *A Geography of Manufacturing*, Englewood Cliffs, N.J.: Prentice-Hall, 1962.

Pred, A., "The Intrametropolitan Location of American Manufacturing," *Annals of the Association of American Geographers* 54 (1964): 165-180.

Richter, C.E., "Impact of Industrial Linkages on Geographic Association," *Journal of Regional Science* 9 (1969): 19-28.

Schultz, G., "Facility Planning for a Public Service System: Solid Waste Collection," *Journal of Regional Science* 9 (1969): 291-308.

Smith, David M., *Industrial Location*, New York: John Wiley, 1971.

Soffer, E. and E. Korenich, " 'Right to Work' Laws as a Location Factor," *Journal of Regional Science* 3 (1961): 41-56.

Steed, G., "Changing Milieu of the Firm: A Study in Manufacturing Geography," *Annals of the Association of American Geographers* 58 (1968): 506-525.

Tiebout, C.M., "Location Theory, Empirical Evidence, and Economic Evolution," *Papers and Proceedings of the Regional Science Association* 3 (1957): 74-86.

Tornqvist, G., "Transport Costs as a Location Factor for Manufacturing Industries," *Lund Studies in Geography*, Series B, 23, 1962.

Williams, W., "Impact of State and Local Taxes on Industry Location," *Journal of Regional Science* 7 (1967): 49-59.

Winsborough, H.H., "Variations in Industrial Composition with City Size," *Papers and Proceedings of the Regional Science Association* 5 (1959): 121-132.

Wonnacott, R.J., "Manufacturing Costs and the Comparative Advantage of United States Regions," Upper Midwest Economic Study Paper 9, 1963.

Zelinsky, W., "A Method for Measuring Change in the Distribution of Manufacturing Activity: The United States, 1939-1947," *Economic Geography* 34 (1958): 95-126.

Theory of Industrial Location

Alonso, W., "Reformulation of Classical Location Theory and Its Relation to Rent Theory," *Papers and Proceedings of the Regional Science Association* 19 (1967): 23-44.

Cooper, L., "Solutions of Generalized Locational Equilibrium Models," *Journal of Regional Science* 7 (1967): 1-18.

Dean, W.H., *The Theory of the Geographic Location of Economic Activities*, Ann Arbor, Mich.: Edward Brothers, 1938.

Denike, Kenneth G. and John B. Parr, "Production in Space, Spatial Competition and Restricted Entry," *Journal of Regional Science* 10 (1970): 49-64.

Friedrich, C.J., *Alfred Weber's Theory of the Location of Industries*, Chicago: University of Chicago Press, 1929.

Greenhut, M.L., *Microeconomics and the Space Economy*, Chicago: Scott-Foresman, 1963.

Hoover, E.M., *Location Theory and the Shoe and Leather Industries*, Harvard Economic Studies, Vol. LVI, Cambridge, Mass.: Harvard University Press, 1937.

Hotelling, H., "Stability in Competition," *Economic Journal* 39 (1929): 41-57.

Isard, W., and T. Smith, "Location Games," *Papers and Proceedings of the Regional Science Association* 19 (1967): 45-82.

Kuhn, H.W., and R.L. Kuenne, "An Efficient Algorithm for the Numerical Solution of the Generalized Weber Problem," *Journal of Regional Science* 4 (1962): 21-34.

Mills, Edwin S., "The Efficiency of Spatial Competition," *Papers of the Regional Science Association* 25 (1970): 71-82.

Orr, E.W., "A Synthesis of Theories of Location, of Transport Rates, and of Spatial Price Equilibrium," *Papers and Proceedings of the Regional Science Association* 3 (1957): 61-73.

Revelle, Charles S. and Ralph W. Swain, "Central Facilities Location," *Geographical Analysis* 2 (1970); 30-42.

Sakashita, N., "Production and Demand Function and Location Theory of the Firm," *Papers and Proceedings of the Regional Science Association* 20 (1968): 109-122.

Scott, Allen J., "Location-Allocation Systems: A Review," *Geographical Analysis* 2 (1970): 95-119.

Steed, Guy P.F., "Plant Adaptation, Firm Environments and Location Analysis," *Professional Geographer* 23 (1971): 324-328.

Stevens, B.H., "An Application of Game Theory to a Problem in Locational Strategy," *Papers and Proceedings of the Regional Science Association* 7 (1957): 143-157.

Teitz, M., "Locational Strategies for Competitive Systems," *Journal of Regional Science* 8 (1968): 135-148.

Resource Orientation

Airov, J., *The Location of the Synthetic Fiber Industry*, Cambridge, Mass.: Harvard University Press, 1959.

Cotterill, C.H., "Industrial Plant Location: Its Application to Zinc Smelting," American Zinc, Lead, and Smelting Co, 1950.

Dinsdale, E.M., "Spatial Patterns of Technological Change: The Lumber Industry of Northern New York," *Economic Geography* 41 (1965): 252-274.

Dienes, L., "Locational Factors and Locational Developments in the Soviet Chemical Industry," University of Chicago Department of Geography, Research Paper 119, 1969.

Lindbergh, O., "An Economic Geographic Study of the Swedish Paper Industry," *Geografiska Annaler* 35 (1953): 27-40.

Mason, P.F., "Some Changes in Domestic Iron Mining as a Result of Pelletization," *Annals of the Association of American Geographers* 58 (1968): 535-551.

Complex Transport Orientation

Alexandersson, G., "Changes in the Location Pattern of the Anglo-American Steel Industry, 1948-1959," *Economic Geography* 37 (1961): 95-114.

Casetti, E., "Optimum Location of Steel Mills Serving the Quebec and Southern Ontario Steel Markets," *Canadian Geographer* 10 (1966): 27-39.

Craig, P.G., "Location Factors in the Development of Steel Centers," *Papers and Proceedings of the Regional Science Association* 3 (1957): 249-265.

Isard, W., "Some Locational Factors in the Iron and Steel Industry since the Early Nineteenth Century," *Journal of Political Economy* 56 (1948): 203-217.

McNee, R.B., "Functional Geography of the Firm, with an Illustrative Case Study from the Petroleum Industry," *Economic Geography* 34 (1958): 321-337.

Isard, W. and J.H. Cumberland, "New England as a Possible Location for an Integrated Iron and Steel Works," *Economic Geography* 26 (1950): 245-259.

General Market Orientation

Boas, C.W., "Locational Patterns of American Automobile Assembly Plants, 1895-1958," *Economic Geography* 37 (1961): 218-230.

Cunningham, W.G., *The Aircraft Industry: A Study in Industrial Location.* Los Angeles: L.L. Morrison, 1961.

Estall, R.C., "The Electronic Products Industry of New England," *Economic Geography* 39 (1963): 189-216.

Gibson, Lay James, "An Analysis of the Location of Instrument Manufacture in the United States," *Annals of the Association of American Geographers* 60 (1970): 352-367.

Pred, A., "The Concentration of High Value-Added Manufacturing," *Economic Geography* 41 (1965): 108-132.

Processing Cost Operations

Hague, D.C., and J.H. Dunning, "Costs in Alternative Locations: The Radio Industry," *Review of Economic Studies* 22 (1955): 203-213.

Krutilla, J.V., "Locational Factors Influencing Recent Aluminum Expansion," *Southern Economic Journal* 21 (1955): 273-288.

Rydberg, H., "The Location of the English Shoe Industry," *Geografiska Annaler* 47B (1965): 44-56.

Manufacturing Regions

Conkling, E.C., "South Wales: A Study in Industrial Diversification," *Economic Geography* 39 (1963): 258-272.

Fuchs, V.R., *Changes in the Location of Manufacturing in the United States since 1929.* New Haven: Yale University Press, 1962.

Krumme, G., "The Interregional Corporation and the Region: A Case Study of Siemens' Growth Characteristics and Expansion Patterns in Munich," *Tijdschrift voor Economische en Sociale Geografie* 61 (1970): 315-333.

Robinson, I.R., "New Industrial Towns on Canada's Resource Frontier," University of Chicago Department of Geography, Research Paper 73, 1963.

Rodgers, A., "Some Aspects of Industrial Diversification in the United States," *Economic Geography* 33 (1957): 16-30.

Specialized Settlement

Deasy, G.F. and P.R. Griess, "Impact of a Tourist Facility on Its Hinterland," *Annals of the Association of American Geographers* 56 (1966): 290-306.

Guthrie, H.W., "Demand for Tourists' Goods and Services in the World Market," *Papers and Proceedings of the Regional Science Association* 7 (1961): 159-176.

Part Four

Spatial
Interaction

In the preceding chapters, static pictures
of the landscape were presented, developing
separately (1) the existence of a density and
activity gradient across the rural landscape;
(2) a regular and hierarchical pattern of central places to serve a dispersed rural population, and (3) a variety of patterns for the
ideal location of processing activities. All
these structures result from the pursuit of
the same goal, maximizing the utility of
places. In the following two chapters, the
other, more dynamic side of the picture is
examined, the structure of flows of goods,
people, and ideas that enliven the pattern of
locations and that make the specialization of
activities at different places worthwhile. In
other words, the alternate goal, to maximize
spatial interaction at least effort, is
emphasized. Some have defined geography
as the study of location, others as the study
of interacting. We shall see that they in
truth are dual aspects of the same process:
how man organizes his affairs over space.

Transportation and Trade

Chapter 6

IMPORTANCE OF TRADE AND TRANSPORTATION

Movements — economic and social, of goods and of people, by means ranging from walking to telecommunication — make possible the specialization of location we have studied thus far. Even though a location may be defined mainly from its special character, that character may be most clearly understood not by the innate qualities of the location itself, but by its relations with other locations. Since relatively little is consumed where it is produced, the pattern of interaction may be the key to the ability of a location to exist.

The goals of spatial organization should determine the optimum structure of **movement.** On the one hand, man desires to minimize distance and the cost of movement, but on the other, he wishes to maximize the value of individual locations. The wealth generated by increasing the value of each location can justify fairly high levels of trade.

For instance, while a producer at a given location wishes to minimize the proportion of his revenues that are needed for transport, society and the provider of the transport consider transport charges payments for services rendered, an alternate form of production. Furthermore, since without transport the goods made at a given location may be worthless, part of the value of the product must be attributed to the transport. It is thus incorrect to view transport costs as a constraint to productivity; rather, transport services and the willingness of producers to use them make possible the high productivity that results from specializing in a location. Society wishes to maximize the total value of both production and transport services, and this goal at times requires more, and at times less, investment in transport.

Improvements in transport have spurred the advance of civilization and have revolutionized patterns of human life. Better transport broadened the range of control and exchange and thus fostered the development of sophisticated social structures. The innovation of the first Phoenician ships made possible the long-distance movement of goods and people and the maintenance of distant supply lines, thereby

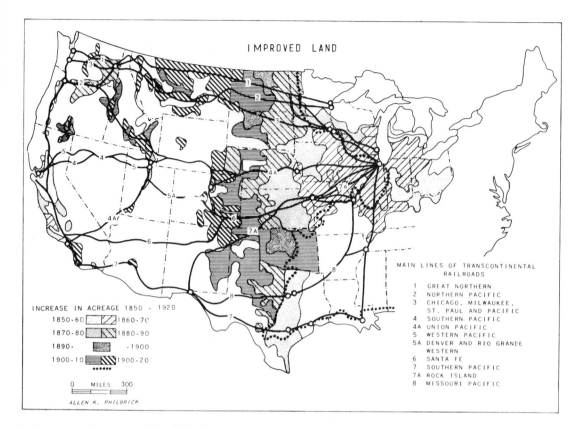

Figure 6.01   Transport and land development. Opening of land for agricultural settlement accompanied the extension of the western railroads. (Reprinted by permission of John Wiley & Sons, Inc., from Allen D. Philbrick, *This Human World*, 1963.)

giving people the freedom to live away from a self-sufficient local area. Investment in road networks made possible the unity of the far-flung Roman Empire, whereas the deterioration of roads in the Middle Ages diminished economic and social exchange. The railroad, by drastically reducing the cost and improving the speed of land transport, stimulated the development of interior resources and farming areas, especially in North America (figure 6.01), Central Europe, and Russia. The car and the truck, creating a demand for improved highways, opened up a wider, more diffuse area and reduced rural and urban cultural distinctions. The incredible development of air transport has truly created "one world" in the geographic sense, because no location — however remote — is more than a few hours away from any other.

Even more significant, perhaps, is the achievement of higher standards of living and greater productivity through better transport. By permitting specialization, improvement in transport leads to greater land and labor productivity and more efficient use of capital; costs of increased trade over longer distances have consistently been lower than the increases in productivity realized through specialization. As entire nations or groups within a nation become willing to abandon self-sufficiency and to exchange their specialties on a broader scale, trade, wealth, and income rise rapidly.

Trade   and   Regional   Development. Trade is both a means for regional development and a consequence of it. Most regions in the early stages of development specialize in the export of primary products (raw materials, foods). Although income leakage is at first common (profits return to the more developed regions), the export-trade income can be used to import manufactures and investment machinery (capital goods), and serves as a basis for the gradual growth of **secondary** (manufacturing) and **tertiary** (service) **sectors,** which in turn leads to a more balanced pattern of trade. Some regions, however, never escape dependence on resource exploitation and on imported higher priced manufactures. In chapter 10 we shall return to a discussion of the problems of regional growth and development and the role of trade (see pp. 241-254).

Factors Influencing Trade

Trade is generated when transport costs become low enough to make local specialization profitable. Most simply, the location of specialized production, the spatial separation that this specialization implies, the cost of overcoming the separation, and the demand for the goods so produced control the extent of trade. Production costs at locations dictate the amount of savings or additional wealth that scale and specialization will generate and thus determine how far apart related activities may be. Specialization and trade may increase so long as the production-cost savings exceed the increase in transport costs. For some activities, diseconomies occur at moderate scale, concentration is limited, and the optimum shipments are very short — even within the plant, for example — but for other activities, almost total concentration of production at a few locations is economic.

THE COST OF DISTANCE

Basically, the economic or social cost of the distance between people or activities where interaction is necessary or desired helps determine spatial structure, or the locations of these activities. Spatial structure as such could not exist without these costs, because any differentiation between areas would then depend only on inherent variations in the land and its owner.

Because distance is no longer such an obvious barrier, it has become common to dismiss its importance. But along with such progress, the *indirect* role played by distance has become greater. For example, the industries that have minute transport costs are tied to the large metropolises because the appropriate labor and management is immobile — in such cases, distance separation obviously does matter. Vast public and private investments have been made to reduce the costs of distance; nevertheless, even in areas that have the best transport, the volume of flows of goods and people drops rapidly with distance.

Measuring distance is not necessarily a simple matter. Its cost to movement and interaction may be expressed in at least these ways:

- *Geodesic distance — the physical mileage between two points.*
- *The time needed to cover the distance via the given mode of transport.*
- *Transport costs — the actual quoted rates or real incurred costs.*
- *Psychological or* **social distance** *— interpreted by individuals.*
- *Combinations of the above — for example, weighing both cost and time.*

Although the impact of distance may be best expressed by time or transport costs, spatial separation is the basic reason for these costs.

Geodesic distance, the length measured as we walk or drive, is the most familiar measure of distance and plays a constant role in the average person's life — going to work, to the store, or to recreation. Yet, whether we consciously realize it or not, we may measure such distance by subtly transforming it to its costs in time; when we say we are willing to go only so many miles, what we may mean is that we are willing to be gone only so long.

Movements of people, such as the journey to work, are more affected by time costs than are movements of goods, but the growth of air freight and innovations in freight handling installed by railroads illustrate that time is becoming very important to shippers, especially as the costs of holding inventories rise. Moreover, central place systems show that changes in the speed of covering a distance can alter the threshold of entry of activities and thus affect the success of places. For example,

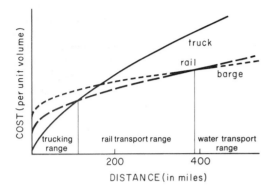

COST (per unit volume)

truck

rail

barge

trucking range

rail transport range

water transport range

200   400

DISTANCE (in miles)

Figure 6.02 Carrier competition. Generally, there is a relation between the capacity of a carrier and the distance at which it is most competitive. Thus, trucking is preferred for short to moderate hauls, higher capacity rail transport for moderate to long hauls, and water transport, if possible, for long hauls of bulk commodities.

range against truckers and at long distance against water and air transport (see figure 6.02).

Carriers in some countries, such as railroads in the United States, typically quote rates by blocks of distance (forming a stair-step function — see figure 5.09 again). This permits rates to be standardized so that only a finite number of rates exist.

The relation of transport rates to distance may vary from area to area because of differences in:

— *Operating costs, due to such factors as topography, volume over routes, and characteristics of goods.*

— *Degree of monopoly control or effect of government regulation and rate-setting policies (figure 6.03).*

— *The characteristics of carriers.*

many hamlets and neighborhood stores have disappeared.

"Real distance" is distorted by our social and aesthetic perceptions: we may tend to consider areas we don't like as being farther away, and perceived distance to shopping centers may be affected by our ability to pay and our image of the centers' quality. Thus, the effective distance between areas of different economic or social status may be quite unlike the geographic distance.

For movements of most goods, the role of distance is best expressed by transport costs, since any business operation must deal with these costs. Transport costs represent either an increase in price to the buyer or a decrease in realized price to the seller, depending on who must absorb the costs.

The relation of transport costs to distance is fairly well known: the rate per mile decreases exponentially as distance increases, because terminal costs are included in the transport rate. Thus, total costs of transport increase more slowly as distance increases (refer to figure 5.09). Alternatively, terminal and haulage costs could be expressed separately. However, many fixed costs are difficult to allocate to individual shipments, and the carrier frequently prefers to undercharge its very close and very far customers. The railroad, for instance, uses its middle-distance shipments — which are most competitive against other carriers — to subsidize competition at close

Topography has a strong influence on the cost of movement — initially, because of the high costs of construction and maintenance in mountainous and swampy areas, and, later, because over-the-road operating costs increase rapidly as gradients and curvatures increase. Rugged topography also incurs indirect costs because the speed of transport is slower. Natural barriers may impose costs (such as tolls on bridges) and thus, in effect, increase distance, although this is usually justified by comparing these costs to those of more roundabout routes.

In addition, rate levels naturally vary by the kind of goods carried. Goods requiring refrigeration, special handling, or packaging incur greater costs and bear higher rates. Shipments of less than standard - carrier size, especially those making up less than a railroad carload or full truckload, have many extra handling costs and are charged much higher rates. Carriers, with the agreement of the government, frequently exaggerate these differences by overcharging finished goods, even to the point of subsidizing some shipments of bulk raw materials.

Unit costs may be set lower where volume is great (figure 6.04). Economies of scale affect transport costs in two ways: individual shipments may be of large size or repeated shipments may reduce carrier overhead and result in lower rates; or a large volume carried over a particular route or to

Figure 6.03 Transport rates for lumber (cost per 1,000 feet) from the Pacific Northwest. Rates increase with distance at a decreasing rate, but there are seeming anomalies due to government regulation (low rates in the Northeast) and competition (high rates in the Southeast). These particular rates are no longer current, but the pattern remains. (Reprinted by permission of the Houghton Mifflin Company, from R.J. Sampson and M.T. Farris, *Domestic Transportation*, 1966.)

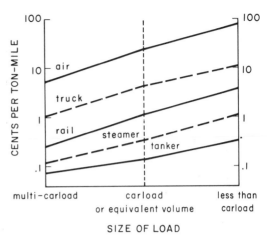

Figure 6.04 Over-the-road transport costs by carrier and volume. Not only do larger capacity carriers enjoy lower over-the-road costs, but for each carrier, costs are much lower if more units (trucks, railcars, ships) are assigned to a single shipment.

and from particular centers may raise the efficiency of shipments.

Where carrier competition to a particular place is keen, rates may be forced down and the difference made up by high prices on routes where the carrier has a monopoly. Governments generally attempt to prevent such high rates by determining prices that yield fair returns, but this method is rigid and often produces inequities.

Error in the Interpretation of Distance

The cost of distance may be incorrectly or only hazily measured by individuals and firms. Even where there is an attempt to minimize distance and transport costs, errors in measurement are common and often result in suboptimal movements of goods. For example, a distributor may assume that a freeway is the better route in a situation actually more suited to delivery via arterials. More commonly, shippers are uncertain about the exact amount of transport costs or tend to see a range of distances or quoted rates as having essentially equivalent costs. Their failure to appreciate these fine distinctions in costs causes some unpredictable patterns of locations and shipping.

Theoretical Transport Networks

Location of the Single Route. Building a link between places is justified if, directly or indirectly, the cost of construction is repaid by the enhanced productivity of the places after trade is established between them. It may be optimal for the routes to depart from the straight line between the two points under certain conditions:

— If the revenue and productivity gained by linking intervening places to the system offset the increased costs of transportation, congestion, and time loss (figure 6.05).

— If the costs of construction and maintenance over a longer route in easier topography are small enough to offset the increased distance of the route (figure 6.06).

Transport costs may actually be lower on the longer route because the gradients will be less steep.

Theoretical Networks. According to the theories of location that we have studied, firms and individuals seek to minimize distances traveled while maximizing both the volume of profitable interaction and the value or productivity at each location. Each movement is assumed to take place

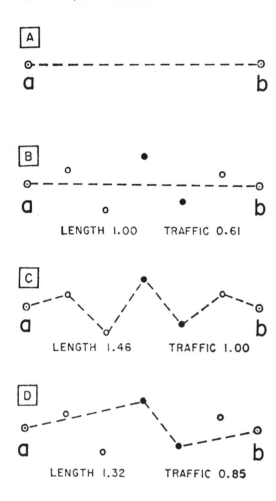

LENGTH 1.00   TRAFFIC 0.61

LENGTH 1.46   TRAFFIC 1.00

LENGTH 1.32   TRAFFIC 0.85

Figure 6.05 Deviation of transport routes for additional revenue. If only places *a* and *b* existed, a direct route would clearly be best. With other towns between (solid dots are larger places), the route may remain direct (with the shortest length and least traffic), deviate fully (the longest route with most traffic), or deviate to the largest places only. Deviation is justified if traffic (revenues) increases more than length (cost), as it does in *D*. (Reprinted courtesy of Edward Arnold [Publishers] Ltd., from Peter Haggett, *Locational Analysis in Human Geography*, London, 1965.)

over the path entailing least cost, subject to competition by other movements wishing to take the same route. It is also assumed that there is a rather complete transport network containing competing modes of travel, although movement associated with any particular activity, given the specialization of locations, should be concentrated on only a small portion of the system.

Agricultural location theory involves minimizing the costs of transporting produce to a central market. Maximum feasible transport cost as a proportion of the market value of a good probably does not vary much from good to good or from center to periphery: the attempt to keep this proportion from becoming unprofitably high results in competitive bidding for land and thus creates the agricultural gradient.

Agricultural gradient theory alone suggests a transport system that is completely center-oriented, radiating outward from the market. Decreasing fineness of the net will reflect the increasing size of farms and the greater distance between them. No crosslinks will be required, since all transport is to the market. The object is to construct the smallest network required both to provide complete access to all agricultural production and to minimize the mileage of higher capacity segments, which are much costlier. Figure 6.07A represents a preliminary attempt to depict such an ideal branching system, but this scheme may be far from being the optimal one. Strictly minimizing distance requires a curved and continually branching system (figure 6.07B), but society places a value on *straight*, direct routes and perceives the costs of indirectness as high enough to justify the slightly longer but more linear system shown in figure 6.07A.

Central place theory is based on minimizing the costs of distributing goods to consumers and of collecting goods from dispersed producers. This theory requires a system oriented to many centers on several levels (figure 6.08). Major roads and flows connect the largest places; lesser roads serve smaller places; and the pattern of transport mirrors the pattern of central places. In pure theory, settlement is homogeneous and the transport pattern strictly regular, except that the volume of transport and the quality of the route reflect the level of the interconnected places. The central place pattern according to the transport principle (shown in figures 4.05 and 4.06) is most efficient because the roads connecting two larger places pass through places of the next lower order. Again, the mileage of the high-capacity, costlier segments is minimized; efficiency is increased by concentrating

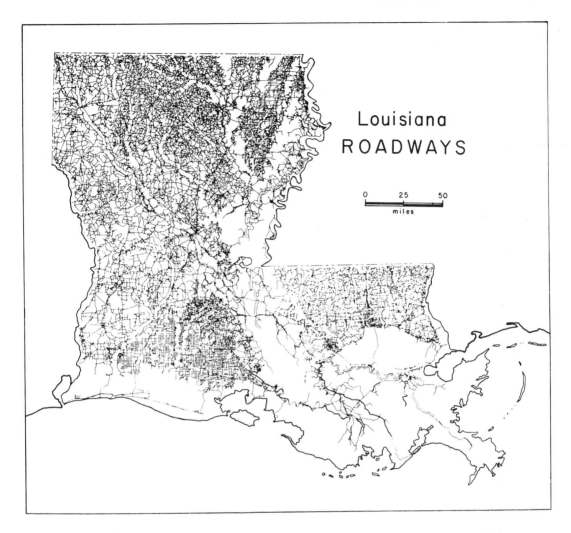

Figure 6.06 Louisiana roads closely reflect local topography. The roads are rectangular in level areas, more complex in rolling areas, and absent from marshy areas along the coast and in the Mississippi delta, where construction is difficult. (Courtesy of the Louisiana Department of Highways.)

transport flows of large volume on major routes and restricting most small flows to local collection and delivery.

Realistically, agricultural gradients and central place systems occur simultaneously and must be considered together. What will the transport network for such a joint surface look like? Figure 6.09 is a first attempt at showing the ideal composite transport net. Essentially, the net is formed by linking laterally at intersections — defining these as central place locations or smaller markets — the branches radiating from a large

agricultural market and also by directing local and regional routes toward nearest central places.

Industrial location theory involves jointly minimizing the transport costs of assembling materials and of shipping products, although the importance of transport costs as a determinant of location varies widely. For some industries, such as sawmills or food processing, raw materials are collected from local areas over small-volume transport routes, and for others, such as urban newspapers, distribution is similarly

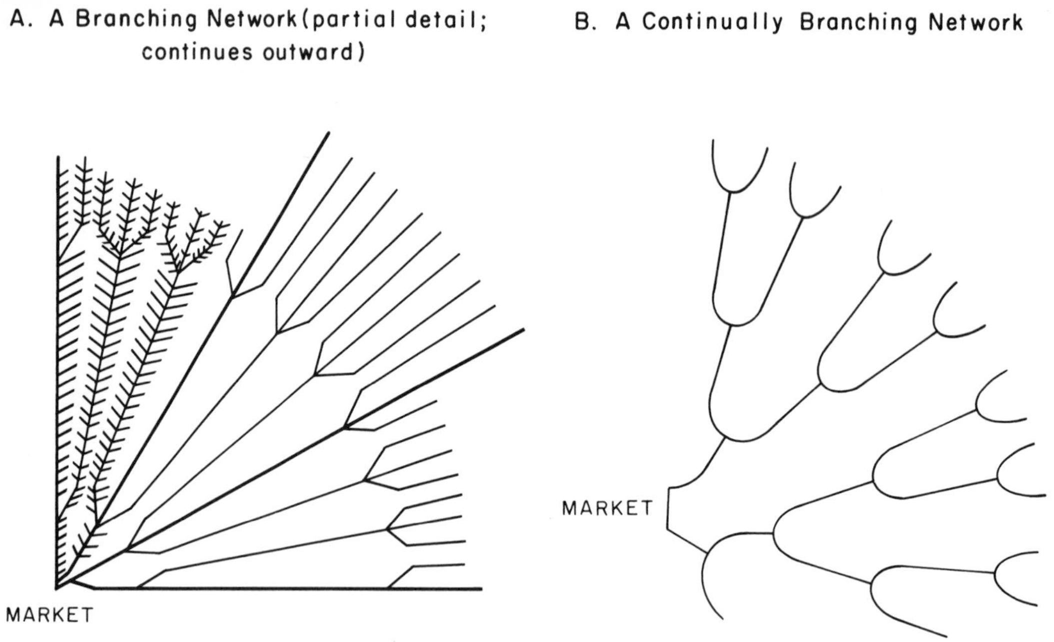

A. A Branching Network (partial detail; continues outward)

B. A Continually Branching Network

MARKET

MARKET

Figure 6.07 *A* and *B* represent two possible networks designed to move produce to a central market. *B* extends to points closest to individual farmers at the least distance to the market, but *A* may be more realistic because of preferences for straighter and more direct roads.

local and small-scale. For the majority of industries, however, interindustry dependence means a pattern of fewer, larger flows, forming a shipping equilibrium that depends on the relative location of suppliers, producers, and markets. See also figure 9.04, p. 216.

Specific patterns of industrial location might not alter the basic structure shown in figure 6.09, but they would tend to destroy its symmetry by creating regional variations in density, such as clusters of strongly linked plants that require particularly strong lateral connections not otherwise needed. Because industrial flows are generally large and less diffuse, transport may be more efficient and also cheaper per unit shipped than for movements of agricultural or central place products.

Evaluating the Transport Network

The amount of movement that may profitably flow on a given route depends greatly on the quality of the transport net.

Components of the quality of a route include:

— *The relative characteristics of the transport modes available — carrier capacity, cost, frequency of service, and speed, for instance.*

— *The vehicular capacity of the routes.*

— **Connectivity** — *how directly places are connected.*

— *Fineness — accessibility to local shippers.*

— *Specific technical quality — surface, curvature, and gradient.*

— **Stress** — *the likelihood that certain routes will be overused.*

— *Density — route mileage per unit area.*

Where it is physically practical, a variety of transport systems over a given route is desirable to assure competition and complementarity of demand (each system is best

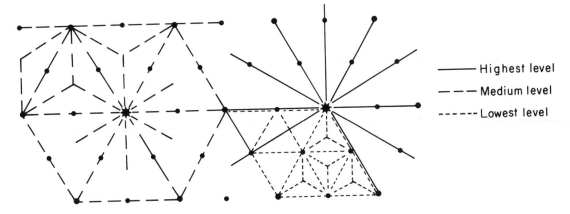

Figure 6.08 Flows in a central place system mirror the geometric arrangement of places. The more important routes and flows converge on the largest (highest level) place (star) from equally large places outside the area (not shown). Medium volume flows and quality routes serve and connect the places of next lower order (large dots, left part of diagram), and local routes and small flows serve the smallest places. More important routes carry local traffic, too, of course.

for some kinds of flows). Demand for transport is also uneven, and transport systems develop stress on links and nodes where topography or accidents of development limit route choice. Thus, roads converge on crucial bridges and mountain passes and around barrier lakes and mountain ranges. Congestion is most likely to develop in such areas or between large neighboring centers. This congestion, however, usually occurs at limited peak traffic periods, such as the daily journey to work, and for seasonal activities, such as beach-going. Queuing analysis can help in finding a capacity that will prevent all but small, acceptable congestion. A capacity adequate for the worst traffic would be extremely excessive most of the time and thus be an inefficient use of capital resources; the cost of providing the capacity for peak demand must be balanced against the costs of congestion, time loss, and deterioration of the system from overuse.

Directness measures the quality of the connections between places; again, the savings from avoiding probable congestion and time loss via indirect routings must be balanced against the costs of providing direct connections. A relatively high level of connectivity implies that the economy is advanced and can afford high-priority bypass links around intervening places.

The fineness of the net refers to its most local portion — its access to farms, homes, forests, and mines. Investment in such local access is costly because of the immense mileage involved, but inadequate access may cost even more by lowering productivity. Poor local access hindered the development of Appalachia in the United States; absence of local all-weather roads has in the past reduced the efficiency of Soviet agriculture.

Since transport networks develop gradually out from areas of greatest development, they commonly exhibit certain problems arising over time. As technology improves, transport networks are subject to obsolescence — excessive curvature or inadequate capacity. Network analysis can reveal congested and circuitous links between places for which improvement is justified — such as on a route between two cities that have strongly linked industries and poor transport between them.

Transport systems can also be analyzed to identify redundancy — overinvested links where revenues do not cover the costs of maintenance and handling traffic. For example, the least efficient 30 percent of America's railway mileage carries only 2 percent of the traffic. Such redundancy may result from a shift in transport mode to competitors or from technological responses

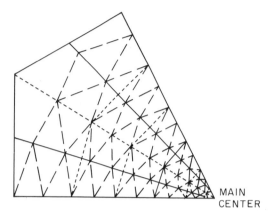

MAIN
CENTER

Figure 6.09   Transport network on a joint agricultural gradient-central place hierarchy surface. This figure shows a possible transport network to serve a landscape in which a central place system is imposed on an agricultural (and population) density gradient (see also figure 9.01).

to scale that make obsolete the too-fine network of an earlier era. In the United States, with its commitment to the private car and large public revenues for roads, there is some risk that roads receive too great an investment relative to alternative possibilities.

The spatial allocation of transport routes has dramatic effects on development. Investment in major through-transport to the neglect of routes for local access risks unproductive agriculture and the depopulation and relative decline of most smaller places, while the reverse situation may foster inefficient **regionalism** accompanied by insufficient national specialization and trade. Any investment in transport will affect the relative optimality of places served, or bypassed, by the new or improved link, and require different adjustments on the part of places (figure 6.10).

Major Transportation Systems

Transport systems both compete with and complement one another. Each has an exclusive province where the others do not compete — ships cross the oceans and major lakes; the rails serve great mineral deposits; roads provide local access and major routes where the amount of traffic will not justify building a railroad; pipelines move bulk

amounts of liquid and gas materials; air serves remote outposts unreachable by other means and allows people to communicate rapidly.

Water transport was the first fairly efficient form of transport. Today, water transport has tremendous capacity, ranging from river barges with from 10 to 100 times the capacity of a rail carload to the giant bulk-petroleum carriers that can carry 200,000 tons of crude oil. Where shiploads are made up of bulk products, and special loading and unloading techniques are available, the efficiency of water transport is unchallenged; costs may often fall below one-tenth of a cent per ton-mile. The costs of handling for general cargoes of mixed goods are rather high, however, even though the actual costs of transport are low. Water transport is also very slow and hampered by storms, ice, and — most important — the very limited location of origins and destinations along shores or major rivers. A great investment in canals took place in China, Europe, and the United States in order to overcome these limitations. However, many canals, and even roads for a while, were rendered obsolete by the development of the railroad. Rail transport has intermediate capacity (20 to 100 tons per car), terminal costs, and over-the-road costs. For multicarload shipments of goods over medium distances, especially if the shipments are between plants or warehouses and no change in mode of transport is required, efficiency is high. The greater the number of train cars between a single origin and destination, the cheaper the rate and the quicker the trip; a train made up of cars with many destinations must be divided at major junctions (classification yards) and reconstituted.

Figure 6.11 shows the railway network in the United States. The great concentration of mileage in the Northeast and Midwest reflects both the richness of agricultural and mineral resources and the historical economic dominance of the regions.

Trucks typically have a lower capacity than do railroad cars, ranging from 1 to 20 tons, and they cannot be linked into trains. Thus, handling costs for large volumes are high, but for truckload volumes they are lower than competing carrier costs. Because

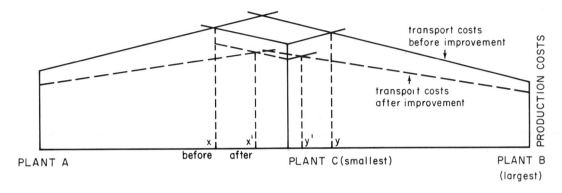

Figure 6.10   Impact of improvement in transport. Suppose that plants *A*, *B*, and *C* are located along a transport route. The size of the market of each is determined by the point where delivered costs from any two plants are equal. Before improvement, delivered costs are equal at points *X* and *Y*. After the route is improved, costs are equal at *X'* and *Y'*, and *A* and *B* are able to expand their markets at the expense of *C* because of their larger size and lower costs.

of truck design and operating characteristics, trucks also have a competitive advantage for lighter, bulkier goods. Their greatest advantage, however, is that they make door-to-door delivery possible with no change in transport mode. The railway network is skeletal and does not serve many good production sites, while motor vehicles can travel on the much finer road network (figure 6.12). Thus, great savings in cost and time are often possible.

On the other hand, however, in spite of many subsidies, operating costs of trucks are high, especially for labor. Piggyback movements of trucks — where fully loaded truck-trailers are carried on railroad flatcars for long hauls — represent efficient cooperation between the two systems, minimizing the costs of both haulage and shifting transport modes, and using the advantages of both systems.

Pipelines cost almost as little as water transport, and they have a high capacity. One technical advantage is their ability to traverse far steeper gradients than can other modes. Other advantages include low labor requirements, use of the pipe itself as storage, low haulage costs, and reduced necessity for a shift in transport mode. However, present pipelines are extremely slow — only three to five miles per hour — and time is becoming more valuable to firms and individuals.

Aircraft have the greatest freedom of movement and far superior speed, but they are limited by the costly equipment needed, restricted airfield location, small capacity, and, thus, high transport rates.

Electric-power transmission is a major source of energy transfer, competing directly with rail and water transport of fuels. Substituting electric power for coal and oil permits some industries to locate away from railways, and long-distance transmission means that remote hydro-electric resources can be developed and perhaps that some low-grade coal can be used without actually moving the coal. Transmission costs are high and usually exceed the cost of shipping and using fuels for power after about 300 miles.

Figure 1.05 indicated the inverse relationship of rates of speed and time needed for transport, and figure 6.02 showed the direct, if variable, relation of rates to distance. Water transport is preferred for low-value bulk commodities with no pressure for quick delivery; these commodities move by rail in areas where water routes are not available. Rails have a theoretical advantage for carrying manufactured goods shipped in lots of at least one carload moderate to great distances. Road transport via trucks is best for products sent local to medium distances or over long, low-volume routes, for collection of farm products and final distribution to retailers, and for local interindustry transfers. As planes have increased in capacity, air transportation has gradually become cheaper and is increasingly used for

Figure 6.11   Pattern of railways in the United States, 1965. Note the concentration of routes in the rich agricultural Midwest and industrial Northeast, the gaps in hilly areas, and the sparseness in the low-density West. (Reprinted by permission of the Association of American Railroads.)

HIGHWAY TRAFFIC

ON PRIMARY ROADS IN THE UNITED STATES·
1969-1970

STEPHEN S. BIRDSALL
Department of Geography
University of North Carolina
Chapel Hill

MAP STUDY NO. 3

10 20 30 40 50 60
Thousand Vehicles per Day

Note: Pennsylvania traffic flows
are for 1964

© STEPHEN S. BIRDSALL 1973

0   50   100   150   200   250
Scale in Miles

Figure 6.12   Highway traffic, 1969-70. Only flows on primary roads are shown. The flows closely reflect the distribution of urban population in the United States. (Reprinted by permission of S. Birdsall, Department of Geography, University of North Carolina.)

transport of higher valued foods and manufactured goods, especially when time savings are important.

Government preferences play a role in the choice of carrier. In the United States railroads are presently at a disadvantage; they have little political "pull" compared with the automobile-petroleum industries and the car-driving public. Government support for individual car owners also indirectly provides a sizable subsidy to the trucking industry by supplying exceptional roads, which enables truckers to capture much of the long-haul bulk commodity business perhaps technically better handled by rail. In countries with state-owned railways, the opposite bias is often apparent.

Development of Transport Systems

Historically, transport-network growth

has both reflected and induced settlement, industrialization, and urbanization (figure 6.13). In long-settled countries dominated by self-sufficient local economies, transport tends to be a complex, poor, but fine network, consisting of partially joined local roads and possibly a few military highways linking the capital to the provinces. With industrialization, penetration lines, usually using rail transport, are built from the earliest point of growth (usually the capital or major port) to the peripheral areas that supply agricultural products and other resources. Processing industries may in turn diffuse outward, and local feeders or access roads may develop for agricultural production. Lines of penetration extend farther, often connecting the major national centers, and industrialization spreads in a leap to these centers. The pattern then proceeds from multiple origins. Even before adequate transport covers the entire territory of the nation, intensive development near the origin demands replacement of the original

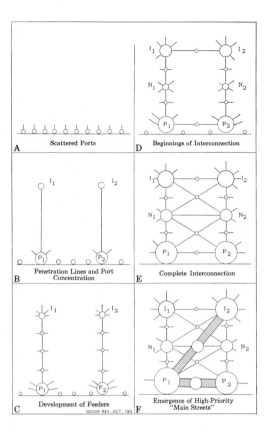

A   Scattered Ports

B   Penetration Lines and Port Concentration

C   Development of Feeders

GEOGR. REV., OCT., 1963

D   Beginnings of Interconnection

E   Complete Interconnection

F   Emergence of High-Priority "Main Streets"

Figure 6.13 This figure illustrates one typical sequence of development, from initial small ports to limited penetration of lines to inland centers (*I*), resulting in consolidation of port activity (*P*), growth of local access feeders, lateral connections, additional nodes (*N*), and, finally, the highest quality direct routes between the most related places. (Reprinted by permission of the American Geographical Society, from Edward J. Taaffe, Richard L. Morrill, and Peter R. Gould, "Transport Expansion in Underdeveloped Countries: A Comparative Analysis," *The Geographical Review*, Vol. 53, 1963.)

penetration lines by higher quality, faster links.

A transport network is developed ostensibly to facilitate movement, but in the long run it modifies location itself. While many transport links are built in response to existing demand, fairly arbitrary decisions on penetration routes frequently may determine the location of future settlements (see figure 6.01).

ACHIEVING A BALANCE BETWEEN SPECIALIZATION AND SELF-SUFFICIENCY

Selectively abandoning local self-sufficiency in favor of greater specialization while continuing to increase trade has traditionally been the direction of greatest efficiency, productivity, and wealth. Certainly, one may observe that lack of transport in many regions prevents the efficient use of resources (that is, the realization of a comparative advantage in a specialty). Trade does cost money, as does transport improvement, but the overriding benefits of specializing in areas follow from variations in inherent natural productivity (such as differences between agricultural and forest land) and in manmade productivity (such as superior and inferior positions on the transport net), and from the realization of economies of scale and agglomeration. A dramatic long-run effect of specialization has been the geographic concentration of economic activity in a few favored sites and areas, notably large urban centers.

Are there limits to specialization? Is there any economic or geographic rationale for greater regional self-sufficiency? The well-known risks of specialization are both military and environmental; dependence on distant sources for strategic materials might be dangerous if enemies could sever those links, and concentrating the growth of an agricultural product in one location may cause serious shortages if weather conditions are too variable. Spatial concentration, along with industrial concentration, also increases the risk of control by a monopoly. If monopoly pricing exists it becomes more difficult to be certain that the location is optimal. Finally, spatial concentration leads to high levels of congestion and pollution, requiring rather expensive means of regulation or abatement if the quality of life and the environment are not to deteriorate.

A critical question concerning specialization, however, is whether it tends to maximize short-run efficiency while not recognizing long-run suboptimality. For instance, it is extremely difficult and far too risky for a small firm to establish in advance whether a location that provides greater self-sufficiency will be more profitable in the long run. In 1800, for example, it was more efficient in the short run for the United States to buy manufactured goods from England than to produce them locally, but in the long run protection of infant industries at home was justified. As another example, in the USSR, construction of new "bases of industry" in Siberia involved costly subsidies at first, but the new industries have since become immensely profitable.

MODELS OF TRADE

In order to describe and explain the patterns of trade, several models have been proposed. A *model* is a formal statement of how factors are interrelated and what outcomes can be expected under particular conditions. The principal models of trade include the following:

— *International-trade or comparative advantage models.*
— *Spatial equilibrium or transportation models.*
— *Descriptive input-output matrices.*
— *Interaction models.*

The last model will be discussed in the following chapter (p. 169-171). The comparative advantage model is the most comprehensive in that the location of production and trade are determined simultaneously, but this has been achieved so far only by using untenable assumptions. Input-output analysis is the most realistic description of trade flows. The transportation equilibrium models are the most satisfactory both theoretically and practically and are also very flexible, but they, too, do not adequately fuse location and trade theory.

The Comparative Advantage Model

The comparative advantage model was developed to explain international trade and included several countries and several commodities. It is nonspatial, that is, the distance between markets and places of production are ignored. It assumes that the available supplies of productive agents — essentially labor — are known for each country and that the productivity of labor with respect to all goods is known — that is, the labor required per unit of output for each product is known. The proportion of the total value of production that each good provides is also known for each country. The problem, then, is to find the output of each good in each country, in that way determining the trade among countries and the net prices of goods that will use labor most fully and achieve the greatest production value. The model quantifies the concept of comparative advantage, and its solutions give both the optimum location and the optimum production volume of many goods in many countries, as well as the ideal levels of trade. For example, imagine two regions with an equal supply of labor and demand for goods, say steel, dairy products, and textiles. Suppose a unit of country A's labor can produce twice as much steel as a unit of B's labor and one and a half times as many textiles, while B's labor unit can produce twice as many dairy products. A has a comparative advantage in steel, and will export it to B; B has a comparative advantage in dairy produce and will export to A; A has a comparative advantage in labor productivity for textiles, and will export some to B, but does not have sufficient labor to fill B's demands. B's extra labor, though less productive, will cover part of its own needs.

The model, however, is limited in many ways. It assumes that labor can be completely substituted among goods; no limits on production except those set by regional labor supplies are admitted. The assumption that prices and consumption patterns are everywhere the same is unrealistic; in particular, transport costs are not included. It also does not admit economies of scale. The model uses the differential quality of regions, but not their spatial separation, and thus while the total amount of trade of each nation can be determined, it may not be possible to determine the geographic pattern of trade.

In summary, the model's ability to yield the location, volume of production, and

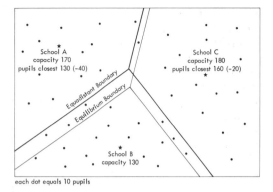

each dot equals 10 pupils

Figure 6.14 School districts according to the assign-ment (transportation) problem. Graphic solution to the assignment of population (pupils) to centers (schools) with constraints on capacity. Equidistant boundaries assign each pupil to the closest school, but this results in too few or too many pupils for the capacities of the schools. Parallel shifting of boundaries, maintaining the three-way junction, shifts pupils in such a way as to minimize travel while meeting the capacity constraints.

trade of many commodities seems im-pressive, but it is severely limited because only one factor of production, labor, is manipulated.

Transportation and Spatial Equilibrium Models

The comparative advantage model allocated production among nations on the basis of variations in labor supply. Transportation models instead allocate trade on the basis of the relative location of sup-ply, demand, and interregional transport costs.

The theory of trade underlying the transportation model is simple and logical, if the location of production and demand are known. Under the simplest conditions, for example, military or perhaps intrafirm trade, where known quantities of goods must be shipped from certain areas and known quantities of goods must be received at other areas, the problem reduces to a basic geographic principle: to minimize the cost of transportation; that is, to find the most efficient, least costly shipments. Finding such solutions, however, is not easy; the relative location of surplus and deficit areas may sometimes require rather costly paths.

For example, in figure 6.14, the problem is to assign known numbers of pupils in the many small areas to one of three schools of a given capacity. If capacity could vary, the minimum-distance (transport cost) solution would simply be to assign each pupil to the nearest school. The constraint of exactly matching pupils to capacities means that many pupils closer to *B* will have to go farther to school *C*, which has a large capacity but too few pupils in its vicinity. Since capacity is difficult to shift in the short run, equilibrium can be achieved by subsidizing (bussing) those pupils who have to travel farther than the closest school.

More generally, once we are given levels of production (supply) and regional demand for a good in a set of areas, we can find the equilibrium prices (as set by supply-demand relations) that would exist if no trade were permitted (figure 6.15). This state of affairs might seem absurd, but it makes a real point: trade will take place (in the two-region example shown in figure 6.15) if the difference between the equilibrium prices in the two regions in the absence of trade ex-ceeds the cost of transporting the product between the regions — the interregional transport cost. As trade flows between the regions prices fall in the importing region as supply increases, and rise in the export-ing region as supply decreases. Because of the lower price, the importing region can consume much more of the good. At the same time, exporting producers in the sur-plus region earn much more because of the higher prices. Consumption is thus evened out between the regions. More trade is justified until precisely that point is reached where the prices in the two regions differ by the interregional transport cost. This equilibrium is stable; if even one more unit were shipped, the cost of transport would exceed the differential in prices, and the shipper would lose money.

Trade can take place then, if oppor-tunities — price differences greater than transport costs — are present; furthermore, if trade takes place between two regions, the price of goods when trade equilibrium is reached will differ by the transport cost between the places. But the particular paths that are used — that is, the opportunities that are actually taken advantage of out of the many possible — will be those that can

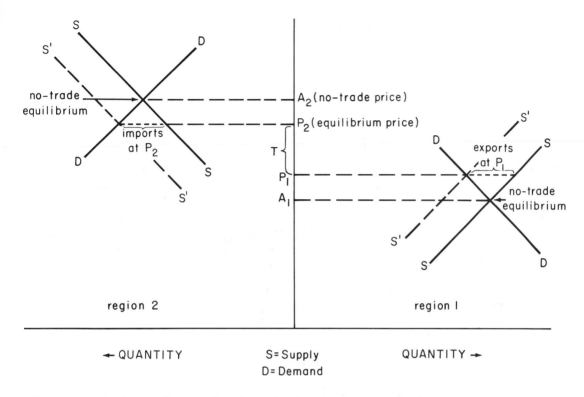

Figure 6.15 This diagram illustrates the volume of trade and regional price levels in two regions under specified conditions of supply, demand, and transport cost. In region 1, supply is too great. Demand will use up the supplies only at the low price, A_1. In region 2, supplies are too short; they can be sold at the high price, A_2. The difference between A_1 and A_2 is greater than the transport cost, T, so it pays region 1 to export goods to region 2. Region 1 exports just enough (and region 2 imports this amount) to raise the price in region 1 up to P_1 (at the reduced supply S') and to lower the price in region 2 down to P_2 (at the increased supply S'). Note that at this stable equilibrium, the prices P_1 and P_2 differ by exactly the amount of interregional transport cost, T.

bring about a trade equilibrium at minimum total transport costs.

Although many specific and more or less complicated forms of the model have been developed, most are dependent on or derive from the simple transportation model. Given a set of regions, their deficits or surpluses with respect to some good, and the pattern of interregional transport costs, the objective is to find the set of routes that will not only minimize total transport costs, but also remove all surpluses and satisfy all deficits. The spatial equilibrium model is a generalized version of the transportation model; specific surpluses and deficits are not given, only regional production and demand. Not only are transport costs minimized and the direction of trade found in this model but also the level and value of trade, final consumption, and the structure of prices.

The Value of Trade. The spatial equilibrium approach to trade not only provides a simple and reasonable theory to account for the volume and direction of trade, but also measures the value of trade to society. The value of final consumption (goods sold) increases, even after discounting the transport cost of the trade itself, because the use of supply is more efficient; consumers in deficit areas get more, supply in surplus areas is not wasted. A reduction in transport rates on a set of routes will similarly increase trade volume — perhaps at no increase in total transport costs.

Evaluation of the Efficiency of Trading Patterns. Since these equilibrium models are normative — they predict what would occur if distances were minimized and value of consumption maximized — it is theoretically possible to estimate the extent

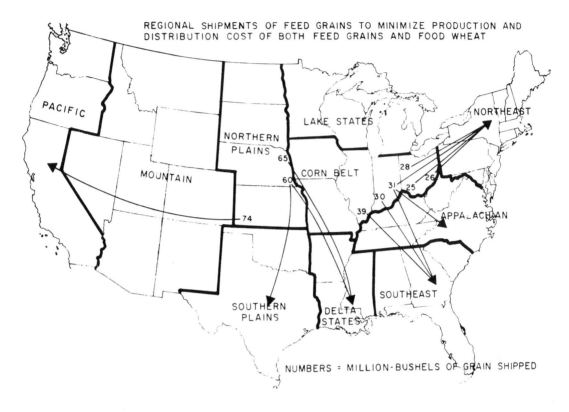

REGIONAL SHIPMENTS OF FEED GRAINS TO MINIMIZE PRODUCTION AND
DISTRIBUTION COST OF BOTH FEED GRAINS AND FOOD WHEAT

NUMBERS = MILLION-BUSHELS OF GRAIN SHIPPED

Figure 6.16 The optimal pattern of shipments of feed grains, using a spatial equilibrium model.
Actual shipments are not known. (Reprinted from Earl Heady and Alvin Egbert, "Spatial Allocation
of Crop Output," *Journal of Regional Science*, Vol. IV, 1962.)

to which the observed trading patterns
depart from the best possible ones (figure
6.16). Also, as in the school example above,
evaluation of the trading pattern may well
suggest changes in the pattern of production or capacity that would reduce or
eliminate some very long and costly flows.

Evaluation of Changing Conditions.
Equilibrium models such as these are particularly useful for short-run prediction of the
impact of changes in transport rates, regional production, and regional demand (from
population shifts, for example) on patterns
of trade, regional consumption, and
prices.

Limitations of Transport Models. The
most serious criticism of equilibrium models
is that a theory of trade as such is necessarily only a partial theory. These models
assume the location of production and from
it predict trade patterns. But making
decisions about location and trade

simultaneously is the central problem of
spatial organization and not easily resolved
(see chapter 9). A study of the trade pattern
of an industry, including production, consumption and prices, can, however, be helpful in estimating shifts in location which
might lead to greater efficiency.

A special difficulty in these models is the
restraints on substitution and variability of
products. For example, where a transport
model might indicate long-distance movement and a high price for a product, the im-
porter might instead substitute another
product for the high-priced one. Also,
possible lower rates for larger flows are not
admitted. Nevertheless the distance-
minimizing models are of real theoretical
and practical importance — theoretically as
an explanation of ideal behavior or process,
and practically, in the evaluation of the efficiency of the patterns of both trade and
production, in estimation of the effects of
changing conditions on these patterns, and
in evaluation of potential locations for new

facilities, factories, roads, or other activities.

Input-Output Estimates of Trade

A table of interindustry flows is a valuable description of trade interdependence for a given year (table 5.01, p. 96). It does not normally indicate distance, direction, and cost of transport. Interregional tables specify flows from the industrial sectors of one region to perhaps a few other regions. No theory of trade is explicit in such a table, but a theory of trade adjustment may be implicit when the matrix is used to evaluate expected changes in demand or output. For example, a rapid increase of production in one sector in a region can be shown to lead to increased flows from backward-linked (supplying) and forward-linked (purchasing) industries, and also to increased imports as well as exports (see table 5.01, p. 97).

KINDS AND PATTERNS OF TRADE FLOWS

Political Influences over Trade

Within a national economy political influences over trade are largely due to transport-rate regulation, government preference for certain carriers, regulation of vehicle size, and variations in local taxation. Trade has nearly always been politically controlled between nations, and, in newly industrializing economies, duties on imports and exports are often an important tool of government action.

In Europe, for several centuries, the road to national wealth and power was often seen to be more through trade than through internal development. In pursuit of more trade, the principal techniques of political control over trade were developed: tariffs and quotas. In the long run these are restraints on trade; they either raise the price of products and the cost of transport or they exclude and limit certain trading paths (figure 6.17). Tariffs on incoming goods have three purposes:

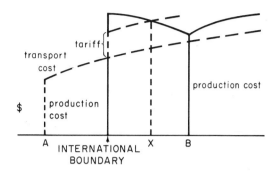

Figure 6.17 Tariffs can restrain trade and keep inefficient plants in production. *A* has much lower production costs (vertical dashed lines) and could sell its products more cheaply than *B* in *B*'s country. By imposing a tariff, the nation to the right prevents *A* from competing any farther than point *X* into its territory.

— *To raise government revenue.*
— *To reduce total imports, thereby improving the balance of trade and fostering the nation's internal development.*
— *To protect internal production from outside competition.*

Naturally, tariffs are conspicuously absent from demanded products not producible within the country. Duties on exports are used in developing countries as major sources of government or private revenue and may be imposed to discourage loss of particular resources. The use of export duties for income however, is limited by the risk of pricing goods above competing exporters of the same good.

Generally, as the internal economy develops, tariffs are used less often for revenue and to achieve a trade balance, but selected tariffs remain to protect infant and/or powerful or nationally desired industries — for instance, essential products that might be cut off in time of crisis.

War or serious political conflict can lead to embargoes against trading with certain countries; the United States, for example, has an embargo against trade with Cuba. Embargoes are a tool of economic warfare, used to hurt the economy of presumed enemies.

Controlled Liberalization of Trade: Common Markets. As nations gain confidence in the competitive strength of their industries or even wish to goad them into

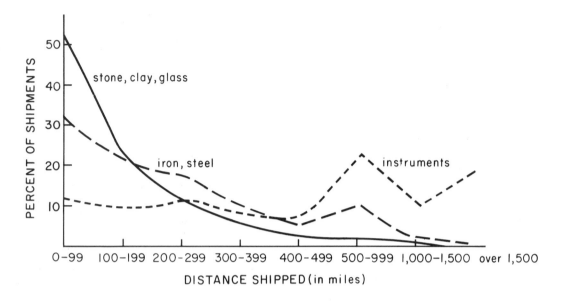

Figure 6.18 Distances traveled by selected commodities, United States, 1963. Although trade volume generally declines with greater distance, the less value per pound, the shorter distance a product is typically shipped.

greater productivity, they may enter into tariff-reduction agreements, such as GATT — the General Agreement on Trade and Tariffs. Smaller groups of nations, especially the small but highly developed nations of Europe, recognized that the large internal markets and resources and absence of trade barriers within the United States and the USSR permitted greater specialization, agglomeration, and scale. To gain the same advantages, the EEC (European Economic Community), composed of France, West Germany, Italy, Belgium, the Netherlands, and Luxembourg, almost completely abolished internal barriers to flows of goods, capital, and labor. The resulting marked increases in trade, income, and economic efficiency are well known. The EFTA (European Free Trade Association) which included the United Kingdom, Portugal, Switzerland, Norway, Sweden, Denmark, and Austria eliminated industrial tariffs but had not dealt with agriculture. So successful has the EEC been that Eire, the United Kingdom, and Denmark have shifted to this more thoroughly integrated economic community.

Free Trade and Protection. It might

seem irrational and self-defeating for nations to have any tariffs at all and for other areas of the world not to form common markets immediately, since tariffs increase transport costs, reduce trade, and restrict profitable specialization. If a country enters a period of excessive imports and imbalance of payments, however, it may have to impose tariffs to restrict imports in order to maintain its national economy. More generally, the disparate levels of economic development presently existing among nations may require some protective tariffs to protect the weaker countries. A common market consisting of very rich and very poor countries would tend to perpetuate the imbalance; unless the more developed nations chose to invest in the less developed ones and to support their industries during a formative period, the more developed countries would almost always maintain an overwhelming advantage in productivity.

Trade and Distance. In advanced economies the vast majority of production enters into trade. Because legal boundaries

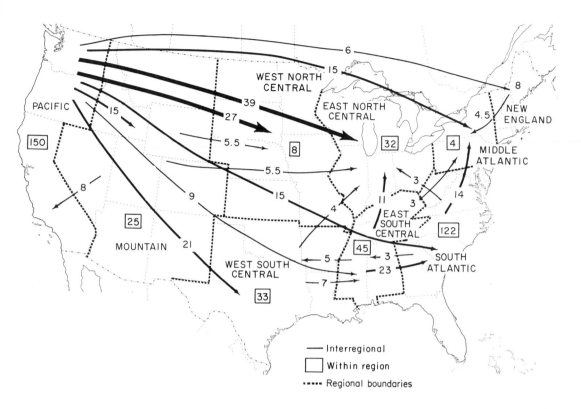

Figure 6.19 Lumber shipments, 1963. Lumber flows centrally toward the northeastern urban-industrial core. In this case, one region, the Pacific Northwest, is an unusually dominant source. (From the U.S. Census of Transportation.)

influence collection of data on trade, one is most aware of international and interstate movements. But the volume of local trade is actually greater; there is a rather regular decay in the value and volume of trade as distance increases (figure 6.18).

These local movements of goods represent a high proportion of total-movement volume and cost because many material suppliers (such as farmers) and most consumer households are spatially diffuse. Intermediate-distance regional and interregional flows directly reflect the specialized structure of an economy. They are large-volume, more skeletal flows, located on only a few routes. International movements of goods reflect mainly the specialization among national economies. International trade remains, however, biased toward raw materials and food; these are about twice as important as they are in most domestic trade.

Flows of Primary Products

Movement of primary products to processing centers is spatially a process of concentrating these products, typically from many scattered units of rural production, into a few urban centers (figure 6.19). In the United States, raw materials are collected locally in most areas, but the large interregional flows tend to be movements from peripheral regions to metropolitan centers.

International flows of primary products require a special discussion, since they have a great influence on economic development. Most simply, a "colonial" trading pattern has developed, in which primary products from less developed countries are sold to processors in more developed countries. Duties on these exports constitute a large share of the national income of less developed countries, emphazing the dual

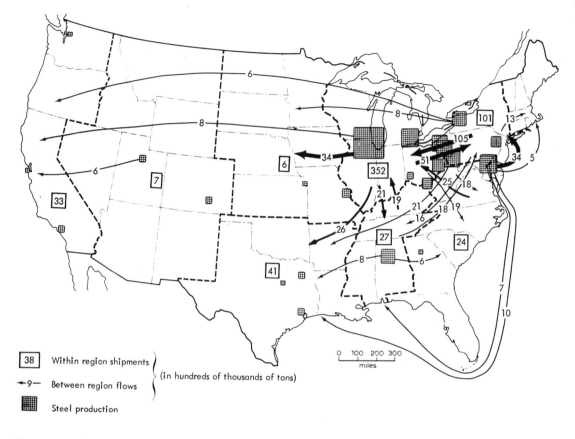

Figure 6.20 Steel shipments, 1968. Most flows are shorter and move within or out of the industrial core — East North Central and Middle Atlantic regions. Please see figure 5.20 for the pattern of iron ore, steel, and coal production in the United States. (From the U.S. Census of Transportation.)

character of many such economies — a commercial export industry grafted upon a generally more subsistent agriculture. While these exports provide capital for development, dependence of this kind courts serious risks: great fluctuations in demand and price prevent stable development and repayment of loans; political considerations may destroy former markets, such as Cuba's loss of the U.S. sugar market; and if the income goes into the hands of a small aristocracy, there may be little incentive for internal development. The weakness of many competing small countries against large industrial, consuming countries is also apparent in the very low prices paid for their primary products in comparison to the high prices the small countries must pay for capital or consumption goods. This trade is not irrational; it does respond to valid demand and trade opportunities, but it is not

strictly fair because of the disparities of power and development.

The major commodities involved in these international flows are petroleum products, agricultural goods (tropical fruits, sugar, rubber, fibers, wheat, meat, livestock, coffee, tea), and minerals (metal ores). These trade patterns exhibit surprising stability, reflecting long-established mother country-colony ties translated into continuing preferential agreements that, to some extent, may not be most efficient for either party.

Primary products also flow in great volume between more developed countries, reflecting surpluses of local resources and production specialties. A few advanced nations that enjoy high resource-to-population ratios, notably the United States, Canada, Australia, New Zealand, and perhaps Sweden, are in the enviable position of possessing both demanded resources and developed manufactures. The resulting trade surpluses help make these five among the richest nations in per capita income.

Flows of Manufactured Goods

The spatial converse to the collection of raw materials is the distribution of manufactured goods to consumers. There are very significant flows between manufacturers; there are also some flows down the urban hierarchy from manufactures to wholesalers, to retailers, and finally to the consumer; and regionally from the industrial core to the periphery. This exchange system operates at great volume imbalance; the bulk of the collected raw materials exceeds many times over the bulk of the manufactured goods, thus some inefficiency in the use of carriers is unavoidable.

Flows of manufactured goods (figure 6.20) can be contrasted with those of primary goods (figure 6.19). Although the most intensive trade occurs within the industrial core itself, there is a sizable outflow to the periphery. On an international scale, manufactured goods from highly industrialized nations tend to be exchanged for the primary products of less developed areas. In addition to the simple colonial exchange discussed above, there is an intermediate kind, typified earlier by Japan and now by India and other developing nations, in which the less developed nations may themselves import some raw materials and then export labor-intensive manufactures.

Exchange of Manufactured Goods

Within and among advanced nations, most of the volume of trade is in manufactured goods. In contrast to early theories of trade, which emphasized the colonial exchange system as the route to wealth, actual experience has shown that greater profitability results from specialized exchange among competing industrial powers. This effect is, of course, merely an extension of the benefits of specialization and scale that can be developed within an economy; to some extent, such trade represents exchange of products for which countries or regions of a country have a clear comparative advantage. For example, paper and basic steel are exchanged between Sweden (specializing in paper) and Germany (specializing in steel); food products and heavy-industry goods between Denmark and Germany; and, within the United States, petroleum products are exchanged for machinery and vehicles between the Southwest and Midwest, and even within regions manufactured goods are exchanged between metropolitan and small-city kinds of manufacturers.

This regional product specialization, however, cannot account for all trade. Even for what is apparently the same product, seemingly inefficient movement of similar goods in opposite directions (cross-hauling) is profitable, usually because some differentiation actually exists. American and European cars vary greatly in size, price, and appeal to consumers, for instance, and most kinds of machinery vary in their specific capabilities. Brand preferences and maintenance programs, such as with aircraft, may tip the balance in favor of certain products. Variations in productivity and price resulting from differences in mechanization, labor costs, and market size may also serve as a short-run creator of trade.

Overall Patterns of World Trade

The pattern of world trade has a striking spatial form. There is an inner web of strong and close ties, generally oriented toward western Europe, with smaller webs around lesser nodes (such as Japan) and only weak links at the periphery — the same kind of pattern observed within a nation and for the internal structure of a city.

Western Europe remains central to and dominant over world trade (figure 6.21). Not only are many of the largest flows internal to western Europe, mainly consisting of manufactured goods, but most of the remaining large flows move to and from Europe, consisting mainly of primary materials shipped to Europe. A few rival trade centers have developed that can challenge this dominance, notably the United States with respect to Canada, Latin

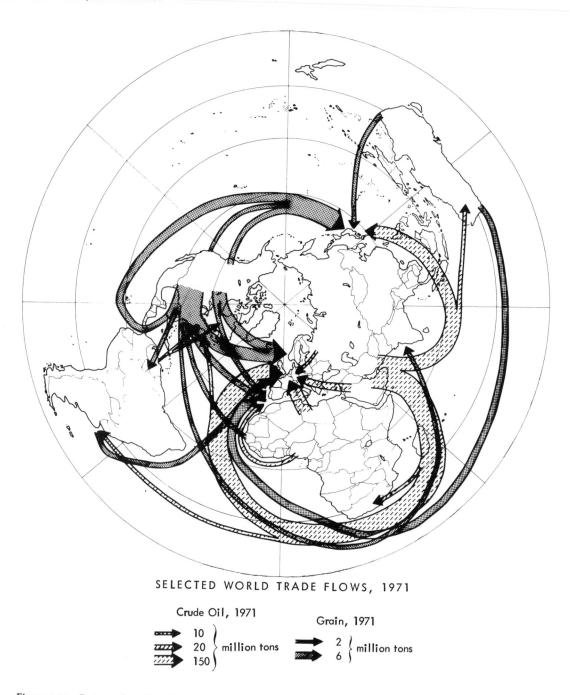

SELECTED WORLD TRADE FLOWS, 1971

Crude Oil, 1971

Grain, 1971

10
20 } million tons
150 }

2
6 } million tons

Figure 6.21 Pattern of world trade in two selected commodities: grain and crude oil, 1971. Flows of goods to and from Europe are dominant. (Data from *World Bulk Trades, 1971,* Fearnley and Egers Chartering Company, Ltd., Oslo, Norway, 1972.)

America and Japan; Japan with respect to much of the world, and the USSR with respect to nations within its sphere. To be sure, the small size of European nations makes their role in international trade seem

even greater than that of, say, the United States and the USSR, but the conclusion holds true even if western Europe is treated as one nation. This pattern of world trade shows much inertia, but it is not necessarily inefficient; it is a reflection of the developmental history of the colonial period and illustrates that economic change can lag far behind political change

Patterns of Internal
U.S. Trade

The internal American pattern of trade movements is similar in structure to the world pattern in that an intense core of trade, some competing centers, and sparse center-oriented flows from the periphery can be observed. However, the American economy is smaller in area, the quality of the transport is fairly high over much of the territory, and disparities in economic development are much less severe. Hence, the American economy is more tightly inter-connected by trade.

The northeastern urban-industrial core is dominated by intense internal movements of manufactures, although local movements of primary products (coal and food) are also significant. From the periphery, foods and other bulk products and some specialty manufactures flow toward the center, while the reverse flow consists largely of machinery and other finished products and consumer goods. Again, competing centers have begun to emerge, notably California and, to a lesser extent, the Gulf Southwest.

Conclusion

Trade is the outcome of the specialization of location; its volume and direction are the result of man's attempt to achieve the highest level of production and consumption. While trade reflects the ideal patterns of location, as modified by the variable quality of resources as well as by political division, the potential profitability of trade is itself a determinant of location.

REFERENCES

General Transportation
and Trade

Cooley, C.H., *The Theory of Transportation*, American Economic Association, 1894.

Fogel, R.W., *Railroads and American Economic Growth: Essays In Economic History*, Baltimore, Md.: Johns Hopkins, 1964.

Fulton, M. and J.C. Hoch, "Transportation Factors Affecting Locational Decisions," *Economic Geography* 35 (1959): 51-59.

Garrison, W.L. et al. *Studies of Highway Development and Geographic Change*, Seattle: University of Washington Press, 1959.

Gauthier, H., "Transportation and the Growth of the Sao Paulo Economy," *Journal of Regional Science* 8 (1968): 77-94.

Perle, E.D., "Estimation of Transportation Demand," *Papers and Proceedings of the Regional Science Association* 15 (1965): 203-215.

Smith, P.E., "A Note on Comparative Advantage, Trade, and the Turnpike," *Journal of Regional Science* 5 (1964): 57-62.

Tattersall, J.N., "Exports and Economic Growth: The Pacific Northwest, 1880-1960," *Papers and Proceedings of the Regional Science Association* 9 (1962): 215-234.

Warntz, W. "Transatlantic Flights and Pressure Patterns," *Geographical Review* 51 (1961): 187-212.

Woytinsky, W.S. and E.S. Woytinsky, *World Commerce and Government*, New York: Twentieth Century Fund, 1955.

Theory of Trade

Alexander, J.W., E.S. Brown, and R.E. Dahlberg, "Freight Rates: Selected Aspects of Uniform and Nodal Regions," *Economic Geography* 34 (1958): 1-18.

Berry, B.J.L., "Recent Studies Concerning the Role of Transportation in the Space-Economy," *Annals of the Association of American Geographers* 49 (1959): 328-342.

Boudeville, J.R., "An Operational Model of Regional Trade in France," *Papers and Proceedings of the Regional Science Association* 7 (1961): 177-190.

Boye, Y., "Collecting and Distributing Commodities: Approaches to Appropriate Systems," *Papers and Proceedings of the Regional Science Association* 12 (1963): 221-224.

Fox, K.A. and R.C. Taeuber, "Spatial Equilibrium Models of the Livestock-Feed Economy," *American Economic Review* 45 (1955): 584-608.

Graham, F., *The Theory of International Values*, Princeton, N. J.: Princeton University Press, 1940.

Henderson, J. M., *The Efficiency of the Coal Industry: An Application of Linear Programming*, Cambridge, Mass.: Harvard University Press, 1958.

Isard, W. and M.J. Peck, "Location Theory and International and Interregional Trade Theory," *Quarterly Journal of Economics* 68 (1954): 97-114.

Mackay, J.R., "The Interactance Hypothesis and Boundaries in Canada," *Canadian Geographer* 38 (1962): 122-129.

Morrill, R.L. and W.L. Garrison, "Projection of Interregional Patterns of Trade in Wheat and Flour," *Economic Geography* 36 (1960): 116-126.

Samuelson, P.A., "Spatial Price Equilibrium and Linear Programming," *American Economic Review* 42 (1952): 283-303.

Vidale, M.L., "A Graphic Solution of the Transportation Problem," *Journal of Operations Research* 4 (1956): 193-203.

Warntz, W., "Transportation, Social Physics and the Law of Refraction," *Professional Geographer* 10 (1958): 6-10.

Wilson, A.G., "Inter-Regional Commodity Flows: Entropy Maximizing Approaches," *Geographical Analysis* 2 (1970): 255-282

Wohl, M., "Transient Queuing Behavior, Capacity Restraints, and Travel Forecasting," *Papers and Proceedings of the Regional Science Association* 21 (1968): 191-204.

Transport Networks and Systems

Black, William, "An Iterative Model for Generating Transportation Networks," *Geographical Analysis* 3 (1971): 283-287.

Burghardt, A.F., "Origin and Development of the Road Network of the Niagara Peninsula Ontario, 1770-1851," *Annals of the Association of American Geographers* 59 (1969): 417-440.

Garrison, W.L., "Connectivity of the Interstate Highway System," *Papers and Proceedings of the Regional Science Association* 6 (1960): 121-137.

Garrison, W.L. and D.F. Marble, "Analysis of Highway Networks," *Highway Research Board Proceedings* 37 (1958): 1-17.

Haggett, P., "Horton Combinatorial Model and Regional Highway Networks," *Journal of Regional Science* 7 (1967): 281-290.

Haggett, Peter and R.J. Chorley, *Network Analysis in Geography*, New York: St. Martins Press, 1970.

Kansky, K., "Structure of Transport Networks," University of Chicago Department of Geography, Research Paper 84, 1963.

Lachene, R., "Networks and the Location of Economic Activities," *Papers and Proceedings of the Regional Science Association* 14 (1965): 197-202.

Mackinnon, R.D. and M.J. Hodgson, "Optimal Transportation Networks: A Case Study of Highway Systems," *Environment and Planning* 2 (1970): 267-289.

Meinig, D., "A Comparative Historical Geography of Two Railnets: Columbia Basin and South Australia," *Annals of the Association of American Geographers* 52 (1962): 394-413.

Newton, Milton, Jr., "Route Geography and the Routes of St. Helena Parish Louisiana," *Annals of the Association of American Geographers* 60 (1970): 134-152.

Quant, R.E., "Models of Transportation and Optimal Network Construction," *Journal of Regional Science* 2 (1960): 27-45.

Sen, Lalita, "The Geometric Structure of an Optimal Transport Network in a Limited City-Hinterland Case," *Geographical Analysis* 3 (1971): 1-15.

Taaffe, E.J., R.L. Morrill, and P.R. Gould, "Transport Expansion in Underdeveloped Countries: A Comparative Analysis," *Geographical Review* 53 (1963): 502-529.

Ullman, E.L., "The Railroad Pattern of the United States," *Geographical Review* 39 (1949): 242-256.

Werner, C., "Role of Topology and Geometry in Optimum Network Design," *Papers and Proceedings of the Regional Science Association* 21 (1968): 173-190.

International Trade, Ports

Alexander, J.W., "International Trade: Selected Types of World Regions," *Economic Geography* 36 (1960): 95-115.

Alexandersson, G. and G. Norstrom, *World Shipping*, New York: Wiley, 1963.

Carter, R.E., "A Comparative Analysis of United States Ports and Their Traffic Characteristics," *Economic Geography* 38 (1962): 162-175.

Desbarats, J.M., "A Geographical Analysis of the Clyde's Forelands," *Tijdschrift voor Economische en Sociale Geografie* 62 (1971): 245-263.

Grotewold, Andreas, "Some Aspects of the Geography of International Trade," *Economic Geography* 37 (1961): 309-319.

Grotewold, Andreas, "The Growth of Industrial Core Areas and Patterns of World Trade," *Annals of the Association of American Geographers* 61 (1971): 361-370.

Johnson, J.F., "Influence of Cost-Distance Factors on Overseas Exports of Corn from the U.S. Midwest," *Economic Geography* 45 (1969): 170-179.

Kenyon, James, "Elements in Inter-Port Competition in the United States," *Economic Geography* 46 (1970): 1-24.

Robinson, R., "Changing Shipping Technology and the Spatial Adjustment of Port Functions," *Tijdschrift voor Economische en Sociale Geografie* 62 (1971): 157-170.

Smith, H.R. and J.F. Hart, "American Tariff Map," *Geographical Review* 45 (1955): 327-346.

Weigend, G.C., "Some Elements in the Study of Port Geography," *Geographical Review* 48 (1958): 185-200.

Yeates, M., "A Note Concerning the Development of a Geographic Model of International Trade," *Geographical Analysis* 1 (1969): 399-403.

Internal Trade

Beckerman, W., "Distance and the Pattern of Intra-European Trade," *Review of Economics and Statistics* 38 (1956): 31-40.

Helvig, M., "Chicago's External Truck Movements: Spatial Interactions between the Chicago Area and Its Hinterland," University of Chicago Department of Geography, Research Paper 90, 1964.

Isard, W., "Regional Commodity Balances and Interregional Commodity Flows," *American Economic Review* 43 (1953): 167-180.

King, L., E. Casetti, J. Odland, and K. Semple, "Optimal Transportation Patterns of Coal in the Great Lakes Region," *Economic Geography* 47 (1971): 401-413.

Olsson, R., "Commodity Flows and Regional Interdependence," *Papers and Proceedings of the Regional Science Association* 12 (1963): 225-230.

Patton, D., "The Traffic Pattern on American Inland Waterways," *Economic Geography* 32 (1956): 29-37.

Pfister, R.L., "The Terms of Trade as a Tool for Regional Analysis," *Journal of Regional Science* 3 (1961): 57-66.

Richmond, S.B., "International Relationships Affecting Air Travel," *Land Economics* 33 (1957): 67-73.

Smith, Robert H.T., "Concepts and Methods in Commodity Flow Analysis," *Economic Geography* 46 (1970): 404-416.

Smith, S.A., "Interaction within a Fragmented State: The Example of Hawaii," *Economic Geography* 39 (1963): 234-244.

Ullman, E.L., *American Commodity Flow*, Seattle: University of Washington Press, 1957.

Wallace, W.H., "Freight Traffic Functions of Anglo-American Railways," *Annals of the Association of American Geographers* 53 (1963): 312-331.

Interaction:
Movements of
People and Ideas

Chapter 7

All theories of location are based in part on the goal of minimizing the distances traveled of both goods and people. Trade in goods, movements of people, and the communication of ideas are indeed predicted by these theories. Since locations are spatially separated and often economically specialized, there is a strong demand for interaction with other persons and for goods and services that are not available at one's own location. Indeed, people are willing to devote much time and income to such movements — at all levels of spatial organization.

Although the movement of people and communications in the main reflects the pattern of specialized location and constitutes the human force which enlivens these patterns, movement of people and ideas may also break out of this structure and initiate, through migration and the spread of innovations, fundamental changes in location.

In a spatially restricted society, interaction is highly localized, and demand can be met within the range of a few villages. Yet, in the absence of telephones and reliable roads, achieving interaction may involve as much effort for local villagers as for members of a highly interdependent economy traveling much greater distances. In advanced economies the quality of the transport system and the cheapness of travel permit more movement over a greater distance for the same effort, thus allowing extensive specialization and greater separation of activities and people.

KINDS OF MOVEMENTS

Many trips for personal interaction and communication are temporary. Such trips include:

- *Personal interactions between businesses.*
- *Interactions between consumers and local businesses — that is, trips for goods and services.*
- *The journey to work.*
- *Interactions between persons for social purposes, much of which can be accomplished by mail or telephone (as can many interbusiness interactions).*

— *Interactions between consumers and distant businesses — such as tourist trips for recreation and "exploration."*

Some moves require a temporary change in residence (transient moves):

— *Military reassignment.*
— *Movement of migrant labor.*
— *Attendance at colleges.*

Some moves are permanent:

— *Migration for economic improvement.*
— *Migration for social and psychological reasons.*
— *Migration because of political necessity or force.*
— *Migration for retirement.*

Temporary movements of people are necessary for the efficient day-to-day functioning of society. If they cannot be made, the volume of production and consumption will fall. If they are excessive, the structure of locations is probably inefficient. But temporary movements do not alter the pattern of location; rather, temporary movements and location mirror each other.

Permanent movements of people, however, are adjustments in location. They may either reflect or initiate shifts in the location of activities. For instance, investment in new activities or, conversely, a decline in established activities may induce inflows and outflows of people, while in pioneering agricultural settlement or the widespread movement to amenity areas like California or Florida, migration stimulated change in the location of activities and increased the value of production in those areas.

Location   Theory   and   Associated Movements

The theory of agricultural location mainly involves minimizing the movements of goods. In extending the theory to urban areas, the focus shifts to personal movements (see chapter 8). The part of location theory that treats of the urban density

gradient involves minimizing the cost of center-oriented journeys to work and to shops; the sector aspect of the theory of urban structure (see chapter 8, pp. 191) entails minimizing intergroup friction and enhancing intragroup social and business interactions. In urban areas we find a gradient of decreasing density caused not by the competition of goods, but because people and businesses differ in their desire and ability to pay for access to more central locations.

Central place theory concerns minimizing transport costs for the interactions of scattered household consumers and farmers with centralized businesses, as well as interactions between agglomerated businesses themselves.

Industrial location also deals mainly with movements of goods; but minimizing the cost of movements of people is vital for certain branches of industry, such as publishing, apparel, and research and development, and it is important enough to many other branches to foster much industrial agglomeration. The differential quality of land and resources influences two kinds of movements of people, tourism and permanent migration:

— *Areas that are perceived as having a high recreation value attract tourists from great distances, and*
— *People may migrate permanently to amenity areas (usually those with mild winters) for work and especially retirement.*

Static location theory, however, does not in general predict migrations. Dynamic modifications in the theory that allow for population growth, increasing demand for land and resources, income growth, shifts in demand, changes in economic structure, and technological change in transport and production all explicitly predict population redistribution through labor migration.

TEMPORARY MOVEMENTS

Interbusiness   Movements.   Businesses of all types are major consumers of each other's services and goods. Those that require the greatest volume of contacts and can least tolerate time lost traveling to each other will tend to agglomerate in central locations. Such contacts include those between publishers and advertisers, apparel makers and designers, courts and lawyers, banks and retailers, and retail and office locations and restaurants.

Shopping and Service Trips. Some shopping and service trips, such as those for gasoline and for quickly needed bread or cigarettes, are usually single-purpose and inflexible in time. Such trips are short and fairly efficient, usually being made to the closest supplier. Travel to elementary schools is similar. Trips for other purposes, however, may require comparison shopping, such as those for clothing, furniture, and weekly groceries, and, in order to save time and travel, the shopper may wish to combine several purposes in one trip. For multipurpose trips, larger nucleations of different activities are preferred. Large centers are better known and offer a greater variety of goods. These and special-purpose centers, such as clusters of furniture stores, automobile dealers, nurseries, and hospitals, will attract customers from greater distances.

Paths of trips frequently overlap (see figure 4.12), since customers may not go to the closest location for a given good or service. Much of this overlap can also be explained by the real — or perceived — differences between centers regarding brand availability, quality, and selection; many persons, for example, skip the closest hospital in order to visit one associated with their religion.

The Journey to Work. The trip to and from work dominates the local travel pattern in advanced societies (figure 7.01). Because their jobs are so important, people are willing to travel farther to work than to shopping centers; consequently, the journey to work is considered to be the key variable in determining urban land use and spatial structure (see chapter 8). In the simplest theory all employment is at the center, and density falls as the more distant resident substitutes more space and lower rent for the higher rent and lower transport cost of the closer resident. In fact there are many industrial and commercial employment centers, both peripherally and centrally located. The larger and more specialized the employment center, the more widespread its **laborshed** — the area from which its workers commute (figure 7.02). So concentrated is the journey to work in peak morning and evening periods (rush hours) that these flows are responsible for severe problems of congestion and pollution in the city. The attempt to solve these problems in part accounts for the very expensive provision of improved freeways and transit systems, which are underutilized at times other than the rush hours.

Trips for Social Purposes. Trips to visit family and friends are between residences and tend to occur within an area of fairly homogeneous socioeconomic status and age, although a family's travel pattern may include visits with friends who have moved to the suburbs or, conversely, with those who have remained in the city (see the movement patterns shown in figure 1.03).

Recreational Trips. Trips for recreational purposes are oriented partly toward nucleated recreational centers, such as a downtown entertainment center, and partly toward space-consuming activities located in the periphery — golf, racing, and rides in the country. Most recreational trips are temporary and limited to the distance an individual can reach and return from in a day.

Tourist Travel. Freedom from work on holidays — increasingly common in the affluent society — permits longer recreational trips, typically of one to three weeks. An important portion of tourists travel from small places to large cities, especially the greatest metropolises. A more obvious portion travel to areas offering some special scenic or recreational quality — distant mountains, beaches, and lakes. The attraction of such areas is partly a function of the degree of difference from home; for example, in winter, tourists travel from the northern cities to Florida, southern California, Hawaii, or the western deserts and mountains. Public awareness of these places increases the tourist trade; national parks and greatly publicized private resorts receive disproportionate amounts of people.

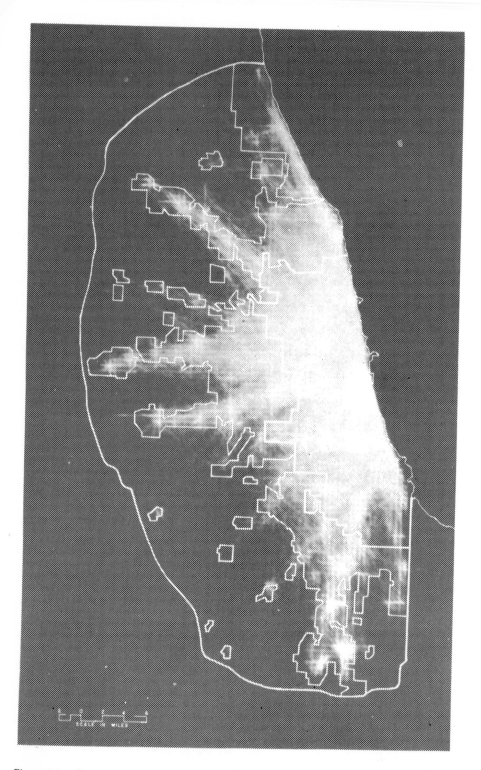

Figure 7.01 Journey-to-work flows, Chicago, 1956. Fuzzy white lines represent work trips, usually toward the center from the periphery. The irregular solid white lines are the boundaries of built-up areas, the outer line is the boundary of the Chicago region. (Reprinted by permission of the Chicago Area Transportation Study from their *Final Report*, Volume 1.)

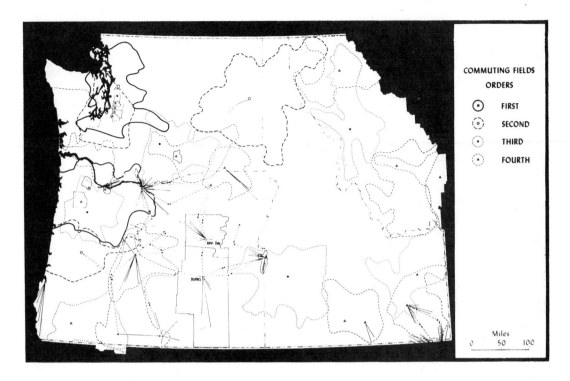

Figure 7.02   Commuting fields for four orders of central places in the Pacific Northwest. Commuting patterns reveal the shape and extent of the **nodal regions** or trade areas of centers. The fields are very extensive in this low-density region. (Reprinted by permission of *Economic Geography*, from Richard Preston, "The Structure of Central Place Systems," Vol. 47, 1971.)

Geographically important effects of tourist travel include the transfer of income (which may constitute much of the income of scenic but otherwise economically limited areas) and the spread of information about other places and opportunities, leading, perhaps, to permanent movements and to the creation of a more unified culture.

Temporary Movements and Choice of Transport Mode

In advanced societies, the automobile is or is becoming the dominant mode of travel at the local level, but poorer and older people must use busses and streetcars. Besides being the most popular form of transportation, the private car can be cheaper than public transport so long as there is more than one person in the car, parking costs are negligible, and the trip accomplishes several purposes. Although a trip by a lone driver is apt to be more expensive than a bus trip, the driver may feel that the greater flexibility,

convenience, and speed of car travel offset the extra cost. Only where parking costs and traffic congestion are high, as in older, very densely populated cities, do public transit trips actually have a clear advantage. Society of course pays for the luxury of the private car through congestion, pollution, urban sprawl, the cost of providing superior roads and freeways, and the deterioration of transport services for those who do not own cars.

Theoretically, trains are more efficient than busses (which are in turn more efficient than cars) because costs are spread among many more passengers. The seeming inconsistency, then, of larger carriers having higher rates than smaller ones is explained by their high fixed costs for personnel and equipment, their relative inflexibility, and the severe problem of providing for peak loads and then dealing with slack capacity the rest of the time. However, where cars must compete on a profit-making basis with the other forms of transportation — taxis, in other words —

they are indeed the costliest.

For long-distance travel, the choice is between personal car, bus, railroad, and plane. Long-distance auto travel is preferred for business purposes when a variety of smaller places must be visited (by a traveling salesman, for instance) and for family recreational travel, because it is both the cheapest and the most flexible kind of transport. In Europe and Japan, because of higher population density, government ownership and subsidy of railroads, lower rates of car ownership, and high auto fuel taxes, the railroads continue to carry much interregional business and pleasure passenger traffic. Air travel is still used chiefly for between-city business trips, since the higher costs are usually covered by expense accounts. As incomes rise and air costs fall relative to other transport, however, a higher proportion of social and recreational trips will be by air. Generally, air travel is efficient for one person traveling alone and whenever time is especially valuable.

*Substitutes for Temporary
Movements: Communications.*

The major geographic role of communications — in the sense of nonpersonal meetings — has always been to maintain widespread organizations, such as large companies and entire nations, which would be impossible to control on a directly personal basis. A wide variety of communications media are available to expedite interaction. Complex decisions can be made and goods and money transferred by mail. The telegraph and later the telephone accelerated communication in a revolutionary way and permitted a much faster and more efficient response to distant problems. The mass media — newspapers and magazines, and particularly radio and television — have national and international connections and are efficiently molding a national, and to some extent an international, culture by disseminating the same information and ideas over a large and diverse territory. Generally, all these means of communication effectively save time and transport costs by substituting for movements of persons, communicating their decisions, demands, and feelings.

While communication is hardly free, it is so much cheaper than personal contact that distance is in effect overcome significantly, at least for many business and governmental transactions. Despite the capability of modern communication, however, it remains a rather imperfect substitute for face-to-face contact.

Thus, even though the money cost of mail remains constant within an economy, the amount of mail declines fairly sharply with distance, partly because the probability of knowing someone declines with distance and partly because mail is relatively slow, especially between smaller places.

Telephone communication is more expensive, and charges, if not real costs, do increase with distance — in the United States, rather sharply within a state and gradually across states. Hence, the frequency of telephone calls diminishes perhaps more steeply with distance than does mail. Again, however, the decreased likelihood of knowing someone far away is a more important reason for the attenuation than the rates charged.

TRANSIENT MOVEMENTS

Military requirements involve the redistribution of large numbers of people. In the United States, over the years, millions of men plus their many dependents are moved away from their original homes and many may prefer not to return home. Within the United States there is a strong military relocation to the West and South, where a majority of the bases are located. Very probably the effect of new information — the knowledge gained while military men were visiting the area — helps explain the postwar and continuous growth of California.

College students represent another large transient group within the United States; perhaps two million are away from home at any one time. Most students go to schools within their home state, although there is a large movement to the older, more prestigious institutions in the Northeast — a population movement opposite to the military transfers to the South and West. As in military movements, shifts to schools often lead to permanent moves, especially since the young and college-educated are at

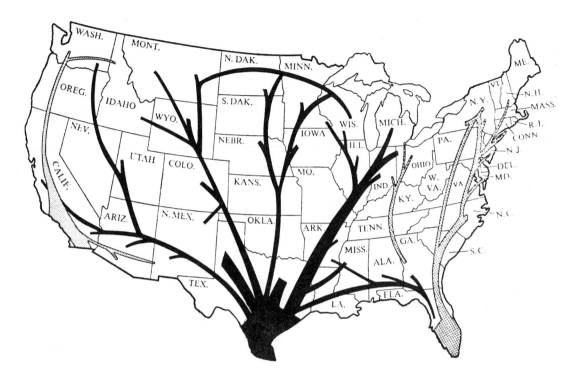

Figure 7.03 Major migrant worker movement in the United States. Migrants originate in Texas, California-Arizona, and Florida and work in these areas during the winter. In spring and summer, the migrants move northward, following planting and harvesting demands. (From the U.S. Department of Labor.)

any rate a most mobile group. However, college graduates do not so much remain in educational centers as become concentrated in the larger cities where white-collar jobs increasingly locate.

Some occupations involve much transiency — for example, airline flight personnel and long-distance rail and truck crews are subject to extensive movement. Another transient is the traveling salesman; his need to meet the maximum number of customers in the least amount of time and shortest distance has led to special models for finding the most efficient paths for such trips (in theory, not practice!).

Migrant, transient labor is common, especially in agriculture, since many crops have heavy demands for seasonal labor; many migrants move from crop to crop as the demand dictates (figure 7.03). Most migrant farm workers are unskilled and uneducated and have not been able to find permanent jobs. In the United States the number of migrants has been maintained by discrimination, prevention of union

organization, and both legal and illegal importation of temporary contract labor. Migrants represent a serious social problem not only because of their extremely low wages and severe poverty, but also because their transience prevents them from obtaining adequate education, health care, and political representation. Such semicontinuous migration is thus very costly and damaging to society, if not to the farmer; where migrant labor is not available, farmers have had to employ workers permanently or have become more fully mechanized. Efforts to organize migrant workers, various aid programs, and increased farm mechnization may reduce the severity of the problem, but the only permanent solution is to end the practice altogether.

In developing countries, however, migrant labor, describing the millions who "circulate" between their home villages and commercial and industrial opportunities in cities, mines, and plantations, represents a probably useful means of aiding the transi-

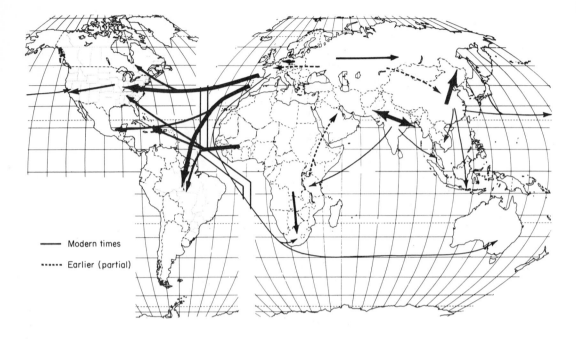

Figure 7.04 World population movements. In recent centuries, colonial and slave movements (from Europe and Africa to the Americas) have been dominant, but, recently, political moves have been sizable (from India and Germany). Flows are consolidated for simplicity; part of Europe's migration, for instance, is shown migrating to all of South America.

tion from a subsistence and tribal to a commercial and urban society.

PERMANENT MOVEMENTS: POPULATION MIGRATION

The migration of people may be viewed as an efficient response to possible dissatisfactions with their present location and to possible opportunities at other locations. Population transfers also depend on the availability of transportation and communication (so that people may be aware of the opportunities at other locations).

Although world history is characterized by constant movements of people, it is apparent that people are less mobile than goods. Inertia is common: many people are willing to accept a lower income than is necessary for long periods or even indefinitely because they fear change, lack knowledge of other places, or consider other values to be of greater importance.

Importance of Migration

Despite these restraints, migration has

been immensely significant.

— *It accompanies and makes possible the spread of settlement and the colonization of new areas.*
— *Rural-to-urban flows make possible rapid industrialization and urbanization.*
— *Transfers of slaves and contract labor for agriculture and mining have brought about new mixtures of people, and have thus had great social and economic impact.*
— *Migration provides the manpower needed to develop new resources.*
— *Migration constitutes a mechanism for alleviating, or at least responding to, inequities in national and regional development.*
— *Migration is the principal mechanism for spreading technology, language, customs, and most other social behavior.*

Migration, then, is one of the primary mechanisms used to achieve or maintain equilibrium in society. Since land is immobile, people must move to the new areas that society evaluates as having greater productivity and more opportunity. To the extent that people respond to the possibility of having higher income or social status, migration can aid in the process of **regional convergence** — lessening the inequalities in income among regions. However, migration will not necessarily lead to such convergence if, for example, the out-migration from the poorer area consists mainly of the most talented groups. Migration may also aggravate the difference in the total level of activity by reducing population in the regions of out-migration.

World Population Movements

In the pursuit of better opportunities, man has continually migrated (figure 7.04) — at times impelled by overpopulation at home, at times attracted by the hope of large rewards, and at still other times forced to move by invasion or defeat. Migrations have been both centrifugal and centripetal — men have sometimes aggressively pushed into new, unsettled areas and have sometimes flowed into already crowded and successful areas.

Population movements typically occur in response to two kinds of motivation — economic and social. In a subsistence village economy, social movements, such as intervillage and intertribal searches for wives and visits to relatives, are dominant. A food crisis may generate long-distance movements of a group for reasons of economic necessity, frequently involving war and the risk of annihilation. When commercial and industrial activities are introduced, a powerful economic motivation — the opportunity for a money income — may take hold.

In developing and advanced economies, the largest volume of movements beyond the local level have been due to expected improvements in income, security, and opportunity. An increasing proportion of movements are being made because of expected improvements in noneconomic conditions, for example, environmental satisfaction. Spatially, such moves are of several kinds: (1) outward moves toward the frontier to help develop agricultural, mineral, or forest resources; (2) moves toward the center, both at the local rural-to-

urban level and toward core urban-industrial areas of the economy; (3) outward moves from the core to the periphery of urban areas themselves; and (4) moves between rural areas, between urban areas, or between "equivalent" metropolitan areas.

Migration for Economic Reasons

Rural-to-Urban Migration.   In this century economic growth has occurred predominantly in towns and cities and has led to the greatest population movements of human history. In most of the world, rural populations were excessive, and poverty severe. The possibility of finding a job in the city, no matter how lowly the job and no matter how filthy and miserable the city slum, has led to the vast rural-to-urban flow that has probably transferred at least 400 million persons to urban areas in this century alone (see figures 7.05 and 7.06). This process of concentration, despite an immense social cost, generally represents an efficient response to existing needs and opportunities and has made possible vast increases in total wealth.

Not all rural-to-urban movements are in response to known opportunities or guaranteed jobs. For instance, one can observe cases where urban growth far exceeds urban opportunities. Since care of the urban jobless is much more costly than that of the rural jobless — who are typically ignored — over-urbanization has become a direct cost, hindering general economic development in many less developed countries.

Intermetropolitan Migration.   During urbanization, migration from rural areas and small towns to cities is dominant, but after a high level of urbanization is reached, migration between urban places becomes greater. Large flows occur between similarly prosperous metropolitan areas, some of these flows consisting of students, military personnel, the young, or the retired heading for amenity areas with better climates or more exciting cities. Some are movements of personnel transferred within companies at the managerial level; some are due to fluctuations in employment in particular industries; and some may be due to the feeling that "the grass is greener on the

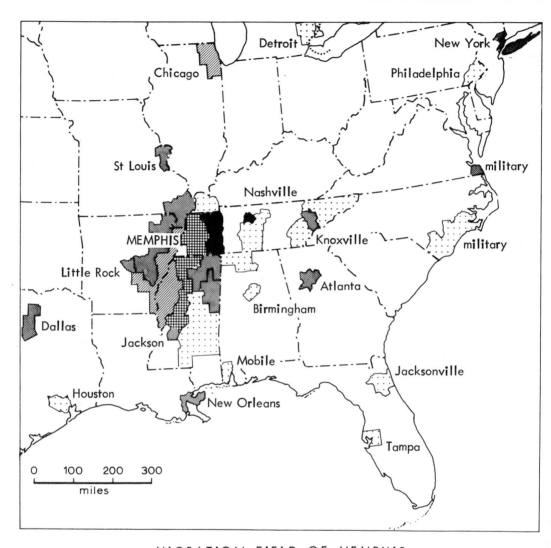

MIGRATION FIELD OF MEMPHIS

Rural – Urban and Urban – Urban Migration
percent of total in-migration

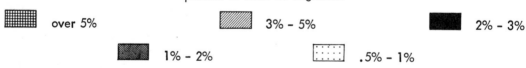

over 5%   3% – 5%   2% – 3%

1% – 2%   .5% – 1%

Figure 7.05   The migration field of Memphis. This migration pattern reveals a dual character: high proportions of incoming migrants (over 3 percent) come from surrounding nonmetropolitan areas, a continuing rural-urban flow within a region; but fair proportions (.5 to 3 percent) also originate in many of the larger metropolitan areas of the South and Northeast. Some of these urban-urban flows are military; many are simply due to the interaction of large places; and some represent fair numbers of native Memphis-area people returning (as from New York and Philadelphia).

other side" or to the desire to get away from home. In any event, the movers believe they will increase their opportunities or satisfac-tion by shifting, and since most of these movements are to areas that are fairly near-by, the cost of movement is low.

Nonurban Opportunities. Not all economic opportunities are urban; millions have migrated from crowded, poverty-stricken rural regions to regions with greater agricultural opportunities. The most dramatic shift was the agricultural settlement of Canada and the United States by Europeans during the eighteenth and nineteenth centuries, when some 50 million persons — who otherwise might never have left their native villages — traveled 5,000 miles to a new and uncertain life in the Americas. Given that the farmer is normally conservative, this movement attests to the extreme gap between local opportunities in Europe and what America was at least perceived as possessing. Perhaps the possibility of owning a large tract of land was a powerful attraction.

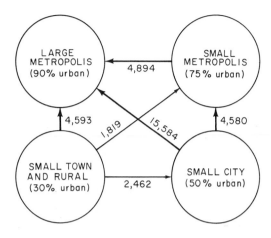

Figure 7.06 Net migration flows from less urban to more urban areas. Counties that are less urbanized have net migration losses — more people migrate from than to them. Thus, there is a net shift in population toward more urban and metropolitan areas. The large metropolis includes Seattle; the small metropolis, Spokane and Tacoma. (Washington state, 1955-1960.)

Migration for Social or Political Reasons

Major population movements have also resulted from political and social persecution. In this century, European and other wars have led to vast redistributions of peoples, such as the expulsion of Germans from eastern Europe, the transfer of Moslems and Hindus within the subcontinent of India, and the settlement of Israel by Jewish migrants from Europe, Africa, and Asia.

Within the United States there has been a vast movement of blacks from the more discriminatory South to the less discriminatory North and West — for both economic and social reasons. Since the First World War, when industrial opportunities in the North were first opened to blacks, several million have left the South. Most moved directly from their extreme poverty as sharecroppers to the large, industrial cities; as unskilled workers, they thus were employed at very low levels. Even the slum dweller segregated in a **ghetto,** however, preferred it to the rural poverty and more pervasive discrimination of the South — partly because he hoped for better education and employment opportunities for his children.

The original importation of slaves, mainly to the Caribbean, Brazil, and the United States, was clearly one of the most colossal forced migrations in human history. Probably some 20 million persons were brought to the New World from 1550 to 1850, and a substantial portion of these evidently died in transit.

Today, movements for retirement represent an increasing proportion of migrations. Many retired families, having more income and greater freedom than in the past, seek urban or suburban locations in zones of warmer climate — Florida, Arizona, and California in the United States, for instance.

The Mechanism of Migration

Migration of people is like trade in the sense that if the potential increase in income or satisfaction — the value differential — is perceived as greater than the economic and social cost of moving, the migration is possible. Or, to state this concept in geographic terms, the interaction between places will depend on their degree of complementarity (value differential) and transferability (cost versus ability to move). In general, the flow of migrants between two places can be considered a function of the perceived qualities of the source and the destination and of the relative location of the places.

When rural opportunities are few, people are more likely to migrate to cities. The

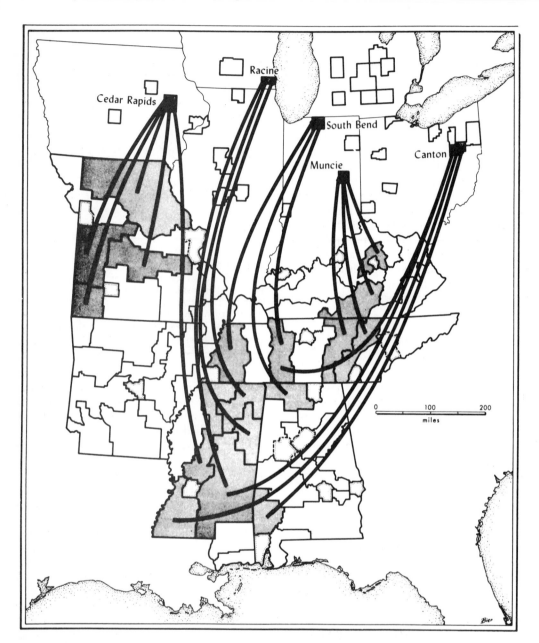

Figure 7.07 Persistence and selectivity in migration streams. This map shows the major sources of migrants to selected cities in the Great Lakes region for the 1955-1960 period. Rather than a diffuse or random pattern of origins, a highly selective pattern is apparent, reflecting mainly the role of friends and relations in encouraging migration along traditional paths for long periods. (Reprinted permission of the Association of American Geographers, from Curtis Roseman, "Channelization of Migration Flows from the Rural South," *Proceedings*, Vol. 3, 1971.)

perceived attractiveness of a city, in turn, depends chiefly on its volume of economic activities, its rate of growth, its income relative to other areas and cities, and the public's image of these factors. The

probability that these opportunities will be acted upon depends on people's awareness of them, as well as on the direct cost of movement, the presence of closer opportunities, and — often — the social cost of a shift in cultural environment. People tend to move away from areas where income is low and unemployment is high or where the prospects of employment for the young are poor.

The public's perception of opportunities is not strictly accurate and is probably biased toward amenity areas and areas of recent growth. The cost of distance *per se* may not be so strong a deterrent to movement as the fact that knowledge of available opportunities declines with distance from them. In order to maintain a stable social and physical environment for their families, many people may prefer to accept nearby but less valuable opportunities.

The Role of Information. Even taking into account these "push-and-pull" factors — dissatisfactions that push migrants out, perceived advantages that pull them in — and the **intervening opportunities** and costs, migration is strongly concentrated on certain favored routes. Such concentration occurs because information available to an individual or group about presumably equivalent places varies greatly. The migration process has an important feedback mechanism; people who have moved write back about opportunities to family and friends still living in their former community. Thus migrants from particular communities and even particular counties tend to follow certain paths (figure 7.07). This mechanism is perhaps even more important in determining the destination of immigrants from overseas.

Although between any pair of places the great majority of migrants travel to the larger or richer place, a reverse flow also exists. This may be economically rational for some population subgroups; for individuals who cannot adjust to urban life, the social gains obtained by returning home compensate for the economic loss.

Effect of Migration on Population

Migration plays a basic role in redistributing population from weak and declining areas to strong and growing ones. Net migration has tended to flow:

"Up the urban ladder" — *from rural*

areas and small places to large cities.

- *From regions of economic stagnation to regions of greater growth.*
- *From discriminatory areas to those of lesser discrimination.*
- *From deprived or rugged areas to areas having more amenities, such as from inner cities to suburbs and from harsher climates to more pleasant ones.*

Population gowth reflects these flows, of course, but natural increase and loss — the other component of population change — can modify the effects of migration (figure 7.08).

In the fastest growing areas of the United States — the amenity regions of Florida, Arizona, Nevada, and parts of California — population increase is due especially to migration. For surburban areas and some rapidly expanding industrial and service cities, both components of growth are large and about equally important. Places growing just a little faster than the national average are apt to have only a very small net in-migration rate.

There are very large areas (see figure 7.08) that have small to average population gains only because a large natural increase offsets net out-migration. In these areas the economy is expanding too slowly to utilize even the region's own natural gain. Several of the older metropolises belong in this category; their fairly large absolute population gains mask their slow rate of growth. Many larger areas consisting of mixed agriculture and small towns and cities also follow this pattern. Here, the large out-migration from the rural areas is concealed by their equally large natural increase or by slight gains from migration to the small cities. However, in the rural areas of the South and Midwest and in isolated hilly areas everywhere, the out-migration is so great — including perhaps one-third of the population in one decade — that natural increase cannot make up the difference. In both this case of absolute population loss and in the preceding case of small population gains due to natural increase, much of the out-migration is of the younger, most productive age groups; thus, prospects of economic growth are even further reduced.

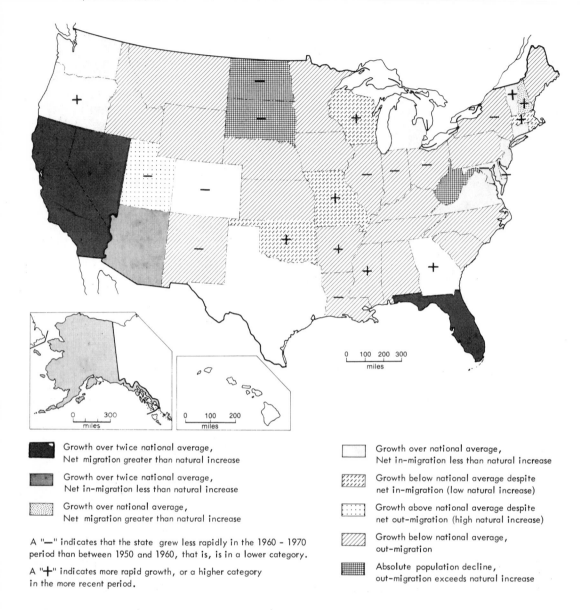

Growth over twice national average,
Net migration greater than natural increase

Growth over twice national average,
Net in-migration less than natural increase

Growth over national average,
Net migration greater than natural increase

A "—" indicates that the state grew less rapidly in the 1960 - 1970
period than between 1950 and 1960, that is, is in a lower category.

A "+" indicates more rapid growth, or a higher category
in the more recent period.

Growth over national average,
Net in-migration less than natural increase

Growth below national average despite
net in-migration (low natural increase)

Growth above national average despite
net out-migration (high natural increase)

Growth below national average,
out-migration

Absolute population decline,
out-migration exceeds natural increase

Figure 7.08   Components of population change: natural increase and migration, 1960-1970. This map reveals the significant redistribution of population within even a ten-year period, and the great variability in experience within one country. The fairly rapid growth in New England, the Ozark region and Mississippi, and Oregon, represents a major change from the previous decade, while the relatively slow growth of the industrial lower Great Lakes is similarly a reversal.

Conclusion

The pure theories of location discussed in earlier chapters do not acknowledge the existence of migration; yet it is one of the most important spatial phenomena of human societies, drastically altering the patterns of location. Migration occurs because of

changes in population, in economic opportunities, and in social and political conditions. A move is made because the individual or group perceives that his quality of life cannot be maintained or improved by any form of adjustment at his present location. Often migration is a response to already changed economic and social conditions, but at other times, the act of migration itself forces these conditions to change.

EFFECTS OF HUMAN MOVEMENTS ON TRANSPORT SYSTEMS

While transport routes are constructed mainly to facilitate the movement of goods, they are also constructed to facilitate the movement of persons. Without doubt, many roads have been built and maintained to permit easier control, both cultural and military, over a territory. In the United States the popularity of the car adds greatly to the demand for more and better roads, and the density and quality of the road network is far higher than is necessary for movements of goods.

Some transport systems have specifically developed in response to the need to move people. The demand for passenger service was great, for instance, during the railroad era. Within and between cities, elaborate streetcar systems laced major arterials, and commuter railroads permitted suburbs and satellite cities to develop in rays about large cities. As the private car met more of the demand and permitted residences to be more widespread, however, the rail and streetcar system, which required high-density traffic, became unprofitable.

The demand for fast movement has contributed to the rapid growth of air travel and the establishment of new routes; many people are willing to pay more for the time savings and greater convenience. Since air routes may be rather direct and, unlike land routes, can ignore intervening places, the route structure fairly closely reflects the demand for connections between any two places.

MODELS OF HUMAN MOVEMENTS

Trips of people, migration, mail, and telephone calls are all interactions between locations of people and locations of other people, businesses, and recreation. The economic cost of such movements is not always the dominant influence, and the number of movements of people is many times greater than those of goods. Thus, whereas goods will tend to be shipped over a restricted number of cheaper paths in order to minimize costs, individuals can merely reduce the frequency of contacts on more expensive paths in order to minimize the cost of the interactions believed necessary (figure 7.09). The psychological benefits of the more expensive routes may outweigh the economic savings of shorter paths. For instance, a shopper can buy his groceries in the closest store only, but the satisfaction he gains from visiting several stores may more than offset the increased distance or time. As another example, all the prospective migrants from some city could travel to the nearest place that offers opportunities, but in fact individual migrants will interpret differently the opportunities existing in a number of places and the cost of reaching them; thus some will be willing to travel farther than others. For these reasons, the models used to find optimal transport patterns, based on minimizing costs, are inadequate for most movements of people.

Most models of human movements, therefore, have been descriptive rather than prescriptive (attempting to optimize movement), in recognition of people's more diffuse movement patterns. In fact, most are modifications of the "law of migration" proposed by E.G. Ravenstein in 1888. Later called the **gravity model**, this inverse relation between frequency and distance has been found in almost countless studies to describe fairly well a wide variety of flows: migrations, vacation trips, shopping trips, mail flows, telephone calls, journeys to work (see figure 7.10 as an example).

The Gravity Model and Related Models of Interaction

The gravity model is based on a theory that contains two principal elements. First, the maximum or ideal number of contacts to or from a group is proportional to the number of people in the group; and the number of contacts between any two groups is at maximum proportional to the product of their sizes. For example, at the extreme, every person in one town could interact with every person in another town. Second, the proportion of the maximum possible

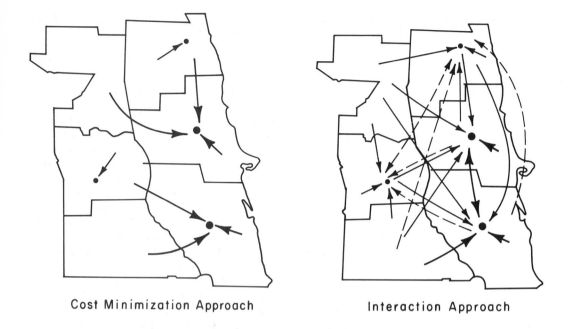

Cost Minimization Approach   Interaction Approach

Figure 7.09 Cost minimization and interaction: two approaches to movements of people. This figure shows movements to hospitals in one part of Chicago. The cost, or distance, minimization approach, useful for goods, is not very appropriate for movements of people because far too few flows are permitted; that is, patients must go to the closest available opportunity. The interaction approach is far more realistic. Patients are as likely to go to a larger, more distant hospital as to a smaller, much closer one. Dots represent hospitals (larger dots are larger hospitals), and lines are flows of people.

contacts actually realized is diminished by some function of the distance between the locations, or an appropriate substitute for that distance. The decay in the number of contacts is definitely not linear as distance increases, but rather exponential or hyperbolic (figure 7.10). Such a form for the decline of contacts with distance may theoretically exist because people perceive distance and the cost of overcoming that distance exponentially (that is, an opportunity 4 miles away is about twice as unattractive as one 2 miles away); greater distances may be seen as longer or shorter, and the cost of overcoming them greater or less than they actually are. Even when the cost of overcoming the distance is significant, the probability that a person knows about an opportunity also decays exponentially with distance. Such a decay in knowledge implies that an individual has an **information field** (pattern of contact) within which the direction and length of trips are not wholly random, but biased toward favored routes and destinations. This occurs because

of the limited number of friends and relatives an individual can have and the limited amount of time he can devote to trips.

Many people perceive the separation of places not as distance but as intervening opportunities. It is logical to argue that, where the direct cost of distance is not very great, the presence of closer opportunities will reduce the perceived advantage of more distant ones somewhat proportionally to the size of the closer opportunities; the more nearby opportunities there are, the less advantageous the farther ones will appear. Intervening opportunities are obviously a restraint to interaction at greater distances, but what constitutes intervening opportunities for the various kinds of interaction has not been very well developed; for the case of economic migration, intervening opportunities may be closer places of equal or larger size and income.

The theory of interaction is not an optimizing model, and distances are not minimized. The model, however, conforms to observed behavior — that is, it is behaviorally rational. Also, since the cost of separation does diminish the likelihood of contact, distance does tend to be minimized, and its predictions are optimal in the sense that the model maximizes the satisfaction of a population. Such satisfaction, however, requires the occasional use of poorer opportunities (that is, some people will perceive an objectively poorer choice, as of a hospital, to be preferable to one that is actually better).

Demands for interaction are closely related to individual preferences for space. Each person evaluates the surrounding world according to its usefulness in satisfying his needs and desires, and ranks his preferences for destinations from among those places that he may visit or contact. For example, a family can choose among a variety of recreation sites around a city. Their satisfaction is not maximized by always going to the closest site, but, instead, satisfaction from a variety of trips to several places will more than offset the added cost of transport. For the individual family, an interaction model can give the probabilities of their going to the various sites; for the mass of people in the city, the model can give the proportions of trips made to each site.

The effect of differential feedback — information about places, usually supplied by friends and relatives — can be included as another element in the model: feedback increases the frequency of travel on some already-used paths and decreases it on others. Barriers to interaction, both physical and cultural, can rather easily be treated in this model.

Interaction models are particularly useful in predicting the demand for or use of new recreation facilities, stores, or shopping centers, and in evaluating the need for new hospitals or other service facilities.

Interaction models do a fair job of predicting the total movement to centers and the distribution of lengths of trips, but since many trips are multi-purpose, and multicentered (to more than one center), these models fail to generate typical shopping patterns. An interaction model can be used to assess the probability of a trip to various centers, but a separate analysis is needed to give the probability of extending the trip for more purposes and to more centers.

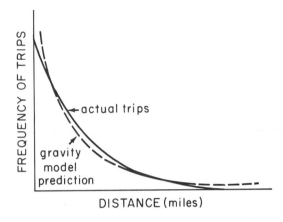

Figure 7.10 Trips to hospitals and distance. The decline in frequency of trips with increasing distance from Chicago general hospitals is well predicted by the gravity model.

A variant of the gravity model, the potential model, is used to sum the expected level of interaction between one place and all others (as in a country) (figure 7.11). This constitutes a useful measure of potential interaction, or accessibility to the population, and is widely used in studies of retail marketing, industrial location, trade, and communication. The pattern in Fig. 7.11 reveals the dominance of megalopolis and the Chicago-New York axis in the United States, and can usefully be viewed in combination with such figures as 5.20, 6.11, and 6.12.

THE SPREAD OF IDEAS AND INNOVATIONS: SPATIAL DIFFUSION

A third class of movements, somewhat different from the flows of goods and people already discussed, includes the gradual spread of ideas, concepts, innovations, rumors, customs, and even settlement itself through a population and across territory. These movements are frequently transmitted through persons traveling for social, business, educational, or military purposes; the movements may also be spread by newspaper, magazine, book, radio, or television. These exemplify the process of **spatial diffusion,** or the spread of a phenomenon in space and time from

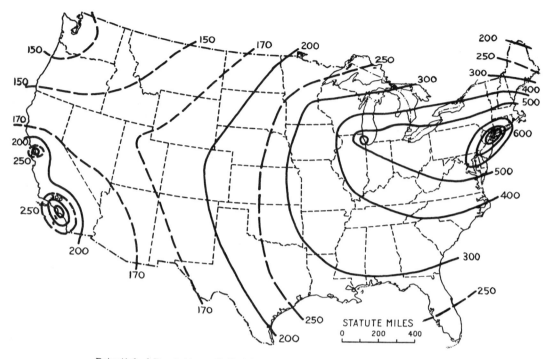

Potential of Population - United States, 1960 (thousands, persons per mile)

Figure 7.11   Population potential, 1960. Population potential is a measure of accessibility to the total population. The total potential at any one point is found by summing the potential interaction (defined as the population of any other place or area divided by the distance to that point) between the given point and all other points. This variant of the gravity model has been found valuable in helping to understand such phenomena as industrial location and airline and highway flows (see figure 6.12). In the figure, "300" can be interpreted as the line along which, according to this mathematical construct, there is a potential volume of 300,000 interactions (contacts, etc.) per year between the population in a typical square mile there and all the rest of the population of the country. The population potential map can also be seen as a highly generalized or simplified description of the relative distribution of population.

limited origins. Most of these phenomena can move through a population and area without altering the landscape. Many others (for example, new house styles) can alter the appearance of the landscape without changing the distribution of people. Such movements are not predicted by theories of location, but neither do they conflict with them.

The spread of a population and its villages, towns, cities, and transport systems — that is, settlement itself — can be viewed as a particularly large and slow process of spatial diffusion from limited origins. In fact, the present landscape can be understood only through the operation of theories of location within a constantly changing distribution of people and activities (see chapter 9, pp. 209).

The spread of innovation — technical change in processing or in ways of doing things — is a phenomenon that is likely to have the greatest effect on the landscape. Since in most countries agriculture is carried out in many small units, the spread of any improvement — whether of tools, seed and animal quality, methods of cultivation, or marketing possibilities — can significantly increase farm income and national output. Knowledge of industrial innovations spreads more quickly, since the number of production units is relatively small, but their application is restricted by the cost of new capital goods, licenses, and royalties. Hence, the spatial effects of innovation are outweighed by economic and technical factors.

Innovations that are used primarily for agriculture or that are basic to economic development and settlement, such as the growth of a rail network, are diffused fairly continuously or "contagiously" over space (figures 7.12 and 7.13). Other examples of contagious diffusion include the spread of logging operations from more to less accessible areas (see figure 3.14, p. 62), the growth of the city into its rural surroundings (where the innovation is urban use: see figures 8.05, 8.13, and 10.02), and the growth of a ghetto (see figure 8.08). Innovations that may be adopted by the entire population, however, are diffused through society's centers of control, the cities. Thus, clubs and organizations, clothing styles, television, and fads seem to spread down the hierarchy of places, from the largest metropolises to their satellite centers and then gradually to surrounding small towns and rural areas. In figure 7.13, for example, the diffusion of television stations rather clearly moved down the urban hierarchy, although there is a contagious or local element within regions (as around New York and Los Angeles), in that some smaller places near early innovators received stations earlier than they would have according to purely hierarchical diffusion. Some innovations, particularly the marketing of new products, may begin in smaller metropolises and less central regions (for example, motel and restaurant chain franchises), and their subsequent diffusion, like that of the railway, is both contagious within regions and hierarchical, with branches appearing early in larger but distant cities.

The most effective means of spreading ideas and innovations are through interpersonal relations. Four major factors control the efficacy of this movement. First, people, even in the same area, vary in their psychological and economic ability to accept change; often, but not always, the more educated and more prosperous will accept change before the less educated or less prosperous. Second, once having accepted change, people vary in their willingness to tell others about it. Third, all persons have a network of contacts (their information field), that is highly restricted spatially. And fourth, physical, cultural, political, and linguistic barriers will affect the relative success of spread in certain directions or environments.

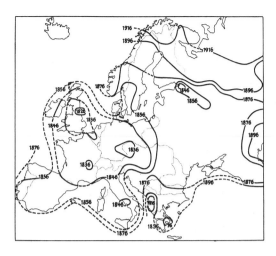

Figure 7.12 Areas within which railways had been built by specified dates, Europe. Note the general spread from the England-Belgium core and the lesser spread from other metropolitan capitals — Rome, St. Petersburg, and Prague. (Reprinted by permission of the Department of Geography, University of Lund, Sweden, from S. Godlund, "Ein innovations Verlauf in Europa," *Lund Studies in Geography*, Series B, 6, 1952.)

The concept of innovation diffusion as a wave arising from an origin and moving outward is a good analogy, where the changing form of the the wave describes the pattern of acceptance at any distance and time from the origin of the innovation (figure 7.14). The crest of the wave — the area of most active acceptance — gradually moves outward from the origin as the population becomes saturated near the origin and as the new accepters of the innovation tell others beyond themselves. Hence, the final level of acceptance often declines slowly with distance. Over time, the cumulative acceptance of the change at any point in space will follow an s-type curve (since the *rate* of acceptance will be very low when the innovation is still far off, will be highest as the innovation reaches an area, and will then fall off because most people who will accept the change have already done so).

The actual movement of the innovation wave is accomplished as the pioneers who first accept the change tell others in their field of personal and business relationships. Thus, nearby acquaintances are the ones most likely to be told about the change and to adopt it (figure 7.15). In turn, these

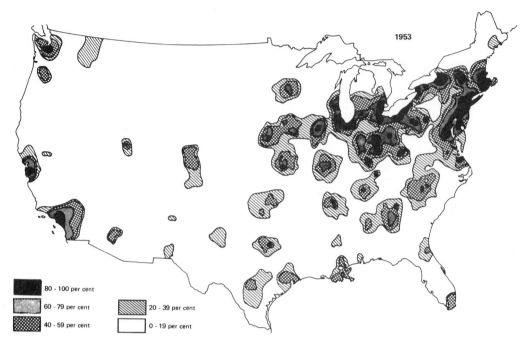

■ 80 - 100 per cent	
▦ 60 - 79 per cent	▨ 20 - 39 per cent
▩ 40 - 59 per cent	□ 0 - 19 per cent

Market penetration: percentage of households having television receivers. Source: A. C. Nielsen, 1953.

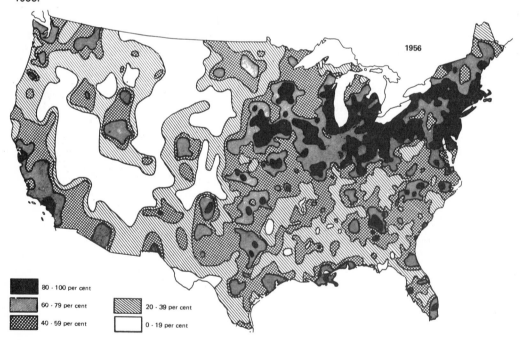

■ 80 - 100 per cent	
▦ 60 - 79 per cent	▨ 20 - 39 per cent
▩ 40 - 59 per cent	□ 0 - 19 per cent

Market penetration: percentage of households having television receivers. Source: A. C. Nielsen, 1956.

Figure 7.13 Diffusion of television, United States, 1953-1962. The market penetration of television in the United States mainly illustrates hierarchical diffusion: that is, it was established first in the largest metropolises and then spread directly to other metropolises, which could meet the initially high threshold. Contagious diffusion is also present; that is, the television market fairly quickly spread to

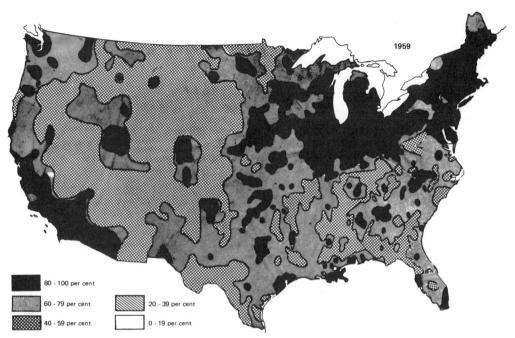

Market penetration: percentage of households having television receivers. Source: A. C. Nielsen, 1959.

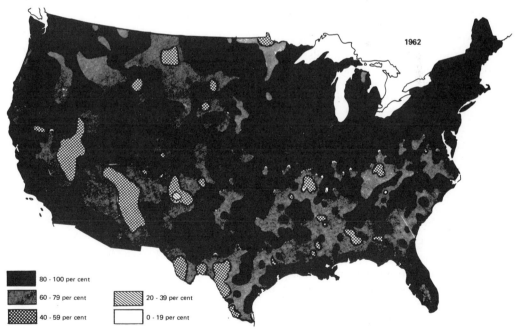

Market penetration: percentage of households having television receivers. Source: A. C. Nielsen, 1962.

smaller centers in the regions of the larger early receivers. (Reprinted by permission of the Macmillan Company, from N. Hansen, editor, *Growth Centers and Regional Economic Development*, Free Press, 1971, from B.J.L. Berry, "Hierarchical Diffusion: The Basis of Developmental Filtering and Spread in a System of Growth Centers.")

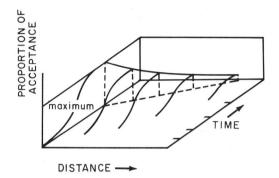

PROPORTION OF ACCEPTANCE

maximum

TIME

DISTANCE ⟶

Figure 7.14 The proportion of people typically accepting an innovation with distance from the origin and time. At any given distance, note how acceptance begins slowly, then speeds up, and later slows again. At greater distances, acceptance begins later and never becomes as complete.

acceptors tell other people, perhaps people beyond the range of the pioneers' contacts. The rate of spread will depend on the persistence in telling about the innovation, on the resistance to change, and on the spatial extent of an individual's **contact field.**

Spatial diffusion has obviously been extremely significant throughout history in the spread of population, language, domestication of plants and animals, and all kinds of technical and cultural practices and beliefs. As man pursues the goal of maximizing interaction at minimum effort, he contributes to the process of spatial diffusion through his sociability, his aggressiveness, and his constant desire for more space and greater security.

Conclusion: Movements of People

As societies become more affluent, they demand higher levels of services. Thus, a greater proportion of movements are of people rather than of goods, and the quality of the transport system is often determined by people's preferences for routes.

The flows of people and ideas reflect, enliven, and at times alter the ideal structure of location. The pattern of flows reflects the complementary needs of locations and people to interact, and the level of flows reflects the intensity of these needs,

REFERENCES

Population Distribution

Aangenbrug, R.T. and F.C. Caspall, "Regionalization of Population Densities in Kansas," *Tijdschrift voor Economische en Sociale Geografie* 61 (1970): 85-90.

Anderson, T.R., "Potential models and the Spatial Distribution of Population," *Papers and Proceedings of the Regional Science Association* 2 (1956): 175-182.

Bogue, D.J., "The Geography of Recent Population Trends in the United States," *Annals of the Association of American Geographers* 44 (1954): 124-134.

Chapman, G.P., "The Application of Information Theory to the Analysis of Population Distributions in Space," *Economic Geography* 46 (1970): 317-331.

Gibbs, J., "Evolution of Population Concentration," *Economic Geography* 39 (1963): 119-129.

Greer, Deon C., "An Assimilation Model of Displaced Population: Finland, an Example," *Proceedings of the Association of American Geographers* 3 (1971): 61-66.

Gregor, H., "Spatial Disharmonies in California Population Growth," *Geographical Review* 53 (1963): 100-122.

Hart, J. F., "The Changing Distribution of the American Negro," *Annals of the Association of American Geographers* 50 (1960): 242-265.

Katzman, M., "Ethnic Geography and Regional Economies," *Economic Geography* 45 (1969): 45-52.

Keyfitz, N., "On the Interaction of Populations," *Demography* 2 (1965): 276-288.

Lee, E.S. et al., *Population Redistribution and Economic Growth, 1870-1950,"* Philadelphia: American Philosophical Society, 1957.

Loeffler, M.J., "The Population Syndromes on the Colorado Piedmont," *Annals of the Association of American Geographers* 55 (1965): 26-66.

Lowenthal, D. and L. Comitas, "Emigration and Depopulation: Some Neglected Aspects of Population Geography," *Geographical Review* 52 (1962): 195-210.

Lowry, Mark, II, "Population and Race in Mississippi, 1940-1960," *Annals of the Association of American Geographers* 61 (1971): 576-588.

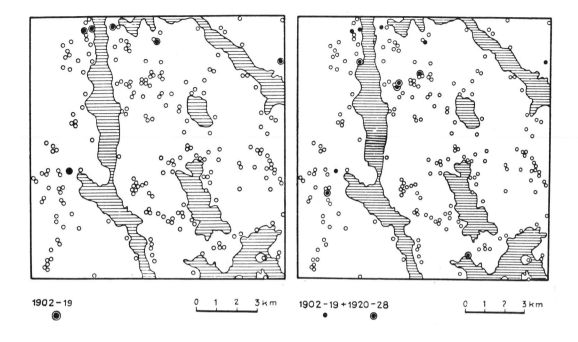

1902 – 19

0 1 2 3 km

1902 – 19 + 1920 – 28

0 1 ? 3 km

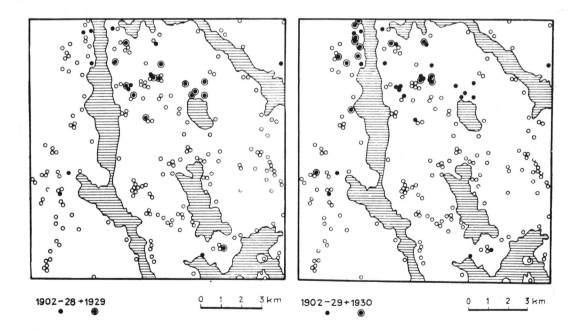

1902 – 28 + 1929

0 1 2 3 km

1902 – 29 + 1930

0 1 2 3 km

Figure 7.15   Importance of information for the spread of innovation. These figures trace the spread of cattle tuberculosis controls in a small area of Sweden. Open circles are potential farm accepters, dots in circles are new adopters, and solid dots are old adopters. Note that the new adopters are in clusters near former adopters, illustrating the importance of information obtained from nearby friends and acquaintances. Migration is also greatly influenced by such an information spread. (Reprinted by permission, from T. Hägerstrand, "On Monte Carlo Simulation of Diffusion," in W. Garrison and D. Marble, eds., *Quantitative Geography*, Studies in Geography, No. 17, 1967, Northwestern University Press.)

Murray, M.A., "Geography of Death in the U.S. and the U.K.," *Annals of the Association of American Geographers* 57 (1967): 301-314.

Northam, R., "Declining Urban Centers in the United States, 1940-1960," *Annals of the Association of American Geographers* 53 (1963): 50-59.

Rogers, A., *Matrix Analysis of Interregional Population Growth and Distribution*, Berkeley: University of California Press, 1968.

Schwartzberg, J.E., "The Distribution of Selected Castes in the North Indian Plain," *Geographical Review* 55 (1965): 477-495.

Stewart, J.Q. and W. Warntz, "Physics of Population Distribution," *Journal of Regional Science* 1 (1958): 99-123.

Webb, J.W., "Natural and Migrational Components of Population Change in England and Wales, 1921-1931," *Economic Geography* 39 (1963): 130-148.

Zelinsky, W., *A Prologue to Population Geography*. Englewood Cliffs, N.J.: Prentice-Hall, 1966.

Zelinsky, W., "An Approach to the Religious Geography of the United States: Patterns of Church Membership, 1952," *Annals of the Association of American Geographers* 51 (1961): 139-193.

Zelinsky, Wilbur, Leszek A. Kosinski and R. Mansell Prothero, *Geography and a Crowding World*, New York: Oxford University Press, 1970.

Temporary Person Movements

Abler, Ronald F., "Distance, Intercommunication and Geography," *Proceedings of the Association of American Geographers* 3 (1971); 1-4.

Ajo, R., "An Approach to Demographical Systems Analysis," *Economic Geography* 38 (1962): 359-371.

Boyce, D.E., "The Effect of Direction and Length of Person Trips on Urban Travel Patterns," *Journal of Regional Science* 6 (1965): 65-80.

Bucklin, Louis P., "Retail Gravity Models and Consumer Choice: A Theoretical and Empirical Critique," *Economic Geography* 47 (1971): 489-498.

Carrothers, G.A.P., "An Historical Review of the Gravity and Potential Concepts of Human Interaction," *Journal of the American Institute of Planners* 22 (1956): 94-102

Chisholm, M.D., "The Geography of Commuting," *Annals of the Association of American Geographers* 50 (1960): 187-8, 491-2.

Claeson, C.F., "Distance and Human Interaction," *Geografiska Annaler* 50B (1968): 143-169.

Dickinson, R.E., "The Geography of Commuting: Netherlands and Belgium," *Geographical Review* 47 (1957): 521-538.

Dodd, S. C., "The Interactance Hypothesis," *American Sociological Review* 15 (1950): 245-256.

Ellis, J.B. and C.S. Van Doren, "A Comparative Evaluation of Gravity and Systems Theory Models for Statewide Recreational Traffic Flows," *Journal of Regional Science* 6 (1965): 57-70.

Golant, Stephen M., "Adjustment Process in a System: A Behavioral Model of Human Movement," *Geographical Analysis* 3 (1971): 203-220.

Hart, J.F. and B.H. Luebke, "Migration from a Southern Appalachian Community," *Land Economics* 34 (1958): 44-53.

Horton, F.E. and R.I. Witticks, "Spatial Model for Examining the Journey to Work," *Professional Geographer* 21 (1969): 223-226.

Huff, D.L. and G.F. Jenks, "Graphic Interpretation of the Friction of Distance in Gravity Models," *Annals of the Association of American Geographers* 58 (1968): 814-824.

Johnsson, B., "Utilizing Telegrams for Describing Contact Patterns and Spatial Interaction," *Geografiska Annaler* 50B (1968): 38-51.

Jordan, T.G., "Population Origins in Texas, 1850," *Geographical Review* 59 (1969): 83-103.

Long, Wesley H. and Richard B. Uris, "Distance, Intervening Opportunities, City Hierarchy and Air Travel," *Annals of Regional Science* 5, No. 1 (1971): 152-161.

Lukermann, F. and P. Porter, "Gravity and Potential Models in Economic Geography," *Annals of the Association of American Geographers* 50 (1960): 493-504.

Moore, Eric G., "Some Spatial Properties of Urban Contact Fields," *Geographical Analysis* 2 (1970): 376-386.

Morrill, Richard L. and Ronald Schultz, "The Transportation Problem and Patient Travel to Physicians and Hospitals," *Annals of Regional Science* 5, No. 1 (1971): 11-24.

Olsson, G., "Distance and Human Interaction," *Geografiska Annaler* 47B (1965): 3-43.

Olsson, Gunnar, "Explanation, Prediction and Meaning Variance: An Assessment of Distance Interaction Models," *Economic Geography* 46 (1970): 223-233.

Ragatz, Richard Lee, "Vacation Homes in the Northeastern United States: Seasonality in Population Distribution," *Annals of the Association of American Geographers* 60 (1970): 447-455.

Taaffe, E.J., "The Urban Hierarchy: An Airline Passenger Definition," *Economic Geography* 38 (1962): 1-14.

Taaffe, E.J., B. Garner, and M.H. Yeates, *The Peripheral Journey to Work*, Evanston, Ill.: Northwestern University Press, 1963.

Wheeler, J., "WorkTrip Length and the Ghetto," *Land Economics* 44 (1968): 107-111.

Williams, Anthony V. and Wilbur Zelinsky, "On Some Patterns in International Tourist Flows," *Economic Geography* 46 (1970): 549-567.

Wilson, A.G., "A Family of Spatial Interaction Models and Associated Developments," *Environment and Planning* 3 (1971): 1-32.

Wolfe, R.I., "Recreation Travel: The New Migration," *Canadian Geographer* 10 (1966): 1-14.

Migration

Adams, J., "Directional Bias in Intra-Urban Migration," *Economic Geography* 45 (1969): 302-323.

Anderson, T.R., "Intermetropolitan Migration: A Comparison of the Hypotheses of Zipf and Stouffer," *American Sociological Review* 20 (1955): 287-291.

Berry, B.J.L. and P. Schwind, "Information and Entropy in Migrant Flows," *Geographical Analysis* 1 (1969): 5-14.

Bogue, D.J. and W.S. Thompson, "Migration and Distance," *American Sociological Review* 14 (1949): 236-244.

Brown, L.A. and J. Holmes, "Search Behavior in an Intra-Urban Migration Context: A Spatial Perspective," *Environment and Planning* 3 (1971): 307-326.

Brown, Lawrence A., John Odland, and Reginald G. Golledge, "Migration, Functional Distance and the Urban Hierarchy," *Economic Geography* 46 (1970): 472-485.

Eldridge, H.T., "Primary, Secondary, and Return Migration in the United States," *Demography* 2 (1965): 444-455.

Hägerstrand, T., "A Monte Carlo Approach to Diffusion," *Archives Europeennes de Sociologie* 6 (1965): 43-67.

Hannerberg, D., ed., "Migration in Sweden: A Symposium," *Lund Studies in Geography*, Series B, 13, 1957.

Hitt, H.L., "The Role of Migration in Population Change among the Aged," *American Sociological Review* 19 (1954): 194-200.

Johnston, R.J., "Latent Migration Potential and the Gravity Model: A New Zealand Study," *Geographical Analysis* 2 (1970): 387-396.

Lee, E.S., "A Theory of Migration," *Demography* 3 (1966): 7-57.

Lövgren, E., "The Geographic Mobility of Labor," *Geografiska Annaler* 38 (1956): 344-394.

Mabogunje, Akin L., "Systems Approach to a Theory of Rural-Urban Migration," *Geographical Analysis* 2 (1970): 1-18.

Morrill, R.L., "The Distribution of Migration Distances," *Papers and Proceedings of the Regional Science Association* 11 (1962): 75-84.

Morrill, R.L. and F.R. Pitts, "Marriage, Migration, and the Mean Information Field," *Annals of the Association of American Geographers* 57 (1967): 402-422.

Nelson, P., "Migration, Real Income, and Information," *Journal of Regional Science* 1 (1959): 43-74.

Ravenstein, E.G., "The Laws of Migration," *Journal of the Royal Statistical Society* 48 (1885): 167-235; 52 (1889): 241-305.

Roseman, Curtis C., "Channelization of Migration Flows from the Rural South," *Proceedings of the Association of American Geographers* 3 (1971): 140-145.

Roseman, Curtis C., "Migration as a Spatial and Temporal Process," *Annals of the Association of American Geographers* 61 (1971): 589-598.

Schwind, Paul, "Spatial Preferences of Migrants for Regions: The Example of Maine," *Proceedings of the Association of American Geographers* 3 (1971): 150-156.

Sjaastad, L., "The Relationship between Migration and Income in the United States," *Papers and Proceedings of the Regional Science Association* 6 (1960): 37-64.

Stouffer, S., "Intervening Opportunities and Competing Migrants," *Journal of Regional Science* 2 (1960): 1-26.

Velikonja, J., "Post War Population Movements in Europe," *Annals of the Association of American Geographers* 48 (1958): 458-472.

Wolpert, J., "Behavioral Aspects of the Decision to Migrate," *Papers and Proceedings of the Regional Science Association* 15 (1966): 159-172.

Wolpert, J., "Distance and Directional Bias in Inter-Urban Migratory Streams," *Annals of the Association of American Geographers* 57 (1967): 605-616.

Yapa, Lakshman and Julian Wolpert, "Time Paths of Migration Flows: Belgium 1954-1962," *Geographical Analysis* 3 (1971): 157-164.

Zelinsky, Wilbur, "The Hypothesis of the Mobility Transition," *Geographical Review* 61 (1971): 219-249.

Diffusion of Settlement and Innovation

Beckmann, Martin J., "The Analysis of Spatial Diffusion Processes," *Papers of the Regional Science Association* 25 (1970): 109-118.

Bowden, L. W., "Diffusion of the Decision to Irrigate: Simulation of the Spread of a New Resource Management Practice in the Colorado High Plains," University of Chicago Department of Geography, Research Paper 97, 1965.

Brown, L., "Diffusion Dynamics," *Lund Studies in Geography*, Series B, 29, 1968.

Hägerstrand, T., *Innovation Diffusion as a Spatial Process*, translated by A. Pred, Chicago: University of Chicago Press, 1968.

Hägerstrand, T., "On Monte Carlo Simulation of Diffusion," in *Quantitative Geography*, W.L. Garrison and D. Marble, eds., Evanston, Ill.: Northwestern University Press, 1967.

Hudson, J.C., "Diffusion in a Central Place System," *Geographical Analysis* 1 (1969): 45-58.

Jordan, T.G., "The Origin of Anglo-American Cattle Ranching in Texas: A Documentation of Diffusion from the Lower South," *Economic Geography* 45 (1969): 63-87.

Katz, E., *The Diffusion of Innovation*, New York: Wiley, 1964.

Kniffen, F., "Folk Housing: Key to Diffusion," *Annals of the Association of American Geographers* 55 (1965): 549-577.

Lamme, Ary J., III, "From Boston in One Hundred Years: Christian Science," *Professional Geographer* 23 (1971): 329-332.

Marble, D.F. and J.D. Nystuen, "An Approach to the Direct Measurement of Community Mean Information Fields," *Papers and Proceedings of the Regional Science Association* 11 (1963): 99-110.

Morrill, Richard L., "The Shape of Diffusion in Space and Time," *Economic Geography* 46 (1970): 259-268.

Morrill, Richard L., "Waves of Spatial Diffusion," *Journal of Regional Science* 8 (1968): 1-18.

Olsson, G., "Complementary Models: A Study of Colonization Maps," *Geografiska Annaler* 50B (1968): 115-132.

Pedersen, Paul Ove, "Innovation Diffusion within and Between National Urban Systems," *Geographical Analysis* 2 (1970): 203-254.

Pred, Allan R., "Large-City Interdependence and the Preelectronic Diffusion of Innovation in the U. S.," *Geographical Analysis* 3 (1971): 165-181.

Pyle, G.F., "Diffusion of Cholera in the U. S. in the 19th century," *Geographical Analysis* 1 (1969): 59-75.

Rogers, E.M., *Diffusion of Innovations*, New York: Macmillan, 1962.

Part Five

Spatial Organization

In the preceding chapters several individual theories of location and interaction
were presented. In the following chapters,
an attempt is made to indicate how these
theories fit together to produce theoretical
and real landscapes. We begin with a discussion of the system of towns and cities and of
the structure of the city itself.

The Urban System and Urban Structure

Chapter 8

THE SYSTEM OF TOWNS

In chapter 4 we discussed the regular locational pattern of towns as central places serving a surrounding dispersed population, and in chapter 5 we examined the variable locational patterns of towns as places of manufacturing. In this section these concepts are combined in a general discussion of urban places and the process of urbanization.

In advanced economies, not only do cities dominate the life of the citizen, but they also contain the vast majority of the population, even though cities occupy only the smallest segment of the nation's land surface. Cities are complexes of those activities — control, exchange, culture, processing — for which efficiency is achieved by intense spatial proximity. In the global perspective cities are but tiny scattered points in a vast area of land and water. Yet these concentrations of people are covering ever-larger areas with high-intensity use, a vast investment in the direct alteration of nature.

In the more advanced areas, cities have become the supporters and organizers of the economy. Not only are up to 80 percent of a nation's population city dwellers, but rural people depend on the city far more than cities depend on the farmer. Cities ultimately depend on farm and mineral resources, to be sure, but the majority of the urban population produces goods and services for other city dwellers.

Cities are vehicles of social, economic, cultural, and administrative control. They are centers of wealth and trade, and they support cultural, educational, and artistic institutions. As focal points of control and culture, cities are also major transmitters of social traditions.

Yet cities contain within themselves the seeds of social change — unrest, social ferment, and even violence. Within their confines are contained a wide variety of people, occupations, and industries, which enriches the experience of city dwellers and also heightens their expectations, giving impetus to both creativity and frustration. As centers for communication and as temporary homes for transients and travelers, cities are pervaded with new ideas and alternate life styles. Their large size embraces the nonconformist — the idealist, the reformer, and

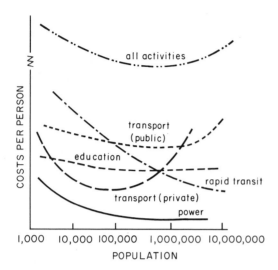

Figure 8.01 Economies of scale with urban size. Moderate-sized cities seem more efficient than either very large metropolises or small cities and towns. Yet all places of every size have a necessary role in the space-economy. Note that the private car is relatively effective in smaller cities, and public transport in larger ones.

the critic — who would be out of place in rural society.

Spatial Patterns of Urban Settlement: Theory of Urban Location

The advantages of agglomeration and scale provide the basic rationale for concentrating population in urban settlements. Whether cities are designed to control a population or to exchange and process goods, costs are reduced and the value of activities enhanced by concentrating them at one point. But because it would be impossible to cluster all activities in one gigantic city, the disaggregation and dispersal of people and activities produces a complex pattern of towns and cities.

We define as *rural* those activities and settlements (homesteads or hamlets) directly engaged in exploiting land and forest resources. The establishment of non-agricultural activities (including mining, services, and processing activities more advanced than family handicraft) gives rise to a different spatial organization that we may call urban, even if the settlement is but a hamlet.

We distinguish two sets of town-building forces: central place activities and processing activities. Central place activities provide services, exchange, distribution, and collection to more dispersed customers. The volume of central place activities varies; the distance people are willing to travel to reach a given activity varies; and different combinations of activities are most profitable for places of varying size. Thus a hierarchy of different town sizes in a network of central places will emerge as the most efficient and profitable way to serve a population. As already discussed, such a network would ideally form a hexagonal structure, distorted, however, in four ways:

— *Variations in productivity affect the frequency and spacing of settlements.*

— *Variations in topography shift settlements toward points of natural communication, such as ports and fords.*

— *Some variations in settlement density are due to developmental history*

— *The presence of processing activities distorts the pattern.*

The alternate set of town-building forces, processing activities, transforms raw materials into demanded products. Clusters of closely spaced urban settlements tend to develop where the resources are concentrated in a few areas.

The freedom of many processing activities from direct need for agricultural or mineral resources and their response to the advantages of large-scale production lead to a preference for location in large urban settlements — that is, cities, — whether the cities are of central place or processing origin. When manufacturing becomes concentrated in such larger places, central place activities will follow, so that in a highly industralized economy a far higher proportion of central place activities may exist to serve the metropolitan population itself than to serve the rural and small-town population.

The composite landscape or set of places then is ideally expected to exhibit a tendency toward dispersed regularity (the central place function) strongly distorted by environmental variation, especially the variable quality and quantity of industrial resources (the processing function).

Variations among Cities and Towns

Cities vary greatly in size and importance, function, form, and relative location. The most obvious variable is size; in theory, larger size may result from the higher order or from the differential response of processing activities to economies of scale (some plants operate well with 10 employees; others may need 10,000).

Central place and processing activities reinforce each other. A larger, higher order place is itself a large market and distribution center. Hence it is attractive to a wide variety of manufacturers, who in turn support a larger population, which increases the demand for and thus the level of services. The metropolis becomes increasingly self-sufficient as the size of the internal market justifies satisfying internally more and more demands. Consequently, many economies exhibit a top-heavy structure of city sizes — a "disproportionate" (from a central place viewpoint) share of the population and the activities resides in the larger metropolises.

An increasing variety of activities becomes profitable with greater size, the proportion of exports and imports decreases, and more economies of scale are realized. As the metropolis continues growing, however, costs increase and the economies of scale are eventually reversed (figure 8.01). Thus the size of metropolises is somewhat limited, reflecting at least these two spatial restraints: the excessive cost and time needed to find sufficient food, water, other raw materials, and markets; and the internal diseconomies, such as pollution, congestion, and blight, resulting from inability to organize space and to disperse wastes efficiently. Therefore, a set of regional metropolises is necessary for the functioning of advanced economies and is able to compete as well.

Primacy.   The size of a territory, especially the one within which an economy developed, influences the distribution of large cities. The smaller the territory, the greater the proportion of economic activity that can optimally be located at one center. Hence the phenomenon of **primacy**, where a high proportion of the total urban population of a country is located in one place. Primacy is essentially a product of territorial size, and it may be economically efficient.

Economies contained in a large territory such as the USSR, the United States, and Canada, or those that have merged several small ones, such as Germany, Italy, and Spain, lack national primacy but may exhibit regional primacy.

Size and Relative Location.   Within an economy, smaller places tend to be more prominent in areas of extensive agriculture, such as the Great Plains of the United States, in areas of extensive forests, and in areas of rugged topography, such as Appalachia and the Ozarks, where most settlements are hamlets. Conversely, larger places are concentrated in the areas of oldest development, such as the northeastern United States, and in positions of high natural accessibility.

Optimum Size of Cities.   Seeking one optimum size for a city conflicts with both the real demand for different levels of central place services and real variations in the scale economies for different forms of processing. One may observe, however, that very small places cannot sustain even minimal services, that people seem unable to live together harmoniously in the dense spatial concentration of the very largest cities, and that at some point economic, social, or environmental costs begin to exceed further gains from agglomeration.

The pursuit of the goals of maximizing the utility of places and level of interaction at least cost and effort results in the existence of places of all sizes. Clearly all these various-sized places have a meaningful role to play in the efficient functioning of human society and belong in the ideal landscape.

Not until a city reaches a size of 250,000 to 350,000 people does it attain a threshold that can provide some self-sufficiency in central place services, support high-quality cultural and educational amenities, and also attract modern industry. It is not surprising, then, that as transportation improves, larger places are the locus of most net growth. Places from about 200,000 to perhaps two million appear most attractive at the present time, evidently because they can support a very wide range of services and activities, are rather self-sufficient, and can support an efficient internal transport system without the severe social costs and congestion of the giant metropolis (see figure 8.01). However, this does not mean that smaller towns and cities do not have a role and cannot be successful and growing.

Classification of Cities. Functional variation in urban activities has led to many systems for classifying cities. Generally determined by a city's employment structure or sometimes by the value of its activities, classification depends on the city's specialized activity — the activity that makes up a disproportionate share of its economy relative to the average for all similar places. Many measures of functional specialization have been proposed; essentially they are useful devices for describing urban emphasis, the distinctive character of a place. In contrast, diversification is the state in which no one activity occurs notably more often than it does on the national average. In general, the larger the place, the greater the likelihood that it will be self-sufficient and thus more diversified.

In the United States, the pattern of urban functional classes is simple: the largest regional capitals are diversified, the core area of the country is dominated by specialized manufacturing places, and the periphery contains centers of trade.

While large cities tend to be diversified, those in the northeastern United States specialize somewhat more in manufacturing, and the "gateway" cities of the Plains and the regional capitals of the South and West specialize more in wholesale and retail trade, transportation, and services. At the small-city level, some peripheral industrial towns based on agricultural, mineral, and forest resources appear. There are also other classes: scattered towns specializing in administration or education, usually containing state capitals or colleges; mining towns, especially in the West, Appalachia, and the Gulf South; and a few transportation cities in crucial transit sites.

Role of the Particular City (Economic Base). More important than its functional class is the role of a city in the regional and national economy. This is revealed largely by the pattern and the strength of its external relations to the surrounding hinterland and to the nation (figure 8.02). The central place usually provides services for a spatial-ly contiguous, limited area; some processing centers, however, serve an entire national economy and even export beyond its borders. In an economic and spatial sense, it is these exports to surrounding areas that make possible the existence of the "unnatural elements" — the cities. Exports provide the income by which a city may purchase the special goods, raw materials, and food that the city does not itself produce.

The population directly engaged in export activities demands other internal products and services and thus indirectly gives rise to another class of activities, so-called nonbasic activities (much retail trade, services, administration, and so forth), which may soon exceed the export or basic group in quantity and value. It is important to understand that this group of internal activities is not parasitic; these activities create value just as do the export activities and are necessary for a high standard of living. Just as the city ultimately depends on the productivity of the country, so do its nonexport activities depend on its exports, since, if city residents could not earn money through export, they would not be able to purchase the foods and other goods that they cannot produce for themselves. However, the larger the place, the greater the proportion of relations carried on internally and the easier it is to sustain a disruption in traditional exports.

The export, or basic, share of the economy may come from any economic sector. From small towns, central place activities are "exported" to the local countryside. The larger the place and the higher its level, the greater the spatial extent of these exports (figure 8.02) and the greater the share of wholesale trade in the city's economy. Excluding the local region, manufactured goods are apt to dominate a city's exports and determine its national importance; thus Detroit is noted as the "automobile capital," Seattle and Los Angeles are famous for aircraft, Pittsburgh for steel, and so forth.

Urbanization

Cities have been in existence throughout recorded history, often functioning as

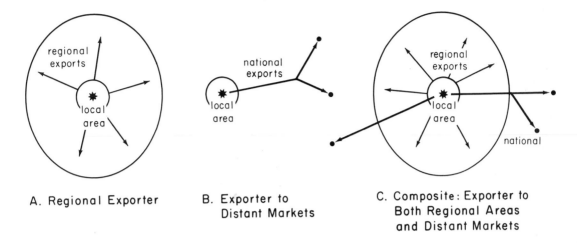

A. Regional Exporter

B. Exporter to
   Distant Markets

C. Composite: Exporter to
   Both Regional Areas
   and Distant Markets

Figure 8.02 Economic base: spatial types. A. Cities emphasizing central place activities export services chiefly to local (up to 10 miles) and regional (10 to 100 miles) markets. B. Cities emphasizing mining or industrial activities export mainly to national markets. C. Most large cities do both.

centers of religious, political, and economic control for the territories on which they depended for sustenance. However, not until the Industrial Revolution vastly raised the productivity of processing and agriculture, so that farmers could produce significant surpluses, did urbanization — the transition to a life dominated by cities — really begin.

Most ancient and medieval cities were small; only a few were able to control food- and material-supply lines of sufficient size to support large numbers of people. When these lines were cut, the cities collapsed. The rise of modern cities began with the development of international commerce and long-distance transport. Some capital, however, had also found its way into internal manufacturing and local communication networks, giving birth to market town and mill town.

The process of urbanization is complex, from its origins in central place and processing activities to its gradual diffusion from points of early political and economic power. Thus a theory of urban location must take into account central place and industrial location theory, resource-use concepts, and the historical process of diffusion.

In moderately rich agricultural areas with few alternate opportunities, such as parts of Europe and America, we can discover a fair-

ly pure geometric central place net. Similarly, in areas with very rich mineral resources, notably coal, we can observe typical industrial clusters of mining centers and heavy industrial towns and cities (figure 8.03).

In regions where processing and central place activities are of about equal importance, historical study often reveals a complicated interplay between different locational forces. One may trace the gradual elaboration of an urban net on a rural population (see figure 1.04, for example). New central places serving agricultural populations commonly developed at midpoints between two already existing places — often in a rather regularly spaced pattern. At the same time, industrial towns based on specific resources or on the entrepreneurial ability of individuals were clustered in districts that were often poor for agriculture, and also along railroads, which connected distant important places. Gradually, these industrial towns took on service functions, distorting the central place pattern and redistributing population along major transport corridors.

In the United States, because of the homestead pattern and the emphasis on local control over schools, rural farm settlement was accompanied by a pattern of small, closely spaced hamlets. Many villages and towns containing a wider variety of ser-

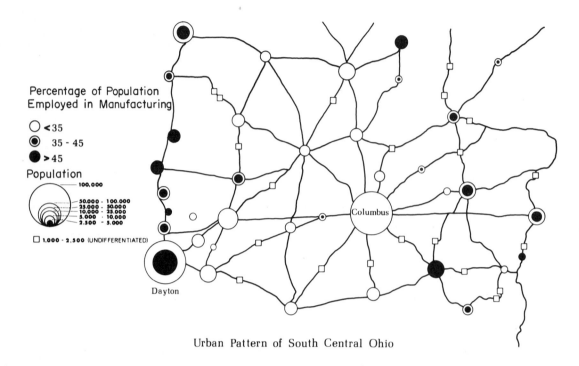

Urban Pattern of South Central Ohio

Figure 8.03 Urban pattern, south central Ohio. This local urban pattern illustrates both a central place pattern (especially the area around Columbus) and an industrial one (the linear set north from Dayton). Places with less than 35 percent of the population employed in manufacturing are primarily service centers.

vice functions were not allowed to develop completely spontaneously but were rather arbitrarily located by the railroad builders and influenced by state decisions locating county boundaries and county seats. Yet, in retrospect, the arrangement has proved surprisingly rational and efficient. Only the most recent period of cheap and fast auto travel has shaken this central place structure and perhaps rendered obsolete the smallest set of places.

In earlier periods, U. S. industries were small and many depended on easily accessible water power. Thus, from New England to the southern Piedmont a fairly fine network of small industrial towns can still be found, especially at falls on streams and smaller rivers. Some of these towns, too, have become obsolete; they have not been able to adjust to shifts in power sources and consumer demands.

Many larger U. S. cities were partially creatures of the railroad. In the interior of the country, sites where early railroads crossed natural barriers, such as the Ohio,

Mississippi, and Missouri Rivers and the Rocky Mountains, often became major cities — Cincinnati, St. Louis, Kansas City, Omaha, and Denver, for instance. Places chosen for railroad junctions or end points often prospered also, including such towns as Los Angeles, Portland, Seattle, Indianapolis, Minneapolis, and Atlanta. Even the old prerailroad port cities were very much affected by railroad development; those with early and good connections to a large interior area flourished — New York, Philadelphia, and Baltimore — while others, such as Charleston and New Orleans, suffered. Other industrial cities were based on concentrations of resources; break-of-bulk ports grew up and spawned linear clusters of manufacturing towns, from which factories gradually diffused outward.

In short, present urban patterns are products of relatively efficient locational behavior, subject of course to adjustments as the economy changes. At any one moment the pattern has inefficiencies; some places are declining because they have lost their original base of people or resources, others because new technology has made their location inefficient. Still other places gain from such developments as shifts in population, use of new resources, responses to new scale economies, and the greater importance of amenities.

Present trends in urbanization reflect both opportunities for developing new central places and manufacturing locations and attempts by existing locations to adjust to change. Very small places are generally declining, even disappearing, because we can travel two or three times as far as we could 50 years ago with the same — or less — effort, and also because many industries prefer larger places in order to use their superior labor supply, business services, and markets (figure 8.04). Conversely, large places are growing disproportionately fast as services multiply, industries become even more market-oriented, and inter- and intrametropolitan transport improves. Yet, even in the most advanced countries, the element of diffusion is still present; regions of a nation are at different stages of urbanization. In the northeastern United States, the first section of the country to be industrialized, a mature pattern consisting of large metropolises and an extensive wealthy **exurban** fringe has emerged. In the South, however, the emergence of central places and the creation of new industrial clusters is just beginning. In the rich agricultural interior, the decline of small centers and the consolidation of population into larger cities is now evident.

Metropolitanization. Some scholars suggest that current trends in city growth are leading, ultimately, to an extreme metropolitanization — a pattern in which most (80 to 90 percent) of the population will reside in a set of regional metropolises, each containing from 1 to 25 million people, and in which the larger portion of territory (95 percent) will be occupied by the minimum rural and small-town population needed to carry on extensive agricultural, forest, and mining activities.

Recent data do not support this theory, however. Cities of all sizes beyond 10,000 people are growing about equally fast, although the smaller metropolises con-

taining 250,000 to 1,000,000 people seem to be growing more rapidly. This trend will cause the metropolises to include a rising proportion of the total population, but the nearby satellite cities that are not part of the great metropolises are growing faster, indicating that some investors and an increasing part of the public are responding negatively to extreme city size. Indeed, a fair proportion of the population seems willing to get along on a much lower income in order to remain in rural areas.

Metropolitanization in the economic and cultural sense, however, in which most of the rural, small-town, and small-city population is dominated by a few large metropolises, seems to be growing. In particular, the increased speed of land travel and the use of air travel in business encourage consolidating higher management, exchange, and financial functions in the largest places with the best connections. These few cities — perhaps only 35 in all the United States — govern the economy and culture of wide territories. This kind of system of metropolitan regions is not at all new, though — the major change in the last half century has been this concentration of power in fewer places, primarily reducing the role of regional centers having from 25,000 to 250,000 people.

Some nations have attempted to control the pattern of urbanization. British attempts date back to the end of the nineteenth century. Since World War II, particularly, government and industry have together built new towns — towns in nonmetropolitan areas — that otherwise would not have existed. The Soviet Union, too, has long had similar policies, and the national government's control over investment has permitted it to establish and encourage a widespread pattern of intermediate-level urban places and smaller metropolises.

Urban Life

Urban life seems in the present age to have overwhelming advantages and attractions. Economic diversity is greater in urban areas; economic opportunities are concentrated there, perhaps to a more than efficient degree. Educational and cultural superiority follow this concentration of talent and

TRADE CENTER CHANGES   1941-1961

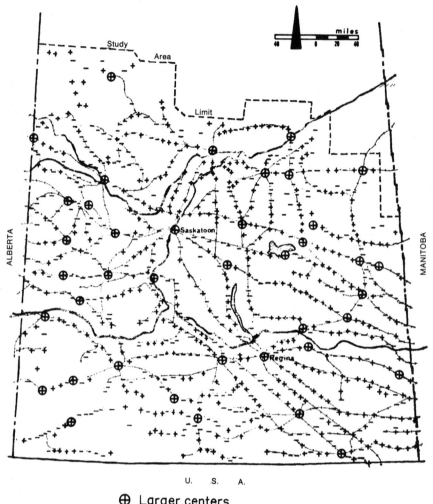

⊕ **Larger centers**

+ **Growing or stable centers**

— **Declining or expired centers**

Figure 8.04   Trade center changes, 1941-1961. On balance, smaller and less accessible centers not near transport junctions are declining. Most larger places are gaining. (Reprinted by permission of the Regional Science Association, from G. Hodge, "Prediction of Trade Center Viability in the Great Plains," *Papers and Proceedings of the Regional Science Association*, Vol. XV, 1962.)

wealth. The efficiencies of agglomeration and greater scale reduce costs and raise living standards. Culturally, mixing ideas and people enriches individual experience, reduces prejudice, encourages innovation and tolerance.

The disadvantages of urban life are notorious, but for most people these do not outweigh the attractions. Many persons, especially those brought up in the country, feel estranged from nature and often live in the rural fringe to get the best of both worlds. Others are accustomed to a close-knit community and strong family ties and cannot adjust to the psychological isolation of the city. The different peoples and cultures are impossible for some to accept, and the sheer concentration of so many people in so little space and the social control needed to regulate them conflict, particularly in the United States, with traditions of individualism. The congestion, speed, noise, and intensity of life contribute to mental and physical illness. The concentration of such a large number of people often makes social and economic differences too obvious, heightens conflict, and leads to social breakdown, delinquency, and crime. In the United States these problems, aggravated by continuous racial conflict, have become severe enough to make many people want to shift back to nonmetropolitan living.

THE INTERNAL STRUCTURE OF URBAN CENTERS

Although the city on the map of a nation is only a point, that point is a significant space — so intensively used that it contains more people and wealth than do all the vast rural lands combined. Moreover, the spatial organization of the city is complex and highly differentiated; it seems to follow the same principles as those governing the development of the rural landscape and the system of central places, so that in a sense the city is a microcosm of this wider landscape. Nothing might seem more unrelated than livestock grazing and the location of jewelry stores in the metropolis; yet, at very different scales, their locations are determined by pursuit of the same goals and by the operation of the same competitive forces. They illustrate the same theories of spatial organizations.

Theory of Urban Structure

Urban land uses are by definition those which respond to the needs or benefits of agglomeration and which themselves need very little space (in comparison to such rural uses as agriculture or forestry). It is not obvious, however, where an urban land use ends and a rural one begins. We may ten-

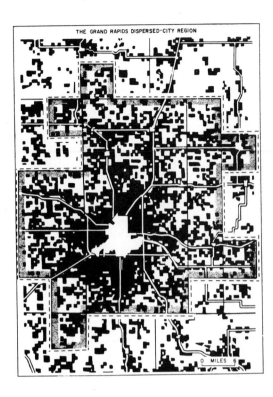

Figure 8.05 The urban-rural continuum. Areas of predominately nonfarm occupance (black areas), including residences of commuters to the city, extend far beyond the city itself. This extension is often termed "the dispersed city." (Reprinted by permission of the Association of American Geographers, from H. Stafford, Jr., "The Dispersed City," *The Professional Geographer*, Vol. XIV, 1962.)

tatively class as urban those activities and areas from which there is much commuting to the city and in which the natural landscape is clearly altered — that is, where the majority of the land is in developed residential or industrial use. But any such arbitrary distinction cannot ignore that there is really a continuum of intensity of activities and land use (figure 8.05), from nonuse in remote rural areas to the most intensively used downtown corner. The urbanized area contains only the more intensive, less space-consuming end of the continuum, those activities that are most able or that most need to compete for a central point. Therefore, the theory of internal urban location will be in part, at least, an extension of agricultural location theory.

The same elements applied to agricultural regions apply in the urban context. The familiar concentric ring concept describes

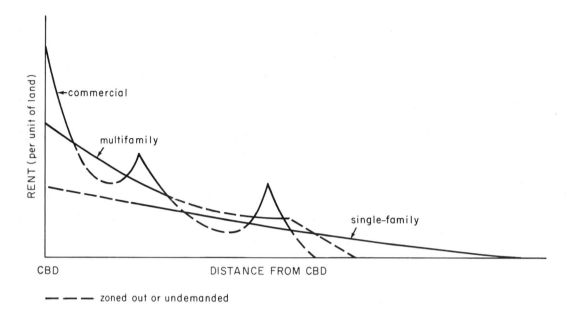

Figure 8.06   Ideal urban-rent gradient. Competition for land results in an ordering of land use from commercial, to multifamily, to single-family residential. Note the equivalence of this model to that for agricultural location. In this simple model, no account is taken of additional commercial centers (but see figure 8.10).

the density gradient of the city, from the point of highest accessibility and value downtown to the least accessible and least valuable areas on the urban fringe. The sector concept stresses the variety of demands for locations that are equally accessible and valuable, just as an agricultural zone of a given intensity may be divided into several parts, as a result of climate, soil, or cultural differences. In addition, central place theory applies to the urban scene and predicts the hierarchy of shopping centers, from the central business district (CBD) to the isolated store.

Gradient Theory.   Urban land uses, like rural ones, vary in intensity and type. Among urban activities, for example, many shops require little space while such uses as parking, cemeteries, and single-family homes require relatively much. Since many activities are located in cities because they benefit from agglomeration, they compete for the limited space around the points of greatest accessibility (figure 8.06). As in agriculture, the "best" locations have the highest price and thus units tend to be small and intensity very great. Shops and services

with a high turnover whose success depends on accessibility to the maximum number of people can afford the highest rents. A home, however, needs to be accessible to only a few people, and residents are willing to accept larger units of land that are less accessible. As in farming, the same total land value per enterprise unit — shop, home, and so forth — may well be found from the center to the edge of the urban area. The area of each unit, though, increases as the land becomes less valuable and less accessible.

The simplest model of urban structure suggests, for example, a zonation of land from:

— *The retail core, to*
— *A wholesale-industrial ring, to*
— *An apartment zone, and*
— *Single-family homes.*

Each activity, however, occurs at a variety of intensities, and a more realistic gradient would be:

— *Central business district commerce.*

Concentric Ring Theory

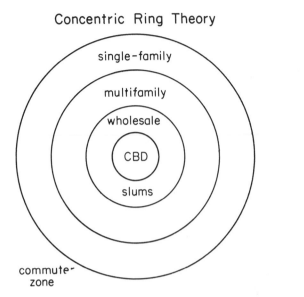

Sector Theory

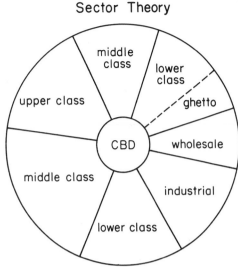

Figure 8.07 Two theories of urban structure. Patterns are based on competition for access and the incompatibility of uses. A combination is more realistic. Please see discussion in text.

— *Wholesaling and central manufacturing.*

— *High-rise apartments.*

— *General multifamily homes.*

— *Outlying business districts*

— *Single-family homes, increasing lot size.*

— *Peripheral manufacturing and wholesale trade.*

— *Exurban residential.*

Many studies corroborate in a general way the existence of the land gradient, but since the gradient theory takes into account only some of the factors affecting location, the observed pattern departs from the predicted one.

As with agricultural activities, physical variations play a role in the location of urban activities. Level land is more suited to manufacturing, and rising and rolling topography to residences (especially land with a view). Arterial roads, when necessary, follow valleys and easy ridges and thus influence commercial location. River and lakefront lands are often desired for industrial, public, and residential use — leading to conflict among the various interest groups. Microclimatic features such as a prevailing wind may affect location; to

avoid smoke, high-value residential buildings are placed to windward, industry to leeward. Physical variations, then, will tend to impose differentials in the use of the land within an intensity zone and, as in agricultural gradients, will distort portions of the zone. A wedge of sloping land with a view, for instance, may have higher land values than its surroundings, and an area of rough topography or swampland may have less value.

Sector Theory. Even without physical variation, however, we should not expect rings of homogeneous activities around the CBD. A variety of somewhat mutually exclusive activities may actually be of similar intensity and thus compete for land at the same distance — for example, manufacturing facilities and apartment houses, different racial groups, or different income groups might compete. This competition leads to a sectorization by class and land use. In its pure form, this sectorization will lead to wedges — sectors — of different uses, with internal variations of intensity within them (figure 8.07). Thus, within the upper-class sector, for instance, the gradient will go from wealthy shops, to expensive high-rise apartments, to older upper-class

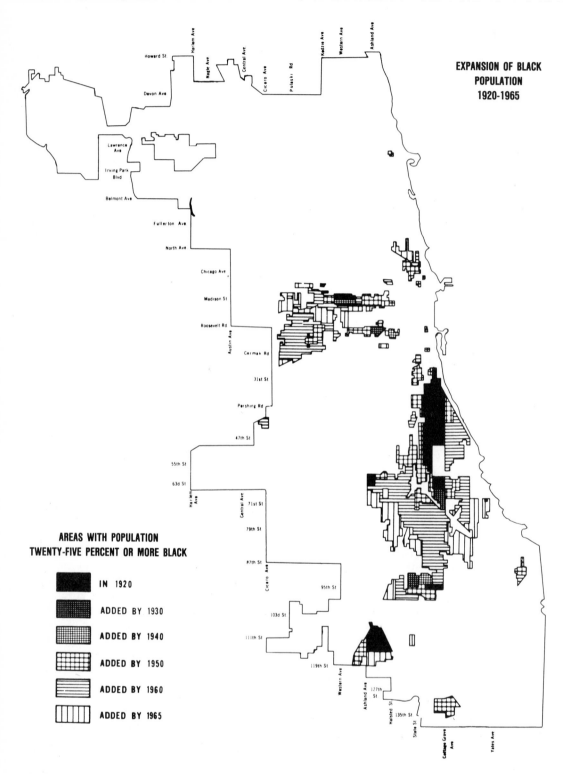

EXPANSION OF BLACK POPULATION 1920-1965

AREAS WITH POPULATION TWENTY-FIVE PERCENT OR MORE BLACK

IN 1920
ADDED BY 1930
ADDED BY 1940
ADDED BY 1950
ADDED BY 1960
ADDED BY 1965

Figure 8.08 Expansion of the black residential area, Chicago, 1920-1965. The development of the Chicago black ghetto well illustrates the pattern of inner-city concentration and expansion as a wedge, primarily into middle-income areas. (Reprinted by permission of P. Rees, ''The Factorial Ecology of Metropolitan Chicago, 1960,'' M.A. Thesis, University of Chicago, 1968.)

apartments, through newer upper-class residential suburbs and industries that utilize professional skills, such as research laboratories. In the lower-class sector, the progression will move from mixtures of inexpensive shops, wholesaling firms, and manufacturing facilities, to older homes that have been subdivided to provide rooms and apartments (including the ghetto), to smaller homes, and finally to suburbs containing low-cost housing and heavy industry. Although racial ghettoes typically occupy a high-intensity zone within the lower-class sector, the ghetto itself may become a wedge after sufficient variation in income develops (figure 8.08).

Another wedge — or more than one wedge — located along the major access railroads may be devoted almost entirely to industry. This separation of manufacturing activities from residential and commercial uses results from both personal preference and zoning laws; historically, however, the need to be near one's place of work led to a mixture of manufacturing plants and lower-class residences, which is still prevalent.

If it were not for racial, religious, and income differences, much of the sectorization would disappear. Social differences are persistent and strong, however, and this joint gradient-sector model offers a reasonable approach to a theory of urban structure. There are other reasons for proposing a **sector theory.** The sector theory most easily allows for growth; increased demand for some activity simply causes an extension of the wedge. Much intraurban migration, such as movements to the suburbs, also evidently occurs within a sector. Finally, even in the absence of social differences, a powerful force for wedge-shaped development is the radial, center-oriented structure of the transport network to the city center.

Central Place Structure of the City. One element is still missing from our urban structure — the hierarchical structure of central place activities that should be imposed on the overall gradient-sector system. The location of shopping centers follows central place structure and at the same time both reflects and modifies the intensity gradient; for example, the distance between shopping centers of equal size increases as one moves outward from the city center, because at lower suburban densities larger

areas are needed for a center to reach its threshold of support.

Since the city is a bounded space, limited in extent, the central business district tends to become the dominant center. A fair time passes before competitive centers begin to emerge. Theoretically, when the total market served by the original center becomes large enough to support seven of the smallest shopping districts, six competitors will simultaneously emerge (figure 8.09). The central business district will support the highest level activities by using the total urban market. Thus, the central place administrative principle generally applies at the highest level in an urban setting, while the arrangement of lower order business districts typically follows the transport principle, with smaller centers approximately midway between larger ones. Since overall density decreases outward from the center of the city, the position of the central business district is further enhanced because it is closest to the area of highest density. The outlying shopping centers will thus have to draw their trade from larger but less concentrated areas farther from the center.

The system of arterials connects major shopping centers first to the central business district and then to each other. The arterials, and especially the centers themselves, locally raise the intensity of land use and the value of the land in proportion to their size. Thus, the intensity gradient is changed by business districts and arterials, so that lesser peaks and ridges of intensity dot the urban landscape (figure 8.10). The central place structure in turn is affected by sectorization, and the structure is weaker in industrial and low-income areas, where purchasing power is less.

The theoretically optimal structure of central places — in this case shopping centers — within an intensity gradient has not yet been fully worked out (discussed more fully in chapter 9; see figure 9.01). Clearly, pure hexagonal trade areas will not be found, although evidence does support the general principle that the smallest centers are located approximately midway between two or three larger ones. In summary, a static theory of urban structure includes an intensity gradient modified by a central place structure of business districts and divided by sectors having different uses and different social groups.

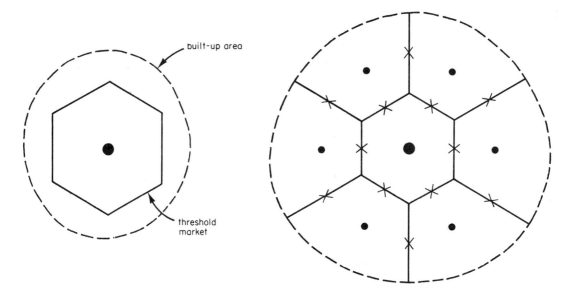

Figure 8.09 Growth of the shopping center hierarchy. When the built-up area of the city grows to many times the threshold necessary to support one center, outlying centers (small dots) will arise. The original center (large dot) continues to dominate the entire market for higher level goods and services. Increasing density or affluence may induce development of more closely spaced neighborhood centers, marked *x* on the figure, midway between the larger business districts.

Urban Land Use

Commercial Uses. Commercial activities require easy access and high visibility. The center of the transport net and other major intersections create the central business district and the major shopping centers, and the routes serving them are sought by arterial-oriented businesses.

The complexity of the commercial structure is a function of city size. A village has only one business center and some arterial business out from it. The town will add some isolated stores, and the small city (population 10,000 to 25,000) will be able to support one or more centers for convenience goods. In the metropolis, at least five levels of commercial structure are commonly recognized:

— *The central business district.*

— *Major outlying shopping centers (at least two or three, and perhaps as many as six), with branch department stores.*

— *District shopping centers, with a variety of specialty stores, banks, movie theaters, and so forth.*

— *Neighborhood shopping centers, emphasizing groceries, drugs,*

cleaners, and the like.

— *Local stores, mainly for gas and groceries.*

In addition, interconnecting arterials may contain two or three levels of businesses, depending on the volume of traffic and the density and income level of the adjoining areas. Arterials thus provide both convenience goods for local residents and goods and services geared to the traveler.

In most cities, business districts developed at a time when streetcars prevailed, and they located at intersections or arterials served by streetcars. Since land use and traffic flows were intensive, the shift to the private car led to severe traffic congestion and parking shortages. Developers of planned shopping centers in the last 25 years adapted to the car by building a new kind of structure: an intensive core of stores with a pedestrian mall, surrounded by parking space. Given the automobile, planned centers are far more efficient than stores lined along roads; congestion is reduced, and more can be accomplished in a given time within shorter walking distance.

The development of outlying shopping centers as a city grows is a natural central place process. At the same time, the nature of the central business district changes as its relative share of all business declines. Auto travel has led to the decline and demise of many local stores, mainly in the inner city, because shoppers can as easily travel to larger, newer suburban centers that provide greater variety (figure 8.11). Some small isolated stores manage to survive by offering special hours, products, or services.

Even more than in the rural landscape, trade areas of business centers overlap (figure 8.12). Since centers are typically not more than a mile or so apart and since they are only subtly differentiated — such as by different grocery, drug store, or bank chains and, at higher levels, by different department store chains — centers that have a spatial monopoly over an area are rare. Other reasons for this overlap of trade areas are that internal urban mobility is great and that many people maintain previously established shopping habits, particularly with regard to doctors, dentists, and banks.

Even the central business district, though small, is highly differentiated internally. There is an inner zone of intensive pedestrian movement for the activities requiring a large volume of customers, and a peripheral ring of stores requiring moderate customer volume, divided into "interest" areas — finance, general office, hotel-entertainment, wholesale, lower-class retail, and high-class shops. This specialization within the central district implicitly recognizes the division of the population into economic and social subgroups.

Residential Use. Residential land use varies in density, quality, racial occupancy, and age. Historically, in the classic city with a rather steep density and land-value gradient, high-density apartments and tenements, with up to 100,000 persons per square mile, could be found closet to the CBD, followed, at increasing distance, by three-story walk-ups (density 25,000), next by two-story apartments, then by houses and duplexes, and finally by single-family homes on progressively larger lots, ranging in density from 10,000 to only 500 people per square mile. Although the gradient was produced through competition, the wealthier classes demanded relatively little of the central area, thus

Figure 8.10 The urban density surface. Land value and intensity peak at points of greater accessibility on major arterials. (Reprinted by permission of the University of Chicago Department of Geography, from J. Simmons, *The Changing Pattern of Retail Location,* Research Paper No. 92, 1964.)

relegating much of it, in degraded form, to the poor.

In the United States, single-family homes extended the circumference of the growing city. In the higher-class sectors of the inner city, older homes were typically replaced with multistory quality apartments. In the poorer sectors, older homes were divided into small apartments and frequently deteriorated into tenements. Although land value and taxes were high and per-family rents low, net revenue per property could be quite large, given high population density and low maintenance costs. Minority groups, often regardless of income, and poorer groups dependent on public transport or who had to walk to get to work were forced to reside in such areas. However, after the inner city deteriorated physically and especially after private car travel became fairly cheap, thus reducing the central area's advantage of accessibility, land values even declined in some central residential districts.

As people began to travel by car rather than by bus, access to the center of the city became less important, and the original gradient of land value and intensity was weakened. Just as with agriculture, when transport cheapens, the quality of the land rather than its accessibility to the center becomes a major determinant of its value. The original gradient was also changed with respect to apartment buildings: the optimal

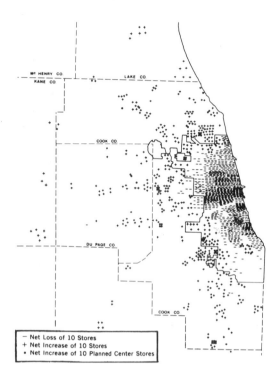

- Net Loss of 10 Stores
+ Net Increase of 10 Stores
• Net Increase of 10 Planned Center Stores

Figure 8.11 Changes in Chicago retail establishments. Retail stores follow the population to the suburbs. (Reprinted by permission of the University of Chicago Department of Geography, from B.J.L. Berry, *Commercial Structure and Commercial Blight*, Research Paper No. 85, 1963.)

The highest income groups have the widest choice of location and type of residence, since their ability to pay enables them to achieve the environment they desire. Middle-income groups may not be able to pay for the newer, more expensive apartments in the central city and are thus likely to move to outer, moderate-quality city districts and suburbs. The poor occupy the oldest, smallest homes and are often closest to industrial areas. Suburban homes are not always available to the poor, and those that are available are apt to be intermixed with surburban industry.

Other Urban Land Uses. Industrial land occurs in wedges or clusters within the metropolis or city and includes an older, inner industrial zone near the central business district that uses little space; adapting to car-driving workers, it also includes newer space-extensive industries in intermediate and fringe locations and along railroads and major highway links.

The observed decentralization of industry in most cities is due to a lack of space and to excessive land costs for the space that is available in the center. Only manufacturing that requires direct contact with other industries and services, that can utilize the labor of nearby poorer groups, and that does not require much space will seek and pay for central locations. Examples of such industries are printing and publishing, apparel, and pottery. On the other hand, industries such as refineries, metal processors, and fabricators prefer more spacious peripheral sites. Specialized small manufacturers whose employees are skilled and for whom local accessibility is not important also prefer peripheral locations in or near middle-income suburbs.

location for that type of housing used to be as close as possible to the center of the city. Because of the locational freedom made possible by car travel and because of employment decentralization, apartment dwellings are located today wherever there is a demand for them, even in suburban areas.

Subpopulations vary in their preferences for housing and amenities and in their ability to pay for them. Some, most often people without children or cars, prefer more central locatons, exchanging higher rent for reduced transport time and cost and proximity to downtown amenities. Others, especially those with young children, are willing to pay more for transport in exchange for more space and cheaper land in the suburbs. They may also be seeking homogenous neighbors — in other words, they are fleeing minority groups — or they may simply desire newer or more modern housing. Indeed, the suburbanite seems willing to spend more for housing and transport combined.

Internal Social Variation

Internal social variation in the sector model reflects the economic, ethnic, and religious differences within a population. Separation of income groups is achieved mainly by the separation of housing of varying values. Similarly valued homes tend to be clustered because of location relative to industry, variation in topographical quality, and the fact that developers construct houses in clusters.

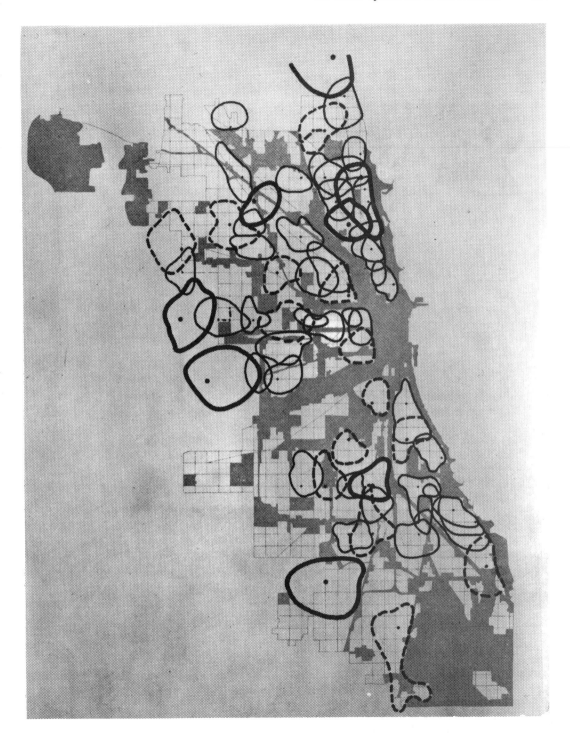

Figure 8.12 Trade areas for convenience goods: Chicago. Overlapping customer trade areas around major Chicago shopping centers. Width of lines indicates size of shopping centers (dots). Dark gray areas are industrial and commercial. (Reprinted by permission of the University of Chicago Department of Geography, from J. Simmons, *The Changing Pattern of Retail Location*, Research Paper No. 92, 1964.)

Incompatibility between social groups, resulting in segregation, is the basis of much internal social variation. Separation of groups by their national origin, color, and religion follows from both the internal preferences within the group and external discrimination against the group. In cities all over the world, minority groups have long been set apart from the rest of the populace — perhaps willingly for self-protection — and the separation has often been legally enforced by the majority. The European Jewish ghettos were the most obvious examples of segregation.

As each different group has immigrated to large American cities, it has been forced to occupy the poorest area, or ghetto, when it arrived. Despite their poverty, these ghettos do offer a community of people to aid in the transition of the group to a new society. The most recent migrants to the American city are blacks and Puerto Ricans. Blacks differ from earlier groups, however, in that color is a greater barrier to assimilation than religion or language ever was. Negro ghettos are maintained by both preference and discrimination; the black minority is not able to disperse because of individual prejudice and real estate, financial, and even legal barriers. Thus black communities have been able to accommodate internal growth only by a slow block-by-block extension. Growth into lower-middle income areas has typically been easiest, since neighboring low-income groups are often the most resistant to black residents, for both psychological and economic reasons, and since the middle-class population can afford to move to the suburbs. In other words, growth most often occurs outward in a wedge rather than through similar housing (see figure 8.08).

Urban Transport

The existing transport routes usually determined the pattern of urban growth and the location of the central business district and major industrial tracts as well. As the size of the city increased, stress was placed on these routes and demand arose for better transport, especially to the central business district. The routes were then modernized by using streetcars, and the center was

enhanced and use intensified along the affected routes; branches of development began to extend outward along these routes in stellate (star-like) fashion (see the pre-auto development pattern, figure 9.07, p. 220). With further growth and a shift to automobile transport, obsolescence and congestion of existing routes again occurred; as the central business district suffered, competing centers arose.

Efforts to improve access to the CBD have led to such transport improvements as rapid transit and freeways. Rapid transit tends to concentrate activities in the downtown area and at outer nodes (stations). It is a viable and efficient system so long as most commuters do not have or use cars and are satisfied with high-density apartment living. However, even in areas having rapid transit and the highest intensity of land use, people demand cars, and severe congestion results (as in New York, Boston, and London). Central densities may then decline as more people demand space for their cars, and the transit system will become less and less profitable.

A freeway system will tend to decentralize people and activities and make transit systems less profitable still; but because of the continuing advantage of the CBD for many activities, freeways will not prevent serious congestion in the large metropolis.

The current dilemma in most American cities is that bus transit became poorer and less popular as busses had to compete with cars on the congested arterials. Yet the popularity of cars and low residential density make traditional subway or other forms of rail rapid transit both financially infeasible and unable to serve significant numbers of people. Until or unless some form of smaller rail transit becomes feasible in a reasonably extensive network, solutions will require greatly improved bus service, together with increasing restrictions on use of the private car.

The Urban Field

The influence of the city extends well beyond the built-up urbanized area. Not only does the city dominate its hinterland through its role as wholesale, retail, service, and communication center, but city residents spend much time and money in the countryside, and most important, a fair proportion of rural people commute to the city to work. From ten to twenty miles away, up to one-third of the workers may commute to the city, profoundly mixing urban and rural values and significantly increasing income and local employment levels in this exurban rural zone. Although commuters may travel as far as 50 miles, favorable influences often give way to "backwash" effects beyond about 25 miles from the smaller metropolis, as the younger and more able migrate to the city.

Growth of the Town or City

Most cities in advanced societies have experienced more or less continuous growth over varying periods of time. Expansion at the edge of the city and change in the use of areas within it are two of the most exciting and dynamic spatial processes.

The growth of population and the increase in activities generate increasing demand for space not only at the edge of the city, but also at good locations within the city. Thus, the city grows in both extent and intensity. The density of the inner areas increases because of competition for the limited, more accessible space. The advent of the automobile, however, caused many cities to spread out more rapidly than they intensified, and overall densities fell.

For short periods and in smaller places, all growth may at times be accommodated by extension of the city alone or, if land is severely restricted (either legally or topographically), by intensification alone; in any longer time period, though, both processes will occur. Central land intensities must rise as the competition for good sites enhances land values and increases rents; and the outer limits of the city must extend because part of the demand is for new single-family houses, and because areas that could intensify often lag in their response.

As intensity increases, older homes and apartments surrounding the CBD will gradually be taken for commercial use. Apartments will extend, especially along arterials, into former single-family areas. In more desired areas, such as sectors of middle or high income, new apartments tend to replace older homes. In less desired areas, homes are often subdivided into small apartments. Together this overintensive use and lack of landlord and tenant maintenance help create slum tenements. In addition, the concentration of low-income residents in one area also hurts preexisting businesses and leads to commercial blight and deteriorating services for the poor. Rehabilitation and code enforcement are attempted, but with little succes. Urban renewal at least shifts the burden of building maintenance to the public sector, even if does not prevent other manifestations of the slum.

Obviously, public officials favor the construction of highrise and townhouse projects designed to attract high-income groups back to the city, but success here is limited by the preference of the rich for the suburbs and open space. At the same time, other residents of older areas move to new housing at the edge of the city. In some cases, the move is impelled by a radical change in the social or economic status of their neighborhood, such as when people escape an advancing ghetto, but more often it reflects their demand for newer and more modern housing.

In the American city at least, which has little central planning, the expansion of the edge and the process of successive uses within the city may be described as a diffusion process. The outer edge is a fairly wide zone of transition from areas that are solidly city to more widely separated homes and subdivisions. Since far more land is available for subdivisions than is demanded, their specific locations are in a sense random. Given a free, speculative land market, the probability that a parcel of land beyond the solid city area will be developed is a complicated function of many factors: housing preferences; distance from the edge, from employment opportunities, and from services; the size of the parcel; topography; and the speculative behavior of the owner. Both premature development and late development are common, and at any one time much land within the suburban fringe is in "speculative nonuse"; it has been sold by the farmer who originally owned it, but not yet subdivided.

The process of succession, too, is complicated. More areas are ripe for renewal,

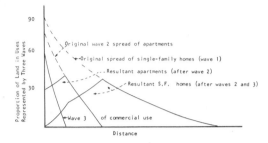

Figure 8.13 Waves of urban expansion. As a place grows, single-family homes spread outward from a small commercial core, and the inner, older homes become replaced by the growing commercial core and a surrounding zone of apartments — the older of which may later be displaced by expanding commerce.

more homes available for replacement by apartments, and more sites available for commercial upgrading than are demanded. Thus, as with subdivisions, their locations are in a sense random.

A microlevel theory of urban growth suggests that the demand for space by new activities may be separated into a series of waves (figure 8.13):

— *A wave front of single-family homes, from the place and time of earliest settlement to the present outermost suburban edge, including necessary supporting facilities: parks, schools, and convenience-goods stores.*

— *A rather slow replacement wave of apartments, which comes a little later.*

— *A wave of poor immigrants from rural areas and from abroad, intensifying the use of existing older housing.*

— *A renewal wave of high-rise apartments for the wealthy and public housing for the poor.*

— *A central commercial expansion, which is as much upward (more intensive use and higher buildings) as outward.*

At any point in time, there is a density gradient (leaving out the subpeaks caused by business districts), and over time this gradient shifts both upward and outward (as in figure 3.07, p. 50).

Conclusion: The Urban Landscape

The city is the result of human activity devoted to intense social and economic productivity and interaction. But the sheer number of men and the need for food and shelter force the countless repetition of urban settlements, from hamlets to the metropolis, to depend on and to serve the dispersed land resources. The sporadic location of industrial resources, too, leads to particular patterns of industrial dispersion. All the towns, cities, and metropolises combined occupy less than one percent of the earth's land surface, yet this tiny space probably contains two billion people, over half of the world's population. Although occupying such a relatively small territory, man's urban activities are organized in ways parallel to and as complex as the structure of the human landscape as a whole.

REFERENCES

Urbanization, Growth, and Decline

Berry, Brian J.L. and Frank E. Horton, *Geographic Perspectives on Urban Systems,* Englewood Cliffs, N.J.: Prentice-Hall, 1970.

Borchert, J.R. and R.B. Adams, "Projected Urban Growth in the Upper Midwest, 1960-1975," Upper Midwest Economic Study, University of Minnesota, 1964.

Cowan, Peter, ed., *Developing Patterns of Urbanization,* Beverly Hills: Sage Press, 1970.

Hance, W.A., *Population, Migration and Urbanization in Africa,* New York: Columbia University Press, 1970.

Harris, Chauncy D., "Urbanization and Population Growth in the Soviet Union, 1959-1970, *Geographical Review* 61 (1971): 102-124.

Lampard, E.E., "The History of Cities in the Economically Advanced Areas," *Economic Development and Cultural Change* 3 (1955): 81-136.

Mayer, H. and C. Kohn, eds., *Readings in Urban Geography,* Chicago: University of Chicago, 1959.

Murphey, R., "The City as a Center of Change: Western Europe and China," *Annals of the Association of American Geographers* 44 (1954): 349-362.

Sjoberg, G., *The Pre-Industrial City*, New York: Free Press, 1960.

Smailes, A.E., *The Geography of Towns*, London: Hutchinson University Library, 1960.

Taylor, G., *Urban Geography*, New York: Dutton, 1949.

Yeates, Maurice H. and Barry J. Garner, *The North American City*, New York: Harper & Row, 1971.

Variation among Cities: Economic Base

Alexander, J.W., "The Basic-Nonbasic Concept of Urban Economic Functions," *Economic Geography* 30 (1954): 246-261.

Alexandersson, G., *The Industrial Structure of American Cities*. Lincoln, Nebr.: University of Nebraska Press, 1956.

Alonso, W., "The Form of Cities in Developing Countries," *Papers and Proceedings of the Regional Science Association* 13 (1964): 165-176.

Bourne, Larry S. and Gerald M. Barber, "Ecological Patterns of Small Urban Centers in Canada," *Economic Geography* 47 (1971): 258-265.

Daly, M.C., "An Approximation to a Geographic Multiplier," *Economic Journal* 50 (1940): 198-199.

Harris, C.D. and E.L. Ullman, "The Nature of Cities," *Annals of the American Academy of Political and Social Science* 242 (1945) 7-17.

Holzner, L., E. Domisse, and J. Mueller, "Toward a Theory of Cultural-Genetic City Classification," *Annals of the Association of American Geographers* 57 (1967): 367-381.

Hodge, Gerald, "Comparison of Urban Structure in Canada, the United States and Great Britain," *Geographical Analysis* 3 (1971): 83-89.

Leven, C.L., "Measuring the Economic Base," *Papers and Proceedings of the Regional Science Association* 2 (1956): 250-258.

Morrissett, I., "The Economic Structure of American Cities," *Papers and Proceedings of the Regional Science Association* 4 (1958): 239-258.

Nelson, H., "Some Characteristics of the Population of Cities in Similar Service Classifications," *Economic Geography* 33 (1957): 95-108.

Smith, R.H.T., "Method and Purpose in Functional Town Classification," *Annals of the Association of American Geographers"* 55 (1965): 539-548.

Stafford, H., Jr., "The Dispersed City," *Professional Geographer* 14 (1962): 8-10.

Stewart, C.T., "The Size and Spacing of Cities," *Geographical Review* 48 (1958): 222-245.

Stone, R., "A Comparison of the Economic Structure of Regions Based on the Concept of Distance," *Journal of Regional Science* 2 (1960): 1-20.

Ullman, E.L. and M.F. Dacey, "The Minimum Requirements Approach to the Urban Economic Base," *Papers and Proceedings of the Regional Science Association* (1960): 175-194.

Urban-Rural Relations

Griffin, P.F. and R. Chatham, "Urban Impact on Agriculture in Santa Clara County, California," *Annals of the Association of American Geographers* 48 (1958): 195-208.

Kikkinen, K., "Change in Village and Rural Population with Distance from Duluth," *Economic Geography* 44 (1968): 312-325.

McGee, T.G., "The Rural-Urban Continuum Debate: The Pre-Industrial City and Rural-Urban Migration," *Pacific Viewpoint* 5 (1964): 159-182.

Muth, R.F., "Economic Change and Rural-Urban Land Use Conversion," *Econometrica* 29 (1961): 1-23.

Thomas, W.L., Jr., ed., "Man, Time, and Space in Southern California," *Annals of the Association of American Geographers* 49, No. 3, Part 2, (1959).

Wheeler, James O., "Commuting and the Rural Nonfarm Population," *Professional Geographer* 23 (1971): 118-122.

Settlement History and Patterns

Borchert, J.R., "American Metropolitan Evolution," *Geographical Review* 57 (1967): 301-332.

Burghardt, A.F., "A Hypothesis about Gateway Cities," *Annals of the Association of American Geographers"* 61 (1971): 269-285..

Clark, W.A.V., G. Rushton, and R.G. Golledge, "The Spatial Structure of the Iowa Urban Network," *Geographical Analysis* 2 (1970): 301-313.

Curry, L., "The Random Spatial Economy: An Exploration in Settlement Theory," *Annals of the Association of American Geographers* 54 (1964): 138-146.

Hart, J.F., N. Salisbury, and E. Smith, "The Dying Village and Some Notions about Urban Growth," *Economic Geography* 44 (1968): 343-349.

Hodge, G., "The Prediction of Trade Center Viability on the Great Plains," *Papers and Proceedings of the Regional Science Association* 15 (1965): 87-118.

Northam, R.M., "Declining Urban Centers in the United States, 1940-1960," *Annals of the Association of American Geographers* 53 (1963): 50-59.

Northam, R., "Population Size, Relative Location, and Declining Urban Centers in the U.S.," *Land Economics* 45 (1969): 313-322.

Trewartha, G.T., "The Unincorporated Hamlet: One Element in the American Settlement Fabric," *Annals of the Association of American Geographers* 33 (1943): 32-81.

Webb, J.W., "Basic Concepts in the Analysis of Small Urban Centers in Minnesota," *Annals of the Association of American Geographers* 49 (1959): 55-72.

The Metropolis

Borchert, J.R., "The Twin Cities Urbanized Area: Past, Present, and Future," *Geographical Review* 51 (1961): 47-70.

Duncan, O.D. et al., *Metropolis and Region*, Baltimore, Md.: Johns Hopkins Press, 1960.

Gottman, J., *Megalopolis: The Urbanized Northeastern Seaboard of the United States*, New York: Twentieth Century Fund, 1961.

Hall, Max, ed., *New York: Metropolitan Region Study*. Cambridge, Mass.: Harvard University Press, 1959.

Harris, B., "City of the Future," *Papers and Proceedings of the Regional Science Association* 19 (1967): 185-198.

Hoover, E.M., and R. Vernon, *Anatomy of a Metropolis*, Cambridge, Mass.: Harvard University Press, 1959.

Park, R.E., E.W. Burgess, and R.D. McKenzie, *The City*, Chicago: University of Chicago Press, 1925.

Wolf, L., "Metropolitan Tidal Wave in Ohio, 1900-2000," *Economic Geography* 45 (1969): 133-154.

Theory of Urban Structure

Alonso, W., *Location and Land Use: Toward a General Theory of Land Rent*. Cambridge, Mass.: Harvard University Press, 1964.

Blumenfeld, H., "Are Land Use Patterns Predictable?" *Journal of the American Institute of Planners* 25 (1959): 61-66.

Blumenfeld, H., "On the Concentric-Circle Theory of Urban Growth," *Land Economics* 25 (1949): 209-212.

von Boventer, E., "The Relationship between Transportation Costs and Location Rent," *Journal of Regional Science* 3 (1961): 27-40.

Burgess, E.W., "The Determination of Gradients in the Growth of the City," *American Sociological Society Publications* 21 (1927): 178-184.

Casetti, Emilio, "Equilibrium Land Values and Population Densities in an Urban Setting," *Economic Geography* 47 (1971): 16-20.

Clark, W.A.V., "Spacing Models in Intra-City Studies," *Geographical Analysis* 1 (1969): 391-398.

Colby, C.C., "Centrifugal and Centripetal Forces in Urban Geography," *Annals of the Association of American Geographers* 23 (1933): 1-20.

Dunn, Edgar S., Jr., "A Flow Network of Urban Structure," *Urban Studies*, 7 (1970): 239-258.

Friedmann, J. and J. Miller, "The Urban Field," *Journal of the American Institute of Planners* 31 (1965): 312-319.

Goldberg, Michael A., "Transportation, Urban Land Values and Rents: A Synthesis," *Land Economics* 46 (1970): 153-162.

Harvey, David, "Social Processes and Spatial Form: An Analysis of the Conceptual Problems of Urban Planning," *Papers of the Regional Science Association* 25 (1970): 47-70.

Hatt, P.K. and J. Reiss, eds., *Cities and Society*, New York: Free Press, 1957.

Herbert, J.D. and B. Stevens, "A Model for the Distribution of Residential Activity in Urban Areas," *Journal of Regional Science* 2 (1960): 21-36.

Huff, D. L., "A Topographical Model of Consumer Space Preferences," *Papers and Proceedings of the Regional Science Association* 6 (1960): 159-173.

Kain, J.F., "An Economic Model of Urban Residential and Travel Behavior," *Review of Economics and Statistics* 46 (1964): 55-64.

Lakshmanan, T.R., "An Approach to the Analysis of Intra-Urban Location Applied to the Baltimore Region," *Economic Geography* 40 (1964): 348-370.

Lynch, K., and L. Rodwin, "A Theory of Urban Form," *Journal of the American Institute of Planners* 24 (1958): 201-214.

Mills, E., "Urban Density Functions," *Urban Studies* 7 (1970): 5-20.

Newling, B.E., "Spatial Variation of Urban Population Densities," *Geographical Review* 59 (1969): 242-252.

Newling, B.E., "Urban Growth and Spatial Structure," *Geographical Review* 56 (1966): 213-225.

Ratcliff, R.U., *Urban Land Economics*, New York: McGraw-Hill, 1949.

Rushton, Gerard, "Behavioral Correlates of Urban Spatial Structure," *Economic Geography* 47 (1971): 49-58.

Scott, A., "Spatial Equilibrium of the Central City," *Journal of Regional Science* 9 (1969): 29-46.

Stevens, B.H., "Linear Programming and Location Rent," *Journal of Regional Science* 3 (1961): 15-26.

Vance, James E., Jr., "Land Assignment in the Precapitalist, Capitalist, and Postcapitalist City," *Economic Geography* 47 (1971): 101-120.

Webber, M.M. et al., *Explorations into Urban Structure*, Philadelphia: University of Pennsylvania Press, 1964.

Studies of Land Use and Urban Structure

Adams, John S., "Residential Structure of Midwestern Cities," *Annals of the Association of American Geographers* 60 (1970): 37-62.

Anderson, T.R., "Scale and Economic Factors Affecting the Location of Residential Neighborhoods," *Papers and Proceedings of the Regional Science Association* 9 (1962): 161-172.

Bourne, Larry S., ed., *Internal Structure of the City*, New York: Oxford University Press, 1971.

Bourne, L., *Private Redevelopment of the Central City*, University of Chicago, Department of Geography, Research Paper 112, 1967.

Brodsky, Harold, "Residential Land and Improvement Values in a Central City," *Land Economics* 46 (1970): 229-247.

Carroll, J. D., "Spatial Interaction and Urban-Metropolitan Regional Description," *Papers and Proceedings of the Regional Science Association* 1 (1955): D1-D14.

Chapin, F.S. and H.C. Hightower, "Household Activity Patterns and Land Use," *Journal of the American Institute of Planners* 31 (1965): 222-231.

Clark, W.A.V., "Measurement and Explanation in Intra-Urban Residential Mobility," *Tijdschrift voor Economische en Sociale Geografie* 61 (1970): 49-57.

Firey, W., *Land Use in Central Boston*, Cambridge, Mass.: Harvard University Press, 1947.

Foley, D.L., "Urban Daytime Population: A Field for Demographic-Ecological Analysis," *Social Forces* 32 (1954): 323-330.

Fuchs, R.J., "Intraurban Variations in Residential Quality," *Economic Geography* 36 (1960): 313-325.

Getis, A., "Temporal Land-Use Pattern Analysis with the use of Nearest Neighbor and Quadrat Methods," *Annals of the Association of American Geographers* 54 (1964): 391-399.

Hansen, W.G., "How Accessibility Shapes Land Use," *Journal of the American Institute of Planners* 15 (1959): 73-76.

Hartshorn, Truman A., "Inner City Residential Structure and Decline," *Annals of the Association of American Geographers* 61 (1971): 72-96.

Haynes, Kingsley E., "Spatial Change in Urban Structure: Alternative Approaches to Ecological Dynamics," *Economic Geography* 47 (1971): 324-335.

Horton, Frank E. and David R. Reynolds, "Effects of Urban Spatial Structure on Individual Behavior," *Economic Geography* 47 (1971): 36-48.

Kain, J.F., "The Journey to Work as a Determinant of Residential Location," *Papers and Proceedings of the Regional Science Association* 9 (1962): 137-160.

Kaiser, Edward J. and Shirley F. Weiss, "Public Policy and the Residential Development Process," *Journal of the American Institute of Planners* 36 (1970): 30-37.

Marble, D.F., "Transport Inputs at Urban Residential Sites," *Papers and Proceedings of the Regional Science Association* 7 (1961): 207-220.

Moore, Eric G., "Comments on the Use of Ecological Models in the Study of Residential Mobility in the City," *Economic Geography* 47 (1971): 73-85.

Muth, R.F., "The Spatial Structure of the Housing Market," *Papers and Proceedings of the Regional Science Association* 7 (1961): 207-220.

Salins, Peter D., "Household Location Patterns in American Metropolitan Areas," *Economic Geography* 47 (1971): 234-248.

Vance, J.E., "Laborshed, Employment Field, and Dynamic Analysis in Urban Geography," *Economic Geography* 36 (1960): 189-220.

Yeates, M.H., "Some Factors Affecting the Spatial Distribution of Chicago Land Values, 1910-1960," *Economic Geography* 41 (1965): 57-70.

Urban Transportation

Fellman, J.D., "Truck Transportation Patterns of Chicago," University of Chicago Department of Geography, Research Paper 12, 1956.

Hoover, R., "Policy Growth and Transportation Planning in the Detroit Metropolitan Area," *Papers and Proceedings of the Regional Science Association* 7 (1961): 223-240.

Lave, Lester B., "Congestion and Urban Location," *Papers of the Regional Science Association* 25 (1970): 133-152.

Meyer, J.R., J.F. Kain, and M. Wohl, *The Urban Transportation Problem*, Cambridge, Mass.: Harvard University Press, 1965.

Retail Business Centers

Berry, B.J.L., "Commercial Structure and Commercial Blight," University of Chicago Department of Geography, Research Paper 85, 1963.

Bowden, Martyn, "Downtown through Time: Delimitation, Expansion, and Internal Growth," *Economic Geography* 47 (1971): 121-135.

Boyce, R.R. and W.A.V. Clark, "Selected Spatial Variables and Central Business District Sales," *Papers and Proceedings of the Regional Science Association* 11 (1963): 167-194.

Goddard, J.B. "Functional Regions within the City Centre: A Study by Factor Analysis of Taxi Flows in Central London," *Transactions of the Institute of British Geographers* 49 (1970): 161-182.

Griffin, D.W. and R.E. Preston, "A Restatement of the 'Transition Zone' Concept," *Annals of the Association of American Geographers* 56 (1966): 339-350.

Horwood, E.M. and R.R. Boyce, *Studies of the Central Business District and Urban Freeway Development*, Seattle: University of Washington Press, 1959.

Huff, D.L., "A Note on the Limitations of Intra-Urban Gravity Models," *Land Economics* 38 (1962): 64-66.

Kersten, E. and D. Ross, "Clayton: A New Metropolitan Focus in the St. Louis Area," *Annals of the Association of American Geographers* 58 (1968): 637-649.

Murphey, P.E., "A Temporal Study of the Spatial Adjustment of a CBD in terms of Central Place Principles," *Tijdschrift voor Economische en Sociale Geografie* 61 (1970): 16-21.

Ward, D., "The Industrial Revolution and the Emergence of Boston's Central Business District," *Economic Geography* 42 (1966): 152-171.

Urban Growth: Political Structure

Bahl, R.W., "A Land Speculation Model: Urban Sprawl," *Journal of Regional Science* 8 (1968): 199-208.

Bourne, L., "Spatial Allocation: Land-Use Conversion Model of Urban Growth," *Journal of Regional Science* 9 (1969): 261-272.

Blumenfeld, H., "The Tidal Wave of Metropolitan Expansion," *Journal of the American Institute of Planners* 20 (1954): 3-14.

Chapin, F.S., "A Model for Simulating Residential Development in Urban Development Models: New Tools in Planning," *Journal of the American Institute of Planners* 32 (1965): 120-125.

Chapin, F.S. and S.F. Weiss, eds., *Urban Growth Dynamics in a Regional Cluster of Cities*, New York: Wiley, 1962.

Clawson, M., "Urban Sprawl and Speculation in Suburban Land," *Land Economics* 38 (1962): 99-111.

Goheen, Peter, "Victorian Toronto 1850-1900: Patterns and Processes of Growth," University of Chicago Department of Geography, Research Paper 127, 1970.

Harvey, R.C. and W.A.V. Clark, "The Nature and Economics of Urban Sprawl," *Land Economics* 41 (1965): 1-10.

Latham, Robert F., and Maurice H. Yeates, "Population Density Growth in Metropolitan Toronto," *Geographical Analysis* 2 (1970) : 177-186.

Morrill, R.L., "Expansion of the Urban Fringe: A Simulation Experiment," *Papers and Proceedings of the Regional Science Association* 15 (1965): 185-202.

Nelson, H., "The Spread of an Artificial Landscape over Southern California," *Annals of the Association of American Geographers* 49 (1959): No. 3, Part 2, 80-99.

Rothenberg, Jerome, "The Impact of Local Government on Intra-Metropolitan Location," *Papers of the Regional Science Association* (1969): 47-84.

Simmons, J.W., "Changing Residence in the City: A Review of Intra-Urban Mobility," *Geographical Review* 58 (1968): 622-651.

Sinclair, R., "Von Thunen and Urban Sprawl," *Annals of the Association of American Geographers* 57 (1967): 72-87.

Thomas, E.N., "Areal Association between Population Growth and Selected Factors in the Chicago Urbanized Area," *Economic Geography* 36 (1960): 158-170.

Ward, D., "A Comparative Historical Geography of Streetcar Suburbs in Boston, Massachusetts and Leeds, England, 1850-1920," *Annals of the Association of American Geographers* 54 (1964): 477-489.

Social Structure

Anderson, T.R. and J.A. Egeland, "Spatial Aspects of Social Area Analysis," *American Sociological Review* 26 (1961) : 392-398.

Berry, Brian J.L., "The Logic and Limitations of Comparative Factorial Ecology," *Economic Geography* 47 (1971): 209-220.

Breger, G.E., "Concept and Causes of Urban Blight," *Land Economics* 43 (1967): 369-376.

Brown, Lawrence A. and Frank E. Horton, "Social Area Change: An Empirical Analysis," *Urban Studies* 7 (1971): 271-288.

Brunn, Stanely D. and Wayne L. Hoffman, "The Spatial Response of Negroes and Whites toward Open Housing: The Flint Referendum," *Annals of the Association of American Geographers* 60 (1970): 18-36.

Brush, J. E., "Spatial Patterns of Population in Indian Cities," *Geographical Review* 58 (1968): 362-391.

Bunge, William, *Fitzgerald*, Cambridge, Mass.: Schenkman Publ. Co., 1971.

Christian, Charles M., John A. Jakle, and Curtis C. Roseman, "The Prejudicial Use of Space: School Assignment Strategy in the United States," *Journal of Geography* 70 (1971): 105-109.

"Cities, the Black and the Poor," *Journal of the American Institute of Planners* 35 (1969), entire issue.

Coulson, M.R.L., "Distribution of Population Age Structure in Kansas City," *Annals of the Association of American Geographers* 58 (1968): 155-176.

Harries, Keith D., "The Geography of American Crime," *Journal of Geography* 70 (1971): 204-213.

Hawley, A.H. and C.D. Duncan, "Social Area Analysis: A Critical Appraisal," *Land Economics* 33 (1957): 337-344.

Jakle, J.A. and J. Wheeler, "Changing Residential Structure of the Dutch Population in Kalamazoo," *Annals of the Association of American Geographers* 59 (1969): 441-460.

Meyer, David R., "Spatial Variation of Black Urban Households," University of Chicago, Department of Geography, Research Paper 129, 1970.

Morrill, R.L., "The Negro Ghetto: Problems and Alternatives," *Geographical Review* 55 (1965): 339-361.

Murdie, R., *Factorial Ecology of Metropolitan Toronto, 1951-1961*, University of Chicago Department of Geography, Research Paper 116, 1969.

Murray, B., "Metropolitan Interpersonal Income Inequality," *Land Economics* 45 (1969): 121-124.

Pyle, Gerald F. and Phillip H. Rees, "Modeling Patterns of Death and Disease in Chicago," *Economic Geography* 47 (1971): 475-488.

Rose, Harold M., "The Development of an Urban Subsystem: The Case of the Negro Ghetto," *Annals of the Association of American Geographers* 60 (1970): 1-17.

Seeley, J.R., "The Slum: Its Nature, Use and Users," *Journal of the American Institute of Planners* 25 (1959): 7-14.

Smolensky, E., S. Becker, and H. Molotch, "Prisoner's Dilemma and Ghetto Expansion," *Land Economics* 44 (1968): 419-430.

Taeuber, K.E., and A.F. Taeuber, *Negroes in Cities*, Chicago: Aldine, 1965.

Ward, David, *Cities and Immigrants*, New York: Oxford University Press, 1971.

Wheeler, James O. and Frederick P. Stutz, "Spatial Dimensions of Urban Social Travel," *Annals of the Association of American Geographers* 61 (1971): 371-386.

Spatial Structure of the Landscape

Chapter 9

THE THEORY OF SPATIAL STRUCTURE: A SUMMARY

We shall now summarize what has been suggested so far to account for the spatial patterns of economic activities. A location is given meaning or identity by specializing, which implies that it forms a set of spatial relations with other locations. We examined locations and the interactions between them in order to discover their structure in space, if indeed there be any. Structure or organization implies on the one hand that a territory may be divided into regions, and, on the other that the regions are arranged in a hierarchical structure. This systematic structure is produced by the rational attempts of a population to achieve some goals of spatial efficiency. These goals are:

— *To maximize the use of each separate parcel of land and, simultaneously, the sum of all parcels of land at least cost or effort, and*

— *To achieve the highest level of interaction between locations at the least possible cost.*

To be sure, other goals and desires also affect the appearance of the landscape, but we will discuss here only what can be understood about the landscape from these two spatial goals.

These goals guide decision making with respect to the following set of interrelated substitutions, the results of which give rise to certain spatial structures:

— *A substitution can be made between land costs and transport costs when seeking accessibility to some point. Expensive sites close to the point can be chosen and then used intensively, or farther sites may be chosen and used less intensively — with the same total costs.*

— *A substitution can be made between production costs at sites and transport costs, when seeking the optimal market size and scale of operations. The cost benefits of larger production volume must be balanced against increased transport costs for procurement of raw materials and distribution of finished goods. Most activities have a limited optimal*

*scale of production, but this varies
greatly by industry.*

— *A substitution can be made between
production-cost savings from agglomeration and transport costs.
The savings gained by proximity to
related industries must be balanced
against the risk of lacking even
partially monopolized supplies or
markets.*

— *A substitution can be made between
self-sufficiency (higher production
costs) and trade (higher transport
costs). Importing higher quality
resources or goods from outside the
region, involving greater transport
costs and the risk of political and
military interference, must be balanced against using lower quality
local resources or producing goods
locally at a higher cost.*

When we attempt to describe the order, or
spatial pattern, of locations and their
interrelations, we observe at least five
elements, together defining the real
landscape. The first two elements constitute
regular patterns induced by the existence of
finite amounts of useful land and the
differential demand of activities for that
land, together with the goals of spatial efficiency:

— *Spatial gradients of land use.*
— *A spatial hierarchy of regions.*

The differential quality of the earth's
surface results in:

— *More irregular but predictable
patterns of location and interaction.*

Elements that distort theoretical patterns
include:

— **Spatial error** *resulting from nonoptimal behavior.*
— *The process of spatial diffusion —
the unfolding of the spatial structure over
time as conditions change.*

Spatial Gradients

In theory, spatial gradients are the inevitable result of the competition between

activities for the limited territory near a
point of maximum accessibility. The
resulting patterns of land use and travel
should maximize the value of the land and
minimize transport costs while satisfying
the demands of society.

A point exists in any area that is central,
and thus at minimum distance, to all other
points in the surrounding area. This central
point is the market. As the distance of any
activity from the market increases, a
producer will incur mounting transport
costs and correspondingly lower net
revenue per unit area until eventually his
activity cannot survive: net revenues will
equal transport costs.

Given activities that are of varying
productivity and transportability, a spatial
ordering of activities results. Activities with
very high transport costs have limited
ranges where they can survive and must be
produced very intensively near the market.
Thus, activities that incur lower transport
costs are displaced to more distant locations,
substituting greater acreage for greater intensity. In theory, at any one point in time
an optimal gradient order will exist. This
equilibrium is brought about by the competitive bidding of potential producers for
the more accessible land, thus raising its
value (the cost of purchase, or rent). Such a
gradient is continuous from the farthest
edge of the agricultural market to the most
intensive urban location. We cannot expect,
however, to observe such a pure gradient
pattern, since the gradient *per se* is but a
partial picture of the theoretical landscape.
The important point to remember is that
competitive behavior exists, and gradient
tendencies may be observed (chapter 3,
Commercial Agriculture; chapter 8, The Urban System and Urban Structure).

Spatial Hierarchy of
Market Areas

Whereas the spatial gradient results from
competition for land around the most central point, the spatial hierarchy includes a
whole system of such points, each attracting
producers and serving consumers within its
market region, but seeking to be separate
from other, similar centers. This behavior
creates an efficient division of space into

regional markets.

A very large number of different economic and social activities, including control, exchange, and other service functions, require little area in which to operate and depend for support on the final consumer market, which is generally scattered. These different activities are mutually attracted, a relationship that is basic to the market concept. Different activities that have similar thresholds (sales needed to sustain the activity) and ranges (distance customers are willing to travel) find it profitable to locate in a cluster, since customers typically wish to minimize the effort needed to consume goods and services. Hence, by enabling customers to satisfy many purposes in the same trip, agglomeration of these activities achieves large economies.

Sellers of the same good or service, however, are mutually repellent. Each seeks a spatial monopoly — an area in which only one seller of the good has all the customers. This competition thus induces sellers to locate just far enough from each other so that each can enjoy a profitable spatial monopoly, but close enough together so that not enough purchasing power remains in the space between the sellers to allow another seller to spring up between them. Ideally, this process results in a triangular arrangement of sellers, each one equidistant from the others, and these triangular patterns will together form a hexagonal network.

When activities require larger markets than in the basic system described above, a hierarchical structure emerges. One rather optimal arrangement is for alternate central places to add the new activity. These alternate places thus become second-level centers. Similarly, for activities requiring even larger markets, alternate second-level centers would acquire the new activity. Thus, an even higher level would be created. In this way, a territory is divided into a hexagonal structure of markets and spatial monopolies having as many hierarchical levels as the economy will support.

Under a given technology, an arrangement of centers will theoretically exist for the entire economy such that the population can satisfy all its demands on all levels at the least possible total distance, while at the same time all activities are profitable. In summary, the central place hierarchy is the result of balancing a number of goals: locating as many activities in as few places as possible and realizing the greatest economies of agglomeration, while at the same time keeping the number of trips and the total distance traveled to a minimum (chapter 4, Towns as Central Places).

Gradient Hierarchies. If land quality were everywhere identical and no activities existed except ones like those already introduced, the landscape would have a joint hierarchical and gradient character (figure 9.01). The gradient results when activities compete for land on the basis of their productivity, and it induces some dispersal of population and activities. However, if the territory of the economy around the main market is large enough to permit the emergence of smaller competing markets and central places, a central place structure emerges. The larger the area within an economy, the more elaborated becomes its hierarchical structure and the less important any single center. Modifying the overall gradient around the main market are local gradients around regional markets. In the United States, for example, we observe a dispersion of central places over the territory, an overall gradient of intensity of population and activities outward from the Northeast, and lesser gradients outward from the other regional centers.

The internal structure of a city also illustrates this structure (figure 8.10 again). When small, the city center contains all the distribution facilities, and there is a gradient of land use outward from the center. As the area of the city increases, the threshold for establishment of competing centers is reached and the original gradient becomes punctuated by areas of greater intensity around district shopping centers. When the city becomes very large, a complex central place hierarchy develops, consisting of hundreds of nodes at many levels with overlapping gradients.

Spatial Quality

The surface of the earth, however, is not homogeneous, but differs markedly in its

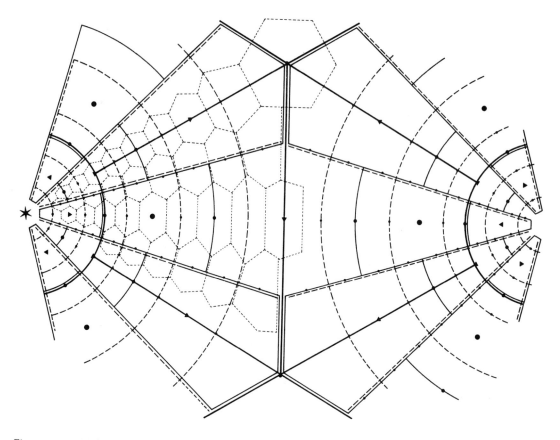

Figure 9.01 Gradient-hierarchy landscape. This is one attempt to combine rent-gradient and central place theories. Central places (dots) and their trade area boundaries (lines) are developed to serve the area between two large centers, which are agricultural markets. The hexagonal shape of the smallest market areas is maintained (for clarity, not all are shown), but the market areas become larger and centers farther apart with distance from the major centers. Compare with figure 4.05 showing the usual central place patterns.

productivity, attractiveness, and — especially — endowment of resources. Variations in spatial quality alter the patterns presented so far, usually by creating variations in the intensity of land use and in the concentration of activities. The gradient-hierarchy landscape will thus change.

Variation in quality works in several ways. If land productivity varies over very wide areas (such as with a seasonal monopoly), it will alter the agricultural gradient and likewise increase or reduce the spacing of central places. More localized differences in land productivity create rather predictable local irregularities, such as upgrading or downgrading the use of the land, or favoring larger or smaller farms than would be expected. Where transport is relatively cheap and differences in land

productivity great, the agricultural land use gradient may be significantly modified.

The Industrial Landscape. Industrial location is especially responsive to variation in spatial quality: raw materials must be obtained from a limited number of specific locations and finished products distributed to other industries with very specific locations, rather than to more widespread final consumer markets. Whereas the gradient-hierarchy landscape consists of central markets serving widely diffused farmers, the industrial landscape shows greater concentration of activities at large markets and material sources. Rather than seeking locations away from each other to obtain spatial monopolies, many industries cluster at locations that have proved

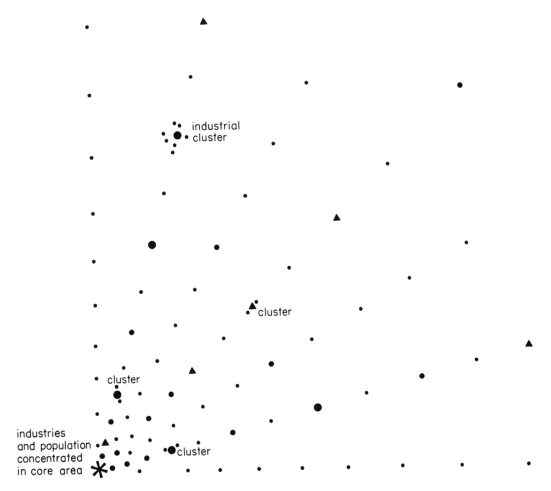

Figure 9.02 Addition of industrial clusters to the gradient-hierarchy surface. When such variation in spatial quality as resource location is considered, the gradient-hierarchy landscape is distorted. Clusters of industrial towns appear. Because of their industrial importance, some larger places are closer together than in figure 9.01. (Only urban places are shown here.)

profitable, hoping to share all or much of a national market.

For industries in which transport costs on finished products are most important and markets are diffuse, location is similar to that for a central place activity. Industries in which the transport costs of raw materials are the dominant expense seek a spatial monopoly, or a local supply area. On a macro-scale, such places will often seem to have located in a cluster, but on a micro-scale, it will be apparent that each plant has sought a separation from the others that will assure it a local supply area.

Industries for which transport costs on both materials and finished goods are significant may locate at either resource or

market or at major junctions between. The less important the transfer costs and the more important other cost differences between sites (such as the quality and cost of labor), the more the industrial pattern will become one of clusters of producers at several locations where costs are least.

The net effect of these patterns of industrial location is, first, to create clusters of urban settlements near major concentrations of resources. Second, industries that share national or large regional markets and for which transport costs are not great tend to locate near the largest single markets — the bigger metropolises. The effect on the landscape is to concentrate population and production in fewer, larger places (figure

9.02) — disproportionately few in comparison to the pure gradient-hierarchy landscape serving an agricultural population.

Distorting Factors

At least two distorting factors complicate the picture still further: spatial error and spatial diffusion. By spatial error, we mean that the optimum locational decision is not always made. Most decisions are made without all the facts, hence they are imperfect. Even with good information, error can be introduced when the data is interpreted. In addition, many persons, governments, and businesses often make decisions that are satisfying rather than optimal; they follow a conservative, safe course that is profitable, even if another, riskier course would be much more profitable.

This error is most apparent in locational mistakes, paid for in extreme cases by economic failure, but more generally by inadequate profits and income and operation at less than capacity. The effect on the theoretically ideal landscape is to blur its precision; to confuse its boundaries between agricultural and urban uses and between market areas, resulting in both zones of interpenetration, such as between crops, and zones of indifference, such as customer choice of a shopping center; and to loosen the rigidity of the hexagonal structure randomly.

Even optimum decisions, once made, may be quickly impaired by the second distorting element: change over time in locational factors and in the locators. If, as history has often shown, population, activities, and knowledge spread outward from a small number of points having greater power, access to markets and capital, and ability to achieve the optimal goals, then a static theory can be considered incomplete. Not only does economic development spread outward from a few origins, but social, political, and economic conditions change over time. Technology, transport quality, productivity, kind and volume of demand, manufacturing processes, and population all change. The effect of these changes on the landscape is to make existing locations obsolete and to force enterprises and individuals to adjust their behavior.

The impact of dynamic spatial growth and diffusion on the landscape creates another kind of gradient. Most obviously here, population and transport density decline outward from the hearth areas of a population to the margin of settlement (figure 9.03) (for example, westward in the United States from the Atlantic seaboard). Moreover, industrialization and urbanization typically diffuse slowly from early centers of economic power (as from Boston-New York-Philadelphia in the United States). As a result, both absolute and per capita income usually follow the same gradient (figure 9.03).

While this summary has focused on the location of activities and people, it should be understood that the whole spatial structure is maintained by interactions between locations — trade, movements of people, and communication. The landscape has become more differentiated, of course, as transport and communications have improved and become cheaper; thus greater advantage can be taken of superior locations and site quality. Organization of locations means specialization of functions, which requires movements to make the specialization profitable. Without movement between places, no organization of locations could exist; there would be only a surface containing individual man-land relationships.

All the locational models and theories discussed could, in fact, be called movement or interaction theories, since the goal of minimizing distance was inherent in each model. The gradients of agricultural and urban land use result from minimizing the costs of supplying agricultural products to markets and the costs of reaching work and shopping within the city. The extent of both the market and the city is governed by transport costs as well as land rent (price).

Central place theory, too, depends on minimizing transport costs when satisfying different sets of central service needs. Again, the extent of one central place level is controlled by the relation of transport costs to possible revenues. However, partly because people are willing to travel much farther for some purposes than for others,

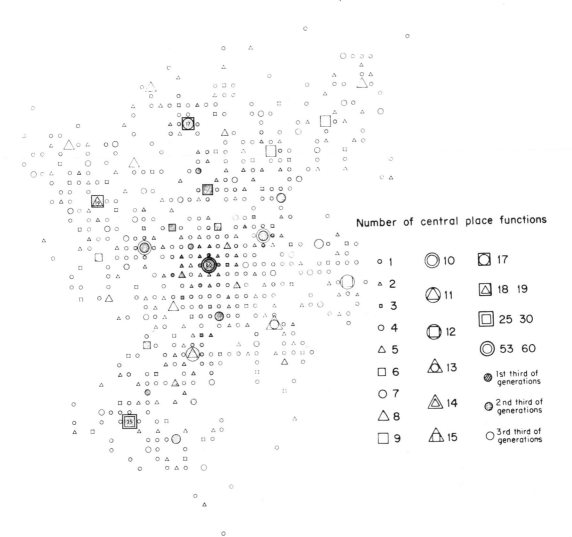

Number of central place functions

o 1	◎ 10	⬟ 17
△ 2	△ 11	△ 18 19
▫ 3		
o 4	⬤ 12	▣ 25 30
△ 5		◎ 53 60
□ 6	△ 13	◍ 1st third of generations
O 7	△ 14	◉ 2nd third of generations
△ 8	△ 15	○ 3rd third of generations
□ 9		

Figure 9.03 Growth of central place systems over time. This figure shows an experimental and hypothetical pattern of central places, as might have developed over perhaps 100 years. Note that the density decreases outward from the center (the distance between the places increases), but that denser clusters of central places occur at various points.

minimizing transport costs applies to a variety of levels. Figure 9.04 depicts movement patterns to agricultural markets on two levels and to central places on three levels for a small area.

Much industrial location involves specific, irregular movements from raw material sources and to markets. Theoretically, industrial location rests heavily on minimizing transport costs, but these costs are to a complex of markets and from a complex of sources, rather than to

just one market. Thus, the resulting location and movement patterns are less regular — they are no longer center-oriented and diffused, but instead, few, larger, and overlapping.

Spatial Organization

In the light of the five spatial elements we have just discussed, that is, gradients, hierarchies, industrial clustering, spatial

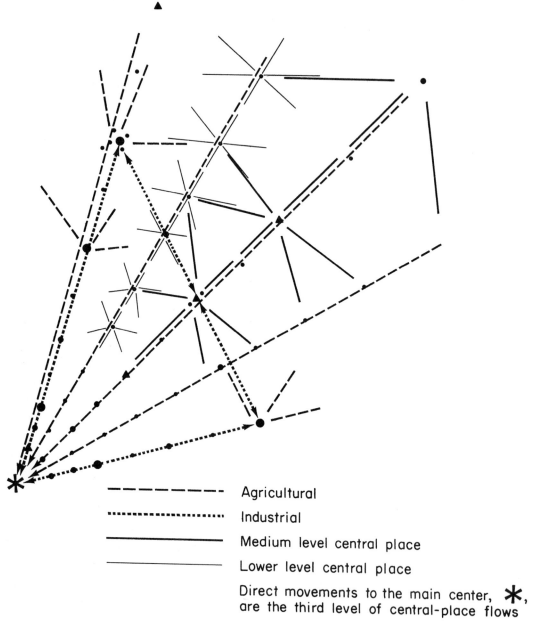

Agricultural

Industrial

Medium level central place

Lower level central place

Direct movements to the main center, ✳,
are the third level of central-place flows

Figure 9.04 Partial movement pattern of a gradient-hierarchy industrial-cluster surface. Movements serve the spatial pattern shown in figure 9.02.

error, and spatial diffusion, the landscape can be seen to show systematic variation in intensity and extent of land use and interaction. The spatial structure of a society is perhaps best described by the patterns of intensity of land use and by the complex pattern of interaction that each location has with the world around it. Try to imagine all

five patterns or elements placed together on one map. It is obviously difficult to analyze such a complex pattern; one component cannot be readily isolated from the others. We attempted here just to summarize the major elements that, in commercial societies at least, seem to interact to produce typical landscapes.

Theory and Reality. There are many ways to test portions of theory. Many of these methods were discussed earlier, and warnings were given not to expect simple patterns, such as hexagonal trade areas, in a real landscape. Finding evidence of efficient behavior in the location of activities requires more sophisticated tests; in the central place example, for instance, adjustments must be made for topography, population density, age of settlement, other activities, and some acceptable range of error.

The evidence given by the more careful tests shows thus far that optimal or nearly optimal spatial behavior and much spatial order can be seen in patterns of location and interaction. However, the effects of rapid changes in technology, population, and other forces are perhaps greater than anticipated, and we have not yet well enough incorporated into our theory the dimension of historical change. On the other hand, the presumed role of irrationality has diminished as we have improved our concept of optimizing behavior, as we have looked at larger sets of relationships, and as we better understand the multiple meanings of distance and other spatial characteristics.

Distribution maps provide the simplest evidence of spatial structure. Distributions of land use, farm size, and per-acre value of farm output corroborate the existence of an agricultural gradient and show the effect of land quality and entrepreneurial differences. Maps of retail and wholesale trade areas in urban centers and analyses of how places are spaced support central place theory, so long as variations in population density and the role of processing activities are taken into account. The locational patterns of individual industries illustrate the kinds of optimal patterns predicted, but they also show the effects of monopoly, brand loyalty, and other distorting factors. The movement patterns of goods and people likewise illustrate the tendency to minimize distance, but they display a degree of indifference to distance as well.

REGIONAL STRUCTURE

In this chapter we first presented a systematic description of locations and interactions so that, when the concept of the region was discussed, it would be clear that in theory the region is only a practical, simplified way of looking at the more complex underlying pattern of behavior. A region is a segment of space that is unified and characterized by some common characteristic — uniformity of land use or dependence upon a particular center, for instance. However, such "pure" common characteristics extend over embarrassingly small amounts of territory, so that we must accept as regions areas with less stringently defined common qualities in order to use the region as a tool in planning and administration.

With respect to theories of spatial structure, two kinds of regions are applicable — uniform and nodal regions. A third kind of region, functional, describes an area unified by a pattern of production and flows; for example, a forest-wood products industry region. Uniform regions are areas having some given use or character or possessing some other common characteristic (the characteristic varies within the region only to some statistically acceptable limit). Whether having in common a single factor or multiple factors, uniform regions may be diverse in other respects.

Uniform regions are the result of spatial agglomeration and the incompatibility of some land uses and social groups. Uniform regions having the same agricultural land use, for example, tend to occur within a certain range in the intensity gradient out from a central market. Specific portions of the zone at that distance tend to specialize in certain crops because of the advantages of agglomeration (specialized markets, research stations, and skilled labor, for instance). The presence of industrial markets stimulates agricultural specialization, and environmental variations also have a significant impact on land use.

Within the city, uniform regions tend to develop naturally because of the benefits of clustering for industries and businesses, because of differential ability to pay rent (or buy homes), and because of perceived incompatibility. The creation of uniform regions of income, religion, and color is strongly motivated by prejudice. Zoning regulations often reinforce the natural trends.

Uniform regions can now be defined by

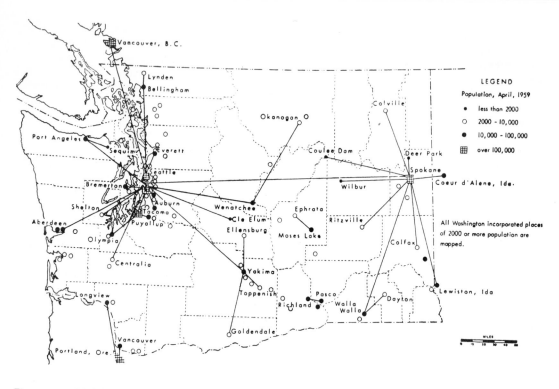

Figure 9.05 Nodal regions of Washington. One clue to the nesting of smaller nodal areas within larger ones is given by an analysis of telephone data. In this example, it was assumed that if one town places more calls than it receives, it depends on that town. Thus, Seattle receives from all places more calls than it sends, including the next most important place, Spokane, which in turn dominates its local region. (Reprinted by permission of the Regional Science Association, from J. Nystuen and M. Dacey, "A Graph Theory Interpretation of Nodal Regions," *Papers and Proceedings of the Regional Science Association*, Vol. VII, 1961.)

fairly simple clustering and grouping techniques that ensure the maximum contrast between the cohesion within the region and the lack of such cohesion with the surrounding areas. Obviously, no territory consists of one unique set of uniform regions; any small area may be part of several different relatively homogeneous regions depending on the criteria used — politics, culture, or land use, for example.

Nodal regions — central places — and their hinterlands, together forming the central place system, have already been discussed at length. They are the chief illustration of the repetitive, hierarchical nature of space. Like uniform regions, nodal regions are not rigidly defined (the zones of influence between competing centers overlap), and boundaries should be defined in terms of strength, or the extent to which a center dominates the customers or suppliers in the region.

Any small area is part of a whole set of nodal regions, from the smallest hamlet to the national economy (figures 9.05 and 9.06). The smaller regions, in general, nest within the larger ones, although there are many cases in which a smaller area is divided in its allegiance to larger ones. The higher the hierarchical level of the region, the more self-contained its culture and its economy.

The structure of metropolitan regions has been the most intensively studied. Metropolitan divisions are based mainly on wholesale and financial patterns (figure 9.07). Although boundaries are typically drawn between these regions, it should be clear that the zones of influence overlap widely, especially where metropolitan centers are close together and their hinterlands are large.

Political regions are legally defined by

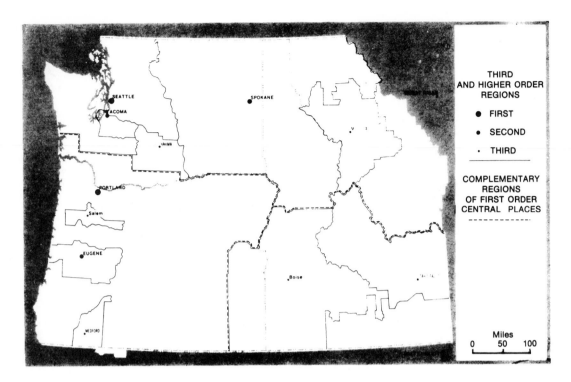

Figure 9.06 Nodal regions of the Pacific Northwest, 1963. This regionalization was based on numbers of branches of firms whose main offices were located in the larger centers. The dominance of Seattle and especially Portland is notable; areas beyond but closer to Eugene are still directly tributary to Portland. (Reprinted by permission of *Economic Geography*, from R. Preston, "The Structure of Central Place Systems," Vol. 47, 1971.)

specific boundaries, and our lives must conform to these boundaries to a degree. Administrative efficiency in large areas requires a hierarchical, repetitive structure, such as in the central place system (nodal economic regions). A question that is interesting theoretically and also important practically is to what extent these sets of regions — political and economic — coincide. Central places often arise at midpoints between large centers. Boundaries between larger places pass through smaller ones, but it is administratively more efficient to include entire subunits within larger ones — for example, to include entire parishes within a diocese, entire schools within a school district. Thus, the economic and administrative principles conflict. If the economic forces are stronger, the later administrative structure will be less than optimal — including too few or too many subdivisions and off-center administrative centers. Administrators and planners generally favor making economic structure subordinate to administrative efficiency, which might be optimal from the viewpoint of the entire society (using social and political as well as economic criteria). Still, political units and economic regions often conflict; the hinterlands of such centers as New York, St. Louis, Kansas City, Omaha, Chicago, Cincinnati, and Portland cross state lines (see figure 9.07).

The solution to this apparent conflict between administrative and economic organization is that economic subareas often nest entirely within higher ones, even though this does not strictly minimize distance. Branch Federal Reserve bank districts, for example, nest within major districts, and retailers in a smaller city midway between larger ones will obtain most wholesale goods from only one of them.

In summary, regions do exist, they do have meaning, and we can delineate them. However, they are not clear-cut areas in

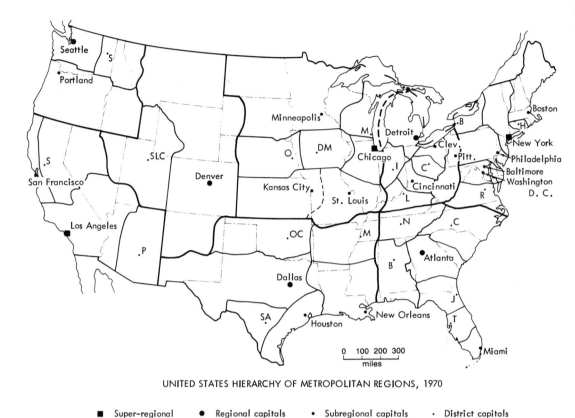

UNITED STATES HIERARCHY OF METROPOLITAN REGIONS, 1970

■ Super-regional   ● Regional capitals   • Subregional capitals   · District capitals

Figure 9.07   Metropolitan regional structure of the United States, 1970. Areas tributary to metropolitan centers at the top three levels of the urban hierarchy. Estimates are by the author, based on wholesale trade data, airline patterns, commuting fields, and related data. The rapid development of the United States over the last century has resulted in a rather unstable structure, in the sense that places of great gateway importance (such as New Orleans, St. Louis, Cincinnati) have declined relatively, after the growth of new centers (such as Dallas, Houston, Kansas City, Denver).

which activities are confined. Rather, regions are useful more as a system of classification. They are imperfect generalizations of the underlying spatial complex, which itself can be better described as the connections of countless individuals, farms, industrial plants, and businesses.

SPATIAL TRENDS IN ADVANCED SOCIETIES

In agriculture, central services, and industry, improvements in transportation have reduced the cost of distance and the dominance of spatial organization by the goal of minimizing transport costs. Thus, in agriculture more attention is paid to en-

vironmental differences and variations in response to inputs. Similarly, amenities (such as view and amount of land), services, and prestige location tend to influence people's choice of homes. Industries and services are responding more and more often to economies of scale and agglomeration, and thus are becoming concentrated in the fewer, larger places with greater market and labor stability and more amenities.

It has become popular to speak of the new locational freedom, to say that the advantages of centrality and accessibility have ceased to play a decisive role, and to ask whether the city, the central business district, the hierarchy of cities and services, and — indeed — much of present theory is becoming obsolete. The fact is, of course, that distance is still important. Our new

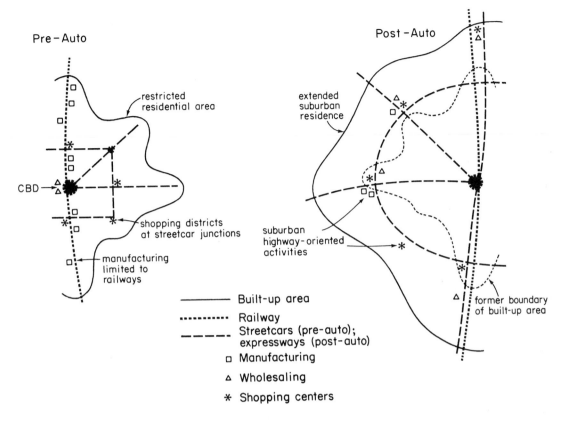

Figure 9.08   The urban pattern: pre-auto and post-auto. The automobile has made possible a more extended residential area and a dispersal of manufacturing and wholesaling activities to suburban locations.

ability to go greater distances for the same cost has extended the range of our activities and lengthened our relationships. But that the goals of accessibility and minimizing distance are still powerful is shown by the even greater concentration of activities today in the few places that are most accessible. Similarly, the structure of distribution of goods and individual shopping is still hierarchical, although the number of levels may have been reduced, and centers of a given level may be farther apart.

A larger portion of manufacturing, as of agriculture, can today respond to local variations in quality and economies of scale in order to penetrate more distant markets and reduce the spatial monopoly of other producers. Yet the growing demand for goods and services that can be delivered immediately — such as entertainment, recreation, and repair work — is stimulating a countertrend toward greater regional self-sufficiency.

Within the city, cheaper transport and the shift to the automobile have had an even more radical impact (figure 9.08); the entire urban area may now be within the range that an individual is willing to travel in his car. The freedom given by the car, however, tends to transform the greatest asset of the center — its accessibility — into a liability — congestion. As a result, some activities are dispersed to more distant points with only moderate accessibility but more space. In this case, a more complicated pattern of rent and land values emerges, showing far more emphasis on local differences in environment and amenities. But the problem of the congested center results from a technical inability to adjust to an altered transport mode; the change in transport does not bestow real "locational freedom" but instead permits competing centers to arise because their freedom from congestion offsets their slightly lower accessibility.

Thus, even with change, spatial order does not disappear. Businesses remain aggregated to maximize the exchange of information and reduce total transport charges, but even more aggregations become appropriate as the city area increases and its density decreases; an individual store that chooses a separate, low-rent site, even though technically accessible, risks lack of awareness by consumers and subsequent bankruptcy because of its spatial isolation. The dispersal of shopping in metropolitan Los Angeles is not the result of "locational freedom," but rather is precisely the result of the difficulty of moving to one center from such a vast, built-up area. Here, stores are not randomly dispersed, but cluster in regional shopping centers rationally located with respect to the distribution of population. The absence of a dominant downtown center, however, may result in having fewer of those goods and services that need the entire metropolitan market for their support, for even in Los Angeles most travel is local, and people are no more willing to travel long distances to a specialized shop than if it were downtown.

Conclusion

Geography as a "discipline in distance" thus concerns the ways in which the fact of space, the cost of overcoming spatial separation, and the differential demand of activities for territory create a complex but ordered structure, exhibiting at world, national, and local scales predictable spatial patterns: characteristic gradients of land use and population; hierarchical patterns of towns, cities, and business districts; hierarchies, clusters, and other industrial patterns. All these patterns can be distorted by the inability and unwillingness of many to follow the underlying goals of maximizing the productivity of places and the level of interaction at minimum cost and travel, which tend to produce the ideal landscape. They can also be distorted by the fact that technological, social, and economic conditions continually change, and that development itself usually diffuses in space from core areas. This book has emphasized the abstract characteristics of space, but it

has frequently recognized that geography is also the study of "man-environment" relations, and that the natural environment continues to condition these ideal structures in very significant ways.

REFERENCES

Spatial Organization

Berry, Brian J.L., "The Geography of the United States in the Year 2000," *Transactions of the Institute of British Geographers* 51 (1970): 21-54.

Berry, B.J.L., *Essays on Commodity Flows and the Spatial Structure of the Indian Economy*, University of Chicago Department of Geography, Research Paper 111, 1966.

Berry, B.J.L., "Interdependence of Spatial Structure and Spatial Behavior," *Papers and Proceedings of the Regional Science Association* 21 (1968): 205-228.

von Boventer, E., "Spatial Organization Theory as a Basis for Regional Planning," *Journal of American Institute of Planners* 30 (1964): 90-100.

von Boventer, E., "Toward a United Theory of Spatial Economic Structure," *Papers and Proceedings of the Regional Science Association* 10 (1963): 163-188.

Curry, L., "Landscape as System," *Geographical Review* 54 (1964): 121-124.

Friedmann, J., "The Spatial Structure of Economic Development in the Tennessee Valley," University of Chicago Department of Geography, Research Paper 39, 1955.

Garrison, W.L., "Spatial Structure of the Economy," *Annals of the Association of American Geographers* 49 (1959): 232-239, 471-482; 50 (1960): 357-373.

Goodey, Brian R., "The Mapping of Utopia: A Comment on the Geography of Sir Thomas More," *Geographical Review* 60 (1970): 15-30.

Hartshorn, Truman, "The Spatial Structure of Socioeconomic Development in the Southeast, 1950-1960," *Geographical Review* 61 (1971): 265-283.

Hodge, G., "Urban Structure and Regional Development," *Papers and Proceedings of the Regional Science Association* 21 (1968): 101-124.

Janelle, D.G., "Spatial Reorganization: A Model and Concept," *Annals of the Association of American Geographers* 59 (1969): 348-364.

Moore, F.T. and J.W. Peterson, "Regional Analysis: An Inter-Industry Model of Utah," *Review of Economics and Statistics* 37 (1955): 368-383.

North, D.C., "The Spatial and Interregional Framework of the United States' Economy," *Papers and Proceedings of the Regional Science Association* 2 (1956): 201-209.

Philbrick, A.K., "Principles of Areal Functional Organization in Regional Human Geography," *Economic Geography* 33 (1957): 299-336.

Pred, Allan R. and Barry M. Kibel, "An Application of Gaming Simulation to a General Model of Economic Locational Processes," *Economic Geography* 46 (1970): 136-156.

Ray, D. Michael, "The Spatial Structure of Economic and Cultural Differences: A Factorial Ecology of Canada," *Papers of the Regional Science Association* 23 (1969): 7-24.

Ullman, E.L., "Regional Development and the Geography of Concentration," *Papers and Proceedings of the Regional Science Association* 4 (1958): 179-200.

Vining, R., "The Description of Certain Spatial Aspects of an Economic System," *Economic Development and Cultural Change* 3 (1955): 147-195.

Warntz, W., *Toward a Geography of Price*, Philadelphia: University of Pennsylvania Press, 1959.

Whebell, C.F.J., "Corridors: A Theory of Urban Systems," *Annals of the Association of American Geographers* 59 (1969): 1-26.

Wolpert, Julian, "Departures from the Usual Environment in Locational Analysis," *Annals of the Association of American Geographers* 60 (1970): 220-229.

Regional Economics

Beckmann, M.J., "The Economics of Location," *Kyklos* 8 (1955): 416-421.

Beckmann, M.J. and T.C. Koopmans, "Assignment Problems and the Location of Economic Activities," *Econometrica* 25 (1957): 53-76.

Bramhall, D.F., "Projecting Regional Accounts and Industrial Locations," *Papers and Proceedings of the Regional Science Association* 7 (1961): 89-118.

Czamanski, Stanislaw and Emil E. Malizia, "Applicability and Limitations in the Use of National Input-Output Tables for Regional Studies," *Papers of the Regional Science Association* 23 (1969): 65-78.

Duncan, O.D. and R. Cuzzort, "Regional Differentiation and Socioeconomic Change," *Papers and Proceedings of the Regional Science Association* 4 (1958): 163-178.

Isard, Walter, *General Theory: Social, Political, Economic and Regional*, Cambridge, Mass.: M.I.T. Press, 1969.

Isard, W., et al., "On the Linkage of Socioeconomic and Ecologic Systems," *Papers and Proceedings of the Regional Science Association* 21 (1968): 79-100.

Isard, W., et al., *Methods of Regional Analysis: An Introduction to Regional Science*, New York: Technology Press, M.I.T., 1960.

Kavesh, R.A. and J.B. Jones, "Differential Regional Impacts of Federal Expenditures," *Papers and Proceedings of the Regional Science Association* 2 (1956): 152-173.

Leven, C.L., "Regional and Interregional Accounts in Perspective," *Papers and Proceedings of the Regional Science Association* 13 (1964): 127-146.

Lianos, Theodore P., "Interregional Allocation of Labor: A Measure of Economic Efficiency," *Annals of Regional Science* 4, No. 1 (1970): 93-104.

Moses, L., "A General Equilibrium Model of Production, Interregional Trade and Location of Industry," *Review of Economics and Statistics* 42 (1960): 376-397.

Nourse, H., *Regional Economics*, New York: McGraw-Hill, 1968.

North, D.C., "Location Theory and Regional Economic Growth," *Journal of Political Economy* 63 (1955): 243-258.

Richardson, Harry W., ed., *Regional Economics*, London: Macmillan, 1970.

Schramm, Gunter, "Regional versus Interregional Efficiency in Resource Allocations," *Annals of Regional Science* 4, No. 2 (1970): 1-14.

Stabler, J.C., "Exports and Evolution: Process of Regional Change," *Land Economics* 44 (1968): 11-23.

Regions and Regionalization

Abler, Ron, "Zip-Code Areas as Statistical Regions," *Professional Geographer* 22 (1970): 270-274.

Berry, B.J.L., "Approaches to Regional Analysis: A Synthesis," *Annals of the Association of American Geographers* 54 (1964): 2-11.

Bogue, D.L. and C.L. Beale, *Economic Areas of the United States*, New York: Free Press, 1961.

Bunge, W., "Gerrymandering, Geography and Grouping," *Geographical Review* 56 (1966): 256-263.

Fox, K.A. and T.K. Kumar, "The Functional Economic Area," *Papers and Proceedings of the Regional Science Association* 15 (1965): 57-86.

Grigg, D., "The Logic of Regional Systems," *Annals of the Association of American Geographers* 55 (1965): 465-491.

Harris, C.D., "Salt Lake City," *Economic Geography* 17 (1941): 204-212.

Horton, Frank E. and Harold McConnell, "A Method for Classification and Regionalization Based on Areal Association," *Annals of Regional Science* 3, No. 2 (1969): 111-126.

Johnston, R.U., "Grouping and Regionalizing: Some Methodological and Technical Observations," *Economic Geography* 46 (1970): 293-305.

Lankford, P.M., "Regionalization: Theory and Alternative Algorithms," *Geographical Analysis* 1 (1969): 196-212.

Lösch, A., "The Nature of Economic Regions," *Southern Economic Journal* 5 (1938): 71-78.

Meinig, D.W., "The Mormon Culture Region: Strategies and Patterns in the Geography of the American West, 1847-1964," *Annals of the Association of American Geographers* 55 (1965): 191-220.

Nostrand, Richard L., "The Hispanic-American Borderland: Delimitation of an American Culture Region," *Annals of the Association of American Geographers* 60 (1970): 638-661.

Nystuen, J.D. and M.F. Dacey, "A Graph Theory Interpretation of Nodal Regions," *Papers and Proceedings of the Regional Science Association* 7 (1961): 29-42.

Perloff, H.S. et al., *Regions, Resources, and Economic Growth*, Baltimore: Johns Hopkins, 1960.

Sabbagh, M.E., "Some Geographic Characteristics of a Plural Society: Apartheid in South Africa," *Geographical Review* 58 (1968): 1-28.

Teitz, M.B., "Regional Theory and Regional Models," *Papers and Proceedings of the Regional Science Association* 9 (1962): 35-52.

Ideal Spatial Organization and Problems of the Real World

Chapter 10

Our principal concern has been to present concepts and models of ideal spatial location and to compare the real landscape with the theoretical one. Ideal locational patterns are those which should result from the successful pursuit of the goals outlined at the beginning of the book: maximizing both the utility of places and the level of interaction at least cost. A landscape following these patterns would be functionally efficient, socially equitable, and, one might hope, ecologically balanced. But, as we have frequently mentioned, observed landscapes tend to deviate from the ideal models. Not only are they distorted with respect to geographic pattern, but they are often inefficient, inequitable, and ecologically imbalanced.

In this chapter we briefly discuss the inefficiency and inequity associated with spatial organization, and the consequent human and environmental problems. Since deviation from ideal spatial organization is particularly evident in regional and world levels of economic development, we also briefly examine the problems attending these broader levels.*

SPATIAL ORGANIZATION: EFFICIENCY AND EQUITY

Although we do not fully understand what constitutes social and economic efficiency, we can compare theoretical landscape patterns with the relative "efficiency" of existing patterns of location and interaction.

Spatial structure would seem to be efficient when the following conditions exist:

— *Enterprises successfully and profitably produce demanded goods and services at least real cost (that is, location is optional and economies of scale are realized).*

---

* The reader is hereby warned that I approach this discussion from a "social democratic" perspective, believing that individual freedom is an essential condition of human progress, but that the higher goal of society must be to ensure an equally good life for all its members, and to live in harmony with nature.

— *The allocation of value (prices, incomes) is fair; thus*
   a. *Land and physical resources are utilized as needed, but not wasted.*
   b. *Individuals and families are allocated value (wages, salaries, rent, royalties, interest, profit) according to their economic and social productivity.*
— *The pattern of interaction simply reflects the structure of economic specialization and social differentiation. Unnecessary cross-movements do not occur.*
— *Regional differences in income are not extreme.*

If these conditions do not hold true, there is an imbalance in the location of either people or economic activities, or both.

Technically, the conditions for optimal location and efficiency are such that no shift in location or intensity of activity or in the level and direction of interaction can occur without some net decrease in total profits or increase in total costs, or both.

Efficiency and Equity

If the conditions listed above really characterized an economy, whether capitalist or centrally planned, the resulting structure would be both efficient and equitable: equilibrium guarantees the "most for the greatest number." The allocation of value, however, might still be considered unfair for those people and regions less able to compete; therefore, government intervention may be desirable to establish greater equity.

For example, if a set of services, such as hospitals, were located according to the principles of industrial location (see pp. 101), the arrangement would be one with minimum total costs (including average cost per patient). Such a minimum may well result, however, in a combination of fewer hospitals with very poor access (and higher costs) and a greater number with very good access (figure 10.01). It would be more equitable to locate the hospitals so that no one has very poor access, even at the cost of lower efficiency (making the many travel a little farther).

Equitable and efficient patterns of location will vary under conditions of uneven density (as in figure 10.01) and even more markedly under conditions of uneven income levels (lower income areas cannot "support" hospitals). But ideal conditions are rare; the real landscape exhibits both inefficiency and a high degree of inequity.

BARRIERS TO EFFICIENCY AND EQUITY

The achievement of efficiency and equity is impeded by several factors, which will be discussed in the sections that follow. These factors include:

— *Technological change and obsolescence.*
— *Human and corporate error.*
— *The precedence of noneconomic values.*
— *Unallocated social costs.*
— *The misallocation of resources.*

Technological Change and Obsolescence

Much inefficiency in the real landscape is due to technological change and obsolescence. A dynamic economy is sustained by constant innovation in products and processes as demand for goods fluctuates. But new processes may render existing capital equipment obsolete, resource deposits become depleted, and the mobility of people and enterprises often forces change in existing uses of land or resources. Moreover, as an economy grows, the increasing scale of enterprises may destroy the viability of countless small factories and stores. Although entrepreneurs try to achieve maximum productivity from their investments, they cannot prevent the encroachment of obsolescence and inefficiency. They tend to maintain nonoptimal locations until profits disappear and even after losses set in.

At any one time many enterprises within an economy are either failing or unprofitable (see figure 8.11). Several factors account for their economic decline. For example, factories unprofitable today may

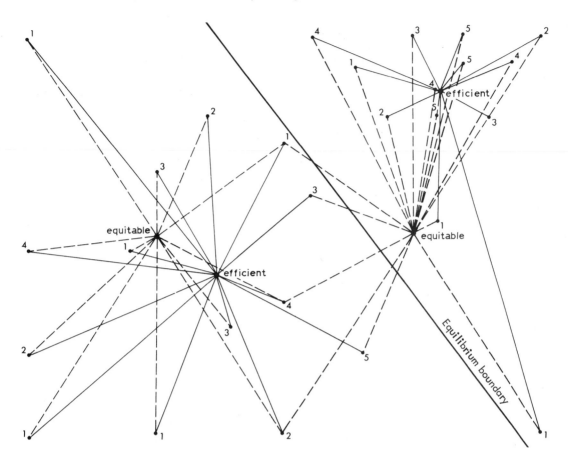

Figure 10.01 Equity versus efficiency in the location of services (such as hospitals or schools). The efficient, or distance-minimizing, solution places a large facility in the densest area and a smaller one in a less concentrated area. Most people (therefore, the average) go a short distance; a few go very far (thin solid lines connect people to a facility). Numbers indicate how many people are at each location. The equilibrium boundary is midway between the efficient locations; all people travel to the closest facility. In the equitable solution, the farthest people travel the shortest distance that is geometrically possible, although this increases total travel, especially from the denser area (dashed lines connect people to the equitably located facilities.

once have been optimally located, but resource and labor costs may have risen, the location of markets shifted, or the best techniques of production altered too rapidly. These external conditions can make adjustment impossible, whatever the behavior of the firm. Similarly, many stores that were favorably located during the streetcar era find it impossible to adapt to the car-oriented transport network. Many firms are unprofitable, however, because they are uneconomically small and their operator is unwilling to shift to a more profitable location or occupation. This problem is common in agriculture, trade, and services.

The shift in carrier priority from trains to trucks has made thousands of miles of local rail obsolete, and, together with improved mobility, has reduced the viability of thousands of smaller trade centers (see figure 8.04). Thus, some obsolescence due to changing times is unavoidable.

Technological changes are responsible for widespread economic and social disruptions. Especially in agriculture and mining, improved technology has displaced millions of people. Here it is the human investment in ways of life or in skills that have been made obsolete, raising the specter of unemployment, underemployment, and poverty.

City-dwellers constitute another group

confronted by the problems of obsolescence and inefficiency. Since urban patterns have developed under constantly changing conditions and urban decision making is notably subject to error and political pressure, cities abound with obsolete and inefficient locations. Many activities located on once optimal sites are unable to adjust to changed conditions: neighborhoods deteriorate when demand falls off for older housing or for sites in older areas.

The adoption of new technology, then, has promoted a trend in economic development toward units (businesses, factories, organizations, farms, cities) of increasingly large size; and toward faster, easier transport. This trend has led and will probably continue to lead to obsolescence and inefficiency in much of the capital and human investment in smaller enterprises and places, as well as in older and poorer housing, particularly in cities.

Human and Corporate Error

One common barrier to the attainment of ideal spatial organization is simple error on the part of individuals or businesses. The fear of making errors may prevent optimal decision making: it is safer to choose satisfactory or profitable locations, for instance, than to take a chance on risky but theoretically optimal sites. The reluctance to take risks is understandable; optimality is notoriously unstable, and changing conditions may eventually erode the value of even the most well-considered course of action.

The effects of error can have far-reaching consequences. For example, private and public investment based on erroneous projections of future population can lead to costly overcapacity in hospitals and schools and to a shortage of capital for needed investment in other areas. Countless farms and businesses are economic disasters because of ignorance and faulty locational decisions. Unfortunately, a great many failures of this kind can be expected in a market economy such as the U.S., where small businesses can be started relatively easily despite the caution of banks in lending capital.

Although most mistakes stem from misinformation or inadequate information, some may be blamed on excessive haste, competitive pressure, lack of entrepreneurial skills, or not following "directions" — a surprisingly common failure. For example, a small entrepreneur may misinterpret marketing information and locate his business in an unprofitable site, or a farmer may accept a useful innovation but implement it ineptly.

Efficient spatial organization presumes that decision makers have equal access to complete information. In reality, complete information is normally unavailable, and misinformation all too prevalent. Decisions are made in the face of uncertainty regarding the future and inadequate information with which to compete effectively in a market economy. If some groups acquire and monopolize new information, they can seize short-term advantages that will destroy producers who are basically more efficient or better located.

Many locational decisions are made on the basis of too little information. For example, a public official may decide to construct a road or a dam at a given location without even considering alternative locations, let alone alternative uses of the investment. Again, people may move to the suburbs without acquiring adequate information about their new location, perhaps simply motivated by irrational fear of certain social or racial groups. On a broader scale, migration is often based on inaccurate and outdated information about distant opportunities. Finally, lack of information about the nature and location of employment opportunities is one of the chief causes of imbalance in the location of people and jobs; hence unemployment and poverty persist even when job opportunities actually exist.

The Precedence of Noneconomic Values

The precedence of noneconomic "irrational" values may result in inequitable conditions, such as social discrimination, against ethnic minorities or women, or in spatial inefficiency, as when firms prefer to remain in familiar but unprofitable locations. Indeed, personal preferences often predominate over economically more rational choices. Farmers or miners technologically unemployed may refuse to leave their homes despite the lack of opportunities; or people may move to a new location for the sake of amenities or "exotic" surroundings rather than for economic reasons. In these examples, the productive potential of firms and people is not realized, location is nonoptimal, and economic imbalance may follow.

The efficiency of spatial interaction diminishes when noneconomic values guide decision making. Many firms, for instance, choose prestigious and expensive downtown locations, requiring costly commuting by suburban labor forces. Unnecessary cross-movements occur when individuals ignore good, nearby shops and services that may project a poor image. Social discrimination may force black patients to travel farther to the few hospitals that will accept them (figure 10.02).

Political factors may interfere with efficient and equitable spatial organization, as illustrated by the fragmentation of services in the metropolis. Several small police and fire departments may exist where fewer, larger ones would be more efficient; school districts may be uneconomically small; and services in border zones may be poorly coordinated. The quality of public services is inferior in some areas because of significant differences in tax base (figure 10.03). Another example of inequity in spatial organization is the political separation between the city and its suburbs: often the majority of costs are borne by the city, but most of the income from the commuting labor force is received by the suburbs.

Perhaps the most deplorable malfunctions in the landscape result from racial discrimination. Depressed local and regional economies and the existence of ghettoes bear witness to the destructive effects of prejudice. In the United States, native Americans (Indians) and blacks have been subject to discriminatory treatment for over three hundred years. Certainly until 1965, education for most Indians and blacks was markedly inferior: schools and equipment were poor, and teachers inadequately trained. But even more serious, the barriers against entering most higher paying businesses, unions, and occupations were so

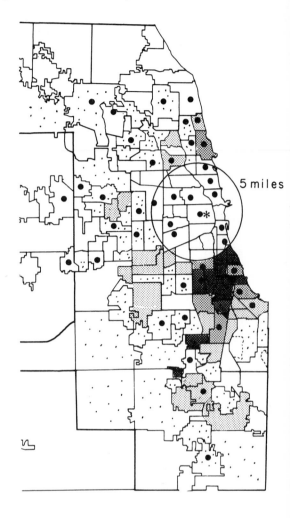

5 miles

* Cook County Hospital

• Intervening hospitals

☐ no patients   ▦ 5-10

⊡ 2   ■ 10-25

▨ 2-5   ■ over 25

Figure 10.02 Unnecessary cross-movements to Cook County Hospital by persons living over five miles away and located closer to other hospitals. Most poor patients have been forced to seek care at the Cook County Hospital. Thus, many patients from the poor south side of Chicago must travel beyond closer intervening hospitals which they cannot afford — an example of spatial inefficiency as well as economic discrimination. Data are from 1968. Patients within five miles to the hospital are not shown.

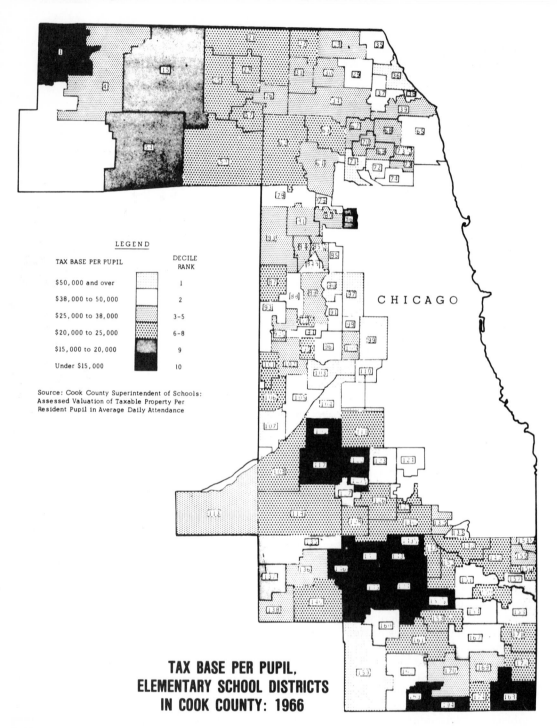

Figure 10.03   Political fragmentation and tax discrimination. Suburban Chicago is divided into scores of school districts. Some areas have formed separate school districts around industrial zones in order to permit good support of schools at a very low tax rate, while other areas without much industry and with many children must endure very high tax rates or poorer schools, or both. (By permission of Pierre de Vise, from *Chicago's Widening Color Gap*, Interuniversity Social Research Committee, Chicago, 1967.)

overwhelming that large proportions of Indians and blacks did not even finish secondary school. Even today, these groups are virtually unrepresented in all but the most menial levels in private sector employment.

The economic and social cost of this underutilization of manpower of some 10 percent of the population is of course enormous. Continuing social inequality breeds hatred, distrust, and violence, and results in high levels of unemployment and severe poverty. Indeed, a vicious cycle of deterioration emerges: the greater discrimination against black males means that family income often depends on the wife's job; family structure is weakened; demands for welfare are expanded; and males often turn to crime and drugs.

Racial discrimination has long hindered the economic development of the South and is by far the major reason for the greater incidence of poverty, illiteracy, crime, and malnutrition found there. Moreover, discrimination and the concentration of minorities in depressed areas is currently leading to decay and financial crisis in many large central cities in the North as well.

The principal geographic effect of racial discrimination is spatial segregation — the restriction of a minority to a ghetto. During the time of slavery, when the inferior status of blacks was legally defined, whites and blacks often lived in close proximity. After legal equality was affirmed, the white majority created a complex structure of sanctions aimed at maintaining inequality. But gradually, as legal "social distance" was reduced, increasing spatial separation was seen as a means of avoiding the perceived social stigma of associating with blacks. As the blacks left a hopeless rural sharecropping life in the South and became unwelcome migrants to the cities, whites felt threatened by black economic and social competition. Blacks were thus relegated to the worst slums, from which whites fled as quickly as they were able. So strong was (and is) racial distrust that even middle class blacks could not escape the ghetto, but were accommodated by its radial extension outward into middle-class housing, whose former residents fled to the suburbs (see figure 8.08).

Separation was enforced by a combination of factors: legal constraints until 1949; the discriminatory behavior of real estate and financial institutions; the threat and practice of terrorism; and the need to remain in segregated communities for self-protection.

The ghetto is spatially inefficient in the sense that it hinders the free operation of the social and economic system: it prevents the optimal use of land; hinders the access of ghetto residents to the labor market and the services of the wider community; and, by restricting interaction, helps maintain the counterproductive duplication of facilities and intergroup fears and prejudices. But even more disturbing, the ghetto is a place of inferior, neglected services; older, shoddy housing; inadequate employment opportunities; and economic exploitation by outside ownership. The spatial isolation, together with employment discrimination, makes the ghetto an area of severe poverty often characterized by unemployment, crime, and disorder. These problems in turn weaken the ability of ghetto residents to escape.

Far from the metropolitan ghetto, Indians are similarly confined to reservations, from which they are supposed to cease competing for desired land and resources. Whereas ghetto residents are reasonably close to at least menial jobs, the reservations are cruelly remote, unproductive tracts in which the traditional forms of Indian life are stifled and productive agriculture and industry are infeasible (figure 10.04). So hopeless is life in most reservations that the Indians are often compelled to join the blacks in the urban ghetto.

Racial discrimination and its effects on people and on the landscape are not encompassed by usual theories of spatial organization; but since spatial organization results from the competition of people and activities for favorable locations, the outcome for racial and other minorities can be understood from their competitive weakness. At a national scale the defeated and powerless Indians were pushed outward virtually beyond the reach of national markets, and opportunities. Until fairly recently, much of the South, largely because of the high black population, had lower levels of

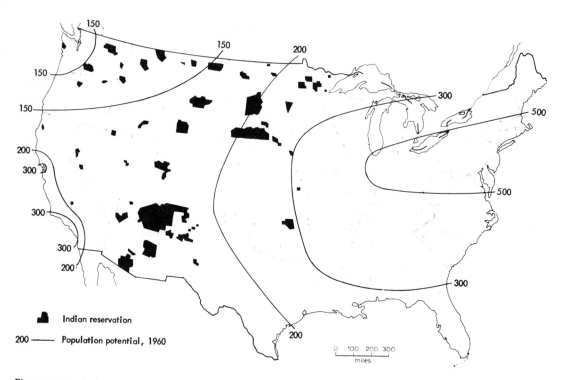

Figure 10.04   Indian reservations and population potential, United States. Note that most Indian reservations are in the zones of lowest accessibility to the rest of the U.S. population. (Sources: U.S. Census of Population, 1960; U.S. Department of the Interior.)

agricultural productivity, urbanization, and income than would be expected from its position relative to such major markets as "megalopolis" or Chicago. Within cities, the location of racial ghettoes can be explained partly by the inability of the minorities to compete equally and by their need for locations near the city center, together resulting in overcrowding into inner city slums, and partly by social discrimination which segregates them from other economically weak groups.

Although this discussion has focused on familiar American problems, similar consequences of social discrimination (not necessarily racial) may be found in most if not all cultures and countries.

Unallocated Social Costs

Pollution, environmental damage, congestion, excessive travel, lack of open space, visual blight, and overcrowding are some environmental and social costs entailed by the activities of individuals and firms but borne by society at large. In the pursuit of maximum profit or satisfaction, firms or individuals are rarely concerned with consequences, except when direct damage can be proved. In particular, firms and individuals benefit appreciably from agglomeration; for example, exposure to customers and sales are increased and transport costs reduced. The landowner, too, benefits from the higher rent that accompanies the concentration of activities and people. But society must bear the inevitable costs of agglomeration, both the direct costs of waste disposal and provision of transport, for instance, and the indirect costs of pollution, noise, delay caused by congestion, and environmental blight.

Theories of spatial organization, which rest on simple goals of profit maximization and cost minimization (including transport), do not take into account these indirect costs and can therefore suggest as optimal a degree of concentration that is not really socially acceptable.

Pollution, or the careless disposal of wastes, not only threatens the environment but impairs human health and reduces productivity. The more concentrated are people and activities, the more severe the pollution (especially in such cities as New York, Chicago, Los Angeles, Tokyo, San Paulo). To reduce pollution to acceptable levels, enterprises and the public must invest heavily in abatement equipment and processes.

Air pollution (figure 10.05) and inefficient waste disposal and provision of water supplies (figure 10.06) illustrate the costs (borne by society) resulting from larger metropolitan agglomerations, the scale economies of which accrue to only a few firms and individuals. Society must also shoulder the long-term costs of environmental damage from strip mining, excessive clear cutting, and overgrazing — practices that are used in the pursuit of short-term profits and may result in deforestation, erosion, visual blight, flooding, and removal of land from productive use. These activities can be carried out, according to theories of spatial organization, so long as direct costs of exploitation and transport do not exceed revenues at the markets; but these practices are inefficient to the extent that it is necessary to assess the damage and rehabilitate the landscape, when it would have been less expensive to use better practices in the first place.

Other social and economic costs of the overconcentration of people and activities are traffic congestion, overcrowding, and lack of open space. Society must invest heavily to overcome congestion, but those who largely benefit from the improved access are the activities whose concentration caused the problem in the first place. Overcrowding and lack of open space occur because private firms and individuals who stand to benefit from agglomeration bid the price of urban land too high. Exorbitant land prices inflate housing costs; people no longer can afford to maintain their homes properly; and slum conditions take over. As the quality of life deteriorates, social disorder and crime grow rampant.

Urban sprawl — the building of homes and subdivisions in an extremely low-density patchwork beyond the central city (figure 10.07) — generates many social and economic burdens caused by the greater distance between individuals and other people, places of work, schools, shopping facilities, and so forth. As a result of urban sprawl, costs of utilities and fire and police protection soar, extensive school bussing is needed, more roads must be constructed, and longer commuting time is required, accompanied by higher levels of pollution. Furthermore, the speculative holding of land for future development has disrupted agriculture, even to the extent of forcing farmers to abandon their land. Such sprawl can occur, according to our ideas of spatial organization, since the commuter bears only the direct costs of his residence and travel.

Visual blight is another problem created by unplanned urban sprawl. But more generally, from the countryside to the central business district we may attribute much of the ugliness of the landscape — particularly in commercial and industrial areas — to the individual who seeks maximum profits for his firm or piece of land without regard to the esthetic consequences.

Problems of Resource Misallocation

Many enterprises are unprofitable while others reap immense profits; resources, including land, are misused; the allocation of resources and income is grossly inequitable; human labor is often not rationally used nor properly valued; and unnecessary cross-movements appear frequently.

These problems, common to most if not all societies, typically result from monopoly control; that is, competition is prevented that would otherwise bring about efficient and equitable patterns. All theories of spatial organization assume the free competition of equals (individuals or firms). Monopoly control tends to prevent an optimal spatial organization from being realized and makes it difficult to assess the efficiency of an economy. It is possible that individuals, firms, or regions that possess disproportionate power may be able to prevent production from being carried on more efficiently elsewhere. One of the primary effects of monopoly is to exaggerate differences in income and wealth among individuals and between regions and coun-

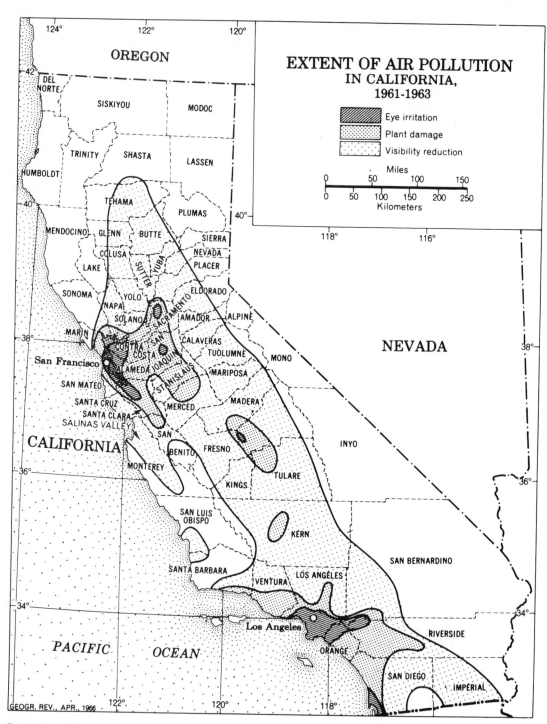

Figure 10.05   Extent of general air pollution in California, 1961-1963. The plant-damage areas are specific, but the eye irritation and visibility reduction may be due in part to forms of general pollution other than photochemical. (Sources: for plant damage, J.T. Middleton: California against Air Pollution (California Department of Public Health, Sacramento, 1961); for eye irritation and visibility reduction, local reports and personal observations up to December, 1963.) (Reprinted permission of *Geographical Review*, from P. Leighton, "Geographical Aspects of Air Pollution," Vol. 56, 1966.)

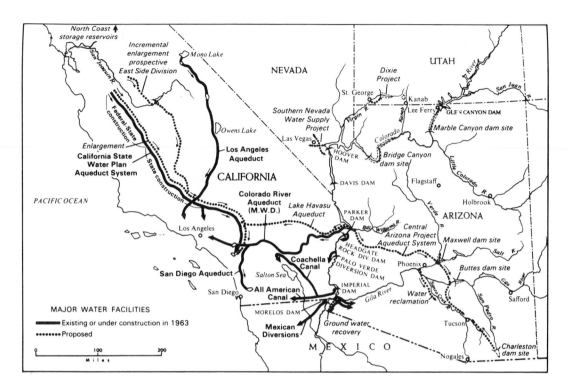

Figure 10.06   Water supply systems serving Southern California and Arizona. Note the extremely long distances involved in supplying metropolitan Southern California. Most of this development was highly subsidized by the federal government, possibly leading to excessive or unfair and inefficient water use. (Source: U.S. Department of the Interior, Pacific Southwest Water Plan Report, 1963.)

tries; and, secondarily, to spread the contagion of blight and decay in both urban and rural landscapes.

Inefficient and Inequitable Capital Allocation. Concentration of investment capital is another barrier to efficiency. In the private sector, investors may show preference for certain regions or cities and ignore others. New products or processes may be denied essential capital, while investment is channeled into relatively unproductive efforts. In the public sector, favoritism and earmarked revenues may result in inefficient investments. For example, excessive road construction in the United States may be encouraged by the exclusive earmarking of federal gasoline taxes. Benefit-cost comparisons for public investments, such as for irrigation systems, are often exaggerated, and alternative investments are rarely considered.

Inefficient Resource Use. Land misuse may result, as noted above, from individual selfishness and irresponsibility or from the short-term maximization of profit — for example, through overgrazing or careless mining and farming methods. Too much or too little taxation may lead to inefficient land use: land near cities may be unnecessarily withdrawn from agriculture, for example, because local governments are tempted to tax according to what might be (maximum zoned use) rather than what is (actual demand for land).

Physical resources, such as water, may be irrationally allocated because of the imbalance of power among competing political divisions and interest groups (resulting, for instance, in costly river-diversion schemes). Discriminatory taxation, such as depletion allowances, encourages the rapacious exploitation of mineral resources. Monopoly ownership of nearby resources may force

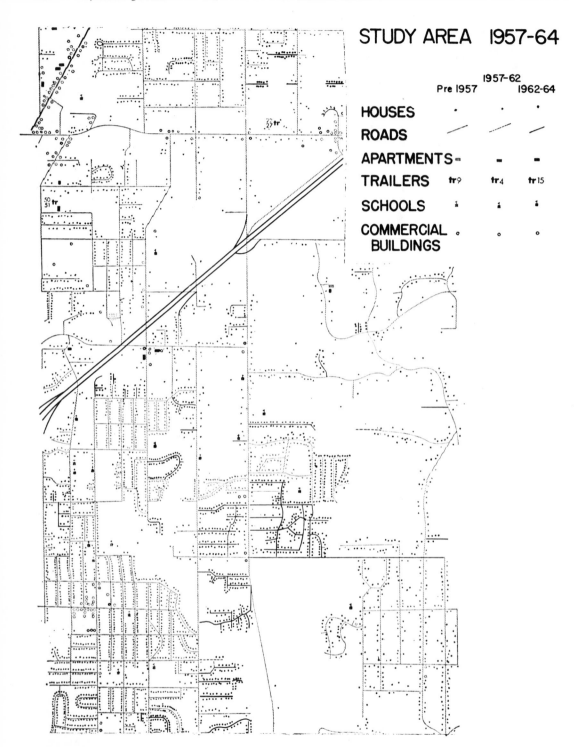

Figure 10.07 Urban fringe settlement. In the sample section from the urban fringe of Seattle, the scattered, sprawling nature of subdivisions can be seen. Most of the vacant areas are held for speculation; none is used for farming. Provision of services and schools to the dispersed suburban population is costly. (Reprinted by permission of the Regional Science Association from Richard Morrill, "Expansion of the Urban Fringe," *Papers and Proceedings of the Regional Science Association*, Vol. XV, 1965.)

competitors to use far distant sources.

Ecologists generally consider that a complex structure of special benefits to the automotive-petroleum sectors (especially a price of gasoline far below what might cover indirect economic and social costs) leads to inordinate use of petroleum products and overdependence on the less efficient private automobile for transportation. If this is true, the effect on the landscape is great, since the competitive advantage of the car and truck currently tends to determine the location of industry, shops, and residences, justifying a low-density city that may not really be efficient.

Other Effects of Monopoly.   Monopoly control permits some individuals, families, or firms to enjoy huge profits or income; examples include many utilities franchises, stores in some urban renewal areas, facilities on tollways, or any monopolistic industry. Because additional production and sales, probably at more locations, are foregone, monopolies are spatially inefficient. And they are inequitable in that some areas and people must do without certain goods and services or incur higher than necessary costs for them.

Monopoly control may also be responsible for excessive movements, as when public or private monopolies (particularly city halls and public clinics) choose one centralized location in contrast to the several locations that would have resulted from competition. Similarly, when hospitals exercise control over the physicians allowed to affiliate with them, many black and poor patients are forced to travel farther for care than would otherwise be necessary (see figure 10.07). Another example of monopolistic control is the basing-point pricing system, that is, the practice of pricing a good in Seattle, for instance, as if it were produced in and transported from another city, such as Los Angeles, when in fact it is produced in Seattle as well. Basing-point pricing systems, because they are not tied to actual costs of production and delivery, may result in the overconcentration of production at nonoptimal locations, as well as in higher costs to consumers.

GEOGRAPHIC EFFECTS OF INCOME INEQUALITY

The most telling sign of spatial inefficiency at local and national levels is excessive inequality of income. If the price system were truly free, if groups and regions had equal access to information, and if their power were balanced, then any inequalities that existed would be the limited and inevitable result of spatial separation and individual differences. But if income variation exceeds what might naturally be expected, the spatial structure of the economy could then be considered inefficient and inequitable.

In spite of almost continuous growth and having perhaps the world's highest per capita income, the United States is beset by incongruent problems:

— *Continuing unemployment,
   beyond that technologically
   induced.*
— *The persistent poverty of as much as
   a quarter of the population within
   a generally affluent society.*

Income levels differ widely among sections of the country (figure 10.08) as well as among areas within cities (figure 10.09). It is generally recognized that these disparities are greater than would be expected under truly optimal conditions in a unified economy. One consequence of regional income inequality, both nationally and within a city, is the distorted pattern of spatial organization, especially the incomplete development of service centers in poorer areas.

Economic Inequality in the City

Ideally, the cityscape should resemble the patterns, suggested in figure 9.01, that would be produced by competition for land and for centers of accessibility. But the ideal surface is distorted by the precedence of noneconomic values, particularly racial discrimination, resulting in the spatial isolation of ghettoes and the inequitable distribution of income. Thus, urban patterns are in reality both inefficient and inequitable.

The major effects of extreme income in-

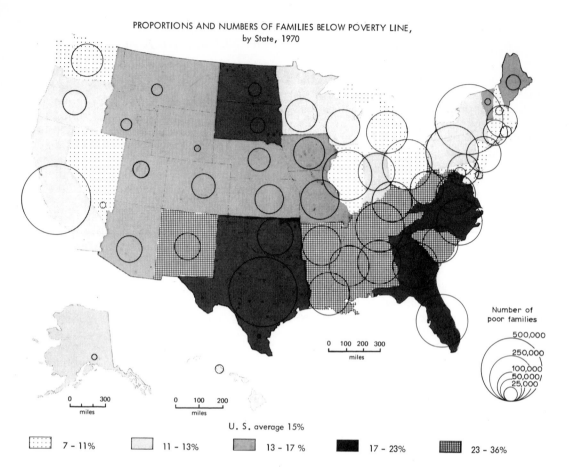

PROPORTIONS AND NUMBERS OF FAMILIES BELOW POVERTY LINE,
by State, 1970

Number of
poor families

500,000

250,000

100,000
50,000/
25,000

0 100 200 300
miles

0   300
miles

0   100   200
miles

U. S. average 15%

7 - 11%   11 - 13%   13 - 17 %   17 - 23%   23 - 36%

Figure 10.08   Distribution of poverty in the United States, 1970. The shading indicates the proportion of the population classified as poor by states in 1970. The circles indicate the absolute numbers of poor persons by state. Note the large numbers of poor in the generally more affluent Northeast and California. (Source: U.S. Bureau of the Census, Census of Population, 1970.)

equality include segregation by class, incomplete business-center development, low accessibility of the poor to services, unnecessary travel, and social and physical decay of urban communities. The rich can and do maintain a quality cityscape wherever they choose to do so. The middle classes can at least move away from undesired areas, while the poor have little choice and are not free to compete for land. Looking back at the evolution of the American city, the poor resided in areas near industry or businesses shunned by the more affluent. As the numbers of poor increased, the middle classes fled outward. Since the poor could not afford the high values (rents) of the former middle-class houses, and yet needed good access to jobs in the central

city, the owners found it necessary and profitable to subdivide the homes. This practice greatly raised density, and the houses eventually were converted into tenements and slums. The departure of the middle classes in turn shifted the location of retail trade and services, and access to goods and services deteriorated for the poor.

Since 1950 the growth of suburban shopping centers and the decline of downtown shopping, services, and employment for lower and lower-middle classes have aggravated unemployment and hastened the physical and economic decay of the inner city (figure 10.10). Vacant, actually abandoned, housing results from both decades of neglect and the inability of the poor to generate sufficient rental income and

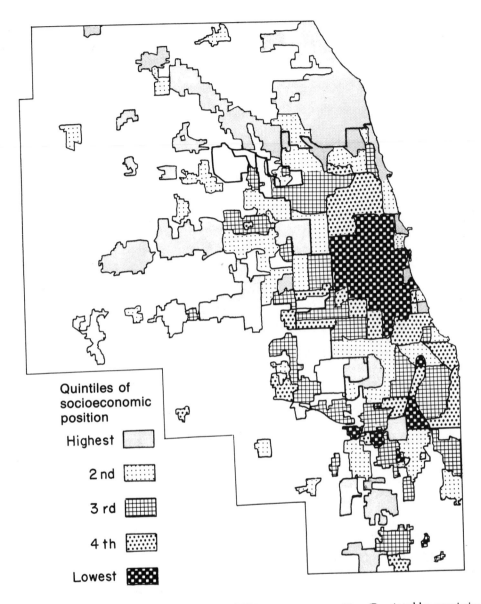

Figure 10.09   The socioeconomic position of Chicago-area communities. (Reprinted by permission of the University of Chicago Department of Geography, from J. Simmons, *The Changing Pattern of Retail Location*, Research Paper No. 92, 1964.)

property taxes. Inefficiencies from this polarization between the inner and outer city include the underutilization of inner city land; the waste of existing investment; and costly transport both for the poor, often to jobs in the suburbs where they cannot live, and for the middle classes, commuting across the inner city to 'downtown white-collar employment. Inequities include the increasingly poor access to employment,

health services, shopping facilities, and so forth; the financial exploitation of the inner city by outside owners; and the central city's subsidy of suburban commuting.

Abandoning the central city to the poor has sharply reduced the accessibility of people to physicians (figure 10.11). High death rates (after adjustment for age and sex) coincide remarkably with inner city areas of poverty, substandard housing, and racial

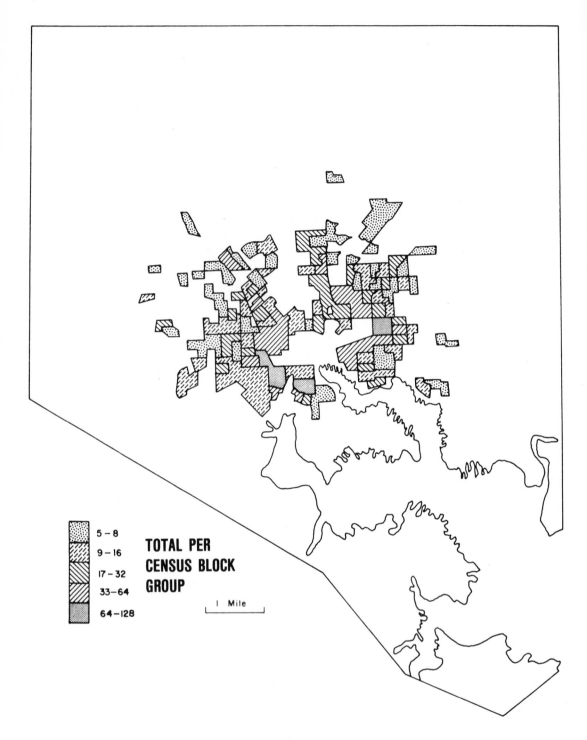

Figure 10.10   Vacant houses, Baltimore, 1968. Most of this housing is abandoned because of long-term neglect or the inability and unwillingness of the poor to pay sufficient rent or cover property taxes. (Reprinted by permission of the Association of American Geographers, from D. Harvey, "Society, the City, and the Space-Economy of Urbanism," College Geography Resource Paper 20, 1972.)

segregation (figure 10.12). The poorer inner city suffers net income losses to affluent suburban areas through rental and proprietary income, regressive local taxation, and other forms of income transfer (figure 10.13). Presumably, if incomes were not so unequal, the social, physical, and economic deterioration and polarization of the inner city need not have occurred.

Regional Inequality in Development and Income

In the United States, fully half the poor and the unemployed live in what are considered prosperous metropolitan areas. This fact suggests that economic inequality is not primarily a regional problem but reflects fundamental distortions in the economic power of different individuals and groups. Nevertheless, regional differences in welfare are significant and illustrate inefficiencies and inequities in the operation of the economy.

Using the United States as an example, the pattern of relative poverty and prosperity is revealed by figure 10.08. A closely related pattern is that of the distribution of hunger (figure 10.14). More prosperous areas include large metropolitan areas in general, California in particular, and Megalopolis (the urban areas from southern New Hampshire to Washington, D. C.), the lower Great Lakes area, and some rural areas in the Northeast and Far West. Relatively poorer areas include nonmetropolitan areas in general, the South and even its smaller urban areas, Appalachia and the Ozarks, peripheral areas in New England and the Great Lakes, the Great Plains, and some areas of the West, most notably Indian reservations.

What explains these patterns? The role of environmental and resource factors is tempting to consider, but poverty in some of the richer natural settings like the Mississippi delta and prosperity in areas like Wyoming and Nevada suggest that other factors must be more important.

A spatial factor, accessibility to major metropolitan markets, is of some significance, since we can note the severity

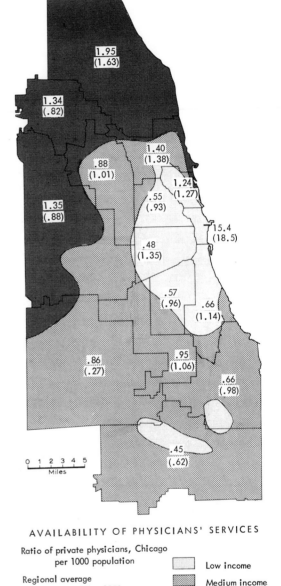

AVAILABILITY OF PHYSICIANS' SERVICES

Ratio of private physicians, Chicago per 1000 population

Regional average
(1.39) = 1950
1.03 = 1970

Low income
Medium income
High income

Figure 10.11 Changing availability of physicians' services, Chicago area, 1950-1970. Except for the high concentration of specialists in downtown Chicago, poorer inner city sections of Chicago have suffered severe declines in the number of physicians and have levels of accessibility less than half those of the affluent inner suburbs. (From data in D. Dewey, "Where the Doctors Have Gone," Research Paper, Illinois Regional Medical Program, 1973.)

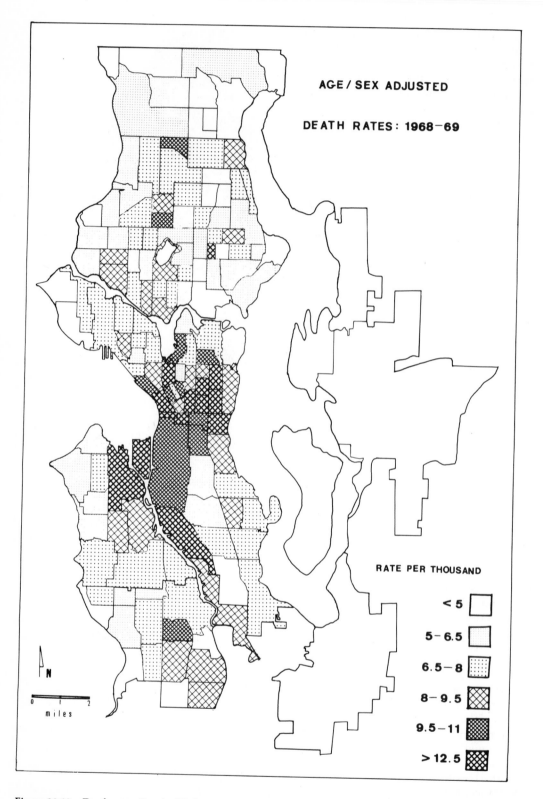

Figure 10.12   Death rates, Seattle, Washington, 1968-1969. These age-sex adjusted death rates show a concentration of higher death rates in the poorest, most industrial parts of the city with the worst housing. (Reprinted by permission of D. Johnson, "Differential Mortality within Cities," M.A. Thesis, University of Washington, 1972.)

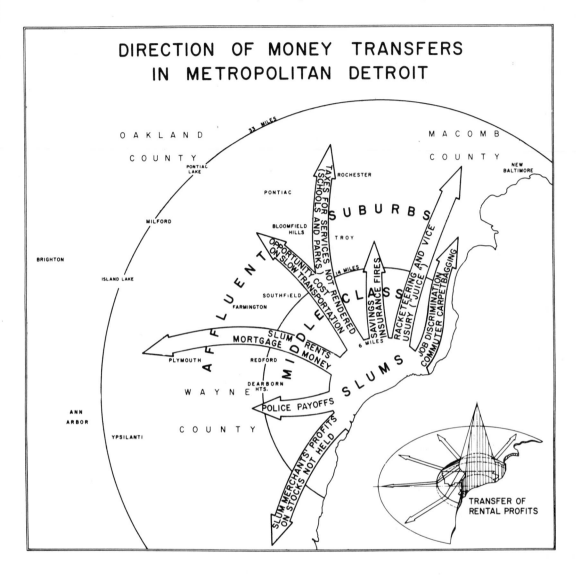

Figure 10.13   Income transfers, Detroit. This figure depicts the pattern of income transfer from the poorer inner city to the more affluent suburbs. Most important are rents, profits from outside-owned business, and the very high incidence of local regressive taxes. Actual figures, however, are very difficult to determine. (Reprinted by permission of Schenkman Publishing Co., from W. Bunge, *Fitzgerald*, Cambridge, Mass., 1971.)

of poverty in the areas of poorest accessibility (the Ozarks and Appalachia, for instance) as well as a tendency for the incidence of poverty to increase with distance from a large metropolis.

Regional Convergence.   One important theory explaining unemployment and income inequality postulates a lag in regional adjustment. According to this theory, as the economy has grown, some rather large areas have not been able to adjust to changing conditions in transport, technology, and de-

mand; consequently these areas have much unemployment and lower per capita income. For example, some mining and lumber areas are declining because demand, labor requirements, and resource levels have fallen. Technological unemployment in such areas is common. Also, many agricultural areas contain inefficient, small farms that cannot generate sufficient income per family. Increasing efficiency and productivity in mining, forestry, and agriculture continually displace labor, but rural economies do not have conditions that attract most industries

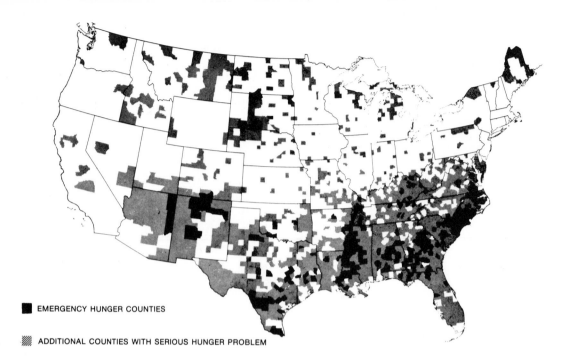

EMERGENCY HUNGER COUNTIES

ADDITIONAL COUNTIES WITH SERIOUS HUNGER PROBLEM

Figure 10.14   Geographic distribution of hunger in the United States, 1967. This map of hunger is closely related to the distribution of poverty. (Reprinted by permission of the New Community Press, from *Hunger, U.S.A.*, Beacon Press, 1968.)

and services. Hence, there is surplus labor, which is either unemployed, underemployed, or can be hired at relatively poor wages.

In the process of adjusting, surplus labor from declining areas has migrated to more successful areas, usually larger cities — not rapidly enough for the declining areas to achieve internal economic equilibrium (including full employment) at a higher income level, but too rapidly for the metropolis to absorb, given the migrants' few skills and lack of education. Thus, although rural out-migration from the poorer farm areas has been rapid, too many small farms remain. Presumably, equilibrium will be reached in the long run in these presently backward areas, and those farms remaining will be large, efficient units. Differences in regional income should gradually disappear.

Rural-Urban Migration. Although relative incomes of regions have already tended to converge, the incidence of unemployment and poverty has not declined very much. Unfortunately the out-

migration from rural areas often includes the more educated and motivated, leaving a high proportion of elderly in the population (or middle-aged who feel it is too late to start anew) and a high ratio of dependency, leading to an absolute decline in the level and variety of services. Despite the poor return in much farming and the lack of alternative opportunities in rural areas, many people prefer their home environment and refuse to leave. Indeed, they know that a shift to the city will not guarantee any real improvement in their quality of life.

Even if the economy is moving toward an equilibrium, in which most people will live in metropolises, some question remains about whether this pattern is truly the most efficient. There may be benefits lost by underutilizing resources in the areas relegated to extensive activities, and there are also enormous, unexamined economic and social costs of congestion in very large metropolises. The United States should perhaps examine the alternative, preferred by many other advanced nations, of developing more evenly across its entire territory.

Moreover, the underlying structural deficiencies in the economy make rural-urban migration futile in itself. There are very large numbers of poor and unemployed in the most prosperous places, such as Chicago and Los Angeles. Even the most successful places are unable to achieve full employment and to eliminate poverty, despite possessing the best transport facilities and economic and cultural opportunities. Thus, merely relocating people from unsuccessful areas to the cities might only aggravate their poverty.

Regional Economic Problems. In view of the deficiencies noted above, depressed regions are not merely products of temporary maladjustment, but, along with richer areas, reflect more fundamental conditions:

- *The price system seems unable to allocate income fairly. Unequal power results not only in widespread poverty among the employed, but also in high levels of unemployment.*
- *There is discrimination — including governmental — against minorities, women, the very old, and the very young.*
- *The economy emphasizes short-run maximization of profits — quick return on investments.*

These three conditions have long been justified by the American tradition of individualism and have been endured because of the remarkable growth that has resulted. To some extent, this growth was based on a continuing stream of cheap labor assured by surplus workers.

The nation has not been able to achieve full employment and greater equality. If the economy sets too low a price for the services of certain workers and then further discriminates against many of them (because of race, for instance), then even in the most prosperous city poverty will never be removed by education or migration alone.

Similarly, if the economy sets too low a price for forest and agricultural products, migration from rural areas will not raise the income levels of those people remaining. This is because individual operators will be unable either to find a profitable production process or to handle an area large enough to be profitable with an existing process.

Prices might be high enough for adequate incomes if all farmers realized high productivity on moderate acreage, but in some highly competitive sectors, distributors may be strong enough to keep prices below even this level.

Apparently, the price system cannot allocate income fairly because of the great variation in the power and bargaining position of different groups and the partly monopolistic control of prices by private industry and government. Weaker groups are paid too little; thus differences in income exceed differences in actual productivity. One consequence is that the economy depends too much on saturating high-income consumers, while much of the population represents enormous latent demand. Surplus capital flees the country. Unemployment and underemployment become chronic. Excessive income inequality can be a deterrent to economic growth, as illustrated by the increase in production, employment, and mass consumption and the reduction in poverty that followed the 1964 American income tax cut. Historically, the development of capitalism and the emergence of the middle class demonstrated the advantage of mass consumption in generating wealth.

Unequal power and income over a long period has obstructed the access of many people to education, health, and other services, which, in a vicious cycle, has reduced the competitive abilities of the poor, who then may withdraw into a state of hopelessness. Education and health are rightly seen as key variables in the reduction of poverty, but it is also apparent that these alone are insufficient, given the chronic lack of jobs.

Uneven distribution of power is also evident in the fact that some groups enjoy preferential treatment, such as mineral depletion allowances and direct and indirect subsidies — perhaps exemplified by a variety of agricultural and transport payments or by investments in highways indirectly aiding long-distance trucking.

The ability of strong unions to help equalize power and raise incomes well illustrates the role of unequal power in the persistence of poverty. In the Pacific Northwest, unionization in the forest products industry results in reasonable income, whereas in the South, lack of unions often means poverty-level wages.

Discrimination against less powerful groups is a basic cause of inequality and poverty in the United States, both nationally and locally. In some cases the young and quite generally women receive low wages or are restricted to lower paying occupations — in laundries, as servants, in textiles, and in apparel and pottery factories in the large metropolises of the North as well as in the South. The elderly are restricted from employment and find their savings depleted by inflation, rising property taxes, and medical bills. Their immobility in an automotive age reduces their access to needed services, in the older sections of central cities as well as in many rural areas where they make up a high proportion of the poor. Discrimination against blacks, native Americans, and other racial minorities entails not only inferior education and health services, but also systematic exclusion from higher paying jobs, particularly at the local and small business level, and an unaccountable waste of resources and potential talent. Emphasis on short-run profits has led, particularly in the past, to excessively rapid or unnecessarily careless resource exploitation and depletion and subsequent decline for regions without alternate resources or opportunities.

Much economic inequality is a consequence of state economic autonomy — minimum wage variations, right-to-work laws, and the like. While low minimum wages attract industry in a state's early stages of industrial development, they are also a deterrent to the state's internal economic growth, since most consumer goods are nationally priced. Right-to-work laws, too, weaken the normal process of increasing income levels through collective bargaining.

Extreme income inequality leads, in a complex way, to the chronic surplus of labor that is responsible for both high unemployment and underemployment and to poverty wages for up to one-fifth of those actually working, but it also helps perpetuate and aggravate social and economic discrimination against minorities.

The labor surplus is a major reason for the very great concentration of economic activities and population in metropolitan areas in the United States. In Sweden, Germany, and Switzerland, in contrast, labor shortages have led to the decentralization of employment and income into smaller cities and towns.

Regional Development

Regional planning and development is action taken to improve equity and efficiency in the economy, specifically with regard to regional imbalances. Even though inefficiency, inequity, poverty, and unemployment exist in the most prosperous cities and regions, other regions are much worse off. The richer cities at least have the resources to aid the disadvantaged; the poorer towns and rural areas could not meet local needs even if they wished to.

The inability to realize economies of scale in small towns and cities, the general surplus of labor and the superior services, facilities, and opportunities (infrastructure) of larger cities suggest that economic expansion will almost always be located in the already successful areas, especially the northeastern core and a few regional metropolises, even if other locations might be more profitable in the long run. In the absence of public intervention to aid weaker regions, the gap between the more and the less successful regions will become even greater, more migration will occur, and the prospects of the weaker areas will be reduced still further.

Recognizing these trends, policy-makers in the United States see two broad alternatives:

- *To encourage present trends of concentration in the larger metropolises and leave a veneer of efficient agricultural and recreational areas on the rest of the land.*
- *To foster more even development over the entire country through programs of regional development.*

Regional development planning is, of course, very limited in a federal system under free enterprise. Past regional planning has been mostly confined to interstate river development, including irrigation and power systems, interstate highway construction, and the allocation of defense contracts. (In the nineteenth century, the Homestead Act policy of free land and mining claims and subsidies for canal and railway construction were very significant means of regional development.)

Some present regional development programs, notably highway construction and education and retraining efforts, may actually encourage greater concentration of people and activities, even if the intention was to spread development; improved roads extend the domination of the larger, more successful centers, and the better trained and educated must necessarily find jobs in the cities. Improvement of access to local areas, such as in Appalachia, may encourage tourists and speed the marketing of farm produce, but it does not provide alternate employment opportunities for those in rural areas.

Programs of first the Area Redevelopment Administration and later the Economic Development Administration required improved local planning, and involved infrastructure investments in smaller cities and towns and some loans to small industries. But because of inherent limitations, these programs cannot be considered very successful.

Without doubt, the most successful examples of regional development and income improvement in the United States have been due to either climate or governmental military action. The sheer number of already skilled and educated people who migrated in search of better climate to Florida, Arizona, and California caused a more general economic expansion, first in services, later in manufacturing. Even more important, the partly deliberate allocation of governmental expenditures for defense and aerospace to selected areas, particularly California, Texas, Alabama, and Florida, induced a level of growth and prosperity in those states that otherwise could not have been achieved.

State and local development efforts, particularly in the South but also in less successful areas of the North and West, have often been based on attracting low-wage (poverty-level) industry, discouraging unions, and evading social responsibilities. Yet over the long run (forty years), this approach has stemmed out-migration, allowed people to remain where they wished, and led to urbanization, better education, and an upgrading of industry and income.

How can regions develop? Normally growth and rising income depend on raising productivity through specialization and mechanization, and increasing export income and trade. In the United States this usually meant more export industry (manufacturing or services). Fairly large and rich regions can also expand internal production of goods formerly imported (for example, clothing, appliances, machinery in California, after World War II). Most nonmetropolitan regions can only raise income by reducing the number of people dependent on the limited land resource.

For regions to develop more evenly, more radical programs would be required — for example, incentives for really significant investments in weaker areas, perhaps by exemption from federal taxation for some period, or conversely, by restricting investments in already overcrowded metropolises (a very difficult task). Since, for competitive reasons, businesses prefer metropolitan locations, which constitute partial markets and offer superior labor, business services, and communications, the most effective regional development strategy appears to be the deliberate fostering of additional metropolitan areas, or "growth centers," in less successful areas (figure 10.15). Rural industrialization or even the spread of investments among smaller towns appears infeasible, but cities of 25,000 to 200,000 people have the potential of acting as catalysts for regional development. They are large enough to reach reasonable economic thresholds while still being located within commuting distance of most of the population. Without the prospect of such moderately sized regional markets, few industries would find it advantageous to decentralize.

Since it is efficient to locate many activities and services in metropolitan centers (many people are willing to work in or near large cities, if they can remain on their farms or in their small towns), a more complete network of "growth centers" offers a means of satisfying many people's desire to live

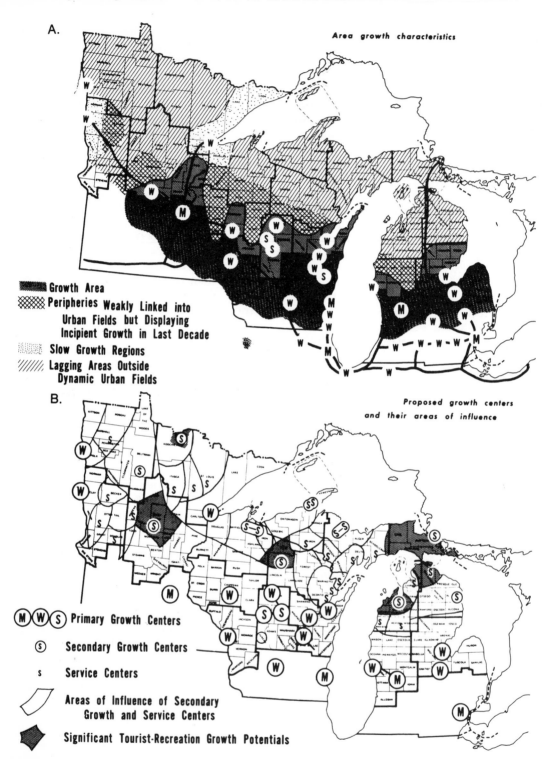

Figure 10.15 Application of the idea of growth centers to the Upper Great Lakes area. In map *A* the region is divided into areas of current strong growth (in or near metropolitan areas) adjoining areas of incipient growth, and areas that are more remote and lagging in growth. In map *B* are identified present or prospective centers of growth in both stronger and weaker parts of the region. *M* refers to metropolitan centers, *W* to wholesale-retail centers, and *S* to retail service centers. (Reprinted by permission of the Upper Great Lakes Regional Commission, from B.J.L. Berry, "Growth Centers and their Potentials in the Upper Great Lakes Region," 1969.)

outside the city and the preference of firms to locate in the city; at the same time, the network enables hinterland incomes to rise to acceptable levels through widespread commuting. This process has already taken place in the Northeast. The task of regional development would be to extend the process to less successful regions. Such a program of "centralized deconcentration" would be expensive, but the investment can theoretically be justified for these reasons:

1. *Resources would be more fully utilized.*
2. *Income levels would rise — more than enough to return the cost of the investment — and consumption would be increased.*
3. *Congestion and pollution costs and diseconomies in the metropolises could be controlled.*

In posing this alternative of regional development, however, it should not be forgotten that the inner portions of large metropolitan areas are also regions of underdevelopment, lacking sufficient jobs and services. The risk of polarization between a rich, white suburbia and exurbia and a poor, black inner city is as severe as that of a rich urban region and a poor periphery. Such planning intervention is intended to lead to a more even development across the nation (or city). To an extent, it would be an attempt to bring about the more regular pattern of urbanization predicted by our theories of spatial organization, but frustrated by historical factors, inequality of power, and environmental differences. Since the competition underlying spatial organization tends to lead to as high a degree of concentration as is profitable, such planning might tend to alter the landscape in favor of greater decentralization than theory would suggest.

THE WORLD ECONOMY: INEQUALITY AND INEFFICIENCY

It is not, of course, strictly possible to evaluate the spatial efficiency of the world economy, because there is not just one world economy or society but national and even local economies having only tenuous connections to each other. These different economies vary greatly in their organizational complexity and spatial interdependence. It is also not possible to unravel these complexities in a few pages, but we will attempt a brief introduction to the problems of world economic development.

International trade may be considered a first step in establishing a world economy. Most international trade is rational in the sense that it is profitable to both sides, but in many ways it is suboptimal. The ideal balance of trade is distorted by ideological conflicts and political loyalties. There may be too much trade within a political bloc, while good opportunities to trade outside the bloc are ignored. The goal of self-sufficiency and the fear of dependence on others may result in more costly internal production, even though greater exchange would be more profitable. Also, the more powerful nations may be able to control prices to their own advantage, thus aggravating international differences in development. In particular this takes the form of low prices for the raw materials of less developed nations, and higher prices for the manufactured goods of the richer nations. In addition, most nations impose barriers against trade from their foreign competitors. It can be argued that at times during the developmental process, barriers to protect infant industries may be required; but too often even the most developed nations use such trade barriers to protect inefficient industries from healthy competition.

The main evidence of economic imbalance and inefficiency is the extreme inequality in the world distribution of income (see figure 1.02). Variations in level of development and income among nations are of course far greater than within a nation. The technology available to a society and the organizational complexity, types of production, and consumption of nations vary greatly.

Although development in an earlier era could be defined by the achievement of a nation's few rich men, in the modern era, when an individual's expectations are no longer bounded by social position, development is better measured by the median income per consuming unit — usually the family. All the other measures of development — energy consumption, literacy, health, quality of transport — are closely related to the typical family's income.

As of 1973, the wealthy countries include

those of northwest Europe and their direct colonies, the United States, Canada, Australia, and New Zealand — all with per capita incomes exceeding $1,500. Their economies and cultures have been closely linked for centuries. They were the first to abandon feudalism, adopt capitalism, and develop open political and social institutions. They are highly industrialized and urbanized; few people remain in agriculture; all citizens are incorporated into the commercial economy; the countries are highly interconnected, internally and externally, and they dominate world trade. Although they have but 12 percent of the world's population, they control perhaps 50 percent of the world's wealth. They have reached a level of affluence that is leading to concern over internal inequality and environmental impact.

A somewhat larger set of countries are moderately developed, enjoying per capita incomes of $500 to $1,500. Included are such diverse areas as southern Europe, eastern Europe, including the USSR, a few countries of Latin America (Venezuela, Argentina), Africa (Union of South Africa), and Asia (Israel, Taiwan, and notably Japan). These countries are fairly industrial and urban, but they retain a large, less productive rural sector. Some therefore have great economic inequalities (most noncommunist countries), an inhibited development of tertiary activities (the communist countries), or severe racial discrimination (South Africa). Although further internal specialization and interconnection may be needed, they have established significant industrial and export bases and will soon be in a position to assure their citizens reasonable material affluence.

The remaining countries, comprising perhaps two-thirds of the world's population but controlling perhaps only one-quarter of the world's wealth, may be considered "developing nations," with per capita income levels of under $500 per year. Included is much of Latin America, most of Africa, and much of Asia, including such major nations as China, India, Indonesia, Pakistan, Nigeria, and Brazil. All are in the process of industrialization, urbanization, and infrastructure development, but may be considered "dual" economies; that is, probably a minority is

moderately affluent and fully involved in the commercial economy, and perhaps the majority remain in a traditional, partially subsistence economy. Consequently, income inequality and regional disparities are unusually great (except, perhaps, in China).

To account for these variations in national development would be a herculean task. We will just suggest some of the major factors.

— *The quality of a nation's land and its endowment of resources vary. Some areas are blessed with rich resources, land or mineral; the preeminent position of America is partly a function of such accidental advantages.*

— *Development and technology diffuse only gradually from more advanced areas. Areas with a head start in development have a great advantage over possible competitors; their existing educational, industrial, and research structures can more readily generate new technology. Whatever the reasons for the developmental headstart of northwest Europe, it has profoundly influenced the nature and extent of development everywhere. During the colonial period of military domination, European institutions spread everywhere, but economic relations were, and perhaps remain, exploitative. The diffusion of medical knowledge and improved health led to a population explosion, which, unlike that earlier in Western Europe, could not be absorbed by colonization in the New World and was not relieved by industrialization, which was often purposefully hindered by the colonial powers.*

— *Nations vary in age, political stability, and damage from past wars. Countries that have stayed out of war and avoided subsequent destruction of property (such as Sweden and Switzerland) seem to develop rather easily. Areas plagued by frequent political change and unrest, accompanied by unstable currency and shifting economic leadership, have difficulty developing. The former colonial powers are largely responsible for this instability, often having prevented the development of internal administrative entrepreneurial and managerial capabilities, let alone economic independence.*

— *Economic and social organization and attitudes toward development vary among nations. In many countries, the leadership has allowed or pursued deliberately antidevelopmental policies — maintaining a feudal land organization or engaging in futile wars against neighbors, for instance. Unfortunately, the former colonial powers have tended to support such leadership, often in an effort to protect overseas investment and sources of raw materials.*

— *The size and population of countries vary. Naturally, a small country has the disadvantage of a small internal market and limited resources. On the other hand, a poor country with a very large population relative to resources will also find it difficult to accumulate a significant surplus for developmental purposes.*

Barriers to Development

By economic development, we mean the interdependent processes of industrialization, urbanization, commercialization, and mechanization of agriculture. Normally these require a rather long period of heavy savings and capital investment to provide an efficient system of education and communication as well as to raise the productivity of labor and land.

Economic development is the goal of most countries. Those who suggest that not all people want to be or are meant to be developed simply do not understand history or human nature. There are *no* people who do not want greater security or material well-being. It is true that most countries are also concerned with questions of security and ideology. The cost of the cold war between the United States and its allies and the USSR, China, and their allies has been far in excess of $1 trillion, a drain that obviously reduces the willingness — and ability — of the larger rich nations to aid the poorer ones. In the extreme case of the Viet-

nam War, although about $200 billion has been spent, Vietnam has been severely damaged — a measure of the perceived superiority of ideological over economic values. Perhaps even more serious, the cold war has caused an aura of insecurity to pervade most nations, rich and poor, who therefore spend an unnecessarily high proportion of their limited capital on nonproductive armaments.

Population Imbalance. Population imbalances are a basic developmental problem of many countries. Many nations have a very small population, so both their markets and their labor forces are too small to allow them to realize even modest scale and agglomeration economies, let alone accumulate enough capital to finance a variety of different industries. No other factor is so important in limiting their development.

Creation of larger nations, or at least formation of cooperating economic blocs, may be necessary to development, but this is difficult to accomplish in the face of the militant nationalism of most new nations. Again, the colonial powers did little to help prevent the proliferation of so many small nations.

Too large a population can also be a problem. Often the ratio of population to arable land is too high, there are few employment opportunities other than farming, and only a low level of technology exists. In many cases the rate of population increase is excessive. In countries where land is already used intensively, most of society's investment and labor is commonly required just to increase food production enough to feed the additional population. In spite of a large potential market and labor force for other kinds of production, not enough surplus food can be generated to provide capital for allocation to alternate activities. In these countries, a birth control program is needed to reduce the rate of population growth below that of economic expansion and capital formation; such a program is often difficult to institute, however, under conditions of little education, traditionally large families (so that the parents will be guaranteed care in their old age), inadequate nutrition, and, in some countries, religious and other kinds of barriers.

In many developing nations, part of the

surplus population has chosen or been forced to leave the overcrowded countryside and move to the cities, even in the absence of employment opportunities. Incredibly bad housing results and may require the diversion of capital needed for creating jobs into minimal housing and services.

Tradition.   In many countries the means necessary for development conflict with existing attitudes and traditions. In some cases, religious practices and beliefs or traditional diets conflict with economic efficiency; for example, India's cattle population is underutilized. More important is the lack of enthusiasm for development often shown in aristocratic social structures; if a ruling group has achieved extreme wealth through the small surpluses of many laborers or by controlling resources, it will gain little from development in the modern sense, which is based on the concept of a mass market. The aristocracy can gain more security and a greater return by investing funds in countries more successful than their own.

A successful transition from such a structure does require land reform, but unless there are simultaneous urban-industrial opportunities for the surplus farm labor, land reform will in itself be futile.

Competition with Wealthy Nations.   A major barrier to development is the superior position of already developed nations. In the short run, a new industry in a poor country will rarely — even with extreme savings on labor costs — be able to compete with a highly efficient industry in a wealthy country. Until the local labor force increases its productivity, and local markets develop as well, such new industries will commonly require financial protection. Unfortunately, deciding whether to support such industries is another problem; it is difficult to know whether a given industry will eventually be competitive or whether it will always be cheaper to purchase a product from another country.

Colonial Trade Patterns.   An underdeveloped nation's existing trade patterns, often inherited from its colonial period, are frequently typified by overdependence on a single or a few exports that are subject to severe price fluctuations; the variations in capital formation make developmental schedules and payments difficult to meet. Also, the colonial pattern of exporting primary goods and importing manufactured products leads to excessive emphasis on imports of consumption goods. Thus there is a persistent conflict between importing capital goods for future gain and importing materials for consumption now.

Lack of Capital

The fundamental barrier to development is lack of capital. Developed nations are not generous with capital, which they perceive as leading to direct competition with their own industries. Internal capital is hard to accumulate if much of the economy remains subsistent and if population and consumption pressures are high. Democratic but uneducated societies are unlikely to restrict consumption sufficiently to encourage the high investment that is necessary for sustained growth. Even dictatorial societies are often unwilling to invest in needed public works — transportation, roads, schools, and water systems — which create the basis for later productivity.

Forces Working toward Development

In spite of this catalog of barriers, development does occur. Strong motivation and a determination to industrialize are common to growing countries. They are aided in this process by the availability of a large body of technology already created by the developed countries

The most successful developing nations are those with very strong governments dedicated to growth and able to enforce an unpopular emphasis on investment to the neglect of present living standards. It is clear that austerity and very high reinvestment levels were common during the industrialization of all the now wealthy nations.

Totally "bootstrap" development seems to be almost impossible, but growth financed by exports is possible, even without outside aid. Less developed countries have also received loans and gifts, which can facilitate development. Some aid, such as technical aid for health, agriculture, and water supplies, is channeled through the United Nations and related agencies. Larger in scope are private investment — primarily to develop exports of desired commodities, such as petroleum and minerals — and government loans and gifts.

Government aid constitutes the most realistic source of general capital, although it may arouse severe political conflict. The donor nation, for example, must spread the available capital over far too many receivers, and the receiving nations resent any strings attached to the aid, even though such control might bring the greatest gain to the country.

There is also some hope that international ideological conflict may be in decline, that trade and investment can occur fairly normally, even between capitalist and communist economies, and that more capital will become available to developing nations through international sources. Raw material shortages in the richest nations may also lead to higher and more stable prices for some exports from developing countries.

*Problems of Internal
Efficiency and Capital
Allocation*

The richer nations are characterized by national economies in which virtually all the people participate commercially. In contrast, most poorer nations have dual economies — the smaller portion of the population participates in the commercial sector, which is often closely tied to exports, and the larger portion remains in the semisubsistence sector, mainly engaged in producing food crops. The distinction between the two groups in income, power, and education is immense, and a major problem of less developed nations is commercializing the subsistence sector of their economies.

Typically, the main sources of capital for such nations are fairly small exports of foods or minerals. As stated above, there is also a temptation to spend heavily on consumer goods and to invest in secure overseas markets, or, at best, to invest in urban services, ignoring the subsistence sector of the economy. This is spatially inefficient because resources are underutilized, and the distribution of income remains inequitable.

Given its desire for widespread development and less dependence on a few overseas markets, the developing nation is faced with the difficult task of finding the optimum allocation of limited capital resources within the country, both geographically and among sectors of industry, agriculture, and services. Spatially, its alternatives are to disperse investment evenly over the entire territory; to concentrate investment in the one best place; or perhaps to distribute it to a set of growth points. Dispersal is a popular choice when political control is diffuse and all parts of the country wish to develop at once. Such a pattern, however, is highly inefficient; the investment in each area will be on an uneconomically small scale and will probably do no more than enable food production to keep up with population growth.

In the short run, in a small country the most profitable use of capital is to concentrate industrial development in the one best place, usually the capital, where threshold markets can be found and adequate labor is available (see figure 10.16). Settlers should then migrate from the countryside to supply additional labor, and the surrounding agriculture will then commercialize in order to serve the urban market. A "primate" center is not inefficient so long as most of the population is within a few hours of the center and an adequate structure of local service centers is encouraged.

In a fairly large and populous country, however, extreme concentration of capital in one place will not lead to the most general development (figure 10.16). Investment must rather be allocated to a set of regional centers, which may in turn commercialize their hinterlands.

Total concentration of investment in strategic growth centers — either one or a few — is, of course, unrealistic. Some more diffuse investment in agriculture (including local transportation) is essential to raise rural efficiency and productivity and to avoid costly food imports. Poor areas not selected for development cannot be ignored without risking social and economic unrest

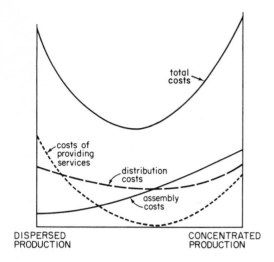

Figure 10.16 Balance between concentration and dispersion. Both extreme concentration of production in a few metropolitan areas or extreme dispersion of production in rural areas appear to be less efficient than a pattern of moderate concentration in a larger set of urban places.

that may drag down the entire economy.

The best sectoral allocation of capital is also a matter of controversy. The traditional emphasis on industry (unbalanced investment) has been criticized in favor of higher allocations to overhead services (roads, education) and agriculture. No simple formula can be applied to all countries. What seems to be true is that there is no real substitute for industrialization, but that industrialization can be most effective only if accompanied by adequate investment in agriculture, services, and the acceptance of improved standards of consumption.

If the chosen strategy is successful, development will spread from the growth centers to their hinterlands, until all the territory and population of the nation are brought into a unified economy. Such an orderly development should lead to a more even distribution of population, production, and income and perhaps even a closer approximation to the theoretical landscape outlined in preceding chapters than is presently true of most advanced countries.

Location Theory:
Reality and the Social Good

In this book, ideal patterns that would

have resulted from following the goals of maximizing the productivity of places and the level of interaction at least cost were described. In the first part of this chapter, departures from the ideal were discussed: on the one hand inefficiency is common, as land and resources are not used efficiently and as productivity is less than it could be; on the other hand, inequity is widespread, even given the pursuit of efficiency, since the power of people and areas is imbalanced.

What about the theories of location themselves? How well do they reflect the real world? According to the gradient theory, from a local to a national scale, all enterprises at all distances should be equally well off. Empirically there is some tendency at the national scale for peripheral areas to be less prosperous, and at the urban scale more prosperous, but this inequality results in the first case from historical biases in power and infrastructure development, and in the latter case from inequality due to a variety of causes. Central place theory is particularly egalitarian, since it presumes equal accessibility regardless of competitive position. Most real world departures are in the direction of unequal accessibility, concentrating services in denser and richer areas. Spatial interaction theories, which can predict this distortion, reflect actual locations and may indicate efficient but unequal, or equal but less efficient patterns of movement. Patterns resulting from the application of most industrial location theories are efficient but not necessarily equitable, since the optimal location (where costs are minimized) will be biased toward the richest and densest areas. If power and income were equal, however, then these patterns would be equitable as well.

Postscript

In *The Spatial Organization of Society*, we emphasized the concept of geography as the study of how man organizes his use of territory, and examined the role of such spatial factors as distance and relative location within an economy. This is not to say that the variable character of the natural environment is not at least as important — frequent recourse to the real environment was often required in the discussions. It seemed worthwhile, however, to have presented the outlines of an ideal spatial landscape so that the role of spatial forces could be appreciated, both with respect to day-to-day behavior and locational decision making and for their part in shaping real landscapes.

REFERENCES

Regional Planning and Development

Alonso, William, "What Are New Towns For?" *Urban Studies* 7 (1970): 37-56.

Brown, H., "Shift and Share Projections of Regional Economic Growth," *Journal of Regional Science* 9 (1969): 1-18.

Brunn, S. and W. Hoffman, "Geography of Federal Grants-in-Aid to States," *Economic Geography* 45 (1969): 226-238.

Casetti, E., L. King, and D. Jeffrey, "Structural Imbalance in the U.S. Urban-Economic System," *Geographical Analysis* 3 (1971): 239-255.

Friedmann J., "Regional Economic Policy for Developing Areas," *Papers and Proceedings of the Regional Science Association* 11 (1963): 41-62.

Gauthier, Howard L., "Geography, Transportation, and Regional Development," *Economic Geography* 46 (1970): 612-619.

Gilmore, D.R., "Development of the Little Economies," Committee for Economic Development, 1960.

Guthrie, J.A., "Economies of Scale in Regional Development," *Papers and Proceedings of the Regional Science Assiciation* 1 (1955): J1-J10.

Hale, C., "Mechanics of the Spread Effect in Regional Development," *Land Economics* 43 (1967): 434-445.

Hansen, N.M., "Regional Planning in a Mixed Economy," *Southern Economic Journal* 32 (1965): 176-190.

Harper, R.A., T.H. Schmudde, and F.H. Thomas, "Recreation-Based Economic Development and the Growth Point Concept," *Land Economics* 43 (1966): 95-102.

Jansen, A.M., "The Value of the Growth Pole Theory for Economic Geography," *Tijdschrift voor Economische en Sociale Geografie* 61 (1970): 67-76.

Leighton, P.A., "Geographical Aspects of Air Pollution," *Geographical Review* 56 (1966): 151-174.

Leven, C.L., J. Legler and P. Shapiro, *An Analytical Framework for Regional Development Policy*, Cambridge, Mass.: M.I.T. Press, 1970.

McNee, Robert D., "Regional Planning, Bureaucracy and Geography," *Economic Geography* 46 (1970): 190-198.

Miernyk, W.H., "Labor Mobility and Regional Growth," *Economic Geography* 31 (1955): 321-330.

Parr, J.B., "Out-Migration and the Depressed Area Problem," *Land Economics* 42 (1966): 149-160.

Parsons, K., "Poverty as an Issue in Developmental Policy," *Land Economics* 45 (1969): 52-65.

Perloff, H., "Key Features of Regional Planning," *Journal of the American Institute of Planners* 34 (1968): 153-159.

Ricks, R. Bruce, "New Town Development and the Theory of Location," *Land Economics* 46 (1970): 5-11.

Sakashita, N., "Regional Allocation of Public Investment," *Papers and Proceedings of the Regional Science Association* 19 (1967): 161-184.

Stilwell, F.J.B., "Regional Distribution of Concealed Unemployment," *Urban Studies* 7 (1970): 209-236.

Thomas, M.D., "Regional Economic Growth," *Land Economics* 45 (1969): 43-51.

Tiebout, C.M., "Exports and Regional Economic Growth," *Journal of Political Economy* 64 (1956): 160-164.

Tornqvist, Gunnar, "Contact Systems and Regional Development," *Lund Studies in Geography*, Series B, No. 35, 1970.

White, G.F., "Contribution of Geographic Analysis to River Basin Development," *Geographical Journal* 129 (1963): 412-436.

Studies of Regional Economic Development

Downs, Anthony, "Alternate Forms of Future Urban Growth in the U.S.," *Journal of the American Institute of Planners* 36 (1970): 3-11.

Hansen, Niles M., *Rural Poverty and the Urban Crisis*, Bloomington; Indiana University Press, 1970.

Hansen, N.M., "Some Neglected Factors in American Regional Development Policy: The Case of Appalachia," *Land Economics* 42 (1966): 1-10.

Klimm, L., "The Empty Areas of the Northeastern United States," *Geographical Review* 44 (1954): 325-345.

Peet, Richard, "Poor, Hungry America," *Professional Geographer* 23 (1971): 99-104.

Saunders, Robert J., "Population Flows, Spatial Economic Activity and Urban Areas in Appalachia," *Annals of Regional Science* 5, No. 1, (1971): 125-136.

Steed, Guy P.F. and Morgan D. Thomas, "Regional Industrial Change: Northern Ireland," *Annals of the Association of American Geographers* 61 (1971): 344-360.

Thompson, J.H. et al., "Toward a Geography of Economic Health: The Case of New York State," *Annals of the Association of American Geographers* 52 (1962): 1-20.

Problems of World Economic Development

Berry, Brian J.L., "Relationship between Regional Economic Development and the Urban System: The Case of Chile," *Tijdschrift voor Economische en Sociale Geografie* 60 (1969): 283-307.

Church, R.J., "Some Problems of Regional Economic Development in West Africa," *Economic Geography* 45 (1969): 53-62.

Friedmann J., "Poor Regions and Poor Nations," *Southern Economic Journal* 32 (1966): 465-473.

Ginsburg, N., "Essays on Geography and Economic Development," University of Chicago Department of Geography, Research Paper 62, 1960.

Gonzalez, Alfonso, "Population Growth and Socio-Economic Development: The Latin American Experience," *Journal of Geography* 70 (1971): 36-46.

Hay, Alan M., "Imports versus Local Production: A Case Study from the Nigerian Cement Industry," *Economic Geography* 47 (1971): 384-388.

James, P.E. and T.J. Wilbanks, "World Culture Regions and Patterns of Change," *Proceedings of the Association of American Geographers* 2 (1970): 77-80.

Melamid, A., "Regional Aspects of Economic Development in Multi-National States," *Papers and Proceedings of the Regional Science Association* 3 (1957): 301-306.

Rodgers, Allan, "Migration and Industrial Development: The Southern Italian Experience," *Economic Geography* 46 (1970): 111-135.

Rostow, W.W., *The Economics of Take-Off into Sustained Growth*, New York: St. Martin's, 1963.

Schwartzberg, J.E., "Three Approaches to the Mapping of Economic Development in India," *Annals of the Association of American Geographers* 52 (1962): 455-468.

Zaidi, I.H., "Toward a Measure of the Functional Effectiveness of a State: The Case of West Pakistan," *Annals of the Association of American Geographers* 56 (1966): 52-67.

GLOSSARY

Accessibility. The relative degree of ease with which a location may be reached from other locations.

Administrative principle. In central place theory, the principle that states that a higher order service area wholly includes seven service areas of the next lower order.

Agglomeration. Spatial grouping of activities or people for mutual benefit. Particular savings, or economies, accrue to such groupings of retailers and industries.

Amenities. Features of the environment — natural or human — that are perceived as pleasant and attractive.

Assembly costs. A manufacturer's transport costs on raw material inputs.

Basic activities. Economic activities, the products of which are exported out of the region; the opposite of nonbasic or service activities, which are produced and consumed internally.

Break-of-bulk. A shipment's division into parts — especially upon transfer from a higher volume to a lower volume carrier, as from ship to rail, or rail to truck.

Central place function. Activity offered from a place to the surrounding hinterland.

Centrality. A state of high accessibility; the quality of being at the center of a transport system.

Cluster. A close spatial proximity of settlements, industries, and so forth.

Colonial. Used here in the limited sense of dependence of a less developed area upon a more developed area.

Comparative advantage. The concept that every location has certain activities which are most successful or profitable; however, some locations may be more productive than other locations for most activities.

Competition. Refers here to more than one place or enterprise seeking the same customers, resources, or whatever; it results in a division of territory.

Complementarity. A state that exists if the varying advantages of two or more locations or areas permit a mutually beneficial linkage, usually by trade.

Concentration. Used here to mean the tendency of people or activities to congregate, or cluster, in space.

Congestion. On a transport link, the condition of retarded flow, resulting in increased costs.

Connectivity. The degree of direct linkage from one location to other locations on a transport network.

Contact field. Refers to the spatial distribution of acquaintances of an individual or group.

Convenience goods. Goods used very frequently, such as groceries or gasoline.

Demand in space. The value of goods and/or services desired by customers; this may be expressed for unit areas or per capita.

Diseconomies. The diminishing returns or profitability that sometimes results from greater size (as of a city) or output (as of a plant).

Dispersed city. A term some authors apply to a cluster of towns with some specialization of function; other authors apply it to a built-up urban area together with its surrounding rural nonfarm population.

Diversification. For firms, refers to a variety of outputs, usually in more than one industrial sector; for cities, indicates there is no unusual dependence on or specialization in particular industries.

Economic margin. In agricultural location theory, refers to the farthest locations from which goods can be profitably shipped to commercial markets.

Efficiency. Best use of territory; inefficiency in space means less than optimal use of territory.

Environment. The natural and cultural setting within which people and firms exist; used here mainly to treat variations in natural conditions, such as landforms, or climate.

Equilibrium. A theoretical state of stability. Any deviation from this state would decrease efficiency or profitability; equilibrium prices are values (for goods, labor, capital, or land) corresponding to these conditions.

Extensive. Refers here to a relatively low level of inputs or outputs per unit area.

Exurban. The zone beyond the urban built-up area, but within which commuters to the urban area are dominant.

Ghetto. An area of the city distinguished by ethnic, racial, or religious character; usually, but not necessarily, a low-income area.

Gravity model. A particular mathematical description of reduced interaction with increasing distance.

Hierarchy. The concept that urban places, together with their trade areas, may be grouped into distinctive levels of functional importance, and that the individual consumer will travel to smaller, closer places for everyday purchases and to larger, more distant places for less-demanded goods.

Gradient. A decline in intensity of land use and/or density of population outward from a major center.

Industrial complex. A set of specific industries that are closely related, usually because each industry makes significant purchases from the others.

Information. Knowledge about the environment, technology, and other conditions that would be necessary for optimal decisions.

Information field. The geographical distribution (around an individual or group) of knowledge about people or areas.

Innovation. An idea that leads to change, typically increasing productivity, in individual or corporate behavior.

Input-output. Refers to the pattern of purchases and sales among sectors of the economy; especially useful in tracing the effects of change in one sector on the behavior of other sectors.

Intensive. Refers here to a relatively high level of inputs and/or outputs per unit area.

Interdependence. Used here to indicate that because of specialization and trade, what occurs at one location affects what happens at many other locations.

Intervening opportunity. In migration theory or shopping behavior, the presence of closer, better opportunities which greatly diminish the attractiveness of even slightly farther ones.

Isodapane. In industrial location theory, a line or contour of constant total cost (assembly, production, and distribution).

Labor productivity. The relative cost of labor per unit of output.

Laborshed. The zone from which workers commute to a plant or city.

Landscape. Refers here to the systematic human pattern of occupance.

Linkages. The pattern of interdependence among industries.

Location. An area which may be treated as a point at the scale of observation used; given meaning by its specialized use.

Locational freedom. The notion that an activity is free to locate anywhere; probably only a theoretical freedom.

Location rent. See **Rent gradient.**

Location triangle. In location theory, a simple diagram of optimum location in the case of three markets and/or material sources.

Marginal farmer. The farm entrepreneur with very low net return per man/hour.

Marginal productivity. The additional output or return from the last added unit of inputs.

Market. A place or location where goods and services are demanded and exchanged.

Market penetration. A firm's share of a market (usually nonspatial).

Marketing principle. In central place theory, that arrangement of the hierarchy of places which will minimize aggregate distance traveled to centers; service areas of larger, higher order places include one-third of the service areas of each of the six neighboring lower order places.

Milkshed. The zone of an urban market's fluid-milk supply.

Movements. Refers to trips by people. These may be temporary (going to work or shopping), transient (going on vacation), or "permanent" (changing residence).

Nesting. In central place theory, refers to the tendency for service areas of lower order places to be wholly included in the service areas of larger, higher order places.

Nodal region. The area which is dependent on or is dominated by a nodal center; a nodal center is the center of a transport network.

Node. An intersection or terminus of routes on a transport network.

Nonoptimal behavior. Any decision making, whether intentional or by default, which results in less than maximum profit outcome.

Oligopoly, spatial. Refers to a fairly stable shared regional market, usually with a common price structure.

Orientation. The tendency for various kinds of industries to locate at markets (market orientation), at resources (resource or raw-material orientation), or because transport costs are decisive (transport orientation).

Peripheral. Located at the edge of a communication system, far from the controlling centers of the culture or economy.

Primacy. An unusually high proportion of population and economic activity in the single largest city of a country, usually the capital.

Primary industry. Manufacturing which specializes in basic processing or conversion of raw materials, as distinguished from secondary industry, which utilizes the outputs of primary manufacturers.

Processing activities. Activities that use a technological process to transform inputs to some demanded output.

Processing or production costs. The actual costs — mainly capital and labor — incurred in the conversion process, not including transport costs.

Queuing. The state in which demanders of a good or service must wait for its delivery because it is already being provided at the limit of capacity (as right-of-way is being provided in rush-hour traffic).

Random. Indicates locational uncertainty or imprecision resulting from many small and unknown factors.

Range. In central place theory, the maximum distance over which a seller will offer a good or service; or from which a purchaser will travel for it.

Region. A portion of space which, according to specified criteria, possess meaningful unity; see **Uniform region** and **Nodal region**.

Regional convergence. Implies that as an economy tends to reach an equilibrium state, prices, incomes, and other measures of value will tend to equalize.

Regional planning. The conscious attempt of government to influence the course of economic and social development; usually it is a result of welfare considerations, more rational use of resources, or alleviation of poverty.

Regionalism. The existence of a regional or sectional identification and loyalty, often resulting in particular kinds of behavior.

Relative location. The advantages or disadvantages of a particular location measured with reference to all competing locations.

Rent gradient. In agricultural and urban-structure theory, a measure of the value to the landowner of the relative accessibility of a certain location; as a result of competition for more accessible locations, a distance-decay gradient in locational rent will develop outward from the central point of greatest accessibility.

Residential farmer. An urban commuter who operates a farm, often at low productivity.

Resources. In an economic sense, any valued aspect of the environment; as used here, demanded natural materials, such as water, minerals, or soil.

Scale, economies of. The concept used to measure the tendency for marginal costs (those of the next unit) and average costs (those of all units) to decrease with increasing volume of output (constant factor proportions); diseconomies may set in at excess volumes.

Secondary sector. Industries making more complex products out of simpler, or primary, raw materials and products. Most construction and manufacturing are secondary industries.

Sector theory. The tendency for sectors or wedges projecting outward from a city's center to be devoted to different uses and social classes.

Self-sufficiency. The attempt of the local economy to provide by itself for all its needs and demands.

Shifting cultivation. An agricultural economy in which fields must be abandoned and hamlets must often migrate, due to exhaustion of soil fertility.

Social distance. Distance as perceived by individuals or small groups from themselves to other individuals or social groups.

Social space. The territory within which a social group carries on most of its interrelations.

Spatial adjustment. Implies changes in the location of a firm or of its suppliers or markets in the face of external change (perhaps change in resources or markets).

Spatial behavior. Refers to the decisions individuals make about their use of and action in space.

Spatial diffusion. The process of the gradual spread over space of people or ideas from critical centers of origin.

Spatial equilibrium. See **Equilibrium.**

Spatial error. Used here to indicate that individuals or firms make mistakes in their locational decisions; see **Nonoptimal behavior.**

Spatial experience. Refers to the extent and intensity of knowledge of territory and travel through it.

Spatial interaction. The interrelation of locations usually in terms of movement of people or communications; the level of interaction varies inversely with distance between locations.

Spatial monopoly. Used here to mean that a given central place's sellers supply most of certain goods and services to its trade area; a processor (for example, of crops or minerals) may similarly have a spatial monopoly over surrounding suppliers.

Spatial organization. The aggregate pattern of use of space by a society.

Spatial relations. The ways in which space and distance influence behavior and locational decisions.

Spatially-restricted society. A culture in which the experience of most members is limited to a small territory and in which local self-sufficiency is required.

Specialization. The commitment of a particular location or area to producing one or very few products.

Stress. In analysis of networks, refers to the degree to which nodes or links must be used in interaction between locations.

Subsistence. The condition of a local economy's ability to provide only for its basic food and shelter needs without significant surplus.

Substitution. In seeking maximum profit or in adjusting to change, it may be possible to use less of a scarcer, costlier input and more of a cheaper, more abundant one.

Suitcase farmer. Urban worker who farms only part of the year, often using inadequate methods.

Technological unemployment. Refers to increasing productivity of labor (such as that due to mechanization of agriculture) displacing workers from activities that are no longer productive relative to other activities.

Tertiary sector. Service activities involving financing, planning, repair, exchange, management, shipping of products. Traditionally, all services (health, education, government) and professions were included, but some scholars use *quaternary* to refer to government and professions.

Threshold. In central place theory, the minimum level of sales needed to attain marginal profitability.

Trade area (or **service area**). The territory from which most of a seller's customers originate.

Transferability. The degree to which a good or service may be transported.

Transhumance. The practice of shifting herds between upland summer pasture and lowland winter pasture.

Transport network. The actual physical system of links and nodes on which movement can take place.

Transport principle. In central place theory, that arrangement of the hierarchy of places which results in the most efficient transport network; see **transport network.**

Underemployment. A case of individuals working either part time or part of the year, but seeking full-time work; or, particularly in agriculture, may refer to full-time occupation which inefficiently uses time and labor.

Uniform region. A territory or space for which the internal variation of specified criteria is appreciably less than the variation between this area and other areas.

INDEX